THE TALMUD OF BABYLONIA

Program in Judaic Studies
Brown University
BROWN JUDAIC STUDIES
Edited by
Shaye J. D. Cohen, Wendell S. Dietrich,
Ernest S. Frerichs, Calvin Goldscheider, David Hirsch, Alan Zuckerman

Project Editors (Projects)

Lenn Evan Goodman, University of Hawaii (Studies in Medieval Judaism)
David Hayes, Coe College (Studia Philonica)

Number 306
THE TALMUD OF BABYLONIA
An American Translation
IX: Tractate Rosh Hashanah

Translated and explained by
Alan J. Avery-Peck

THE TALMUD OF BABYLONIA
An American Translation
IX: Tractate Rosh Hashanah

Translated and explained by

Alan J. Avery-Peck

Scholars Press
Atlanta, Georgia

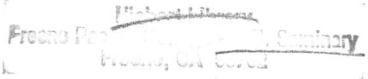

THE TALMUD OF BABYLONIA
An American Translation
IX: Tractate Rosh Hashanah

© 1995
Brown University

Library of Congress Cataloging-in-Publication Data
Talmud. Rosh ha-Shanah. English.
    Tractate Rosh Hashahah / translated and explained by Alan J. Avery-Peck.
    p. cm. — (Brown Judaic studies ; no. 306) (The Talmud of Babylonia ; 9)
    Includes bibliographical references and indexes.
    ISBN 0-7885-0172-0 (cloth ; alk. paper)
    1. Talmud. Rosh ha-Shahan—Introductions. I. Avery-Peck, Alan J. (Alan Jeffery), 1953– II. Title. III. Series. IV. Series: Talmud. English. 1984 ; 9.
[BM506.R5E5]
296.1'250521 s—dc20
[296.1'25]
                                    95-20613
                                    CIP

Printed in the United States of America
on acid-free paper

In memory of

Robert and Lillian Zinder

TABLE OF CONTENTS

Preface ix

Abbreviations and Bibliography xiii

Transliterations xxi

INTRODUCTION 1
The Content of Mishnah Rosh Hashanah 1
The Plan and Program of Bavli Rosh Hashanah 7
The Ideology of Bavli Rosh Hashanah 29
Theory of Translation and Explanation 56
Manuscripts, Editions, Commentaries 60

I.   ROSH HASHANAH CHAPTER ONE 61
II. ROSH HASHANAH CHAPTER TWO 275
III. ROSH HASHANAH CHAPTER THREE 313
IV. ROSH HASHANAH CHAPTER FOUR 375

Index to Biblical and Talmudic References 463

General Index 471

PREFACE

This translation and explanation of Tractate Rosh Hashanah in the Babylonian Talmud ("Bavli") is meant to facilitate study of the history, religion, and culture of the people of Israel in Babylonia from the redaction of the Mishnah, ca. 200 C.E., into the sixth century, when the Talmudic text itself was completed. My decision to undertake this translation is based upon the particular needs of recent scholarship on early Rabbinic Judaism. Recent study increasingly has worked to evaluate Rabbinic documents viewed as wholes. The texts, that is, are recognized to be the creations of specific groups of people who, in ways unique to their own circumscribed historical periods, addressed and answered questions of importance to their society. Study of these groups requires a clear understanding of the literary character and substantive interests of each document of the Rabbinic corpus. While viewed comparatively in relationship to the other documents in the corpus, each text is interpreted in light of its own principle interests and from the perspective of the historical context in which it came into being. This new translation and explanation of Bavli Rosh Hashanah represents one aspect of that interpretative task, so as to be instrumental in explaining the Talmud and the Judaism that document so richly reveals.

In light of its scholarly context, the volume has two goals, 1) presentation of Tractate Rosh Hashanah in clear English and 2) analysis of the interpretative agendum and principle thematic interests of the Babylonian masters who created the text before us. Let me explain in turn each of these purposes.

This translation, the first of Tractate Rosh Hashanah in almost sixty years, aims to correct the major shortcomings of the presently standard translation of M. Simon (*Rosh Hashanah, Translated into English with Notes, Glossary and Indices* [London, the Soncino Press: 1938]). These shortcomings are 1) Simon's failure to provide the step-by-step commentary needed to explain the extremely terse and abstruse language of individual Talmudic dicta and 2) his decision not to detail the flow of the argument within each complete unit of Talmudic discourse (sugya).

Simon, this is to say, quite accurately reproduces the bare substance of the Talmudic text. There is little to be corrected in his rendering of individual words or phrases. His footnotes, further, which routinely cite Rashi, briefly clarify the meaning of particularly elusive legal statements. The problem is that, besides his inconsistency in explaining these individual rules, Simon rarely comments on the logical flow of the sugya as a whole. He does not provide the additional language necessary to make clear, for instance, where a question ends and the answer begins, to explain how a rejoinder relates to the original premise, or even to clarify where one argument ends and the next begins. The result is that, while technically accurate, Simon's translation, if not supplemented by the original text and its commentaries, often does not allow the reader to understand the issues addressed by the Talmudic masters or to follow the progression of ideas through which those issues are explored.

Simon's approach to translation may be rationalized as having pedagogical value. It forces readers to work unaided through a largely unembellished text, drawing their own conclusions about the Talmudic masters' legal theories and interests. The problem is that the extreme terseness of the document being translated makes it difficult for anyone who needs a translation in the first place to comprehend it. This being the case, the possible merit of Simon's translation seems to me to be overshadowed by its shortcomings. In spite of its accuracy and the beauty of its language, Simon's translation does not adequately explain the Talmudic discourse. It therefore can neither meet the needs of many readers who turn to it nor serve as the basis for research that aims to characterize the legal and conceptual agenda of the Talmudic tractate viewed as a whole.

A primary contribution of the present volume, therefore, is to supply the text with a point-by-point commentary that 1) details the larger issue of each unit of Talmudic discourse, 2) indicates the relationships among the individual steps through which the argument is developed, and 3) explains the individual laws or legal concepts of which the argument is composed. The specifics of how this work is carried out are explained in detail in the fourth section of the Introduction, which discusses Theory of Text and Translation.

The second major contribution of this study is to present a typology of Bavli Rosh Hashanah's materials, an analysis of the structure of the Talmudic commentary, and, on this foundation, a description of the distinctive theological program of the Talmudic authorship. Found in the Introduction, these analyses point out the tractate's central exegetical concerns and chief substantive interests. We begin with a listing of the tractate's units according to their relationship to the underlying Mishnaic text. This shows that, rather than being primarily exegetical, more than half of the tractate supplements Mishnah Rosh Hashanah's laws, applying to new cases the legal principles and interests that account for the Mishnah's own legislation.

Alongside this listing, an outline of the unfolding substantive interests of the Talmudic tractate allows identification of long agglomerates of materials through which the Talmudic masters express a distinctively Amoraic point of view. In these materials, the Talmudic rabbis break away from the central focus of the Mishnah upon Temple, priest, and cult, viewed as the loci of sanctification in Israelite life and as the context through which salvation ultimately will be achieved. The Talmud, by contrast, speaks of the efficacy of the rabbi and Rabbinic learning as paths to salvation, arguing that the Messiah will come in response not to the priests and priestly worship but to the people's adherence to Rabbinic teaching. In this message we see the extent to which the Talmudic masters propose a theological point separate from that which is found in the Mishnah and particularly appropriate to the age in which they spoke.

The idea for a new translation of the Talmud of Babylonia came from Professor Jacob Neusner, of the University of South Florida. I appreciate his invitation to participate in this project, and I thank him for the encouragement he has given me throughout my preparation of this volume. His warm personal friendship and assistance are a source of inspiration to me, for which I am always grateful.

Professor Gary Porton, of the University of Illinois, Urbana, kindly read the entire manuscript, an arduous and time consuming task. His corrections of style and content improved this volume immeasurably. I thank him for his assistance with this project as well as for his constant guidance and help, beginning when I was his undergraduate student at the University of Illinois, over twenty years ago. It is also a pleasure to thank Professor Frederick R. Murphy, College of the Holy Cross, who suggested many improvements to the Introduction, and my student, Jessica Madore, who painstakingly reviewed the entire manuscript and corrected many errors that would otherwise have escaped attention.

The majority of the work on this volume was completed during my first year as Kraft-Hiatt Professor in Judaic Studies at the College of the Holy Cross. Through this chair, Jacob Hiatt and Robert and Myra Kraft have created a concrete and lasting opportunity for dialogue between Jews and Christians, which will do much to further the causes of mutual understanding and appreciation so vital in our world. I am thankful for their vision and for the opportunity to carry out my research and teaching in the stimulating setting of this wonderful college. I express my gratitude to the College's administration, to my colleagues in the Religious Studies Department and on the faculty as a whole, and to our students, all of whom have warmly and graciously welcomed me and helped to make the Kraft-Hiatt Chair's inaugural year so productive and exciting.

Alan J. Avery-Peck

June 21, 1995
23 Sivan 5755
*Lisa's and my fourteenth
wedding anniversary*

ABBREVIATIONS AND BIBLIOGRAPHY

Ah.	=	Ahilot
Albeck	=	Albeck, H., *The Six Orders of the Mishnah* (Jerusalem and Tel Aviv, 1957-1959). *Vol. 2: Seder Moed.*
Ar.	=	Arakhin
Aruch	=	Kohut, Alexander, ed., *Aruch Completum,* 8 vols. (Vienna, 1878-92; second ed., 1926).
Avery-Peck, *Besah*	=	Avery-Peck, Alan J., *The Talmud of Babylonia. An American Translation. Volume VII. Tractate Besah* (Atlanta, 1986).
Avery-Peck, *Terumot*:	=	[Avery-]Peck, Alan J., *The Priestly Gift in Mishnah: A Study of Tractate Terumot* (Chico, 1981).
Avery-Peck, *Y. Shebiit*	=	Avery-Peck, Alan J., *The Talmud of the Land of Israel. A Preliminary Translation and Explanation. Vol. 5. Shebiit* (Chicago, 1991).
Avery-Peck, *Y. Terumot*	=	Avery-Peck, Alan J., *The Talmud of the Land of Israel. A Preliminary Translation and Explanation. Vol. 6. Terumot* (Chicago, 1988).
A.Z.	=	Avodah Zarah
B.	=	Bavli, Babylonian Talmud
b.	=	*ben*, "son of"
B.B.	=	Baba Batra
Bek.	=	Bekhorot
Ber.	=	Berakhot
Bes.	=	Besah
Bik.	=	Bikkurim
B.M.	=	Baba Mesia

B.Q.	=	Baba Qamma
Chron.	=	Chronicles
Cracow	=	Babylonian Talmud, Cracow edition (Cracow, 1602-1605), cited by Rabbinovicz.
Dan.	=	Daniel
Danby	=	Danby, Herbert, *The Mishnah, Translated from the Hebrew with Introduction and Brief Explanatory Notes* (London, 1933).
Dem.	=	Demai
Dt.	=	Deuteronomy
Eccles.	=	Ecclesiastes
Ed.	=	Eduyyot
Erfurt	=	Tosefta, Erfurt Manuscript (see Lieberman, vol. 1, pp. 8-11).
Erub.	=	Erubin
Es.	=	Esther
Ex.	=	Exodus
Ezek.	=	Ezekiel
Gen.	=	Genesis
Ginsberg	=	Ginsberg, M., *Besah: Translated into English with Notes, Glossary and Indices* in Isidore Epstein, ed., *The Babylonian Talmud: Seder Mo'ed* (London, 1938).
Git.	=	Gittin
Haas	=	Haas, Peter J., *A History of the Mishnaic Law of Agriculture: Tractate Maaser Sheni* (Chico, 1980).
Hag.	=	Hagigah
Hal.	=	Hallah
Hor.	=	Horayot
Hos.	=	Hosea

Hul.	=	Hullin
Is.	=	Isaiah
Jaffee	=	Jaffee, Martin, *Mishnah's Theology of Tithing: A Study of Tractate Maaserot* (Chico, 1981).
Jastrow	=	Jastrow, Marcus, *A Dictionary of the Targumim, the Talmud Babli and Yerushalmi, and the Midrashic Literature*, 2 vols. (New York, 1895-1903; reprint: New York, 1975).
Jer.	=	Jeremiah
Josh.	=	Joshua
Kel.	=	Kelim
Ker.	=	Keritot
Ket.	=	Ketuvot
Kgs.	=	Kings
Kil.	=	Kilaim
Krauss	=	Krauss, Samuel, *Talmudische Archäologie*, 3 vols. (Leipzig, 1910-12; reprint: New York, 1979).
L	=	Babylonian Talmud manuscript London, British Museum, Harley 5508 (12th century), cited by Rabbinovicz.
Lev.	=	Leviticus
Lieberman	=	Lieberman, Saul, ed., *The Tosefta According to Codex Vienna with Variants from Codex Erfurt, Genizah MSS. and Edition Princeps*, 4 vols. (New York, 1955).
Lieberman, TK	=	Lieberman, Saul, *Tosefta Ki-Fshuta: A Comprehensive Commentary on the Tosefta*, 7 vols. (New York, 1955).
Lit.	=	Literally

M	=	Babylonian Talmud, Codex Munich 95; Facsimile edition: Hermann L. Strack, *Talmud Babylonicum Codicis Hebraica Monacensis 95* (Leiden, 1912; reprint: Jerusalem, 1971).
M.	=	Mishnah
Ma.	=	Maaserot
Mak.	=	Makkot
Makh.	=	Makhshirin
Mal.	=	Malachi
Me.	=	Meilah
Meg.	=	Megillah
Meiri	=	Hameiri, Menahem, *Beth Habehira on the Talmudical Treatise Rosh Hashanah. Edited from MS 3551/56 in the Bibl. Palat. in Parma and Annotated by Isaac S. Lange and Kalman Schlesinger* (Jerusalem, 1969).
Men.	=	Menahot
Mic.	=	Micah
Mid.	=	Middot
Miq.	=	Miqvaot
M.Q.	=	Moed Qatan
M.S.	=	Maaser Sheni
MS.	=	Manuscript (pl.: MSS.).
Naz.	=	Nazir
Ned.	=	Nedarim
Neg.	=	Negaim
Neusner, *Appointed Times*	=	Neusner, Jacob, *A History of the Mishnaic Law of Appointed Times*, 5 vols. (Leiden, 1981).

Neusner, *Damages*	= Neusner, Jacob, *A History of the Mishnaic Law of Damages,* 5 vols. (Leiden, 1981).
Neusner, *Holy Things*	= Neusner, Jacob, *A History of the Mishnaic Law of Holy Things,* 5 vols. (Leiden, 1981).
Neusner, *Judaism*	= Neusner, Jacob, *Judaism: The Evidence of the Mishnah* (Chicago, 1981).
Neusner, *Purities*	= Neusner, Jacob, *A History of the Mishnaic Law of Purities,* 22 vols. (Leiden, 1974-77).
Neusner, *Rosh Hashanah*	= Neusner, Jacob, *The Talmud of Babylonia. An Academic Commentary. Vol. VIII. Bavli Tractate Rosh Hashanah* (Atlanta, 1994).
Neusner, *Tosefta*	= Neusner, Jacob, *The Tosefta Translated from the Hebrew*, 6 vols. (New York, 1977-86).
Neusner, *Women*	= Neusner, Jacob, *A History of the Mishnaic Law of Women,* 5 vols. (Leiden, 1979-80).
Nid.	= Niddah
Num.	= Numbers
Oh.	= Ohalot
Or.	= Orlah
P	= Babylonian Talmud, Romm Edition (Wilna, 1880-86, and numerous reprints).
Par.	= Parah
Pes.	= Pesahim
Ps.	= Psalms
Qid.	= Qiddushin
Qin.	= Qinnim

R.	=	Rabbi
Rabbinovicz	=	Rabbinovicz, Raphaelo, *Sefer Dikduke Soferim. Variae Lectiones in Mischnam et in Talmud Babylonicum*, 2 vols. (reprint: New York, 1976).
Rashi	=	Solomon b. Isaac of Troyes (France, 1040-1105), commentary to the Babylonian Talmud, in standard editions.
R.H.	=	Rosh Hashanah
RH	=	Hananel b. Hushiel (Kairwan, ca. 990-1050), commentary to the Babylonian Talmud, in standard editions.
Rif	=	Isaac b. Jacob Alfasi (Spain, 1013-1103), *Sefer Rab Alphas* (Venice, 1521 and numerous reprints).
Rosh	=	Asher b. Yehiel (Germany and Spain, c. 1250-1327), commentary to the Babylonian Talmud, in standard editions.
S	=	Babylonian Talmud, Soncino Edition (Soncino, Barco, and Pesaro, 1488-1519); cited by Rabbinovicz.
Sam.	=	Samuel
San.	=	Sanhedrin
Shab.	=	Shabbat
Shav.	=	Shavuot
Sheb.	=	Shebiit
Sheq.	=	Sheqalim
Silia	=	Babylonian Talmud, Silia Edition (Silia, 1578-81); cited by Rabbinovicz.

Simon	=	Simon, M., *Rosh Hashanah: Translated into English with Notes, Glossary and Indices* in Isidore Epstein, ed., *The Babylonian Talmud: Seder Mo'ed* (London, 1938).
Song	=	Song of Songs
Sot.	=	Sotah
Strack	=	Strack, Hermann L., *Introduction to the Talmud and Midrash* (Philadelphia, reprint: 1959).
Suk.	=	Sukkah
T.	=	Tosefta
Ta.	=	Taanit
Tam.	=	Tamid
Tem.	=	Temurah
Ter.	=	Terumot
Toh.	=	Toharot
Tosafot	=	Exegetical compilation to the Babylonian Talmud (Germany and France, 12th and 13th centuries), in standard editions.
T.Y.	=	Tebul Yom
Uqs.	=	Uqsin
V	=	Babylonian Talmud, *Editio Princeps* (Venice, 1520-23; facsimile edition: Jerusalem, 1967-72).
Y.	=	Yerushalmi, Talmud of the Land of Israel, "Palestinian Talmud"
Yad.	=	Yadaim
Yeb.	=	Yebamot
Yom.	=	Yoma
Y.T.	=	Yom Tob
Zab.	=	Zabbim
Zeb.	=	Zebahim

Zech.	= Zecharia
Zuckermandel	= Zuckermandel, Moses Samuel, *Tosefta, Based on the Erfurt and Vienna Codices, with Parallels and Variants* (Trier, 1881-82; revised edition with supplement by Saul Lieberman, Jerusalem, reprint: 1970).

TRANSLITERATIONS

א	= ʾ		ל	= l
ב	= b		מ, ם	= m
ג	= g		נ, ן	= n
ד	= d		ס	= s
ה	= h		ע	= ʿ
ו	= w		פ, ף	= p
ז	= z		צ, ץ	= ṣ
ח	= ḥ		ק	= q
ט	= ṭ		ר	= r
י	= y		שׁ	= š
כ, ך	= k		שׂ	= ś
		ת = t		

Transliterations generally represent the consonantal structure of the Hebrew or Aramaic word, with no attempt made to vocalize. I do not distinguish between the spirantized and non-spirantized forms of *b, g, d, k, p,* and *t*. Verbal roots are indicated by capitalization. When, on occasion, a word is vocalized, the following notation is used:

a	= *qamaṣ, pataḥ*	i =	*ḥiriq*
ei	= *sere-yod*	o =	*ḥolem, ḥolem ḥaser, qamaṣ qatan*
e	= *sere, segol, vocal shewa*		
	u = *šuruq, qubbuṣ*		

INTRODUCTION

The Content of Mishnah Rosh Hashanah

Lacking an encompassing theoretical issue or legal theme, Mishnah Tractate Rosh Hashanah presents two distinct topics. The first concerns the court proceedings that lead to the proclamation of the new month (chapters 1-2), while the second details the rules for the sounding of the shofar on the New Year festival (chapters 3-4). This latter concern is central to the topic announced in the tractate's title, since Scripture describes this festival as "a memorial proclaimed with the sounding of the shofar" (Lev. 23:23-25; see Num. 29:1-6). In chapters 3-4, the Mishnah responds by defining a valid shofar, describing how and when in the worship service it is to be sounded, and by detailing how one fulfills the obligation of hearing the shofar-blasts.

Unlike the material on the shofar, the tractate's initial discussion, on the procedure for proclaiming the new month, is related only tangentially to the topic of the New Year festival. The connection is that New Year is the only festival that commences on the first day of a month, a day that, in Mishnaic times, was ascertained by the court, which examined witnesses who claimed on the preceding night to have observed the new moon.[1] The need through this procedure to determine whether or not the new month had commenced complicated the New Year celebration. This was the case since one could not know whether or not it was in fact the first day of the new year until sometime in the middle of the day, after the court had examined witnesses and completed its deliberation. Perhaps for this reason the

---

[1] Already in Mishnaic times, physical observation of the moon was coordinated with a system of reckoning that determined the limits within which an extra day could be added to a month and that established the insertion every second or third year of an entire additional month (second Adar). Despite continued, limited, dependence upon the physical appearance of the new moon, the lunar year thus was fixed to the solar year. This assured that the festivals would occur not only on the correct date in the lunar calendar but also in the right season, e.g., Passover at the time of the wheat harvest.

rules for the proclamation of the new month were associated in the minds of the Mishnah's framers with the observance of the New Year festival, the topic announced in the title of the tractate.

A short prologue to the tractate locates an additional thematic association between the procedure for proclaiming the new month and the rules for preparing and sounding the shofar on the New Year. This prologue states that there are four new year days, on each of which God judges the world and imposes a sanction appropriate to the particular season. The court's determination of the start of the new month thus regularly demarcates a time of judgment. According to the tractate's prologue, the festival celebrated on the first of Tishre, discussed in the second half of the tractate, is the most important of these times, since on this day all who enter the world pass before God in judgment (M. R.H. 1:2).[2] The tractate's prologue thus suggests the logic of discussing the declaration of the new month in conjunction with a consideration of the New Year celebration. New months in general mark points at which God judges of the world. Since the New Year celebrated on the first of Tishre is the festival of judgment *par excellence*, consideration of its traits in particular is appropriately associated with the discussion of the procedures for the proclamation of the new month.

The redactor's effort through this prologue to create a theme that unites the two distinct discussions that follow is weakened by the failure of the remainder of the tractate to refer to the character and consequences of God's judgment[3] or even to mention three of the four listed new year days or times of judgment. As a result, the tractate ultimately provides neither distinctive legal conceptions nor

---

[2]Scripture, for its part, refers to the first day of the seventh month neither as New Year nor as a day of judgment, but only as a "memorial proclaimed with the sounding the shofar," on which no work is to be performed (Lev. 23:23-25). The Rabbinic association of this day with judgment derives from its connection with the Day of Atonement, Lev. 23:26-28.

[3]As we shall see, by contrast, these concerns become central in the Talmudic discussion.

expands upon the theological point with which it begins. We have instead simply a listing of facts, albeit important ones, pertinent to two distinct topics, the proclamation of the new moon and the sounding of the shofar on the New Year. In this regard, this tractate contrasts with those that establish and work out their topics within the framework of a single legal or theological problematic that stands behind the bulk of their materials.[4] The absence here of such a generative issue suggests that the decision that the Mishnah should contain a tractate on the New Year celebrated on the first of Tishre depended on the importance of that festival within the Israelite calendar. This decision was made by the Mishnah's redactors without regard for whether or not they conceived of a specific legal or theoretical concern that would be particularly elucidated through discussion of that topic.[5]

The following outline clarifies the unfolding of the tractate's two topics and indicates in brief the point of each of its pericopae. Insofar as the Talmudic discussion of Tractate Rosh Hashanah closely follows the Mishnah's order and topical concerns, this outline serves as well as an initial introduction to Bavli Rosh Hashanah.

I. *The designation of the new month.* 1:1-3:1

A. *Prologue: The four new years.* 1:1-2

    1:1   There are four new years.

    1:2   Four times in the year the world is judged.

---

[4]See for instance, Avery-Peck, *Terumot*, pp. 1-7, and Avery-Peck, *Besah*, pp. 1-3, and Jacob Neusner's discussion of the underlying problematic of the each of the Mishnah's tractates in his *History of the Mishnaic Law*.

[5]Neusner, *Appointed Times* (vol. 4, p. 61), puts it this way: "In all, even though the tractate has a sizable share of information on both its themes, it is yet another one which raises forcefully the question of why, having so few important, and no distinctive, conceptions to lay forth, anyone would have wanted to make such a tractate to begin with."

B. *The new moon. Rules for witnesses of the appearance of the new moon.* 1:3-9

    1:3   On six new moons, messengers go forth to make the announcement.

    1:4   On two new moons, witnesses violate the prohibitions of the Sabbath in order to testify in the court in Jerusalem.

    1:5   Whether or not the new moon appeared clearly, they violate the Sabbath. Yose: Only if it appeared clearly.

    1:6   When more than 40 pairs of witnesses came, Aqiba held them back at Lud. Gamaliel disagreed.

    1:7   A father and son go together to give testimony but may not testify together. Simeon: They may. Yose: Precedent.

    1:8   These five are invalid to testify about the appearance of the new moon....

    1:9   On the Sabbath, a witness who cannot walk may ride an ass or palanquin; they carry food and weapons for self-defense.

C. *Changes necessitated by sectarian interference in the procedures for receiving testimony and announcing the new moon.* 2:1-4

    2:1   If people in Jerusalem will not recognize the witness, they send someone to testify to his good character. This was needed because of the Minim.

    2:2   At first they kindled flares to announce the new moon. After Samaritans spoiled matters, they determined to send messengers.

    2:3   How did they kindle flares?

    2:4   At what locations did they kindle flares?

D. *The new moon. The court proceeding.* 2:5-3:1

    2:5   The witnesses gathered in a large Jerusalem courtyard.

    2:6   How did they examine the witnesses?

    2:7   Proclaiming the new month: The head of the court says, "It is sanctified." The crowd responds by saying this twice.

    2:8   Gamaliel had pictures of the moon to show witnesses; he accepted testimony that others rejected.

    2:9   Gamaliel forced Joshua to submit to Gamaliel's decision regarding the new moon.

    3:1   Sanctification of the new moon is done solely by the court on the basis of the testimony of witnesses.

II. *The shofar.* 3:2-4:4

A. *The rules for the shofar.* 3:2-8

    3:2   All shofars are valid except for that of a cow.

    3:3   The shofar for the New Year derives from an antelope + additional features.

    3:4   The shofar for fast days derives from a ram + additional features.

    3:5   The proclamation of the Jubilee is equivalent to the New Year in regard to the sounding of the shofar and the blessings.

    3:6   A shofar that cracked or was otherwise damaged and repaired is invalid.

    3:7   One must hear the shofar, not an echo. One who hears must intend to fulfill the obligation.

    3:8   Scriptural evidence for the significance of intention.

B. *Practices altered because of the destruction of the Temple.* 4:1-4

    4:1   On a New Year festival that coincided with the Sabbath, they sounded the shofar in the Temple but not in the provinces. Yohanan b. Zakkai ruled that they should continue to sound it wherever there is a court.

    4:2   Jerusalem was ahead of Yavneh. In the latter they sound the shofar only in the court.

    4:3   The *lulab* was taken up in the Temple for seven days but in the provinces for one day. Yohanan b. Zakkai ruled that they should take it up for seven days in the provinces, as a memorial to the Temple.

    4:4   Late arriving witnesses caused the Levites to be mixed up, so they began to receive testimony only until the afternoon offering. Yohanan b. Zakkai ruled that they should again receive testimony all day long.

C. *Sounding the shofar in the liturgy of the New Year.* 4:5-9

    4:5   The order of the blessings and sounding of the shofar in the New Year Additional Service (*Musaf*).

    4:6   They do not recite fewer than 10 Sovereignty-verses, Remembrance-verses, and Shofar-verses.

    4:7   The one who leads the *Musaf*-service is responsible for sounding the shofar.

    4:8   Rules for fetching and preparing the shofar for use on the festival day.

    4:9   The proper way of blowing the shofar is to sound three sets of three blasts.

Beyond the short prologue at M. R.H. 1:1-2, the Mishnah's framers make no effort to tie together the distinct topics discussed in the tractate's two main units. These units' mutual independence is highlighted by the redactional placement of M. R.H. 4:4, which concerns the problem created by the uncertainty on the morning following the twenty-ninth of Elul regarding whether or not the new month of Tishre has started, such that the day is to be celebrated as the New Year. Pertinent to the discussion of the celebration of the festival of New Year and representing a ruling of Yohanan b. Zakkai (M. R.H. 4:1-4), this pericope appears with the rules for the shofar. It would, however, more appropriately have been placed at the beginning of the tractate, with the other rules for the receiving of witnesses and the court proceedings that determine the start of the new month. Such placement would have signaled the redactional integration of the two issues considered here, the procedure for determining the start of the new month and the rules for the celebration of the New Year, which occurs on the first day of the month. The failure of the tractate's redactors to make this connection means that, on formal as well as substantive grounds, the tractate's two topics are presented as independent discussions, each concerned with its own distinct topic and issues.

The Plan and Program of Bavli Rosh Hashanah

The preceding outline of Mishnah Rosh Hashanah serves as an initial introduction to Bavli Rosh Hashanah as well. For, as we shall see in detail in the following, the Talmudic treatise comprises a careful commentary on and supplement to the Mishnaic tractate. The Bavli takes up in turn almost all of the Mishnah's rules and indicates their origins in Scripture, explains what they mean, and frequently provides additional regulations to facilitate the application of the Mishnah's rules and practices. We shall see below the extent to which, through this commentary, the Talmudic masters express a theological program quite distinctive from that of the Mishnah. However, even as they express their own points of view, their line-by-line and often word-by-word reading of the Mishnah remains slavishly dependent upon the antecedent text. The Mishnah establishes the framework for the Talmudic masters' own writing, which is dedicated to comprehending the Mishnah's rules, on the one hand, and to supplementing them, on the other, by providing additional laws, parallel in topic to and generally illustrating the same legal principles as those that appear in the Mishnah.

The relationship between the Talmudic and Mishnaic tractates thus stands in marked contrast to the relationship between Mishnah Rosh Hashanah and Scripture. Mishnah Rosh Hashanah has only the slightest foundation in Scripture. The Bible refers to the use of the shofar on the first day of the seventh month (Lev. 23:24, Num. 29:1) but provides no information regarding the court's declaration of the new month. Nor does Scripture call this day "New Year" or refer to it or to the other periods listed in the Mishnah as times of judgment. Those who worked out the Mishnaic rules and concepts in this tractate were compelled to do so largely on their own, with no guidance from Scriptural legislation. The Talmudic masters, by contrast, faced the clearly demarcated task of interpreting the Mishnaic text, a task they accomplished by remaining almost entirely within the topical and theoretical interested expressed in that text. The result is a book of exegesis very different from that represented by Mishnah Rosh Hashanah. The Mishnaic and Talmudic tractates at hand accordingly illustrate very different methods of adapting an antecedent holy text to one's own contemporary needs.[6]

The interests of the framers of Bavli Rosh Hashanah are revealed through a classification of each of the Bavli's individual units according to its relationship to Mishnah Rosh Hashanah. Specifically, I divide the Talmud's discussions into three basic types, organizing each type, in turn, into its constituent categories. This classification shows that the greatest number of Talmudic units (51.02% of the Talmudic tractate) are supplementary, providing additional rules and theoretical discussions that carry forward the themes introduced by the Mishnah. Within this category, most of the materials (63.34%) contain the Amoraic masters' own rules and considerations. The rest of the category is comprised of citations from the Mishnah and Tosefta (9.33%) and laws cited in the names of Tannaim but not found in early texts (24.67%).

---

[6]On this issue, see below, pp. 29ff., and Avery-Peck, *Besah*, p. 21.

The tractate's second central focus is exegetical, with 41.16% of its units pertaining to the meaning of Mishnah Rosh Hashanah's laws and disputes. Here we find a focus on Amoraic exegesis (41.32% of the category) and a significant interest in locating in Scripture the sources of the Mishnah's ideas (40.5% of the category). The remaining units in this category locate the meaning of Mishnah Rosh Hashanah elsewhere in the Mishnah or in the Tosefta.

Only a small percentage of the tractate falls into the third category, which I term synthetic materials. Comparing and contrasting rules taken from diverse contexts within Mishnah Rosh Hashanah and throughout the Rabbinic corpus, these discussions account for only 7.82% of the tractate.

In the following, each of the Talmud's units is listed under the applicable category. In individual cases, especially those involving long and complex units, assignment to a specific classification may be debated. In the course of an Amoraic dispute over the meaning of a Mishnaic rule, for instance, parallel rules may be cited from the Mishnah or Tosefta. In the same way, a supplementary Amoraic rule may introduce a separate, though related, rule from the Mishnah along with a dispute over that rule's meaning. Placement of such units represents my judgment concerning the unit's central function. It seems unlikely, however, that different assignments of debatable entries would radically change the overall results of this survey concerning the central focus of the Talmudic materials found in this tractate.

I. Exegetical Material
A. Amoraic exegesis[7]
1. 1:1 XVII   Meaning of M. R.H. 1:1B.
2. 1:1 XXXVI   Why did the authority behind M. R.H. 1:1B not include the rule given at 1:1 XXXV?

---

[7]Here I include only Aramaic interpretation that does not depend upon Scripture. For the Amoraic use of Scripture in the interpretation of the Mishnah, see below, section C.

3.	1:1 XXXVIII	Why did the authority behind M. R.H. 1:1B not include the rule given at 1:1 XXXV?
4.	1:1 XLI	Why did the authority behind M. R.H. 1:1B not include the rule given at 1:1 XXXV?
5.	1:1 XLIV	Explanation of parallel rules at 1:1 XXXV.A and M. R.H. 1:1B.
6.	1:1 XLVII	Point of the rule at M. R.H. 1:1E.
7.	1:1 LXXXI	M. Sheb. 2:7 cited and analyzed.
8.	1:1 LXXXIII	Interpretation of M. R.H. 1:1G-H.
9.	1:1 LXXXV	Interpretation of the actions of Aqiba, unit 1:1 LXXXIV.
10.	1:2 I	Interpretation of M. R.H. 1:2B.
11.	1:2 XXXVI	Meaning of *Benei Maron* at M. R.H. 1:2D.
12.	1:3 I	Explanation of M. R.H. 1:3.
13.	1:3 IX	Explanation of M. R.H. 1:3B.
14.	1:7 III	The law follows the view of Simeon, M. R.H. 1:7D.
15.	1:8 I	Point of M. R.H. 1:8C.
16.	2:1 I	Significance of word "another," M. R.H. 2:1A.
17.	2:1 II	Same issue as in preceding entry.
18.	2:2-4 VIII	Meaning of "Bet Baltin," M. R.H. 2:4C.
19.	2:2-4 IX	Meaning of "Exile," M. R.H. 2:4D.
20.	2:2-4 XI	Distance between locations listed at M. R.H. 2:4.
21.	2:6 I	Why and how are specific questions asked of witnesses, M. R.H. 2:6C?
22.	2:7 V	At M. R.H. 2:7D, the law follows Eleazar b. Sadoq.
23.	2:8a I	Why the procedure described at M. R.H. 2:8A is permitted.

24.	2:8b-9 I	Explanation of approach of Gamaliel, M. R.H. 2:8B.
25.	3:1 I	Significance of rule of M. R.H. 3:1A.
26.	3:1 II	Point of M. R.H. 3:1A-B.
27.	3:1 III	Point of M. R.H. 3:1A-B: the court's decision must be made by day.
28.	3:1 IV	Rationale behind M. R.H. 3:1C.
29.	3:1 V	Rationale behind M. R.H. 3:1E.
30.	3:2 II	Why a cow-horn may not be used as a shofar, M. R.H. 3:2A-B.
31.	3:2 III	Why a cow-horn may not be used as a shofar, M. R.H. 3:2A-B.
32.	3:2 IV	Why a cow-horn may not be used as a shofar, M. R.H. 3:2A-B.
33.	3:3-5 IV	Explanation of M. R.H. 3:3C.
34.	3:3-5 V+VI	Implication of M. R.H. 3:3C, as interpreted by preceding entry.
35.	3:3-5 VII	Interpretation of M. R.H. 3:7.
36.	3:6-7 VI	Application of rule of M. R.H. 3:7A-C.
37.	3:6-7 VII	Application of rule of M. R.H. 3:7A-C.
38.	4:1-2 IV	Meaning of "with a court," M. R.H. 4:1F.
39.	4:1-2 V	Meaning of "and in this regard also," M. R.H. 4:2A.
40.	4:1-2 VIII	Meaning of M. R.H. 4:2A.
41.	4:5 I	Meaning of Aqiba's statement, M. R.H. 4:5B.
42.	4:5 V	Meaning of term "second" at T. R.H. 2:11.
43.	4:6a I	Reason one recites ten Sovereignty-verses, M. R.H. 4:6A.
44.	4:6b I	What verses does M. R.H. 4:6C exclude from use?
45.	4:6b II	What verses does M. R.H. 4:6C exclude from use?

46.	4:7 II	Why the Hallel is not recited on the New Year festival and the Day of Atonement, M. R.H. 4:7C.
47.	4:8 I	Why are the actions listed at M. R.H. 4:8B-G forbidden?
48.	4:8 II	Point of M. R.H. 4:8D-E.
49.	4:8 III	Point of M. R.H. 4:8G.
50.	4:9 XIII	Point of M. R.H. 4:9E.

B. Amoraic disputes over meaning

1.	1:1 XCV	Discussion of Tannaitic rule at unit 1:1 XCIV.
2.	1:3 VIII	Dispute over meaning of M. R.H. 1:3B.
3.	1:7 II	Dispute over decided law at M. R.H. 1:7.
4.	4:1-2 I	M. R.H. 4:1A+C does not derive from Scripture (Hama bar Hanina) but from Rabbinic authority (Rava).
5.	4:1-2 III	Conflicting interpretations of M. R.H. 4:1E-F.
6.	4:4a I	What is the "mix-up" referred to at M. R.H. 4:4A?
7.	4:9 XVI+XVIII	Whose view represents the decided law at M. R.H. 4:9F-G?

C. Explanation from Scripture

1.	1:1 VIII	Scripture proves that the years of kings are counted from Nissan (M. R.H. 1:1B).
2.	1:1 IX	Scripture proves that the New Year festival is in Nisan, not Iyyar.
3.	1:1 X	Scripture proves that the New Year festival is not in Sivan.
4.	1:1 XI	Scripture proves that the New Year festival is not in Tamuz.
5.	1:1 XXIII-XXVIII	Scriptural source of T. Ar. 3:17.

6.	1:1 XXXIX	Scriptural source of B. R.H. 1:1 XXXV.A.
7.	1:1 XLVI	M. R.H. 1:1C vs. D: both views depend upon Ps. 65:13.
8.	1:1 XLVIII	Scripture proves that M. R.H. 1:1E refers to the final judgment.
9.	1:1 XLIX	Ps. 8:14 proves that heavenly judgment depends upon an earthly court's declaration of the new month.
10.	1:1 L	Ps. 8:14 proves that God will judge all nations.
11.	1:1 LI	Source in Scripture of M. R.H. 1:1E.
12.	1:1 LIV-LV	Scripture proves that one lengthens sanctified time by continuing it into secular time (unit 1:1 LIII) + alternate interpretation of Aqiba.
13.	1:1 LIX	M. R.H. 1:1F derives from Scripture.
14.	1:1 LXI	The view of Meir, 1:1 LX, derives from Scripture.
15.	1:1 LXII	The view of Eleazar, 1:1 LX, derives from Scripture.
16.	1:1 LXIV	We know from Scripture that the world was created in Tishre or, alternatively, Nisan (unit 1:1 LXIII).
17.	1:1 LXV	We know from Scripture that the patriarchs were born in Tishre or, alternatively, Nisan (unit 1:1 LXIII).
18.	1:1 LXVI	We know from Scripture the month in which the patriarchs died.
19.	1:1 LXVII	Scripture indicates when Isaac was born.
20.	1:1 LXVIII	We know from Scripture when Sarah, Rachel, and Hannah were visited.
21.	1:1 LXIX	We know from Scripture that Joseph left prison on New Year.

22.	1:1 LXX	We know from Scripture that the bondage in Egypt ended on New Year.
23.	1:1 LXXI	Scripture indicates that redemption from bondage in Egypt occurred in Nisan.
24.	1:1 LXXII	Eliezer: Scripture proves that in Tishre the Israelites will be redeemed; Joshua: Nisan.
25.	1:1 LXXIII	Development of preceding item.
26.	1:1 LXXVI.C-W	Scripture stands behind T. R.H. 1:9.
27.	1:1.LXXVIII	M. Ma. 1:3 cited and explained primarily through Scripture.
28.	1:1 LXXIX	Development of preceding item.
29.	1:1 LXXX	Development of #27.
30.	1:2 III	Scriptural foundation of position of Yose, cited in unit 1:2 II.
31.	1:4 II	Lev. 23:4 stands behind M. R.H. 1:4.
32.	1:5-6 I	Ps. 12:6 indicates meaning of term at M. R.H. 1:5A.
33.	1:7 I	Scripture stands behind disputing views at M. R.H. 1:7A-C+D.
34.	2:2-4 I	Source of the word "flare" at M. R.H. 2:2A.
35.	2:7 I	Scriptural source of M. R.H. 2:7A.
36.	2:7 II	Scriptural source of M. R.H. 2:7B.
37.	2:7 III	Scriptural source of M. R.H. 2:7B.
38.	3:2 I	Dt. 33:17 stands behind view of rabbis, M. R.H. 3:2A-B.
39.	3:3-5 VIII	Num. 10:2 explains M. R.H. 3:4A-C.
40.	3:3-5 IX	M. R.H. 3:3-5 applies only in the Temple.
41.	4:3 I	Scripture allows one to create a memorial to the Temple, M. R.H. 4:3B.
42.	4:3 II	Reason for the rule at M. R.H. 4:3C.
43.	4:3 III	Different reason for the rule at M. R.H. 4:3C.

44.	4:7 I	Prov. 14:28 stands behind M. R.H. 4:7.
45.	4:9 III	Lev. 25:9 proves that trumpet sounds on New Year must be made with a shofar, M. R.H. 4:9.
46.	4:9 IV	Lev. 25:9 proves that shofar sounds on New Year are preceded by a plain blast.
47.	4:9 V	Lev. 25:9 proves that on the New Year festival there are three sets of blasts, M. R.H. 4:9A.
48.	4:9 VII	Separate proof that shofar sounds on New Year are preceded by a plain blast.
49.	4:9 VIII-IX	Review of Scriptural foundations of preceding rules.

D. Explanation from the Mishnah

1.	1:1 I (+ II-III)	M. Sheb. 10:5 explains M. R.H. 1:1B.

E. Explanation from Tannaitic statements

1.	1:1 XII	Claim that units 1:1 VIII-XI all represent Tannaitic teachings.
2.	1:1 LX	T. R.H. 1:8 explains M. R.H. 1:1E-F.
3.	1:4 III	Tannaitic statement explains M. R.H. 1:4E-F.
4.	1:5-6 III	Tannaitic statement disagrees with M. R.H. 1:6A-B.
5.	2:2-4 II	When were flares used (M. R.H. 2:2-2)? + Amoraic explanation.
6.	2:2-4 X	Meaning of "Lit up like a bonfire," M. R.H. 2:4D.
7.	2:5 I	Nature of Bet Ya'azeq, M. R.H. 2:5A.
8.	2:8b-9 IV	Explanation of M. R.H. 2:9B.
9.	2:8b-9 VI	What happened at meeting of Joshua and Gamaliel, M. R.H. 2:9H?
10.	3:2 V	Aqiba proves that *yovel*, M. R.H. 3:2D, means "ram."
11.	3:3-5 III	T. R.H. 2:4 clarifies M. R.H. 3:3C.

12.	4:1-2 II	Story of how Yohanan b. Zakkai imposed the rule at M. R.H. 4:1D.
13.	4:6a II	Meaning of M. R.H. 4:6B from T. R.H. 2:12.
14.	4:9 XV	Tannaitic discussion of reasoning for views of Gamaliel and sages, M. R.H. 4:9F-G.

The exegetical materials focus upon Amoraic exegesis, frequently with attention to the foundation in Scripture of the Mishnah's rules. While the Talmud is filled with disputes about specific rules and the meaning of Rabbinic statements, these issues only infrequently extend to direct argumentation about the meaning of passages in Mishnah Rosh Hashanah. Accordingly, I identify only seven instances of Amoraic disputes over the meaning of a Mishnaic statement. With the Amoraic authorities generally providing their own explanations of the Mishnah, neither passages from the Mishnah nor other Tannaitic statements often are cited to explain Mishnah Rosh Hashanah.

II. Supplementary Material
A. Rules cited from the Mishnah and Tosefta

1.	1:1 IV+V-VII	T. R.H. 1:1 is cited and explained; supplements M. R.H. 1:1B.
2.	1:1 XVIII	M. R.H. 1:1B parallels T. R.H. 1:2, concerning the failure to fulfill a vow in a timely manner.
3.	1:1 XIX-XXXI	T. Ar. 3:17's rule for fulfilling a vow + Amoraic explanation.
4.	1:1 LXXVI.A-B	T. R.H. 1:9 supplements M. R.H. 1:1E-F.
5.	1:1 LXXVII	T. R.H. 1:10 supplements M. R.H. 1:1E-F + brief Amoraic explanation.
6.	2:1 IV	T. R.H. 1:15 provides details behind M. R.H. 2:1.
7.	2:8b-9 V	T. R.H. 1:18: rules concerning the authority of the court.

8.	3:6-7 I	T. R.H. 2:4 supplements M. R.H. 3:6: preparation and repair of a shofar.
9.	3:6-7 II	Continuation of preceding entry.
10.	3:8 I	T. R.H. 2:5 supplements M. R.H. 3:8I-J + Amoraic interpretation.
11.	3:8 II	T. R.H. 2:5 + Amoraic explanation.
12.	4:5 IV	Procedure for sounding the shofar on the New Year, T. R.H. 2:11.
13.	4:6b IV	T. R.H. 2:13: passages that may be used in the Remembrance-verses.
14.	4:6b VI	T. R.H. 2:13: use of verses appropriate to more than one category.

B. Other Tannaitic rules and homilies

1.	1:1 XXXV	Other events for which the first of Nisan is the New Year + Amoraic dispute over Scriptural foundation.
2.	1:1 XLII-XLIII	The first of Nisan begins the new year for the renting of houses.
3.	1:1 LVI	Rules for the Jubilee year + Scriptural foundation.
4.	1:1 LVII	Meaning of the word "liberty" at Lev. 25:10.
5.	1:1 LXIII	List of significant events that occurred in Tishre.
6.	1:1 LXXIV	Israelite and non-Israelite approaches to dating the flood.
7.	1:1 LXXXII	Yose and Aqiba dispute rules for tithing + Amoraic explanation.
8.	1:1 XCIV	Rules for the new year of trees.
9.	1:2 XVII	Houses: treatment of different types of people on Day of Judgment.
10.	1:2 XIX	Houses: manifestation of God's mercy on Day of Judgment.

11.	1:2 XXI	How is God's mercy made manifest on the Day of Judgment?
12.	1:2 XXX	Yose: For individuals, repentance is efficacious only until their final judgment has been passed.
13.	1:2 XXXI	Rule indicated in preceding item is disputed by Tannaitic authorities.
14.	1:2 XXXIII	Members of the House of Eli would die at 18 years. Gamaliel instructed them to study Torah.
15.	1:3 II	Dispute between Simeon b. Yohai and Aqiba over meaning of verses pertinent to M. R.H. 1:3.
16.	2:6 II	How specific statements of witnesses regarding the new moon are evaluated.
17.	2:6 III	Same issue as preceding entry.
18.	2:6 IV	Same issue as preceding entry.
19.	2:6 V	Same issue as preceding entry.
20.	2:7 IV	Tannaitic statement disagrees with M. R.H. 2:7D.
21.	2:8b-9 III	Court's decision regarding the new moon is binding even if it is incorrect.
22.	3:2 VI	People's use of certain words explains biblical verses.
23.	3:2 VII	People's use of certain words explains biblical verses.
24.	3:2 VIII	People's use of certain words explains biblical verses.
25.	3:2 IX	People's use of certain words explains biblical verses.
26.	3:6-7 XXII	Statement on the requirement of intention for fulfilling the obligation to hear the shofar.
27.	3:8 III	Circumstances under which one may repeat an act in order to fulfill the

		obligation on behalf of some other person.
28.	3:8 IV	One should not break bread to say the blessing on behalf of some other person, unless he intends himself to eat.
29.	3:9 V	One may repeat the Hallel to fulfill the obligation on behalf of some other person.
30.	4:4a II	Which psalm is recited on each day of the week?
31.	4:4b II	Listing of ordinances of Yohanan b. Zakkai + Amoraic discussion.
32.	4:5 II	Source in Scripture for each benediction of the New Year Amidah.
33.	4:5 III	Dispute regarding placement in worship service of sanctification of the day.
34.	4:8 IV	Urine may not be put in a shofar.
35.	4:9 XII	The consequence of not hearing all of the shofar blasts in the correct order.
36.	4:9 XIX	Eleazar: One must always prepare to pray + Amoraic discussion.
37.	4:9 XX	Situation in which prayers recited by the agent of the community fulfill the obligation of absent members of the community.

C. Rules and homilies in the names of Amoraim

1.	1:1 XIII-XVI	Hisda states that M. R.H. 1:1B applies only to Israelite kings + extended Amoraic dispute.
2.	1:1 XXIX	Rava's rule regarding when one must sacrifice an animal he has consecrated.
3.	1:1 XXX	Rava's rule regarding the prohibition against delaying fulfillment of vows.

4.	1:1 XXXII	Application to an heir of rule against delaying fulfillment of a vow.
5.	1:1 XXXIII	Application to a woman of rule against delaying fulfillment of a vow.
6.	1:1.XXXIV	How to count the year within which a firstling must be sacrificed.
7.	1:1 XL	Communal sacrifices should be purchased with contributions received in that same year + Tannaitic parallel.
8.	1:1 LII-LIII	Rules for Jubilee years (M. R.H. 1:1E) derived from Scripture.
9.	1:1 LXXXVIII	Yannai's rule for citron tree.
10.	1:1 LXXXIX	Nahman/Yannai's rule for a leap year.
11.	1:1 XC	Rabbah's rule for tithing of citron.
12.	1:1 XCI	Hamnuna's different rule for tithing of citron.
13.	1:2 IV	Hisda: rule for the judgment of a king and the community.
14.	1:2 VI	Reasons for a number of practices required by Scripture.
15.	1:2 VII	Discussion of use of the shofar.
16.	1:2 VIII	Discussion of use of the shofar on the New Year.
17.	1:2 IX	Failure to sound shofar on the New Year leads to evil.
18.	1:2 X	A year that begins in poverty ends in riches.
19.	1:2 XI	God judges people only on basis of their past actions.
20.	1:2 XII	Three things call to mind a person's iniquities.
21.	1:2 XIII	Four things cancel a person's judgment.
22.	1:2 XIV	A person is obligated to pay respect to his master on each festival.

23.	1:2 XV	A person is obligated to purify himself on each festival.
24.	1:2 XVI	God opens three books on the New Year.
25.	1:2 XVIII	Fate of sinners on the Day of Judgment.
26.	1:2 XX	Categories of sinners.
27.	1:2 XXII	God pardons iniquities of people who pardoned others.
28.	1:2 XXIII	Development of preceding.
29.	1:2 XXIV	God is "just" and "kind."
30.	1:2 XXV	Similar to preceding item.
31.	1:2 XXVI	Similar to preceding items.
32.	1:2 XXVII	Explanation of Ex. 34:6: God appeared to Moses like one who leads the community in prayer.
33.	1:2 XXVIII	Explanation of Ex. 34:6: the power of repentance.
34.	1:2 XXIX	The power of repentance.
35.	1:2 XXXII	Repentance of a community is efficacious even after the final judgment has been passed.
36.	1:2 XXXIV	Same point as in preceding unit.
37.	1:2 XXXV	Ten days between the New Year and the Day of Atonement are most effective for repentance.
38.	1:3 III	Dispute concerning whether or not the Scroll of Fasting has been nullified.
39.	1:3 IV	The Scroll of Fasting has not been nullified.
40.	1:3 V	The Scroll of Fasting has not been nullified.
41.	1:3 VI	The Scroll of Fasting has not been nullified.
42.	1:3 VII	Continuation of dispute regarding the Scroll of Fasting.

43.	1:3 X	Rule for intercalation of Adar.
44.	1:3 XI	Continuation of preceding entry.
45.	1:3 XII	Continuation of preceding discussion.
46.	1:3 XIII	Continuation of preceding discussion.
47.	1:3 XIV	Can a month be intercalated to prevent the occurrence of a Sabbath-festival sequence?
48.	1:3 V	Continuation of preceding item.
49.	1:3 VI	Samuel asserts that he can fix the calendar. Abba rejects this claim.
50.	1:3 XVII	Appearance of the new moon.
51.	1:3 XVIII	Conditions for proclamation of the new moon.
52.	1:3 XIX	Proclamation of the new moon in the diaspora.
53.	1:3 XX	Conflicts in calendar between the land of Israel and the diaspora.
54.	1:3 XXI	Rules for observing two festival days.
55.	1:3 XXII	Application of preceding rule.
56.	1:3 XXIII	Problem of observing the Day of Atonement when the correct calendar is unknown.
57.	1:3 XXIII	Development of theme of the preceding.
58.	1:3 XXV	How to determine the leap year.
59.	1:3 XXVI	How those at sea are to determine the calendar.
60.	1:5-6 II	Dispute over meaning of Dt. 34:10.
61.	2:1 III	Those who report sighting the new moon do not require character witnesses, contrary to M. R.H. 2:1.
62.	2:2-4 III	Delineation of types of cedar, supplements M. R.H. 2:3.
63.	2:2-4 IV	How coral is raised from the sea bed.
64.	2:2-4 V	God will restore trees gentiles removed from Jerusalem.

65.	2:2-4 VI	The value of teaching Torah.
66.	2:2-4 VII	Idol-worshippers have no atonement.
67.	2:8a II	Permissibility of making images.
68.	2:8a III	Permissibility of making images.
69.	2:8a. IV	Permissibility of making images.
70.	2:8b-9 II	A court's decision regarding the new moon is binding even if it is incorrect.
71.	3:6-7 III	Rule for preparation of a shofar.
72.	3:6-7 IV	Rule for preparation of a shofar, including some Tannaitic statements.
73.	3:6-7 V	Rule for preparation of a shofar.
74.	3:6-7 XI	Rule for use of horn of a burnt-offering as a shofar.
75.	3:6-7 XII	Rule for use of horn of animal used for idolatry as a shofar.
76.	3:6-7 XIII	Vows have no impact upon the obligation to hear the shofar.
77.	3:6-7 XIV	Requirement of intention for fulfillment of religious obligation.
78.	3:6-7 XV	Rava: intention is not required.
79.	3:6-7 XVI	Rava's notion is challenged.
80.	3:6-7 XVII	Rava's notion is challenged.
81.	3:6-7 XVIII	Rava's notion is challenged.
82.	3:6-7 XIX	Rava's notion is challenged.
83.	3:6-7 XX	Rava requires intention in some instances + discussion.
84.	3:6-7 XXI	Zera on the issue of intention.
85.	4:1-2 VI	Nature of the obligation to sound the shofar.
86.	4:1-2 VII	Application of requirement that the shofar be sounded on the Sabbath only before a court.
87.	4:4a III	Which psalm is recited on the Sabbath at the time of the additional sacrifice?

88.	4:4a IV	Which psalm is recited on Sabbath afternoon?
89.	4:4a V	Method of reading the indicated psalms.
90.	4:4a VI	The divine presence made ten journeys in leaving Israel prior to the first destruction.
91.	4:6b III	Passages inappropriate for use in the Remembrance-verses.
92.	4:6b V	Use of Ps. 24:7-10 in the Sovereignty-verses.
93.	4:9 X	Abbahu ordained a particular sequence for sounding the shofar + discussion.
94.	4:9 XI	What must one hear to fulfill the obligation to hear the shofar?
95.	4:9 XIV	Rules for sounding of shofar on behalf of a different person.

D. Tannaitic rules applied to new cases

1.	4:8 VII	Application of M. R.H. 4:8K.
2.	4:8 VIII	Application of M. R.H. 4:8L.

E. Application of the Mishnah's and Tosefta's rules

1.	1:1 LXXXIV	Aqiba's application of the rules at M. R.H. 1:1G-H.
2.	4:4b I	Application of M. R.H. 4:4G.

The largest number of units here, and in the tractate as a whole, consists of Amoraic rules and homilies that supplement the Mishnah's own materials. While covering a variety of situations, the majority of these units follow and develop themes and legal principles expressed within the Mishnah itself. Within the supplementary material, the Talmud cites a fair number of rules from other Mishnaic tractates and from the Tosefta. It is, by contrast, hardly interested in the actual application of Tannaitic rules to concrete situations (II.D, E).

III. Synthetic Materials
A. Discussion of contradictory or parallel Tannaitic statements

1.	1:1 XXXVII	T. San. 2:7 appears to contradict the rules introduced at unit 1:1 XXXV.
2.	1:1 LXXV	Coordinating of M. R.H. 1:1E-F and related Tannaitic statement.
3.	1:1 LXXXVI	Determination of the view of Gamaliel based upon a number of his statements.
4.	1:1 LXXXVI	Coordinating of interpretations of several Tannaitic statements.
5.	1:4. I	Coordinating of rules of M. R.H. 1:3A and 1:4A.
6.	3:1 VI	M. R.H. 3:1C-D+E appears to contradict the view of Aqiba.
7.	3:3-5 I	Relationship of the statement of Levi to M. R.H. 3:3A-B and the view of Judah.
8.	3:3-5 II	Nature of the dispute between Judah and rule at M. R.H. 3:3A-B.
9.	4:6b VII	Relationship between M. R.H. 4:6D-E and the distinct Tannaitic statement of Yose's opinion.
10.	4:8 V	Relationship of M. R.H. 4:8I and a Tannaitic statement.
11.	4:8 VI	T. R.H. 2:16 appears to contradict itself.
12.	4:9 I	M. R.H. 4:9B appears to contradict a Tannaitic statement.
13.	4:9 II	M. R.H. 4:9C appears to contradict a Tannaitic statement.
14.	4:9 VI	Discussion of a contradiction in the statements cited at B. R.H. 4:9 III-V.

B. Which Tannaitic authority?

1.	1:1 XLV	Which authorities stand behind M. R.H. 1:1B and 1:1C?

2.	1:1 LVIII	Unit 1:1 LVI is the views of Judah and Yose. Others disagree.
3.	1:2 II	Which authority stands behind M. R.H. 1:2?
4.	1:2 V	Which Tanna accounts for the Amoraic practice of praying daily for the sick?
5.	3:3-5 X	Who stands behind a contemporary liturgical practice + coordination with a different Tannaitic rule.

C. Coordination of Amoraic rules

1.	1:1 XCII+XCIII	Systematization of rules from units 1:1 LXVI, XC, and XCI.
2.	3:6-7 VIII	Relationship of B. R.H. 3:6-7 VI to B. R.H. 3:3-5 V-VI.
3.	3:6-7 IX	Relationship of B. R.H. 3:6-7 VI to B. R.H. 3:3-5 V-VI.
4.	3:6-7 X	Relationship of B. R.H. 3:6-7 VI to B. R.H. 3:3-5 V-VI.

Synthetic discussions are best suited to the identification of overarching theories that account for several Mishnaic or Amoraic rules. One might think that the infrequency of such discussions here results from the absence in the tractate as a whole of any encompassing legal theories that can explain its individual rules. The fact of the matter, however, is that studies of other tractates show that even those with carefully worked out legal principles exhibit a similar paucity of synthetic units.[8] This suggests that we are dealing here with a characteristic trait of Talmudic discourse, which, despite the impression created by the Talmudic dialectic, does not frequently compare and contrast rules deriving from diverse Tannaitic contexts.

The synoptic table that follows delineates the overall result of the preceding classification of this tractate's materials.

---

[8]See Avery-Peck, *Besah*, pp. 18-20, *Y. Terumot*, pp. 33-36, and *Y. Shebiit*, pp. 34-36.

SYNOPTIC TABLE

		# of units	% of category	% of Rosh Hash-anah
I. Exegetical Material				
A.	Amoraic exegesis	50	41.32	17.01
B.	Amoraic disputes over meaning	7	5.79	2.38
C.	Explanation from Scripture	49	40.50	16.67
D.	Explanation from the Mishnah	1	.82	.34
E.	Explanation from Tannaitic statements	14	11.57	4.76
Totals:		121	100.00	41.16
II. Supplementary Material				
A.	Rules cited from the Mishnah and Tosefta	14	9.33	4.76
B.	Other Tannaitic rules and homilies	37	24.67	12.59
C.	Rules and homilies in the names of Amoraim	95	63.34	32.31
D.	Tannaitic rules applied to new cases	2	1.33	.68
E.	Application of the Mishnah's and Tosefta's rules	2	1.33	.68
Totals:		150	100.00	51.02
III. Synthetic Material				
A.	Discussion of contradictory Tannaitic statements	14	60.87	4.76
B.	Which Tannaitic authority?	5	21.74	1.70
C.	Coordination of Amoraic Rules	4	17.39	1.36
Totals:		23	100.00	7.82
Final Totals:		294		100

The synoptic table indicates in detail the interests of Bavli Rosh Hashanah. The greatest percentage of the tractate's material, slightly over half of the tractate, supplements the Mishnah's rules with thematically related materials. Within this category, the majority of rules are stated in the names of the Amoraim themselves. The Talmudic authorities, this is to say, did not define as their central purpose recording and transmitting Tannaitic statements other than those found in Mishnah Rosh Hashanah, which forms the center of their work. Instead, their commentary on Mishnah Rosh Hashanah provided the context in which to offer laws that answered their own questions regarding appropriate and required festival observance. While the Talmudic tractate is structured as a commentary to Mishnah Rosh Hashanah, direct elucidation of the Mishnah's specific rules takes up slightly less space than supplementation. The exegetical materials comprises 41.16% of the tractate; the synthetic materials, which in essence represent a more sophisticated form of exegetical analysis, comprise another 7.82%.

Notably, this typology of Bavli Rosh Hashanah yields figures almost exactly parallel to those obtained when Bavli Besah, found in this same division and concerning the rules for food preparation on a festival day, is evaluated according to the same criteria. In the case of Bavli Besah, I found that 41.16% of the tractate was devoted to exegetical issues, 51.02% to supplementary materials, and 7.82% to synthetic issues.[9] The only significant difference within these categories is that Bavli Besah contains almost no examples of Explanation from Scripture, so significant an element of Bavli Rosh Hashanah. This probably results from the fact that Bavli Besah is dedicated to the working out of a set of legal principles distinctive to the Mishnah and completely unknown to Scripture. Bavli Rosh Hashanah, by contrast, contains no such principles or generative problematic at all, leaving open a greater potential for locating in Scripture the sources of its individual rules. Indeed, since the rabbis'

---

[9] See Avery-Peck, *Besah*, pp. 7-21.

New Year festival is quite a different celebration from the Bible's "memorial proclaimed with the sounding of the shofar" (Lev. 23:23-25), the Talmudic authorities may have felt a much stronger than usual compulsion to find a scriptural foundation for their distinctive rules. Be this as it may, the overall parallel between the percentages of each tractate devoted to Exegetical, Supplementary, and Synthetic materials suggests the extent to which Talmudic tractates emerged on the basis of a single plan and program that determined the Amoraic authorities' interests and approach.

The Ideology of Bavli Rosh Hashanah

Typologies such the one just presented indicate the overall interests of the Talmud's framers and suggest the extent to which a single plan and program stand behind the Talmud as a whole. A typology cannot, however, point out the specific concerns of or points made by the Talmudic authorship within each of the listed categories. It falls short of suggesting whether or not any Talmudic tractate, or, ultimately, the Talmud as a whole, makes a distinctive legal or theological point, separate from that which is found in the Mishnah. A typology cannot yield information regarding what the Talmudic redactors wished to say through their analysis of and supplement to the Mishnah.

To answer that question, in the following I provide an outline in which Bavli Rosh Hashanah is summarized so as to show its thematic and conceptual relationship to Mishnah Rosh Hashanah.[10] Each line of the Mishnah appears as a sub-head and is followed by a unit-by-unit summary of the points made by the Talmud pertinent to that Mishnaic statement. In this way, the outline shows graphically the extent to which the framework of the Mishnaic discourse

---

[10] The concept of outlining tractates of the Talmud so as to identify their ideology was developed by Jacob Neusner, in his *The Talmud of Babylonia. An Academic Commentary*. My conclusions regarding Bavli Rosh Hashanah are commensurate with those he reached in his study of this tractate. See Neusner, *Rosh Hashanah*.

determines both the organization and contents of the Talmudic discussions.

At the same time, this approach allows the distinctive message of the Talmud to emerge. This occurs because the outline allows us to recognize the few points at which the Talmudic redactors diverge from their usual close adherence to the Mishnah's ideas. In these instances they present instead significant agglomerates of materials containing ideas that stand outside of the range of the Mishnah's interests. Standing outside of the topical framework of the Mishnah, these agglomerates clearly express the Talmudic authorship's own distinctive ideas. In Bavli Rosh Hashanah, three significant agglomerates occur:[11]

> 1. B. R.H. 1:1 XVIII-XXXIV. The prohibition against delaying the payment of a vow or other obligation to God. The Talmud details the obligations subject to this prohibition and, for each type, discusses the point at which one is considered guilty of delaying. Significant material focuses upon fulfillment of the obligations to offer sacrifices, but the discussions also include vows to give to charity and to fulfill other obligations pertinent in the rabbis' own day.
>
> 2. B. R.H. 1:1 LXIII-LXXIV. Listing of the months in which redemptive events took place in Israelite history, culminating with a discussion of the month in which God's final redemption will occur in the future.
>
> 3. B. R.H. 1:2 IV-XXXV. The longest independent thematic unit of the tractate develops the theme of M. R.H. 1:2D-F, God's judging of the entire world on the New Year. The

---

[11]The rest of the Talmudic tractate yields but one significant independent composition: B. R.H. 1:3 X-XXVI, which discusses the procedures for intercalating the calendar. This topic is fully in line with the Mishnah's own interests, to which the Talmudic considerations add nothing unexpected. By contrast, a short agglomerate at B. R.H. 2:3 IV-VII moves beyond the Mishnah's interests. Like the materials discussed here, it concerns God's ultimate acts of redemption and the means of atonement available to the Israelite people.

Talmud begins by discussing the judgment on the New Year and then considers the nature and result of God's final judgment on the day when the dead will rise. The unit ends with discussions of repentance, focusing on when acts of repentance are most efficacious for individuals and communities.

These discussions all occur in the context of the Talmudic treatment of the Mishnah's prologue, in conjunction with which they develop a unified theme and theological point. Of concern to the Talmudic masters is the centrality of the New Year festival in God's larger scheme of salvation. When the Talmudic masters think about the New Year, their distinctive interest is that which is only hinted at in the prologue to Mishnah Rosh Hashanah: the process through which God will judge the world and redeem Israel. In line with this, they present at B. R.H. 1:1 LXIII-LXXIV the calendar of redemption and, at B. R.H. 1:2 IV-XXXV, a detailed discussion of what will happen on the day of judgment itself, including an analysis of people's ability, through repentance, to assure God's acting out of his attribute of mercy.

The Talmudic agglomerate at B. R.H. 1:1 XVIII-XXXIV, on the need to fulfill in a timely fashion one's obligations to God, develops one practical aspect of the theological perspective presented at B. R.H. 1:1 LXIII-LXXIV and B. R.H. 1:2 IV-XXXV. At issue is how Israelites are to assure God's favorable judgment. Within the Rabbinic, no less than the biblical, concept of covenant, this depends upon the fulfillment of all of one's obligations to God: commitments made in the form of vows or pledges to charity, observance of ritual and social requirements and, in the time of the Temple, presentation of all required sacrificial offerings. Here the Talmud addresses a primary question concerning the people's meeting of these obligations: what is the time period within which such commitments must be fulfilled? In the present context, this question is significant because of its implication for God's judging of each individual. A favorable or negative judgment will be determined by whether or not the individual has completed his obligations to God in a timely manner.

We see that, in tractate Rosh Hashanah, when the Talmud moves away from the close consideration of the Mishnah, it focuses narrowly on the question of how the people can assure God's positive judgment and thereby achieve salvation. This interest is introduced in the first two pericopae of Mishnah Rosh Hashanah, the discussion of which takes up a full half of the Talmudic treatment of the tractate, much of which is comprised of the three major agglomerates referred to here. But while taking up the themes of judgment and salvation that introduce the Mishnaic tractate, the Talmudic authorship diverges significantly from the focus and concern of the Mishnah's framers. While referring to each individual's being judged on the New Year, the Mishnah's larger concern is God's judging of the community as a whole and his executing punishment through his control of nature—providing or withholding grain at Passover, fruit at Pentecost, and water at Tabernacles.[12] Further, while introducing the concept of judgment, the Mishnah here does not complete the picture by speaking of God's ultimate saving of the Israelite nation. The Talmud's interest, by contrast, shifts quickly from the broader question of judgment to a treatment of the individual's ability effectively to atone and, finally, to the nature of the ultimate reward or punishment that will come with the advent of the messianic age.

In pursuing this distinctive interest, the authorship of Bavli Rosh Hashanah expresses the program for Judaism prominent in the Talmudic literature as a whole, a program that clearly demarcates Talmudic ideology from that of the Mishnah. The main foci of the Mishnah are Temple, priests, and cult. While these aspects of Judaism are central to biblical religion, despite their prominence in the Mishnah, they are clearly disjunctive from the needs of the community to which the Mishnah and later Rabbinic texts spoke in the aftermath of the destruction of the Jerusalem Temple. The Talmuds, by contrast, have at their heart a concept that is well-fitted to the post-

---

[12]On this and the following, see Neusner, *Rosh Hashanah*, chapter 5.

Temple Jewish communities in which they were promulgated. The Talmuds of the Land of Israel and Babylonia speak of the efficacy of the rabbi and of Rabbinic learning as paths to salvation. At the foundation of the Talmudic message is the claim that, "when Israel does what sages teach, *the* Messiah will come."[13]

This message is expressed forcefully in Bavli Rosh Hashanah, which speaks of the Israelites' need to fulfill their obligations to God and of the certainty that God will bring judgment and, ultimately, redemption. At exactly those points at which the Talmud moves beyond the orbit of issues and rules defined by the Mishnah, it expresses an ideology distinctive to its own authorship and appropriate to the period in which that authorship spoke, long after the destruction of the Temple and the cessation of priestly worship.

While formulated as a careful commentary on and supplement to the Mishnah, Bavli Rosh Hashanah thus moves well beyond the topics and concerns introduced by the antecedent text, bringing into play issues and questions unique to its own authorship. The existence of these concerns and the way in which they are melded into a carefully organized and narrowly designed commentary is shown in the following outline. The outline indicates both the care with which the Talmudic tractate has been redacted and the extent to which its few substantive digressions express the theme I have identified. Talmudic units that do not present commentary to and close supplementation of the Mishnah are marked by the indenting of their numerical designation and description.

Mishnah Rosh Hashanah 1:1

A. M. R.H. 1:1B1: *The first day of Nisan is the new year for kings.*

    I   Why this rule?

    II   How do we know this from Scripture?

        III   Different rule for non-Israelite kings.

---

[13]Neusner, *Bavli*, p. 197. On these ideas in general, see pp. 195-210.

| | | XIV-XVI | Special case of Cyrus. |

B. M. R.H. 1:1B2: *The first day of Nisan is the new year for ... festivals.*

    XVII   Is this indeed the case?

                XVIII-XXXIV   Long sub-unit on the prohibition against delaying the payment of a vow or other obligation to God.

    XXXV-XXXIX   The first of Nisan is also the new year for months, leap years, and heave-offering of the *sheqel*. How do we know this, and why is it not included in the Mishnah?

C. M. R.H. 1:1C-D: *The first day of Elul is the new year for tithing cattle. Eleazar and Simeon say it is the first day of Tishre.*

    XL   Which Tannaitic authority stands behind the anonymous rule?

    XLVI   Eleazar and Simeon both depend upon Scripture.

D. M. R.H. 1:1E1: *The first of Tishre is the new year for the reckoning of years.*

    XLVII-XLVIII   What is the purpose of this rule?

    XLIX-L   Thematically related development of the preceding.

E. M. R.H. 1:1E2: *The first of Tishre is the new year for the reckoning of ... Sabbatical years.*

    LI   How do we know this from Scripture?

F. M. R.H. 1:1E3: *The first of Tishre is the new year for the reckoning of ... Jubilees.*

    LII-LVIII   Is this indeed the case? + related materials regarding the inception of the Jubilee year.

G. M. R.H. 1:1F1: *The first of Tishre is the new year for ... planting trees.*

LIX	From what verse do we know this?
LX-LXII	Application of this rule in determining the age of trees.
LXIII-LXXIV	List of months in which significant events took place and in which redemption will occur. Eliezer and Joshua dispute. Extended analysis of the list, including biblical foundation for each view.

H. M. R.H. 1:1F2: *The first of Tishre is the new year for ... vegetables.*

LXXV-LXXXII	Meaning and implications of this rule.

I. M. R.H. 1:1G-H: *Houses of Hillel and Shammai: date of new year of trees.*

LXXXIII	Why is this new year in Shevat?
LXXXIV-LXXXVII	Aqiba applies both Houses' views.
LXXXVIII-XCIII	Special rules for the citron tree.
XCIV-XCV	Other anomalous cases.

Two groupings of pericopae move beyond the range of interests of a commentary: XVIII-XXXV, on the prohibition against delaying the payment of a vow, and LXIII-LXIV, on the determination of the months in which God's redemptive actions were experienced in Israelite history. The former draws directly on the rule stated at M. R.H. 1:1B, that Nisan is the new year for festivals. This date accordingly has important implications for determining the point at which one has in fact "delayed." The second group of materials, on the dating of redemptive events in Israelite history, is connected to the Mishnah only in that it shares a general concern for the significance of specific months. Rather than a close connection to the Mishnah's themes, it seems tightly connected to the Talmud's own concern, made explicit in the following, for the association of the New Year festival and God's judging and saving of the Israelite people.

Mishnah Rosh Hashanah 1:2

A. M. R.H. 1:2A-B: *At four seasons the world is judged: at Passover through grain.*

    I   Which grain is meant?

B. M. R.H. 1:2D-F: *At New Year, the entire world is judged.*

II-III	Which authority stands behind this passage? At issue is when judgment in fact occurs.
IV	Who is judged first, king or community?
V-XV	How do people move God towards a favorable judgment?
XVI-XXVIII	The nature of God's judgment.
XXIX-XXXIV	The power of repentance: distinction between individual and community.
XXXV	When should people repent?

C. M. R.H. 1:2D: *On the New Year all who enter the world pass before Him like troops.*

XXXVI	Nature of God's judgment, as reflected in the term translated here as "troops."

While flowing from the general interests of the tractate, the large collection of material in section B moves far beyond the Mishnah's specific concern for the liturgical and ritual practices pertinent to the New Year. The Talmud's reflections are much broader, for it discusses theological issues concerning the nature of God's judgment, the end of days, and the ways in which people, through repentance and proper behavior on earth, can prepare for God's scrutiny of their deeds.

Mishnah Rosh Hashanah 1:3

A. M. R.H. 1:3A-B: *On six new moons messengers go forth.*

    I+II   Why only in these months? Because they contain fast days.

            III-VII   Discussion of the Scroll of Fasting.

B. M. R.H. 1:3B3-4: *Messengers go forth at Elul and at Tishre.*

    VIII   Why both months?

C. M. R.H. 1:3B5: *Messengers go forth at Kislev.*

    IX   But no messengers go forth at Second Adar.

            X-XII   Rules for intercalating first and second Adar.

            XIII-XV   Rule for intercalating a month so as to avoid a Sabbath-festival sequence.

            XVI-XXVI   Procedure for establishing the calendar.

D. M. R.H. 1:3C: *When the Temple stood, they would go forth also at Iyyar.*

The Bavli's major contribution is at section C, a detailed discussion of the rules for intercalating the calendar and of the rights of the court to intercalate a month despite evidence that no extra day should be added. Additionally, Amoraic authorities move beyond the framework of the Mishnah in their short discussion of the Scroll of Fasting, which indicates the dates on which miraculous events occurred in Israelite history and on which, therefore, fasting is prohibited.

Mishnah Rosh Hashanah 1:4

A. M. R.H. 1:4A-D: *To present testimony in two months they profane the Sabbath, Nisan and Tishre.*

    I   Only these months? This seems to contradict M. R.H. 1:3A.

    II   Scripture proves that they profane the Sabbath only for Nisan and Tishre.

B. M. R.H. 1:4E-F: *When the Temple stood, they profaned the Sabbath for all the months.*

    III   Edict of Yohanan b. Zakkai that changed this rule.

Mishnah Rosh Hashanah 1:5

A. M. R.H. 1:5A-C: *Whether or not the moon appeared clearly they violate the Sabbath vs. Yose.*

    I   Meaning of term "clearly."

Mishnah Rosh Hashanah 1:6

A. M. R.H. 1:6A-C: *Aqiba kept witnesses back at Lud; Gamaliel scolded him.*

    II   Court must make a judgment regarding the new moon based upon the testimony of witnesses.

    III   Contrary to M. R.H. 1:6B, Aqiba did not hold witnesses back.

Mishnah Rosh Hashanah 1:7

A. M. R.H. 1:7A-D: *A father and son who saw the new moon go together to give testimony; Simeon: they even testify together.*

    I   Source in Scripture for both views.

    II-III   The law follows Simeon.

B. M. R.H. 1:7E-G: *Incident illustrating the opinions cited in M. R.H. 1:7A.*

Mishnah Rosh Hashanah 1:8
A. M. R.H. 1:8A-C: *Five individuals may not testify regarding the new moon. Any evidence that a woman is not valid to offer, they also may not offer.*

    I   The converse is true: testimony a woman may give, such individuals may give.

Mishnah Rosh Hashanah 1:9
A. M. R.H. 1:9A-E: *The obligation of witnesses of the new moon to take all steps necessary to appear before the court.*

Mishnah Rosh Hashanah 2:1
A. M. R.H. 2:1A: *If the people in Jerusalem are not going to recognize the witness, they send another to give evidence about him.*

    I   "Another" means two people must testify.

    II   Is the testimony of one individual not trusted?

    III   Contrary to the Mishnah, witnesses need not attest to the honesty of the one who testifies regarding the new moon.

B. M. R.H. 2:1B-C: *On account of the minim, they began to accept testimony only from those who are recognized.*

    IV   Story of how sectarians hired witnesses to mislead the court.

Mishnah Rosh Hashanah 2:2
A. M. R.H. 2:2A: *At first they would kindle flares.*

    I   From Scripture we know the word "flare" signifies "burning."

    II   Were flares lit to mark the beginning of full months, defective months, or both?

B. M. R.H. 2:2B: *Once the Samaritans had spoiled matters, they made the rule that messengers would go forth.*

Mishnah Rosh Hashanah 2:3

A. M. R.H. 2:3A-B: *They kindle flares with long cedar wood sticks, reeds, oleaster, and flax tow.*

    III   Kinds of cedar.

        IV   Method of farming coral from the ocean bottom.

        V   God is destined to restore the trees of Jerusalem destroyed by gentiles.

        VI   The futility/value of teaching Torah where there are no students.

        VII   The value of Rabbinic scholars, who serve as a means of atonement for sin.

B. M. R.H. 2:3C-E: *Preparation and use of the flares.*

In section A, the Talmudic discussions briefly shift to interests outside of those expressed by the Mishnah but totally in keeping with those of the other, longer agglomerates of material that have distinguished the Talmud's independent interests. Here again the focus is upon God's ultimate acts of redemption and the means of atonement available to the Israelite people. The Rabbinic class sees itself as central in assuring God's favorable judgment of the nation.

Mishnah Rosh Hashanah 2:4

A. M. R.H. 2:4A-C: *Where did they kindle flares?*

    VIII   Meaning of *Bet Baltin*.

B. M. R.H. 2:4D: *From Bet Baltin one waves them to and fro until he sees the whole Exile lit up like a bonfire.*

    IX   What is meant by "Exile"?

    X   What is "lit up like a bonfire"?

XI Distance between locations listed at M. R.H. 2:4A-C.

Mishnah Rosh Hashanah 2:5

A. M. R.H. 2:5A-B: *In Jerusalem, the court examined witnesses in a courtyard called Bet Ya'azeq.*

  I The character of Bet Ya'azeq.

B. M. R.H. 2:5C-G: *The treatment of the witnesses at Bet Ya'azeq.*

Mishnah Rosh Hashanah 2:6

A. M. R.H. 2:6A-C1: *How do they examine the witnesses? .... "Was it facing the sun or turned away from it? Was it to the north or to the south?"*

  I Why the apparently redundant questions?

B. M. R.H. 2:6A-C2: *"How high was it, and in which direction was it leaning?"*

  II Answers to these questions suggest whether the witness is truthful.

C. M. R.H. 2:6D: *If he said, "It was facing the sun," he has said nothing at all.*

D. M. R.H. 2:6E-F: *Afterwards they would bring in the second party and examine him. If the testimony coincided, it was confirmed.*

  III Acceptable range of difference between testimony of the two witnesses.

  IV Unacceptable witnesses, e.g., those who saw only a reflection.

  V Unacceptable witnesses, e.g., those who saw it only for a moment.

E. M. R.H. 2:6G-I: *Unneeded witnesses are questioned briefly, so they will feel it was worth coming.*

Mishnah Rosh Hashanah 2:7

A. M. R.H. 2:7A: *The head of the court says, "It is sanctified."*

	I		Scriptural proof.

B. M. R.H. 2:7B: *The people respond, "It is sanctified. It is sanctified."*

	II		Scriptural proof that the people's response is required.
	III		Scriptural proof that the people must say "It is sanctified" twice.

C. M. R.H. 2:7C-D: *Whether it appears at the expected time or not, they sanctify it. R. Eleazar b. Sadoq says, "Only when not expected."*

	IV		Tannaitic statements that disagree with Eleazar b. Sadoq.
	V		The law follows Eleazar b. Sadoq.

Mishnah Rosh Hashanah 2:8

A. M. R.H. 2:8A: *Gamaliel had a picture of the shapes of the moon to show to witnesses.*

	I		Is making a picture of the shapes of the moon really permitted?
	II		Is it permitted to make images of heavenly attendants one can't reproduce?
	III		Is it permitted to make images of the other heavenly attendants?
	IV		Is it permitted to make them without worshipping them?

B. M. R.H. 2:8B-D: *Witnesses rejected by Yohanan b. Nuri were accepted by Gamaliel.*

	I		Reason Gamaliel accepted the testimony.

C. M. R.H. 2:8E-J: *Further cases of conflict over witnesses.*

	II		A decision of the court to sanctify the new month is valid even if the new moon has not actually appeared.

III	Same point.

Mishnah Rosh Hashanah 2:9

A. M. R.H. 2:9A-B: *Gamaliel decrees that Joshua accept his determination regarding the calendar. Aqiba meets Joshua.*

    IV   Who was troubled, Aqiba or Joshua?

B. M. R.H. 2:9C: *Aqiba tells Joshua he can prove that Gamaliel has acted properly.*

C. M. R.H. 2:9D-G: *Dosa b. Harkinas tells Joshua that one cannot take issue with a court.*

    V   Dosa's view derives from Scripture: statement on the authority of the court in each generation.

D. M. R.H. 2:9H-J: *Joshua goes to Gamaliel on the Day of Atonement. Gamaliel calls him "my master and my disciple."*

    VI   Detailed description of what happened in this meeting.

Mishnah Rosh Hashanah 3:1

A. M. R.H. 3:1A-B: *No matter when the new moon appears, if the declaration "It is sanctified" is not made before it gets dark at the beginning of the thirty-first day, the month coming to an end is an intercalated month.*

    I   Even though everyone saw the new moon, the declaration "It is sanctified" is necessary.

    II   M.'s rule applies if the court and all the people saw the new moon or if witnesses saw it and were examined. If the public and court saw the new moon, additional witnesses are not required.

    III   Unlike in commercial cases, even though witnesses already have been examined, the matter may not be completed at night.

B. M. R.H. 3:1C-D: *If the court alone saw it, two of them give testimony in the presence of the rest.*

| IV | Testimony is required only if, at the time of the sighting, the court was not in session. If the court was in session when the sighting occurred, no witnesses are needed. |

C. M. R.H. 3:1E-F: *If the entire court of three saw it, let two of them arise, and let them seat some of their colleagues with the remaining judge, and give testimony before them.*

| V | Same issue as at unit IV. A decision regarding the month may not be made by a single judge acting alone. |
| VI | Tannaitic dispute concerning whether people who witnessed an event may serve as judges. |

Mishnah Rosh Hashanah 3:2

A. M. R.H. 3:2A-C: *All shofars are valid, except for that of a cow, because it is a horn. Yose says, "But are not all shofars called horns?"*

| I-III | Scriptural sources of both positions. |
| IV | Abayye: cow's horn may not be used because it is comprised of layers. |

B. M. R.H. 3:2D: *Yose's view based on Josh. 6:5.*

| V | How we know that the word *yovel* at Josh. 6:5 actually means "ram." Incident involving Aqiba. |
| VI-IX | Series of incidents in which rabbis hear in common usage a word from the Mishnah or Scripture the meaning of which they had not known. |

Mishnah Rosh Hashanah 3:3

A. M. R.H. 3:3A-B: *The shofar for the New Year derives from an antelope. It is straight.*

    I   Levi says it is curved + relationship of his view to that of Judah.

    II   Evaluation of dispute between M. R.H. 3:3A-B, 3:4A-B, and view of Judah.

B. M. R.H. 3:3C: *...its mouth is overlaid with gold.*

    III   T. R.H. 2:4 clarifies the Mishnah.

C. M. R.H. 3:3D: *At the sides of the one who blows the shofar are two who blow trumpets.*

    IV-V   How are the shofar and horns used so the distinct sounds can be heard?

    VI   No matter how long the blast, each sound counts only for its own set.

    VII   To fulfill the obligation, one must hear the shofar, not an echo.

D. M. R.H. 3:3E-F: *Shofar is sounded for a long note; trumpets are sounded for a short note.*

Mishnah Rosh Hashanah 3:4

A. M. R.H. 3:4A-C: *Shofars used on fast days derive from rams, are curved, and overlaid with silver.*

    I   Why gold for the New Year festival and silver for fast days?

B. M. R.H. 3:4D-E: *In the middle of those who blow the shofar are two who sound trumpets.*

    IX   Trumpets and shofars were used together only in the Temple.

C. M. R.H. 3:4F: *Shofar sounds short note; trumpets sound long note.*

Mishnah Rosh Hashanah 3:5

A. M. R.H. 3:5A: *Proclamation of the Jubilee is equivalent to the New Year in regard to the sounding of the shofar and the blessings.*

X	In what specific regard are they equivalent?

B. M. R.H. 3:5B: *Judah: On New Year they sound a ram's horn; on the Jubilee, an antelope's horn.*

Mishnah Rosh Hashanah 3:6

A. M. R.H. 3:6A-E: *Rules for repairing a damaged shofar.*

I-V	Supplementary rules detailing ways of preparing or repairing a shofar.

Mishnah Rosh Hashanah 3:7

A. M. R.H. 3:7A-C: *He who sounds the shofar into a cistern, cellar, or large jar: to fulfill his obligation he must hear the shofar, not an echo.*

VI	Circumstances in which this rule applies: depends on where he is standing.
VII	Circumstances in which this rule applies: what if he is moving?
VIII-IX	Development of preceding: a shofar blast is not divisible.
X	Refutation of unit VII.
XI	Use of horns from sacrificial animals prohibited but valid if restriction against trespass applies.
XII	Shofar from animal used in idolatry or taken from a city under a ban of destruction.
XIII	Impact of vow to receive no benefit from a particular shofar or person who sounds it.

INTRODUCTION 47

B. M. R.H. 3:7A-J: *One near a synagogue who hears the shofar or the reading of the Scroll of Esther fulfills his obligation only if he directs his heart.*

	XIV	Parallel case of a person compelled to eat unleavened bread.
	XV	Rava: performance of religious obligations does not require intention.
	XVI-XVIII	Rava's view challenged.
	XIX	Rava's view rejected.
	XX	Rava revises his original statement: in some cases intention is required.
	XXI	One who sounds the shofar and one who hears it both must formulate intention.
	XXII	Same point on Tannaitic authority.

The short sub-unit on intention focuses upon and ultimately rejects Rava's view, holding instead that a ritual act is valid only if performed with the specific intention of fulfilling the pertinent religious obligation. This notion of the centrality of intention is a familiar Mishnaic and Talmudic theme.

Mishnah Rosh Hashanah 3:8

A. M. R.H. 3:8A-H: *So long as the Israelites set their eyes upward and submit their hearts to their Father in heaven, they grow stronger; if not, they fall.*

B. M. R.H. 3:8I-J: *Shofar blasts of a deaf-mute, idiot, and minor do not fulfill the obligation of the community; whoever is not obligated to carry out a deed cannot fulfill the obligation of the community.*

	I	Who is obligated to hear the shofar?

	II	Rule for one who is half slave and half freed.
	III-V	Circumstances in which one may or may not repeat a religious act so as to fulfill the obligation on behalf of others.

Mishnah Rosh Hashanah 4:1

A. M. R.H. 4:1A-C: *If the New Year coincided with the Sabbath, in the Temple they would sound the shofar, but not in the provinces.*

    I   We know from Scripture that the shofar is not sounded on the Sabbath.

B. M. R.H. 4:1D: *When the Temple was destroyed, Yohanan b. Zakkai ordained sounding of the shofar wherever there is a court.*

    II   Circumstances of Yohanan's decree; how he prevailed.

C. M. R.H. 4:1E-F: *Eleazar: Yohanan b. Zakkai ordained regarding Yavneh alone; sages: wherever there is a court.*

    III   Do sages entirely concur with Yohanan?

    IV   Meaning of sages' position.

Mishnah Rosh Hashanah 4:2

A. M. R.H. 4:2A-C: *In this regard also Jerusalem was ahead of Yavneh: in every town within sight and sound of Jerusalem and able to come up, they sound the shofar. But in Yavneh, they sound it only in the court alone.*

    V   Meaning of "In this regard also."

    VI   Nature and extent of obligation to sound the shofar.

    VII   Secondary issues regarding sounding of the shofar on the Sabbath in the presence of a court.

	VIII	Meaning of "within sight and sound and able to come up."

Mishnah Rosh Hashanah 4:3

A. M. R.H. 4:3A-B: *The lulab was taken up in the Temple for seven days; in the provinces, for one day. When the Temple was destroyed, Yohanan b. Zakkai ruled that in the provinces the lulab should be taken up for seven days, as a memorial to the Temple.*

	I	From what verse do we know one should create a memorial to the Temple?

B. M. R.H. 4:3C: *Yohanan also ruled that the day on which the omer is waved should be wholly prohibited in regard to the eating of new produce.*

	II	Why should the day the omer was waved in the Temple be wholly prohibited?
	III	Yohanan's ordinance actually represents a scriptural prohibition.

Mishnah Rosh Hashanah 4:4

A. M. R.H. 4:4A-C: *In olden times they would receive testimony about the new moon all day; once, witnesses came late, and the Levites were mixed up as to what psalm they should sing; then they determined to receive testimony only up to the afternoon offering.*

	I	What was the "mix up": did they recite the wrong psalm or no psalm?
	II	Which psalm did the Levites recite for each day of the week?
	III	Which psalm did they recite for the Sabbath additional sacrifice?
	IV	Which psalm did they recite for the Sabbath afternoon sacrifice?
	V	Did they recite the entire psalm or only one passage each week?

| | VI | The divine presence left the Temple in ten stages; in similar stages, the Sanhedrin was removed from Jerusalem into a place of exile. From the lowest point of banishment they are destined to be redeemed. |

B. M. R.H. 4:4D-E: *If witnesses came late, they treated that and the following day as holy; when the Temple was destroyed, Yohanan b. Zakkai ruled that they should again receive testimony all day long.*

C. M. R.H. 4:4F-G: *Joshua b. Qorha: Yohanan b. Zakkai ruled: Even if the head of the court is elsewhere, the witnesses should come to the location of the council.*

| | I | This applies only to witnesses regarding the new moon. Others are obligated to go wherever the head of the court is. |
| | II | Listing and discussion of ordinances of Yohanan b. Zakkai. |

Once again, at B. R.H. 4:4 VI, where the Talmud moves away from the immediate interests of the Mishnah, it takes up the theme of God's judgment and the coming redemption of the Israelite people.

Mishnah Rosh Hashanah 4:5

A. M. R.H. 4:5A-D: *The order of the blessings of the New Year additional service: Patriarchs, Powers, Sanctification of the Name including the Sovereignty-verses without the shofar; Sanctification of the Day and shofar, Remembrance-verses and shofar, Shofar-verses and shofar; then the blessing of the sacrificial service, the thanksgiving, and the priestly blessing; so Yohanan b. Nuri. Aqiba: If he does not sound the shofar in connection with the Sovereignty-verses, why does he mention them at all?*

I	Meaning of Aqiba's statement, which, on the surface, is unconvincing.

B. M. R.H. 4:5E-H: *Aqiba: one says Patriarchs, Powers, Sanctification of the Name, and includes the Sovereignty-verses with the Sanctification of the Day and then sounds the shofar; Remembrance-verses and sounds the shofar; Shofar-verses and sounds the shofar; then the blessing of the sacrificial service, the thanksgiving, and the priestly blessing.*

II	Passages in Scripture that instruct about the recitation of the benedictions of the Amidah and the Sovereignty, Remembrance, and Shofar-verses.
III	Proper placement of the Sanctification of the Day.
IV-V	How Tannaitic masters followed the view of Yohanan b. Nuri, A-D, or Aqiba, E-H.

Mishnah Rosh Hashanah 4:6

A. M. R.H. 4:6A: *They say no fewer than ten each of Sovereignty, Remembrance, and Shofar-verses.*

I	Two explanations for why ten of each kind of verse is required.

B. M. R.H. 4:6B: *Yohanan b. Nuri: Three of each fulfills the obligation.*

II	Interpretation of Yohanan's view.

C. M. R.H. 4:6C: *They do not use verses of Remembrance, Sovereignty, or Shofar that speak of punishment.*

I	Examples of verses that speak of punishment.
II	Verses that speak of punishment of idolaters are permitted + examples.

	III	They do not recite a verse that concerns the remembrance of an individual, even if it is favorable + examples.
	IV	Verses referring to visitations are like verses that refer to remembrance + examples and disagreement.
	V	Ps. 24:7-10 includes many Sovereignty references.
	VI	Verses that serve multiple purposes.

D. M. R.H. 4:6D-E: *One begins with verses deriving from the Pentateuch and finishes with verses deriving from prophetic writings. Yose: One may finish with verses deriving from the Pentateuch.*

	VII	Yose means his statement to apply only *post facto* + dispute over whether the Pentateuch contains four Sovereignty-verses.

Mishnah Rosh Hashanah 4:7

A. M. R.H. 4:7A-C: *On New Year the one who leads the additional prayer orders the sounding of the shofar; on other festivals, the one who says the morning service leads the Hallel.*

	I	Why the shofar is sounded late in the worship service while Hallel is recited early.
	II	Why the Hallel is not recited on the New Year and the Day of Atonement.

Mishnah Rosh Hashanah 4:8

A. M. R.H. 4:8A-G: *To provide a shofar for New Year they do not cross the Sabbath boundary, dig up debris, climb a tree, ride a beast, or swim; they do not cut it either with a tool that is forbidden on account of the rules of Sabbath or by a negative commandment of the Torah.*

	I	These things are forbidden because the shofar derives only from a positive commandment while the festival day restrictions derive from both positive and negative commandments.
	II	Why must all these restrictions be listed? Some appear to be obvious.
	III	What tool is meant by M. R.H. 4:8G?
B.	\multicolumn{2}{l}{M. R.H. 4:8H: *But if one wanted to put water or wine in it, he may do so.*}

B. M. R.H. 4:8H: *But if one wanted to put water or wine in it, he may do so.*

    IV   Who stands behind this rule?

C. M. R.H. 4:8I: *They do not keep children from sounding the shofar.*

    V   Rule for women may be based on this.

D. M. R.H. 4:8J: *But they practice with them until they learn how to do it.*

    VI   Even on the Sabbath.

E. M. R.H. 4:8K: *One who is practicing has not thereby fulfilled his obligation to sound the shofar.*

    VII   If he sounds it to produce proper notes, he has fulfilled his obligation.

F. M. R.H. 4:8L: *One who hears the shofar sounded by the person who is practicing also has not fulfilled his obligation.*

    VIII   To fulfill the obligation, one who sounds the shofar must formulate the intention to satisfy his own as well as other listeners' obligations.

Mishnah Rosh Hashanah 4:9

A. M. R.H. 4:9A-B: *The shofar is sounded in three sets of three blasts. A sustained blast is equal to three quavering blasts.*

	I	A Tannaitic rule does not contradict M. R.H. 4:9B.
B.	\multicolumn{2}{l	}{M. R.H. 4:9C: *A quavering blast is equal to three alarm blasts.*}

B. M. R.H. 4:9C: *A quavering blast is equal to three alarm blasts.*

    II   This is subject to dispute.

    III   From where in Scripture do we know that a shofar is used on the New Year?

    IV   From where in Scripture do we know that the sounds are preceded by a plain blast?

    V-VI   From where in Scripture do we know that there are three sets of three blasts (= M. R.H. 4:9A)?

    VII   From where else in Scripture do we know that the sounds are preceded by a plain blast (unit IV)?

    VIII-IX   Sequence and number of blasts derives from Scripture.

    X   Question of actual practice: Abbahu in Caesaria.

C. M. R.H. 4:9D: *If one sounded the first sustained blast and then sounded the second sustained blast for twice as long, he has credit only for one set.*

    XI   Supplementary rule: one fulfills the obligation by hearing nine blasts at nine different hours of the day.

    XII   Omission of some blasts impairs the validity of all the blasts.

D. M. R.H. 4:9E: *He who recited Musaf and afterward was assigned a shofar should sound a sustained blast, a quavering blast, and a sustained blast, three times.*

INTRODUCTION 55

XIII	If he had a shofar all along, he must sound the blasts during the course of the blessings.
XIV	One may sound the shofar on another's behalf but not recite the blessings on another's behalf.

E. M. R.H. 4:9F-G: *Just as the congregation's agent is liable to recite the daily prayers, so each individual is liable. Gamaliel: The agent of the community carries out the obligation on behalf of the community.*

XV	Debate between Gamaliel and anonymous authorities.
XVI-XVIII	Did sages concede to Gamaliel?
XIX	A person should put his prayer in order and then pray.
XX	Only people who cannot recite prayers themselves are exempted by the recitation of the agent of the community.

The preceding outline of the interests of Bavli Rosh Hashanah and of its relationship to the Mishnah illustrates three significant points about the Talmudic tractate: 1) It is carefully organized and laid out as a commentary on and supplement to the Mishnah, the organization of which it follows line-by-line. 2) It has a narrow range of interests in the elaboration of the Mishnah's law, a point shown equally by the typology of the Talmudic materials presented above. 3) The points at which the Talmudic discourse diverges from its usual interest in explanation and supplementation reveal a cogent ideology concerning the processes through which the people of Israel will be judged by God and ultimately will experience God's salvation. Bavli Rosh Hashanah articulates this ideology through its calendar of redemption (B. R.H. 1:1 LXIII-LXXIV), its depiction of God's judgment on the day the dead will rise (B. R.H. 1:2 IV-XXXV), and the idea that, from the lowest point of Israel's banishment, the people are to be redeemed (B. R.H. 4:4 VI).

Another aspect of the Bavli Rosh Hashanah's messianic message appears as only a small note. But this is a note that signals a concept central in the Talmudic masters' larger understanding of the importance of their work in explicating and supplementing Mishnaic law. The point, expressed at B. R.H. 2:3 VII, is that the study and pious lives of Rabbinic sages serve the people of Israel as a means of atonement from sin. The rabbis themselves thus are central in God's process of judgment, atonement, and redemption. In this notion, the shift in the Talmud from the ideology of the Mishnah is manifest. Within the Mishnah, priest and cult are the loci of sanctification and, hence, of redemption.[14] In Bavli Rosh Hashanah, as in the Talmud as a whole, the focus moves from priest and cult to the Rabbinic sage and to all who study and observe the law. The Talmud is clear that, as the Mishnah stated, on the New Year, God judges all people. But for the Talmud's authorities, the important point is that proper adherence to the Torah, as expressed and interpreted by the Talmudic rabbis themselves, can assure a positive evaluation, bringing with it the end of exile and the achieving of redemption.

Theory of Translation and Explanation

This translation aims to reproduce in colloquial American English the content and flow of the Talmudic discussions found in Bavli Rosh Hashanah. My hope is to render the Talmudic materials accessible even to individuals who are both unaccustomed to the general characteristics of Talmudic discourse and unfamiliar with the technical terms and concepts through which that discourse is expressed. Use of this translation, without additional reference to the original text or to other commentaries, should provide a basic understanding of the Talmudic discussions found in this tractate.

To attain this goal, a word-by-word translation is supplemented by the extensive use of interpolated comments. These com-

---

[14] See Neusner, *Judaism*, pp. 230-283, and Avery-Peck, *Terumot*, pp. 2-21.

ments, set off from the Talmud's own words with two different types of brackets, serve three distinct purposes:

1) Square brackets [...] mark words I have added in order to transform the Talmud's abstruse and often fragmented clauses into complete English sentences. These rather basic additions a) supply words clearly assumed by, but missing from, the original text and b) spell out completely the point expressed by technical terms or other Talmudic shorthand.

2) I also use square brackets when I interpolate explanatory comments or references within individual Talmudic sentences. Supplying this information within the translation itself permits the reader easily to grasp the point of each Talmudic statement without the distraction of constant reference to footnotes. Marking these, and all, additions with brackets allows the reader to reconstruct exactly what is found in the original text and thereby to formulate an independent judgment about the meaning of the passage.

3) Rounded brackets {...} surround my own extended exegetical comments. Found before and after individual Talmudic stichs, these comments make explicit the logical links implicit in Talmudic discourse. At the beginning of many Talmudic units a bracketed explanation introduces the issue about to be discussed. At each step in the argument such comments explain the present state of the discussion and indicate the direction it is about to take. These interpolations thus form a running commentary to the text, facilitating intelligent reading and evaluation of each Talmudic argument, viewed as a whole.

The use of brackets, particularly the rounded type, distinguishes this translation from previous ones. To clarify individual Talmudic statements Simon, for instance, uses footnotes, in which he routinely cites Rashi. He also provides, without brackets, the words needed to create sentences of disjointed Talmudic prose. But, besides being inconsistent in supplying the important information just described, Simon hardly ever provides an overview of the Talmud's larger arguments or of the individual steps in logic of which those debates are composed. Readers therefore are left on their own to discern the structure and point of the Talmudic *sugya*.

Simon's approach requires readers to struggle unaided through a largely unembellished text and forces them independently to formulate views concerning that text's meaning. This method of translation has, perhaps, some, chiefly pedagogical, merit. The problem is that the extreme economy of Talmudic language means that, without access to the commentaries printed on the Talmudic page, most individuals, especially those who wish to begin with a translation in the first place, cannot be expected to attempt such an evaluation. My own approach therefore appears to me much preferable and, in fact, to correct the principle shortcoming of Simon's otherwise excellent translation. My bracketed comments give the reader easy access to the Talmudic arguments. By setting aside these interpolations, the reader likewise has use of a careful, word-for-word translation, against which exegetical possibilities other than the one I provide may be tested.

Other specific aspects of this translation too are designed to increase intelligibility of the Talmudic discourse. First, I break the undifferentiated text of the Talmud into its smallest complete units of discourse. Designated by Roman numerals, these are the shortest units of Talmudic discussion that a) address and resolve a single issue and b) are logically independent of the materials that precede and follow. Dividing the text in this way is a significant improvement over Simon's translation, in which there is little relationship between the paragraphing of the English and the content of the text being translated. Marking these divisions in the text also facilitates study by isolating the proper focus of interpretation, the individual unit of discourse, or *sugya*. Finally, my division of the text forms the basis both for the typology and the outline of the Talmud's materials, presented above. Carefully dividing the text facilitates determination of the relationship between each of the Talmud's discussions and the pertinent pericope of the Mishnah.

To allow analytical reading of each unit, its materials too are broken into their smallest component parts. These are the individual sentences or thoughts from which the larger discussion is created. Division of the material in this manner facilitates study by isolating each stage in the *sugya* and providing the context for my extended comments. Designation of the individual components by letter also permits easy reference to any of the lines of the text. In conjunction with the Roman numerals that mark units of discourse, my lettering provides a complete system of references for this Talmudic tractate.

To promote further the translation's central goal of intelligibility, three typefaces are used. Mishnaic pericopae appear in italics. Citations of Tosefta are in boldface. The Talmud's own words, as well as my bracketed comments, are in regular type. The use of different typefaces highlights points at which the Talmud cites and explains antecedent materials or uses them in building its own arguments.

The form and goal of this translation determine the content of the comments that precede the Talmudic materials on each individual pericope of the Mishnah. Since the Talmudic materials themselves are explained in the course of the translation, my additional comments serve a separate purpose altogether. They briefly describe the relationship of each Talmudic unit to the Mishnah and focus as well upon the agendum of Talmudic issues as it unfolds within the Talmud's several units pertinent to each Mishnaic passage. These comments form the basis for the preceding synoptic classification and description of the Talmud's materials.

Summary: The goal of this translation is to render Bavli Rosh Hashanah accessible even to those who are not familiar with Talmudic discourse at all or who simply do not wish to turn to the original text and its relevant commentaries. To accomplish this, a word-for-word translation is liberally augmented 1) with the information required to understand the legal and conceptual basis of individual Talmudic statements and 2) with a step-by-step evaluation of the flow of each unit of Talmudic discourse. I hope, through this approach, to have improved the availability to scholars and all interested parties of a document that richly portrays the inner-life and ideals of Rabbinic Judaism.

Manuscripts, Editions, Commentaries

This translation is based on the printed edition (hereafter: P), which is corrected and annotated to indicate variants from the Munich manuscript (hereafter: M) and other manuscripts and editions cited by Rabbinovicz. In the vast majority of cases, the textual issues are minor and have no impact upon the meaning of the Talmud's discussions. Still, variants from MS. M of even minor significance are listed in the notes. One common substantive textual issue concerns the correct name to which a statement of law is attributed. Unless there is a clear reason to prefer one name over another, I translate P and list the alternatives in a note.

My translation of Mishnah Rosh Hashanah is based upon that of Jacob Neusner, *Appointed Times*, Part IV, pp. 64-95, which I have liberally revised in line with the style of my translation of the Talmud's passages. In rendering other pericopae cited from the Mishnah and Tosefta I also referred to Neusner's work on five of the Mishnah's six divisions as well as to the other recent translations and commentaries listed in the bibliography. The availability of these modern studies of the Rabbinic literature greatly eased my own work in translating Bavli Rosh Hashanah.

I assume throughout that the Talmudic discourse has a rather obvious meaning that can be drawn out from its own words and the flow of its particular ideas. Where the meaning of the text is not implicit in the information it itself provides, I generally cite Rashi, who tends to propose a straightforward interpretation of the text. If there are genuine issues of meaning, I choose the interpretation that seems most reasonably to explain the text at hand, even if, on occasion, that interpretation leaves unresolved apparent contradictions with other Talmudic passages. I cite alternative explanations in a note. Since this translation intends to provide access to the world of the Talmud, not to that of medieval Judaism, it is beyond its scope consistently to cite the views of post-Talmudic commentaries. While important in their own right, for purposes of this study, those exegetes serve only when their work is needed to elucidate a particular passage.

CHAPTER ONE

ROSH HASHANAH CHAPTER ONE

1:1

[A] [2a] *There are four new years:*
[B] *(1) the first day of Nisan is the new year for kings and festivals;*
[C] *(2) the first day of Elul is the new year for[1] tithing cattle.*
[D] *R. Eleazar and R. Simeon say, "It is on the first day of Tishre."*
[E] *(3) The first day of Tishre is the new year for the reckoning of years, for Sabbatical years, and for Jubilees,*
[F] *for planting [trees] and for vegetables;*
[G] *(4) the first day of Shevat is the new year for trees, in accord with[2] the opinion of the House of Shammai.*
[H] *The[3] House of Hillel say, "On the fifteenth day of that month [is the new year for trees]."*

M. R.H. 1:1 lists the starting points of four distinct annual cycles. These cycles pertain to the determination of the fiscal year, which is based upon the reign of the king (B), establish which animals may be given as tithe on behalf of other animals (C+D; see Lev. 27:32), demarcate the annual religious and ritual calendar (E), and establish the year to which produce belongs (F). This affects the procedure by which specific foods are tithed and, in the case of recently planted trees, determines the point at which the fruit may be eaten at all (see Lev. 19:23). The new year for trees (G vs. H) determines the tithing year for the fruit of trees.

---

[1] M adds: [for the reckoning of] years, for Sabbatical years, and for....

[2] M and other sources lack, "in accord with," reading the preceding as direct discourse.

[3] M and other sources introduce the line: But.

An exceedingly long and detailed Talmudic treatment of this pericope provides each rule's foundation in Scripture and outlines its application in religious, communal, or commercial life. The resulting discussion forms a line by line commentary that neither yields any protracted theoretical discussions of the Mishnah's issues nor locates overarching principles or implications that emerge from the pericope as a whole. The material pertinent to the Mishnah, rather, remains narrowly exegetical, reviewing each line of the Mishnah's passage in turn and indicating its significance without questioning the theory that stands behind it.

The Talmudic discourse breaks away from its narrowly exegetical interests only at two points. Units **XVIII-XXXIV** consider the prohibition against delaying payment of a vow or other obligation to God, and units **LXIII-LXXIV** discuss the months in which redemptive acts occurred in past Israelite history and in which the final redemption will occur. Moving away from the directly exegetical concerns that mark the rest of the Talmudic discussion, these essays point to the distinctive interests of the Talmudic masters themselves. These interests concern 1) the manner by which Israelites are to comply with the covenant so as to assure that God's redemptive actions will be forthcoming and 2) the calendar by which that redemption has begun to unfold and will continue to occur. Later in the tractate, when the Talmudic authorities again break away from the interests of M. Rosh Hashanah, they discuss the actual process of God's judgment and the fate awaiting those who are righteous and those who sin. So we see here the introduction of a theme that recurs whenever the Talmud's masters move away from the narrowly exegetical interests that concern such a large percentage of the tractate.

The following outline details the specific interests of each Talmudic unit, viewed in relationship to the Mishnaic pericope on which it comments.

A.	M. R.H. 1:1B: *The first day of Nisan is the new year for kings*		
		I	Why this rule?
		II	How do we know this from Scripture?
		III	Different rule for non-Israelite kings (+ XIV-XVI: special case of Cyrus).
B.	M. R.H. 1:1B: *The first day of Nisan is the new year for ... festivals*		
		XVII	Is this indeed the case?
		(XVIII-XXXIV	Long sub-unit on the prohibition against delaying payment of a vow or other obligation to God.)
		XXXV-XXXIX	The first of Nisan is also the new year for months, leap years, and heave-offering of the *sheqel*. How do we know this and why is it not included in the Mishnah?
C.	M. R.H. 1:1C-D: *The first day of Elul is the new year for tithing cattle. Eleazar and Simeon say it is the first day of Tishre*		
		XL	Which Tannaitic authority stands behind the anonymous rule?
		XLVI	Eleazar and Simeon both depend upon Scripture.
D.	M. R.H. 1:1E: *The first day of Tishre is the new year for the reckoning of years*		
		XLVII-XLVIII	What is the purpose of this rule?

(XLIX-L   Thematically related development of the preceding.)

E.   M. R.H. 1:1E: *The first day of Tishre is the new year for the reckoning of ... Sabbatical years*
   LI   How do we know this from Scripture?

F.   M. R.H. 1:1E: *The first day of Tishre is the new year for the reckoning of ... Jubilees*
   LII-LVIII   Is this indeed the case? + related materials regarding the inception of the Jubilee year.

G.   M. R.H. 1:1F: *The first day of Tishre is the new year for ... planting trees*
   LIX   From what verse [in Scripture] do we know this?
   LX-LXII   Application of M. R.H. 1:1F in determining the age of trees.
   (LXIII-LXXIV   List of months in which significant events took place and in which redemption will occur. Eliezer and Joshua dispute. Extended analysis of this list of dates, including establishment of the biblical foundation for each view.)

H.   M. R.H. 1:1F: *The first day of Tishre is the new year for ... vegetables*
   LXXV-LXXXII   Meaning and implications of this rule.

I.   M. R.H. 1:1G-H: *Houses of Hillel and Shammai: date of new year of trees*
   LXXXIII   Why is this new year in Shevat?

LXXXIV-LXXXVII	Aqiba applies both Houses' views.
LXXXVIII-XCIII	Special rules for the citron tree.
XCIV-XCV	Other anomalous cases.

The Talmudic commentary follows the order of the Mishnah's presentation, with only two agglomerates of pericopae moving beyond the explicit interests of the Mishnah itself: **XVIII-XXXV**, on the prohibition against delaying payment of a vow, and **LXIII-LXIV**, on the determination of the months in which significant events occurred in Israelite history. The former occurs here because it draws upon the rule stated at M. R.H. 1:1B, that the first of Nisan is the new year for festivals. This date accordingly has important implications for determining the point at which one has in fact "delayed." The second group of materials, on the dating of significant events in Israelite history, is even less closely connected to the issues at hand here, drawing only upon the Mishnah's general concerns for the significance of specific months. Accordingly, we see the extent to which these materials stand outside of the Talmud's otherwise narrowly exegetical interests, forming independent statements of concerns distinctive to the Talmudic masters' own thinking.

[I.A] *[The first day of Nisan is the new year] for kings* [M. R.H. 1:1B]—

[B] What is the purpose of this rule? {Rashi: Instead of a set day designated to mark the anniversary of all kings' reigns, the anniversary should be marked by the day on which the particular king actually assumed the throne.}

[C] Said Rab Hisda, "It is because of legal documents.

[D] "For we have taught on Tannaitic authority [M. Sheb. 10:5]: *Antedated bonds are invalid, but postdated bonds are valid.*" {Documents are dated according to the day, month and year of the reign of a specific king. Counting all reigns from the first of Nisan makes it easy to determine when a legal document was created, even for people who do not know the day on which a specific king assumed the throne.}[4]

[II.A] {The implications of the preceding are spelled out.} Our rabbis have taught on Tannaitic authority: [As for] a king who ascended [to the throne] on the twenty-ninth of Adar—as soon as the first of Nisan has arrived, a [full] year [in office] is credited to him.

[B] But if he ascended [to the throne] on the first of Nisan [itself]—they do not count a [full] year of his [reign] until the next first of Nisan arrives.

[C] A master said, "'[As for] a king who ascended [to the throne] on the twenty-ninth of Adar—as soon as the first of Nisan has arrived, a [full] year [in office] is credited to him':

[D] [2b] "This teaches us[5] that Nisan is the new year for kings,

[E] "and a single day in the year can be considered a full year."

[III.A] {Unit II.B is explained.} "But[6] if he ascended [to the throne] on the first of Nisan [itself]—they do not count a [full] year of his [reign] until the next first of Nisan arrives."

[B] This is obvious [and need not be stated]!

[C] No, it is necessary for a case in which they appointed him [to be king] while it was still Adar, [but he did not actually assume the throne until Nisan].

---

[4]In a system in which years always begin, for instance, on January 1, the month of June necessarily precedes the month of July. But in a system in which months are counted from a particular event, this is not necessarily so. Imagine a case in which dating follows the actual day on which a king ascends to the throne. If a king were appointed on July 1, then, in the counting of that king's reign, the month of July, the first month of his reign, would always precede the month of June, which would be the last month before the anniversary of his rule. In this system, a person who did not know the date on which the king assumed the throne could not tell whether a date in July is earlier or later than a date in June.

[5]Rashi's text and the marginal correction in M read: What does this teach us?

[6]An addition written between the lines in M introduces this line: A master said.

[D] [Had A's rule not been taught explicitly] what might we have thought?

[E] [Since] they appointed him [before Nisan, once Nisan arrived, it is as though he had been king for] two years!

[F] Therefore we are [explicitly] taught [the contrary]. {Even if the king had been appointed to rule some time before, his reign is dated from the beginning of Nisan of the year in which he actually assumed the throne.}

[IV.A] Our rabbis have taught on Tannaitic authority [T. R.H. 1:1]: **If [the king] died during Adar, and another [king] arose in his place during Adar, [in writing legal documents during that same month] they count [the year as the last year in the reign of] this one [who died] and [as the first year in the reign of] that one [who assumed the throne].**

[B] **If [the king] died during Nisan, and another arose in his place during Nisan, [in writing legal documents during that same month] they count [the year as the last year in the reign of] this one [who died] and [as the first year in the reign of] that one [who assumed the throne].**

[C] **If [the king] died during Adar, and another [king] arose in his place during Nisan, they count the former [period, up to Nissan, as the reign of] the first [king], and [they count] the latter [period, after the beginning of Nisan, as the reign of] the second [king].**

[V.A] {Unit IV.A is explained.} A master said: **If [the king] died during Adar, and another [king] took power in his place during Adar, [in writing legal documents during that same month] they count [the year as the last year in the reign of] this one [who died] and [as the first year in the reign of] that one [who assumed the throne].**

[B] This is obvious [and need not be stated]!

[C] [No, it is necessary, since, had A's rule not been taught explicitly] what might you have thought?

[D] In [the middle of] a year, we do not [begin to] count [according to the reign of] a second [king].

[E] [To prevent this wrong assumption, at T. R.H. 1:1, cited at A] we are [explicitly] taught [the contrary].

[VI.A] {Unit IV.B is explained.} **If [the king] died during Nisan, and another arose in his place during Nisan, [in writing legal documents during that same month] they count [the year as the last year in the reign of] this one [who died] and [as the first year in the reign of] that one [who assumed the throne].**

[B] This is obvious [and need not be stated]!

[C] [No, it is necessary, since, had A's rule not been taught explicitly] what might you have thought?

[D] When we said [above, unit II.E], "A single day in the year can be considered a full year"—[this applies] at the end of the year, [so that a king who assumes power at the end of Adar is credited with a full year on the first of Nisan].

[E] But at the beginning of a year we do not apply [this rule, so that a king who dies at the beginning of Nisan does not have the new year counted within his reign].

[F] [To prevent this wrong assumption, at T. R.H. 1:1, cited at A] we are [explicitly] taught [the contrary].

[VII.A] {Unit IV.C is explained.} **If [the king] died during Adar, and another [king] arose in his place during Nisan, they count the former [period, up to Nissan, as the reign of] the first [king], and [they count] the latter [period, after the beginning of Nisan, as the reign of] the second [king].**

[B] This is obvious [and need not be stated]!

[C] No, it is necessary for a case in which they appointed him [to be king] while it was still Adar, and [this] king was the son of the [recently deceased] king.

[D] [Had A's rule not been explicitly taught] what might you have thought?

[E]   [Since] they appointed him [before Nisan, once Nisan arrived, it is as though he had been king for] two years!

[F]   [To prevent this wrong assumption, at T. R.H. 1:1, cited at A] we are [explicitly] taught [the contrary, that the years of his reign are counted only beginning in Nisan, when he actually assumed power].

[VIII.A] Said R. Yohanan, "From what [verse in Scripture do we know] concerning kings, that they count [the years of their reign] only from Nisan?

[B]   "For it is said [1 Kgs. 6:1]: 'In the four hundred and eightieth year after the people of Israel came out of the land of Egypt, in the fourth year, in the month of Ziv, which is the second month, of Solomon's reign over Israel, [he began to build the house of the Lord].'

[C]   "An analogy is made between the reign of Solomon and the Exodus from Egypt.

[D]   "Just as the [years from the] Exodus from Egypt are [counted] from Nisan, so the [years of the] reign of Solomon are [counted] from Nisan."

[E]   Now, as for the Exodus from Egypt itself: How do we know that we date it from Nisan?

[F]   Perhaps[7] we should date it from Tishre! {See M. R.H. 1:1E. Rashi: even though the Exodus occurred in Nisan, one might imagine that Tishre, the new year of years, marks its anniversary.}

[G]   Do not even think that, since it is written [Num. 33:38]: "And Aaron the priest went up Mount Hor at the command of the Lord and died there, in the fortieth year after the people of Israel had come out of the land of Egypt, in the fifth month [that is, Ab], on the first day of the month."

---

[7]Rashi's text begins this line: I might say....

[H]	And it is written [Dt. 1:3]: "And in the fortieth year, in the eleventh month [that is, Shevat], on the first day of the month, Moses spoke [to the people of Israel...]."
[I]	Since [what is described at G] took place in Ab [which is before Tishre], and it is called the fortieth year, and since [what is described at H] took place in Shevat [which is after Tishre], and it is called the fortieth year, we may conclude that the new year [in regards to the Exodus] does not begin in Tishre. {If Tishre marked the anniversary of the Exodus from Egypt, then what is described at H would have taken place in the forty-first year.}
[J]	{I's conclusion is challenged.} Certainly this [incident, referred to at G] explicitly [is indicated as being counted] from the Exodus from Egypt.
[K]	But this [incident referred to at H]: On what basis [do you know that it represents forty years counted] from the Exodus from Egypt?
[L]	Perhaps[8] [it counts] from the construction of the [wilderness] tabernacle, [which took place in the year after the Exodus]!
[M]	{J-L is rejected.} [We know that I is correct on the basis of] that which Rab Pappa said: "[The appearance of the expression] 'twentieth year' in two separate passages allows for an analogy based upon verbal congruities."[9] {See below, unit **XIII**.I, 3b.}
[N]	So here [at G-I, I can argue that the two appearances of the term] fortieth year [at Num. 33:38 and Dt. 1:3] allow for an analogy based upon verbal congruities:
[O]	Just as here[10] [at Num. 33:38, in the case of the death of Aaron, the years are being counted] from the Exodus from

---

[8]M adds: it refers to a different counting [of years]. Comparably....

[9]*Gezerah shavah.* In M this line is garbled.

[10]M reads: There.

Egypt, so here [at Dt. 1:3, in reference to Moses' speech, the years are being counted] from the Exodus from Egypt.

[P] {Another challenge to I is presented. This again supports F's proposal that the number of years since the Exodus from Egypt should be counted from Tishre.} But on what basis [do you conclude that] the incident that took place in Ab [the fifth month, recorded at Num. 33:38, cited at G] occurred first [that is, prior to the incident recorded at Dt. 1:3, referred to at H]?

[Q] Perhaps the incident that took place in Shevat [the eleventh month, recorded at Dt. 1:3] occurred first! {In this scenario, Moses' speech took place before Aaron died. It was counted as taking place in the fortieth year because the fortieth anniversary of the Exodus, in Tishre, already had passed.}

[R] Do not even think that, since it is written [Dt. 1:4, in the continuation of the passage referring to Moses' speech]: "after he had defeated Sihon [the king of the Amorites]."[11]

[S] But when Aaron died, Sihon in fact was still alive. {Clearly, then, the event recorded in Dt. 1:4 happened after Aaron's death, reported at Num. 33:38.}

[T] [We know that Sihon was alive when Aaron died] since it is written [Num. 21:1]: [3a] "When the Canaanite, the king of Arad, [who dwelt in the Negeb], heard [that Israel was coming by the way of Atharim...]."

[U] What report did he hear?

[V] He heard that Aaron had died and that the clouds of glory had left [the people of Israel]. He therefore determined that it now was permitted to fight against [the people of] Israel.

[W] And this is[12] as it is written [Num. 20:29]: "And all the congregation saw that Aaron was dead...."

---

[11] The final bracketed words appear explicitly in M.

[12] M lacks the beginning of this line.

[X] Now,[13] said R. Abbahu, "[At Num. 20:29] do not read, 'saw.' Rather [by adding one letter, read it as], 'were seen.'" {That is, once the clouds of glory departed, the Israelites became visible to their enemies.}

[Y] [This reading is] in accordance with Resh Laqish, for said Resh Laqish, "'*Ki*' [the word in the verse following 'saw,' translated as 'that'] has four [additional] meanings: 'if,' 'perhaps,' 'but,' [and] 'since.'" {Hence, the verse may be read: And all the congregation was seen, since Aaron was dead....}

[Z] Is this [exposition at T-Y] an appropriate proof [that Sihon was alive when Aaron died]?

[AA] There [at Num. 21:1] reference is to Canaan, while here [at Dt. 1:4 we speak of] Sihon!

[BB] [To resolve this problem, we recall that] it is taught on Tannaitic authority: [The names] Sihon, Arad, and Canaan all refer to the same individual.

[CC] [He was called] Sihon, since he resembled a *sayyah* [that is, a foal] in the wilderness.

[DD] [He was called] Canaan after his nation.

[EE] And what was his [given] name? His name was Arad.

[FF] There are those who say:

[GG] [He was called] Arad because he resembled an *arad* [that is, wild ass] of the wilderness.

[HH] [He was called] Canaan after his nation.

[II] And what was his [given] name? His name was Sihon.

[IX.A] Now, might I not reason [that] New Year is [in] Iyyar, [the second month]?

[B] Do not even think such a thing, since it is written [Ex. 40:17]: "And in the first month [that is, Nisan], in the second

---

[13]M reads: Now, this accords with what R. Abbahu said.

year,[14] on the first day of the month, the tabernacle was erected."

[C] And it is [further] written [Num. 10:11]: "And in the second year, in the second month [that is, Iyyar] [on the twentieth day of the month],[15] the cloud was taken up from over the tabernacle of the testimony."

[D] [Insofar as], when speaking of [the construction of the tabernacle, in] Nisan, [Ex. 40:17] calls it the second year, and when speaking of [the removal of the cloud, which took place immediately thereafter, in] Iyyar, [Num. 10:11 still] calls it the second year, this proves that New Year is not in Iyyar. {If it were, the event reported at Num. 10:11 would have been described as taking place at the beginning of the third year.}

[X.A] Then might I not reason [that] New Year is [in] Sivan, [the third month]?

[B] Do not even think such a thing, since it is written [Ex. 19:1]: "On the third new moon after the people of Israel had gone forth out of the land of Egypt, [on that day they came into the wilderness of Sinai]."

[C] Now, if [new year] were in the third month, [Ex. 19:1 would have indicated that they had entered the wilderness of Sinai], "*in the second year* after [the people of Israel] had gone forth[16] [out of the land of Egypt]."

[XI.A] But why not propose [that New Year is in] Tamuz [the fourth month], Ab [the fifth month], or Adar [the twelfth month]? {Unit **VIII** already has shown that Ab and Shevat are the fifth and eleventh months of the same year. This

---

[14]M lacks the remainder of this line.

[15]The preceding bracketed words appear explicitly in M.

[16]M lacks: had gone forth.

	proves that New Year does not occur in any of the intervening months.}
[B]	Rather [to reject A's proposal entirely], said R. Eleazar, "[We learn that New Year is in Nisan] from this verse [2 Chron. 3:2, referring to Solomon's building of the Jerusalem-Temple]: 'He began to build in the second month, *in the second*, of the fourth year of his reign.'
[C]	"What is the meaning of 'in the second'?
[D]	"Is it not the second month, by which they count his reign?"
[E]	Rabina objected to this: "Let me rather argue [lit.: say] that [it refers to] the second day of the month."
[F]	[Rejecting E]: If that were the case, [Scripture] would have written explicitly, "On the second [day] of the month."
[G]	Then I might rather argue [lit.: say] [that reference is to] the second day of the week!
[H]	This[17] [is unacceptable] since [in Scripture] we never find it written, "the second day of the week."
[I]	And, further, one must make an analogy between the latter and former occurrences of [the word] "second."
[J]	Just as the former occurrence of the word "second" refers to a month, so the latter occurrence of the word "second" must refer to a month.
[XII.A]	{The following argues that all of the preceding biblical proof texts derive from Tannaitic authority.} A Tannaitic teaching concurs with R. Yohanan [see above, unit **VIII**]: From what [verse in Scripture do we know] concerning kings, that they count [the years of their reign] only from Nisan?
[B]	For it is said [1 Kgs. 6:1]: "In the four hundred and eightieth year after the people of Israel came out of the land of Egypt [in the fourth year, in the month of Ziv, which is the second

---

[17] M reads this line: Said R. Ashi, "No. [In Scripture] we never find [reference to] the first (*sic*) of the week."

	month, of Solomon's reign over Israel, he began to build the house of the Lord]."
[C]	And it is written[18] [Num. 33:38]: "And Aaron the priest went up Mount Hor at the command of the Lord, [and died there, in the fortieth year after the people of Israel had come out of the land of Egypt, in the fifth month (that is, Ab), on the first day of the month]."
[D]	And it is written [Dt. 1:3]: "And in the fortieth year, in the eleventh month [(that is, Shevat), on the first day of the month, Moses spoke to the people of Israel...]."[19]
[E]	And it is written [Dt. 1:4, in the continuation of the passage referring to Moses' speech]: "after he had defeated Sihon [the king of the Amorites]."
[F]	And it says [Num. 21:1]: "When the Canaanite, [the king of Arad, who dwelt in the Negeb], heard [that Israel was coming by the way of Atharim...]."
[G]	And it says [Num. 20:29]: "And all the congregation saw that Aaron was dead...."
[H]	And it says [Ex. 40:17]: "And in the first month [that is, Nisan], in the second year, [on the first day of the month,[20] the tabernacle was erected]."
[I]	And it says [Num. 10:11]: "And in the second year, in the second month [(that is, Iyyar) on the twentieth day of the month, the cloud was taken up from over the tabernacle of the testimony]."
[J]	And it says [Ex. 19:1]: "On the third new moon [lit.: month] after the people of Israel had gone forth [out of the land of Egypt, on that day they came into the wilderness of Sinai]."

---

[18]Here and at D and E, M reads: it is said.

[19]In the printed edition, this line is added in brackets.

[20]M explicitly states: on the first day of the month.

[K] And it says [2 Chron. 3:2]: "He began to build [in the second month, in the second, of the fourth year of his reign]."[21]

[XIII.A] Said Rab Hisda, "They taught [that Nisan is the new year for kings] only for the case of Israelite kings.

[B] "But in the case of kings of[22] other nations, we count [the years of their reign] from Tishre,

[C] "as it is stated [Neh. 1:1]: 'The words of Nehemiah the son of Hacaliah. Now it happened in the month of Kislev, in the twentieth year....';[23]

[D] "and it is written [Neh. 2:1]: 'In the month of Nisan, in the twentieth year of King Artaxerxes....'

[E] "[Insofar as], when speaking of Kislev, [Neh. 1:1] calls it the twentieth year, and, when speaking of Nisan, [Neh. 2:1 still] calls it the twentieth year, this proves that new year [for non-Israelite kings] is not in Nisan." {If it were, the event reported at Neh. 2:1 would have been described as taking place at the beginning of the twenty-first year.}

[F] {The argument of C-E is rejected.} Granted that [Neh. 2:1] refers explicitly to Artaxerxes.

[G] But how do you know that [Neh. 1:1 also] refers to [the reign of] Artaxerxes?

[H] Perhaps [3b] it refers to some other enumeration! {If this is the case, no conclusions may be drawn from these verses regarding the new year for non-Israelite kings.}

[I] [Rejecting G] said Rab Pappa, "[The appearance of the expression] 'twentieth year' in two separate passages allows for an analogy based upon verbal congruities.

[J] "Just as there [at Neh 2:1] reference is to Artaxerxes, so here [at Neh. 1:1] reference is to Artaxerxes."

---

[21]The bracketed words appear explicitly in M.

[22]In error, M adds here: Israel.

[23]M adds the continuation of the verse: while I was in Susa the capital.

[K] {Another challenge to C-E is presented.} But on what basis [do you conclude that] the incident that took place in Kislev [recorded at Neh. 1:1] occurred first [that is, prior to what is recorded at Neh. 2:1]?

[L] Perhaps the incident that took place in Nisan [which is reported at Neh. 2:1] occurred first! {In this scenario, the twentieth year indeed commenced with Nisan, as indicated at Neh. 2:1. What is reported at Neh. 1:1 took place later on, in Kislev of that year.}

[M] Do not even think that, since it is taught on Tannaitic authority: The things Hanani told Nehemiah in Kislev, [Nehemiah in turn] told the king in Nisan.

[N] "The things Hanani told Nehemiah in Kislev"—this is as it is said [Neh. 1:1-3]: "The words of Nehemiah the son of Hacaliah.[24] Now it happened in the month of Kislev in the twentieth year, while I was in Susa the capital,[25] that Hanani, one of my brethren, came with certain men out of Judah. Now, I asked them concerning the Jews[26] that survived, who had escaped exile, and concerning Jerusalem. And they said to me, 'The survivors there in the province who escaped exile are in great trouble and shame. The wall of Jerusalem is broken down, and its gates are destroyed[27] by fire.'"

[O] "[Nehemiah in turn] told the king in Nisan"—this is as it is said [Neh. 2:1-6]: "In the month of Nisan, in the twentieth year of King Artaxerxes, when wine was before him, I took up the wine and gave it to the king. Previously I had not been sad[28] in his presence. And the king said to me, 'Why is

---

[24] M lacks the beginning of the citation.

[25] M adds here: And it is written. In the following, M lacks: with certain men out of Judah.

[26] M adds, "etc.," and continues the citation with, "And they said...."

[27] A scribal error (Rabbinovicz), M reads: have been consumed.

[28] Literally: bad. A scribal error (Rabbinovicz), M reads: good [that is, happy].

your face sad, since you are not sick? This is nothing other than a sadness of the heart.' Then I was very much afraid and said to the king, 'Let the king live for ever! Why should my face not be sad when the city, the place of my fathers' sepulchers, lies waste, and its gates have been destroyed by fire?' Then the king said to me, 'What do you request?'[29] So I prayed to the God of heaven and said to the king, 'If it pleases the king, and if your servant has found favor in your sight, [I request] that you send me to Judah, to the city of my fathers' sepulchers, that I may rebuild it.' And the king said to me, the queen sitting beside him, 'How long will you be gone, and when will you return?' So it pleased the king to send me, and I set him a time."

[P] Rab Joseph proposed [yet another] challenge [to A-B's theory, that the reigns of non-Israelite kings are counted from Tishre, the seventh month: "Hag. 1:15 states],[30] 'On the twenty-fourth day of the month, in the sixth month, in the second year of Darius the king.'

[Q] "And it is written [in the following verse, Hag. 2:1], 'In the seventh month,[31] on the twenty-first day of the month, [the word of the Lord came by Haggai the prophet].'[32] {Since Scripture does not explicitly state the year, we assume that it intends the second, referred to in the preceding verse, Hag. 1:15.}

[R] "Now, if [the new year for non-Israelite kings in fact] is [Tishre, the event referred to at Hag. 2:1] would have to be in the seventh [month] of the third year!"

---

[29]In M the remainder of the citation is abbreviated.

[30]M explicitly adds: It is written.

[31]P adds in parenthesis, marked for deletion: in the second year.

[32]The bracketed words appear explicitly in M.

[S] [Rejecting P-R's argument] said R. Abbahu,³³ "Cyrus was a worthy king.³⁴ Therefore they counted [the years of] his [reign] like those of the kings of Israel." {The example of Cyrus is unique and does not disprove the contention of A-B.}

[T] Rab Joseph challenged this [response at S]: "For one thing, if it is as you state, two Scriptural passages are contradictory:

[U] "For it is written [Ezra 6:15]: 'And this house was finished on the third day of the month of Adar, in the sixth year of the reign of Darius the king.'

[V] "And [concerning this verse] it is taught on Tannaitic authority: At that same time in the following year, Ezra went up from Babylon along with his group of exiles.

[W] "And it is written [Ezra 7:8]: 'And he came to Jerusalem in the fifth month, which was in the seventh year of the king.'

[X] "Now, if it is [as you say, that the reigns of non-Israelite kings are counted from Tishre], this would have to be the eighth year!

[Y] "And for another thing, what is the relationship [between your proposal, at S, and the verses cited at P-Q]?

[Z] "There [at Neh. 1:15-2:1, cited at P-Q, reference is to] Cyrus, while here [in your challenge to the conclusion based upon Neh. 1:15-2:1, reference is to] Darius." {P-R's argument stands. The fact that Cyrus is treated as an Israelite king has nothing to do with the counting of the years of Darius' reign. On the basis of that counting, we know that the reigns of non-Israelite kings, like those of Israelites, are counted from Nisan.}

[AA] {Y-Z is rejected.} It has been taught on Tannaitic authority: Cyrus, Darius, and Artaxerxes are all the same individual.

---

³³M reads: Abba.

³⁴This is a play on words. In Hebrew, the name Cyrus and the word for "worthy" contain the same consonants, in a different order.

[BB] [He was called] Cyrus, since he was a worthy king;

[CC] Artaxerxes, after the name of his empire;[35]

[DD] and what was his [given] name? Darius.

[EE] {We now take up the example from the book of Ezra, T-X, which, contrary to P-R, but in line with the original proposition of A-B, suggests that Cyrus' reign was counted from Tishre.} Despite [AA-DD's resolution of the problem raised at Y-Z] there remains [at U-W] a contradiction [to P-R's example].

[FF] Said R. Isaac, "There is no contradiction. Here [at P-R, in the verses from Haggai, reference is to the period] before [Cyrus] became wicked, [while] here [at U-W, in the verses from Ezra, reference is to the period] after [Cyrus] became wicked." {In the former period, Cyrus was treated like an Israelite king and therefore was not subject to the usual rule. But in the latter period, he was treated like all non-Israelite kings, whose reigns are numbered from Tishre, just as A-B originally proposed.}

[GG] Rab Kahana[36] challenged [FF's explanation]: "Did [Cyrus] in fact become wicked?

[HH] "But [indicating the contrary] thus it is written [Ezra 6:9, recording Cyrus' decree regarding the rebuilding of the Jerusalem Temple]: [4a] 'And whatever is needed—young bulls, rams, or sheep for burnt-offerings to the God of heaven, wheat, salt, wine, or oil, as the priests at Jerusalem require—let that be given to them day by day without fail.'[37]

---

[35]Simon, p. 9, explains this by claiming that the Persian "Artaxerxes" means "By whom empire is perfected."

[36]M reads: Rabina.

[37]In M, the conclusion of the verse, cited below at JJ, appears here as well.

[II] Said to him R. Isaac, "Rabbi, I borrow from your own argument:[38]

[JJ] "[The continuation of HH's passage, at Ezra 6:10, reads]: '...that they may offer pleasing sacrifices to the God of heaven, and pray for the life of the king and his sons.'" {The implication is that Cyrus acted for his own benefit, not for the sake of God. In this way, he had indeed become wicked.}

[KK] {JJ's conclusion is shown to be unacceptable.} But is one who acts in this way not in fact meritorious?

[LL] For so we have taught on Tannaitic authority: [As for] one who says, "This *sela* is [given] for charity, so that my sons may live, and so that I may merit a place in the coming world"—lo, this person is in every respect righteous. {Contrary to JJ, one who performs a pious deed with the expectation of reward still is deemed meritorious.}

[MM] {The Talmud claims that the Tannaitic precept cited at LL does not apply to Cyrus, JJ.} There is no contradiction [between LL and JJ].

[NN] This [precept, LL] applies to an Israelite, while this [ruling, JJ] applies to gentiles.[39] {We conclude that Cyrus really did become wicked, which explains the distinct ways in which his reign was counted. Accordingly the original contention of A-B stands. The reigns of non-Israelite kings normally are counted from Tishre. Only while he acted meritoriously was Cyrus' reign counted from Nisan, like the reigns of Israelite kings.}

---

[38] So Jastrow, p. 524, s.v., *twn'*. In M, this line and JJ read simply: He said to him, "I borrow from your argument." The citation at JJ is abbreviated and, in part, incorrectly transcribed.

[39] So M, which reads "*omot haolam*," and early printings, which read "*nokrin*." Most printed editions read: idol worshippers.

[XIV.A] {The Talmud cites additional sources that suggest that Cyrus became wicked.} And it you wish, I can argue: From what [Scriptural verse] do we know that [Cyrus] became wicked?

[B] For it is written[40] [Ezra 6:4, which cites Cyrus' edict indicating how the Jerusalem-Temple is to be rebuilt]: "with three courses of great stones and one course of new timber; let the cost be paid from the royal treasury."

[C] Why did he want it done this way, [including timber in the construction]?

[D] He reasoned: If the Jews rebel against me, I can burn it down!

[E] {D's inference is rejected.} But [in building the Temple] did Solomon not do the same?

[F] For thus it is written [1 Kgs. 6:36]: "He built the inner court with three courses of hewn stone and one course of cedar beams."

[G] [The difference is that] Solomon placed [the wood] on top, whereas the other [that is, Cyrus] placed it on the bottom; Solomon sunk it in the building, whereas the other did not sink it in the building; Solomon plastered over it, whereas the other did not plaster over it.

[XV.A] Said Rab Joseph, and some say R. Isaac,[41] "From what [Scriptural verse] do we know that [Cyrus] became wicked?

[B] "From here [Neh. 2:6]: 'And the king said to me, the *shegel*[42] sitting beside him....'"

[C] What is the meaning of "*shegel*"?

---

[40]M reads: From here.... M continues by citing 1 Kings 7:12: "The great court had three courses of hewn stone round about." P's reading is preferable (Rabbinovicz), since the point here is to contrast Cyrus' actions, B, with those of Solomon, F+G.

[41]M, in error, reads: Said Rab Isaac, and some say Rab Nahman.

[42]Usually: queen.

[D] Said Rabbah[43] bar Lema in the name of Rab, "A female dog."

[E] {D's interpretation of *shegel* is problematic.} Rather, based on this, thus it is written[44] [Dan. 5:23]: "But you have lifted up yourself against the Lord of heaven; and the vessels of his house have been brought in before you, and you and your lords, your *shegel*, and your concubines have drunk wine from them."

[F] If *shegel* means female dog—does a female dog drink wine? {Since it does not, *shegel* clearly does not mean what D claims.}

[G] There is no problem, since [we can assume that Dan. 5:23 refers to a case in which] they trained it, and it drinks [wine].

[H] Rather [one can challenge the notion that *shegel* means female dog] on this basis [Ps. 45:9, referring to the Israelite king]: "daughters of kings are among your ladies of honor; at your right hand stands the *shegel* in gold of Ophir."

[I] Now, if *shegel* means female dog, what is the prophet[45] trying to tell [the people of] Israel?

[J] This is what he is saying: Since the Torah is as dear to [the people of] Israel as a *shegel* is to the idol worshippers, you[46] [Israelites] have earned the gold of Ophir.

[K] But if you wish, I can argue [that], in fact, *shegel* means queen, but Rabbah[47] bar Lema [D] learned a [particular] teaching [that, in the case of Cyrus, the term refers to a female dog].

---

[43]M lacks the preceding line and presents the name here as "Rava bar Lema." The correct name of this authority is unclear.

[44]M lacks: Thus it us written.

[45]M and other sources lack: the prophet. Instead, the word "it" is understood.

[46]M and other sources read: they.

[47]M again reads: Rava.

[L] And why was [this dog] called *"shegel"*? For she was as dear to him as a queen.

[M] Similarly, [it was because] he had her sit in the queen's place.

[XVI.A] {The Talmud cites yet an additional source that suggests that Cyrus became wicked.} And it you wish, I can argue: From what [Scriptural verse] do we know that [Cyrus] became wicked?

[B] From here [Ezra 7:21-22: "And I, Artaxerxes the king, make a decree to all the treasurers in the province Beyond the River: Whatever Ezra the priest, the scribe of the law of the God of heaven, requires of you, be it done with all diligence], up to a hundred talents of silver, a hundred *kors* of wheat, a hundred baths of wine, a hundred baths of oil, and salt without prescribing how much."

[C] Initially, he placed no limit [on how much could be spent], but now he placed a limit.

[D] {C's interpretation of the verse is rejected.} But perhaps at first he had not decided upon the limit, [even though he intended all along to have a limit]?

[E] Rather, the best explanation [for how we know that Cyrus became wicked] is the one we taught first. {See unit **XIII**.HH-NN.}

[XVII.A] *[The first day of Nisan is the new year for kings] and festivals* [M. R.H. 1:1B].

[B] Is [the new year] for festivals [indeed] on the first of Nisan?

[C] [Certainly] it is [rather] on the fifteenth of Nisan! {The fifteenth of Nisan is the first day of Passover, which is the first festival in the liturgical year.}

[D] [Agreeing with C] said Rab Hisda, "[M. R.H. 1:1B means that] the festival that is in it [that is, Nisan] is the new year for festivals."

[XVIII.A] This [rule, M. R.H. 1:1B] has implications[48] for determination of the point at which one who makes a vow has transgressed [Dt. 23:21's prohibition against delaying fulfilling an obligation to God].

[B] And this [follows the perspective of] R. Simeon,[49] for it is taught on Tannaitic authority [T. R.H. 1:2]: **All the same are one who vows, one who consecrates an object, and one who pledges a Valuation [but has not yet carried out what he has said]. Once the festivals of an entire year have gone by, he has violated [the precept that one] not delay [in fulfilling his obligation].**

[C] R. Simeon says, "[This is so in the case of] three festivals in their proper sequence, with the festival of unleavened bread coming first."

[D] And so would R. Simeon[50] say, "Sometimes they are three, sometimes they are four, and sometimes they are five.

[E] "How so?

[F] "[If] one vowed before Passover, [he violates the law after] three [festivals have passed: Passover, Pentecost, and Tabernacles].

[G] "[If he vowed] before Pentecost, [he violates the law only after] five [festivals have passed: Pentecost, Tabernacles, Passover, Pentecost, and Tabernacles].

[H] "[If he vowed] before the Festival [that is, Tabernacles, he violates the law only after] four [festivals have passed: Tabernacles, Passover, Pentecost, and Tabernacles]."

---

[48]M and other manuscript sources read: What are the implications?

[49]The beginning of this line is lacking in M and a number of early exegetical sources.

[50]So T. R.H. 1:2. Sources for B. add: b. Yohai.

[XIX.A] Our rabbis have taught on Tannaitic authority [T. Ar. 3:17, with variations in the order of the entries]: **Those who owe the assessment of an object to be redeemed and Valuations, things that have been declared *herem* and things that have been declared sanctified, sin-offerings and guilt-offerings, burnt-offerings and peace-offerings, gifts of charity and tithes, firstlings and tithe of cattle and the Passover, [4b] gleanings, forgotten sheaves, and that which is left growing in the corner of a field—one has violated [the precept that one] not delay [in fulfilling his obligation] only once the festivals of an entire year have gone by.**

[B] [T. Ar. 3:18]: **R. Simeon says, "[This is so in the case of] three festivals in their proper sequence, with the festival of unleavened bread coming first."**

[C] [Disagreeing] R. Meir says, "As soon as one festival has gone by, [the person] has violated [the precept that one] not delay [in fulfilling his obligation]."

[D] [Disagreeing] R. Eliezer b. Jacob says, "As soon as two festivals have gone by, [the person] has violated [the precept that one] not delay [in fulfilling his obligation].

[E] [T. Ar. 3:18]: **R. Eleazar b. R. Simeon says, "As soon as the festival of Tabernacles has passed by, [the person] has violated [the precept that one] not delay [in fulfilling his obligation]."**

[F] What is the reasoning of the first Tannaitic authority [at A]?

[G] {The following refers to Dt. 16, which describes the festival calendar and states, vs. 16: "Three times a year all your males shall appear before the Lord your God at the place that he will choose."} Since [the Scriptural rules] emerge from this context [that is, of a description of the three festivals], why does it need to repeat itself and write [Dt. 16:16]: "at the feast of unleavened bread, at the feast of weeks, and at the feast of booths. [They shall not appear before the Lord empty-handed]"?

[H] Learn from this the precept of not delaying [payment of one's obligations]!

[I] Now,[51] R. Simeon says, "[Dt. 16:16] need not have referred [by name] to the festival of Tabernacles, since the Scriptural passage [in which Dt. 16:16 is found already] is talking about [Tabernacles, at Dt. 16:13-15].

[J] "Why [then] is [Tabernacles explicitly] mentioned [at Dt. 16:16]?

[K] "To teach that, [in the sequence of festivals, Tabernacles] is last, [coming after Passover and Pentecost]." {This interpretation of Scripture accounts for Simeon's view above, at B.}

[L] But [as for] R. Meir—what is his reasoning [C, for holding that one is in violation of the precept against delaying after only one festival has passed]?

[M] As it is written [Dt. 12:5-6: "But you shall seek the place that the Lord your God will choose...;] there you shall go, and there you shall bring [your burnt-offerings and your sacrifices, etc.]." {The implication is that what you owe must be brought at the next possible opportunity, whichever festival it is.}

[N] But [how do the] rabbis [at A understand this verse]?

[O] It is a positive commandment. {Dt. 12:5-6 indicates what one should do. But one who does not has not violated the restriction against delaying.}

[P] But [in the view of] R. Meir—since the Merciful told him to bring [what he owes], and he did not bring [it], he has immediately transgressed the precept that one not delay.

[Q] But [as for] R. Eliezer b. Jacob—what is his reasoning [D, for holding that one is in violation after two festivals pass]?

---

[51]M and all early sources for B correctly (Rabbinovicz) read here: Now, [as for] R. Simeon, what is his reasoning? It is as it is taught on Tannaitic authority—R. Simeon says....

[R] For it is written [Num. 29:39]: "These you shall offer to the Lord at your appointed feasts...."

[S] [Eliezer b. Jacob argues that] the smallest [number of festivals that can be referred to by the plural] "appointed feasts" is two.

[T] But [how do the] rabbis [at A understand this verse]?

[U] [They hold that] this [plural "appointed feasts"] accords with [the interpretation proposed by] R. Jonah. For R. Jonah said, "All of the appointed feasts were put on the same footing,[52] to show that they all atone for the uncleanness of the sanctuary and its holy things."

[V] But [as for] R. Eleazar b. R. Simeon—what is his reasoning [E, for holding that one is in violation only after Tabernacles has passed]?

[W] As it is taught on Tannaitic authority: R. Eleazar b. R. Simeon says, "[Dt. 16:16] need not have referred [by name] to the festival of Tabernacles, since the Scriptural passage [in which Dt. 16:16 is found already] is talking about [Tabernacles, at Dt. 16:13-15].

[X] "Why [then] is [Tabernacles explicitly] mentioned [at Dt. 16:16]?[53]

[Y] "To teach that this [specific festival] is determinative." {This interpretation of Scripture accounts for Eleazar b. Simeon's view above, E.}

[XX.A] Now, [as for] R. Meir and R. Eliezer b. Jacob—this [verse, Dt. 16:16]: "at the feast of unleavened bread, at the feast of weeks, and at the feast of booths"—how do they interpret it?

---

[52]The end of this line is lacking in all manuscript sources. It appears to have been unknown to Rashi as well.

[53]M lacks this line. It introduces the following line: Rather.

[B]54 They use it [for the same purpose] as R. Eleazar said [in the name of] R. Oshaia.

[C] For said R. Eleazar said R. Oshaia, "From what [Scriptural verse do we know that a sacrifice omitted on] Pentecost may be made up for on the [following] seven days?

[D] "Scripture says: 'at the feast of unleavened bread, at the feast of weeks, and at the feast of booths.'

[E] "This equates the festival of Pentecost with the feast of unleavened bread.

[F] "Just as [a sacrifice omitted on] the feast of unleavened bread may be made up for on the [following] seven days, so [a sacrifice omitted on] Pentecost may be made up for on the [following] seven days."

[G] {E-F's interpretation is challenged.} But [instead] one should equate [the festival of Pentecost] with the festival of Tabernacles!

[H] [The result would be to say that] just as there [in the case of Tabernacles] there are eight days [on which a missed offering may be made up], so here [in the case of Pentecost] there are eight days, [not the seven suggested at E-F].

[I] {H is rejected.} The eighth day [following Tabernacles, referred to at Lev. 23:36] is an independent festival. {Tabernacles itself has only seven days.}

[J] [Disagreeing with I], I can say that the eighth day of Tabernacles is an independent festival in regard to (1) casting lots [to determine which priestly course will officiate]; (2) [reciting the benediction thanking God for bringing us to this] time; (3) [the name of the] festival, [that is, Azeret, not Tabernacles]; (4) the [festival] offering; (5)

54At B-C, M reads simply: They use it [for the same purpose] as R. Hoshaia, for said R. Hoshaia.... This appears to be a scribal error, since in the parallel passages at B. Hag. 17a and B. M.Q. 24b M's reading is the same as that of the printed edition.

the psalm [chanted by the Levites; and] (6) the blessing [for the king; 1 Kgs. 8:66].

[K] But as for making up [for a missed sacrifice],[55] all agree [that a sacrifice missed on] the first day [of Tabernacles] may be made up on it [that is, the eighth day].

[L] [This is] as we have taught on Tannaitic authority [M. Hag. 1:6]: *He who did not make a festal offering on the first festival day of Tabernacles makes festal offerings throughout the entire festival, including the last festival day of the festival [of Tabernacles].*

[M] If you grasp a lot, you will not [successfully] grasp [it all]; but if you grasp a little, you can grasp [it]. {The point of this is not clear.}[56]

[N] [If, as we have seen, Dt. 16:16 does not indicate that Pentecost and Tabernacles are comparable], for [the purpose of] what law did the Merciful include [in that verse reference to] the festival of Tabernacles?

[O] It is to equate it with the festival of unleavened bread.

[P] [5a] Just as on the festival of unleavened bread [the celebrant] must stay overnight [in Jerusalem], so on the festival of Tabernacles [the celebrant] must stay overnight [in Jerusalem].

[Q] Now, there [in the case of Passover] from what [verse] do we know [that the celebrant must stay overnight in Jerusalem]?

[R] As it is written [Dt. 16:7, referring to the paschal offering, "And you shall boil it and eat it at the place the Lord your God will choose]; and in the morning you shall turn and go to your tents." {The implication is that the individual must

---

[55]M, other manuscript sources, and the parallel at B. Hag. 17a lack the end of the this line. There is no difference in meaning.

[56]Simon, p. 14, comments: "A proverbial saying, indicating that Pentecost should be put on a level in this respect with Passover which has the smaller number of days, not with Tabernacles."

stay in Jerusalem, at the place of the sacrifice, throughout the night.}

[**XXI**.A] {We turn to a question left open by the preceding unit.} But [as for] the first [cited] Tannaitic authority [unit **XIX**.F-G] and R. Simeon[57] [unit **XIX**.I-K, both of whom depend upon Dt. 16:16 to derive the prohibition against delaying payment of one's obligations]—from where do they derive [the right] to make up [for a missed sacrifice] on Pentecost?[58]

[B] They derive it from that which Rabbah bar Samuel taught on Tannaitic authority. For Rabbah bar Samuel taught on Tannaitic authority: "The Torah said: Count the days and sanctify the new month. {Reference is to Num. 11:19-20: "You shall not eat [meat] one day, or two days, or five days, or ten days, or twenty days, but a whole month." The verse is taken to suggest that months are counted a day at a time. The actual sanctification is accomplished through a sacrifice (Num. 28:11).}

[C] "[Comparably, the Torah states]: Count days and sanctify the festival of Pentecost. {Reference is to Lev. 23:15: "And you shall count from the morrow after the Sabbath, from the day that you brought the sheaf of the wave offering; seven full weeks shall they be." This suggests that the period to Pentecost is counted by weeks. The sanctification is marked by an offering of grain, Lev. 23:16.}

[D] "[This suggests that] just as the month is [sanctified] for a period that accords with the unit of time by which it is counted [that is, a day], so the festival of Pentecost is [sanctified] for a period that accords with the unit of time by

---

[57]Following Rabbinovicz, delete "b. Eleazar," found in parentheses in the printed text and lacking in M and other manuscript sources.

[58]So R. Hananel, followed by Simon, as required by the sense of the passage. Here and in the following, the text reads: Tabernacles.

	which it is counted [that is, a week]." {Since Pentecost is sanctified for a full week, the compensation period is also a week.}
[E]	{B-D is rejected.} [Following this same argument], should I not state that [the compensation period for][59] Pentecost is [only] one day? {This can be derived from Lev. 23:16, which refers to "counting fifty days."}
[F]	{Rava rejects E.} Said Rava, "Is it indeed the case that for Pentecost we count only days and do not count weeks [as well]?
[G]	"Rather, [indicating that we in fact counts weeks], thus said a master,[60] 'It is an obligation to count days and an obligation to count weeks.'
[H]	"And moreover, [at Dt. 16:16] it states, 'The festival of Pentecost.'" {In Hebrew, the term for Pentecost is literally "weeks," suggesting that the week is the operative unit.}

[XXII.A] {At issue is the inclusion at T. Ar. 3:17, cited at unit **XIX**.A, of the Passover offering as an item that, after three festivals have passed, is subject to the prohibition against delaying fulfillment of one's ritual obligations.} Now, can the Passover sacrifice be offered on any of the [other] festivals?

[B] [Does not] the Passover sacrifice have a fixed time, [the fourteenth of Nisan, so that] if one offers it [at that time], he has offered it [and fulfilled the obligation], but if he fails to offer it [at that time and offers it instead at a different point], it is rejected? {Indeed this is the case. It therefore appears that the Passover offering does not belong in the list at T. Ar. 3:17. It cannot be brought beyond the fourteenth of Nisan.}

---

[59]M has the bracketed words explicitly.

[60]Manuscript sources and the parallel passages at B. Hag. 17a and B. Men. 66a read: thus said Abayye.

[C] Said Rab Hisda, "Passover [was included in the list] incidentally. {Its appearance there should not be taken seriously.}

[D] [Explaining in a different way the appearance of Passover at T. Ar. 3:17] Rab Sheshet said, "Which Passover offering [is referred to there]? The peace-offering [that one brings in lieu] of a Passover offering." {See M. Pes. 9:6 and B. Pes. 97b. If a Passover offering is lost and not brought at the appropriate time, a peace-offering is designated in its place. This peace-offering comes under the restriction against delaying and so appropriately is listed at T. Ar. 3:17.}

[E] {This solution to the problem is rejected.} If [what Sheshet says] is [in fact] the case, then reference is to a peace-offering! {But at T. Ar. 3:17 peace-offerings are listed independently. So the Passover offering mentioned in that list cannot signify a peace-offering. That would create a redundancy.}

[F] {The problem raised at E is resolved, showing D's explanation to be correct.} [T. Ar. 3:17] taught [concerning] peace-offerings brought in place of a Passover offering as well as peace-offerings brought for their own sake. {Hence the two different terms at T. Ar. 3:17.}

[G] {We conclude with an explanation of why peace-offerings brought in place of a Passover offering needed to be included explicitly at T. Ar. 3:17.} You might have thought that since [the peace-offering] is brought in place of a Passover offering [5b], they deemed it equivalent to a Passover offering [which only may be sacrificed on the fourteenth of Nisan itself]. {In this case, one who fails to make the offering has transgressed the prohibition against delaying immediately upon the conclusion of Passover itself.}

[H] Therefore we have been instructed [explicitly at T. Ar. 3:17, that one has transgressed the prohibition against delaying only by failing to offer the peace-offering that replaces a

Passover offering within a period of a full year after Passover].

[XXIII.A] From what [verse in Scripture] are these rules [at T. Ar. 3:17 derived]?

[B] It is as our rabbis have taught on Tannaitic authority: [Dt. 23:21 states]: "When you make a vow [to the Lord your God, you shall not be slack to pay it;[61] for the Lord your God will surely require it of you, and it would be sin in you]."

[C] [From the beginning of this verse] I only know the rule for a vow.

[D] [As for] a freewill-offering—from what [verse in Scripture do I know that it is subject to the same obligation not to delay in paying it]?

[E] Here [at Dt. 23:21] it says, "vow," and in another place it says [Lev. 7:16]: "If the sacrifice of his offering is a votive offering [using the same word as 'vow'] or a freewill-offering...."

[F] Just as in that other place [Lev. 7:16] the freewill-offering is included with it [that is, with the vow], so here [at Dt. 23:21, we deduce that] the freewill-offering is included with it [and so is subject to the same rule against delaying payment that applies to a vow].

[G] [Dt. 23:21 continues]: "To the Lord your God." This refers to [T. Ar. 3:17] **the assessment of an object to be redeemed and Valuations, things that have been declared *herem*, and things that have been declared sanctified.** {Thus we know from Scripture these items too are subject to the prohibition against delaying payment.}

[H] [Dt. 23:21 continues]: "you shall not be slack to pay it." [This means you must pay] *it* and not its substitute. {See unit **XXIV**.}

---

[61]M explicitly contains the continuation of the cited verse up to this point.

[I] [Dt. 23:21 continues]: "For [the Lord your God] will surely require it of you." This refers to [T. Ar. 3:17] **sin-offerings and guilt-offerings, burnt-offerings, and peace-offerings.**

[J] [Dt. 23:21 continues]: "the Lord your God." This refers to **gifts of charity and tithes,** and **firstlings**.[62]

[K] [Dt. 23:21 continues]: "of you." This refers to **gleanings, forgotten sheaves, and that which is left growing in the corner of a field.**

[L] [Dt. 23:21 continues]: "and it would be sin in you." [This means that the sin will be attributed to you],[63] but the sin will not be accounted to your offering. {Hence, the offering still may be used, even after the owner has violated the prohibition against delaying.}

[XXIV.A] {We continue with an exposition of unit **XXIII.H.**} A master said, "[Dt. 23:21 states]: 'You shall not be slack to pay it.' [This means you must pay] *it* and not its substitute."

[B] To what substitutes [is reference made]?

[C] If [reference is to] the substitute of a burnt-offering or peace-offering—these certainly are offered [subject to the restriction against delaying]. {Accordingly, the statement at A cannot apply to these things.}

[D] If [reference is to] the substitute of a sin-offering[64]—it is left to die [and cannot be offered at all]. {Accordingly, it would make no sense for the text to exclude this offering from the rule against delaying. Since it cannot be offered, no one would assume that it is subject to that rule.}

[E] Therefore, to what substitutes [is reference made]?

[F] [Reference is to] the substitute of a thank-offering.

---

[62] M reads: tithes, firstlings, tithe, and the Passover [offering].

[63] The bracketed words appear explicitly in M and other sources.

[64] In error (Rabbinovicz), M reads: sin-offerings and guilt-offerings.

[G] For R. Hiyya taught on Tannaitic authority: "[As for] a thank-offering that was [lost, replaced, found, and then] mixed up with its substitute, and [then] one of the offerings died—there is no remedy for the remaining [offering].

[H] "What course can the individual follow?

[I] "To offer it together with the bread [required in the case of a thank-offering]?

[J] "[This is unacceptable, since] it might be the substitute, [in the case of which the bread is not offered; B. Men. 79b].

[K] "[Alternatively, is it possible] to offer it without the bread?

[L] "[This is unacceptable, since] it might be the [original] thank-offering, [in which case the bread is required]."

[M] {F is rejected. Given the circumstance described at G-L, why would the substitute of a thank-offering be covered by Dt. 23:21?} Indeed, since this [substitute] cannot be offered at all, why would I need the verse [at Dt. 23:21 specifically] to exclude it [from being subject to the rule against delaying]? {The case appears similar to that of the sin-offering, explained at D.}

[N] [To solve the problem of the meaning of A]⁶⁵ said Rab Sheshet, "In fact, [contrary to C, A's rule is meant] to exclude the substitute of a burnt-offering or peace-offering [from the restriction against delaying].

[O] "And here, with what situation are we concerned? [A case] such as one in which [an individual had designated one of these offerings and, before he offered it] two festivals had passed. Then it developed an [invalidating] blemish, and [the owner] deconsecrated it [by substituting it] with a different [animal], after which another festival passed [without the substitute's being offered].

[P] "You might think that, since this [substitute] comes as a replacement for the prior [animal], it is as though three

---

⁶⁵M introduces this line: Rather. In the following, it lacks the words "to exclude."

festivals have passed, [so that the individual is guilty of violating the precept against delaying].

[Q] "Therefore we are informed, [that the substitute of the burnt-offering or peace-offering is not subject to the restriction against delaying based upon the point at which the original offering was designated]."

[R] But according to R. Meir, who said [that] as soon as one festival has passed, he has violated the prohibition against delaying, what can one say? {In Meir's view of the law, Sheshet's explanation of A makes no sense.}

[S] Said Rava, "Here [taking account of Meir's view], with what situation are we dealing? [With a case] such as one in which [the offering] developed an invalidating blemish during the festival period, and [the owner] deconsecrated it by substituting it with a different [animal], after which the festival passed.

[T] "You might think that, since this [substitute] comes as a replacement for the prior [animal], it is as though it had been kept over the entire [period between one] festival [and the next]. {In this interpretation, the individual now would be guilty of violating Meir's interpretation of the restriction against delaying.}

[U] "Therefore we are informed, [that the substitute of the burnt-offering or peace-offering is not subject to the restriction against delaying according to the point at which the original offering was designated]." {The individual violates the prohibition against delaying only if he fails to offer the animal before a second festival has passed.}

[XXV.A] {We turn to an exposition of unit **XXIII**.L.} [Dt. 23:21 reads]:[66] "And it would be sin in you." [This means that the sin will be attributed to you], but the sin will not be

---

[66]M introduces this line: A master said. In M additionally the biblical citation is abbreviated.

accounted to your offering. {Hence, the offering still may be used, even after the owner has violated the restriction against delaying.}

[B] Is this [conclusion] in fact derived from this [verse]?

[C] [Certainly not; rather] it is derived from [the statement attributed to] "Others."[67]

[D] For it is taught on Tannaitic authority [T. San. 3:6]: **Others say, "Is it possible to suppose that a firstling, the proper time for [the offering of] which has passed after the first year, should be in the status of unfit Holy Things and so be invalid [to be brought to Jerusalem]? Scripture says [Dt. 14:23], 'And you will eat before the Lord your God[68] the tithe of your grain, wine, and oil, and the firstborn of your herd and flock.'**

[E] **"The text draws an analogy between the firstling and [second] tithe. Just as [second] tithe does not become invalid, [so that it may be brought to Jerusalem and eaten] from one year to the next, so the firstborn does not become invalid [and may be kept] from one year to the next."**

[F] [Despite the conclusion based upon Dt. 14:23], it was still necessary [to derive this rule from Dt. 23:21, as at A].

[G] You might have thought that this conclusion [derived at D-E from Dt. 14:23 applies only to] a firstling, which is not for appeasement;

[H] but in [the case of] consecrated things, [such as burnt-offerings and sin-offerings], which are for appeasement, you might say [that if they are kept over from year to year] they

---

[67]M reads: Certainly it is derived from there [that is, the source cited at D]. At D, in place of "Others say," M reads: R. Meir says. This appears to be a scribal error. In the parallel passages at B. Zeb. 29a, M's reading is the same as that of the printed edition.

[68]M lacks the beginning of the citation.

	will not appease[69] [and so are invalid]. {The notion that these offerings are for appeasement derives from Lev. 1:3: "If his offering is a burnt-offering from the herd...; he shall offer it at the door of the tent of meeting, that he may be accepted before the Lord."}
[I]	Therefore we are taught [by Dt. 23:21 that the contrary is true]. {Even consecrated things such as burnt-offerings and sin-offerings may be offered after their appointed time. The owner has violated the restriction against delaying, but the offering itself remains valid.}
[J]	But even so [I might propose that A's interpretation of Dt. 23:21 is unnecessary, insofar as the same conclusion] [6a] can be derived from [the statement] of Ben Azzai.
[K]	{The following is based upon Lev. 7:18: "If any of the flesh of the sacrifice of his peace-offering is eaten on the third day, he who offers *it* shall not be accepted, neither shall it be credited to him." The italicized word "it" is unnecessary and therefore is subject to interpretation.} For it is taught on Tannaitic authority: Ben Azzai says, "'...it....'[70] Why does Scripture state [this word]?
[L]	"Since it is said [Dt. 23:21]: '[When you make a vow to the Lord your God], you shall not be slack to pay it,' I might reason that even one who delays paying his vow is subject to [the penalty indicated at Lev. 7:18, that] 'he [who offers it] shall not be accepted.'
[M]	"[Therefore] Scripture [at Lev. 7:18 needed explicitly to] state, '...it...,' [meaning] 'it' [that is, a sacrifice left beyond the third day] is subject to [the penalty that] 'he [who offers it] shall not be accepted.'

---

[69]M lacks this word.

[70]M adds the prior word of the citation ("offers") and lacks the question that follows, continuing directly with L. The meaning is the same.

[N] "But he who delays fulfilling his vow is not subject to [the penalty that] 'he [who offers it] shall not be accepted.'"

[O] {We see that, contrary to A, Lev. 7:18, not Dt. 23:21, yields the rule that a transgression of the prescription against "not delaying" is attributed to the individual, not the offering. What then is the implication of Dt. 23:21, cited at A?} Rather [the conclusion of Dt. 23:21], "and it would be sin in you" [means that the sin of delaying payment of a vow is in you], but the sin is not in your wife.

[P] You might have thought: Since R. Yohanan, and some say R. Eleazar, said, "A man's wife dies only if money is demanded from him and he does not have it, since it says [Prov. 22:27], 'If you have nothing with which to pay, why should your bed be taken from under you?,'" therefore, for his violation of [the precept that one] not delay [in fulfilling his obligation], she also dies.

[Q] Therefore we are informed [by Dt. 23:21 that this is not the case]. {Only the one who delays in paying the vow is punished for that sin.}

[XXVI.A] {Dt. 23:23 reads: "That which has passed your lips you shall be careful to perform, and you shall do what you have voluntarily vowed to the Lord your God, a freewill-offering that you have stated with your mouth." The verse is elucidated.} Our rabbis have taught on Tannaitic authority:[71] "That which has passed your lips"—this refers to the positive commandments.

[B] "You shall be careful to perform"—this refers to the negative commandments.

[C] "And you shall do"—this is an admonition to a court, that it should compel you to do [what you have vowed].

---

[71]M adds here an introductory citation of the verse about to be analyzed a clause at a time: That which has passed your lips you shall be careful to perform, and you shall do....

[D] "What you have voluntarily vowed"—this refers to a vow.

[E] "To the Lord your God"—this refers to sin-offerings, guilt-offerings, burnt-offerings, and peace-offerings.

[F] "A freewill-offering"—this refers to [the word's] literal meaning.

[G] "That you have stated"—this refers to the things sanctified for the repair of the Temple.

[H] "With your mouth"—this refers to charity.

[XXVII.A] {The interpretations of the clauses of Dt. 23:23 given in the preceding unit appear to be redundant. In the following, the citations of unit **XXVI** are in italics.} A master said, "[As for the interpretation]: *'That which has passed your lips'—this refers to the positive commandments*—why do I need this?

[B] "[This same point] derives from [Dt. 12:5-6: 'But you shall seek the place that the Lord your God will choose out of all your tribes to put his name and make his habitation there]; there you shall go, and there you shall bring [your burnt-offerings and your sacrifices...]. {The verse is read to mean: "Each time you come, you shall bring...."}

[C] "*'You shall be careful to perform'—this refers to the negative commandments*—why do I need this?

[D] "[This same point] derives from [Dt. 23:21: 'When you make a vow to the Lord your God], you shall not be slack to pay it.'

[E] "*'And you shall do'—this is an admonition to a court, that it should compel you to do [what you have vowed]*—why do I need this?

[F] "[This same point] derives from [Lev. 1:3: 'If his offering is a burnt-offering from the herd...]; he shall offer it [at the door of the tent of meeting...].'"

[G] {G explains F. Then H-K raises and resolves a problem suggested by F+G.} For it is taught on Tannaitic authority:

"He shall offer it"[72]—this teaches that they compel him [to offer it].

[H] Is it logical [to claim that they should make him offer it] against his will?

[I] [Suggesting the contrary, in the continuation of Lev. 1:3] Scripture states, "That he may be accepted [literally: 'of his own will']."

[J] Therefore, how [can they force him]?

[K] They compel him up to the point at which he states, "I wish to do it [of my own accord]."

[L] {We turn to the issue raised at A, C, and E: why do we require these interpretations as well as those proposed in unit **XXVI**?} One [set of interpretations, in unit **XXVI**, applies in a case in which] he said [the vow] but had not [yet] designated [the animal needed to pay it]. The other [at B, D, and F, applies when] he had [made the vow and] designated [the required animal] but had not [yet] offered it.

[M] Now [to indicate that in either case the individual must not delay in fulfilling his obligation, both Scriptural interpretations] are needed!

[N] For if we knew [only the case in which] he said [the vow] but had not [yet] designated [the animal to pay it, I might believe that] the reason [he is required to pay the vow without delay] is that he has not yet acted on his word.

[O] But, [if N were the only case I explicitly knew, then, if] he had [made the vow and] designated [the required animal] but had not [yet] offered it, I might say[73] [that he is not subject to the prohibition against delaying, since, I could argue],

---

[72]In M this line is garbled, possibly the result of the scribe's having copied into the text a gloss found in the margin of his source (Rabbinovicz). M additionally adds here: What is the point [of this verse]?

[73]M lacks the preceding clause.

wherever [the animal] is, it is in the treasury of the All-Merciful.[74]

[P] [To avoid O's incorrect understanding, both interpretations] are needed.

[Q] Further, if we knew [only the case in which] he had [made the vow and] designated [the required animal] but had not [yet] offered it, [I might believe that he is subject to the prohibition against delaying], since he is keeping [the animal] with him [instead of completing the required offering].

[R] But [if Q were the only case I explicitly knew, then, if] he had said [the vow] but had not [yet] designated [the animal to pay it], I might say [that he is not subject to the prohibition against delaying, since, I could argue], his word alone is of no weight[75] [and has not obligated him to the vow at all].

[S] [To avoid R's incorrect understanding, both interpretations] are needed.

[T] {L's solution to the problems raised at A, C, and E is rejected.} How can you claim [that in unit **XXVI** reference is to a situation in which] he had said [the vow] but had not [yet] designated [the animal to pay it]?

[U] For [at Dt. 23:23, explained at unit **XXVI**.F, the term] "freewill-offering" is written. {As we see in the following, an individual is not responsible for a freewill-offering that dies or is stolen. This suggests that there is no act of obliging oneself to a freewill-offering outside of actually designating the animal.}

---

[74]M and other manuscript sources appear here to be garbled. Rabbinovicz prefers the reading of the printed edition.

[75]M reads: it is mere speech and of no weight. The meaning is the same.

[V] And we have taught on Tannaitic authority[76] [M. Qin. 1:1G-M]:[77] *What is deemed [to be a pair of birds brought in fulfillment of] a vow?*[78] *He who says, "Lo, I pledge myself to bring a burnt-offering."*

[W] *And what is deemed [to be a pair of birds brought]*[79] *as a freewill-offering? He who says, "Lo, this is a burnt-offering."*

[X] *What is the difference between vows and freewill-offerings? In the case of vows, [if the birds] died or were stolen, he is answerable for them [and must replace them, as he said at V]. In the case of freewill-offerings, [if] they died or were stolen, he is not answerable for them [and need not replace them, in accordance with his words at W].*

[Y] Said Rava, "A case exists [in which he has obligated himself to a freewill-offering without having set the animal aside] in a situation in which he says, 'I am obligated to a burnt-offering on the condition that I am not answerable for it [in a case in which it dies or is stolen].'"

[XXVIII.A] {We return to the issue of unit **XXVI**.H, cited here.} *"With your mouth"—this refers to charity.*

[B] Said Rava,[80] "One becomes obligated immediately [to fulfill a vow to give] charity.

[C] "What is the reason?

---

[76]M, other manuscript sources, and the parallel at B. Hul. 139a introduce the citation as though it were a non-Mishnaic Tannaitic source: Thus it is taught on Tannaitic authority. The Tosafot apparently had this same reading. Their comment, "This is a passage of the Mishnah...," indicated that the term needed to be amended to read as it now appears in the printed edition (Rabbinovicz).

[77]See also M. Meg. 1:6.

[78]M and other sources add: and what is deemed a freewill offering? [Birds brought in fulfillment of] a vow.... The meaning is the same.

[79]M lacks the beginning of this line.

[80]M reads: Rabbah.

[D] "The poor are standing [waiting for help]."

[E] This is obvious [and goes without saying]!

[F] What might you have thought [that necessitated the explicit statement of this rule]?

[G] Since [the rule for charity] occurs in the context of [the discussion of] sacrifices, therefore, as in the case of sacrifices, [one has] until three festivals have passed [to fulfill one's obligation to give charity].

[H] Therefore we are informed [to the contrary]:

[I] [Only] there [in the case of offerings] did the All-Merciful make them dependent upon the festivals. But here, [in the case of charity, he did] not [make it dependent upon the festivals], since the poor are numerous.[81]

[XXIX.A] Said Rava, "As soon as any one festival has passed, [an individual who has not sacrificed an animal he consecrated] has transgressed a positive commandment."

[B] They objected [on the basis of M. Ed. 7:6]: *Testified R. Joshua and R. Pappias concerning an offspring of peace-offerings, that it is to be offered as peace-offerings.*[82] {If the animal was pregnant while consecrated and gave birth before being sacrificed, the offspring shares its consecrated status.}

[C] *Said R. Pappias, "I give testimony that we had a cow in the status of peace-offerings, and we ate it on Passover and ate its offspring as peace-offerings on the Festival [of Tabernacles]."* {Pappias reports that the consecrated offspring was available for sacrifice on Passover but nevertheless was kept over that and the following festival, Pentecost. It finally was offered on Tabernacles. This suggests that, contrary to what Rava claims, A, one does not

---

[81] M and other sources lack this line entirely.

[82] The text of M. Ed. 7:6 continues: *For R. Eliezer says, "The offspring of peace offerings is not to be offered as peace offerings." And sages say, "It is to be offered."*

transgress by delaying sacrifice of a dedicated animal beyond a single festival.}

[D] {D and E-F claim that what Pappias describes may not have been contrary to A's rule at all. A therefore stands.} Granted, on Passover they did not sacrifice it, for, I can argue, it was not yet old enough. {A new-born animal must remain with its mother for seven days and is acceptable as a sacrifice only from the eighth day on (Lev. 22:27). If the offspring was born on the eve of Passover, it could not have been offered on that festival.}

[E] But [as for this] offspring, [born on the eve of Passover], how could it have been kept over Pentecost, so as to involve a transgression of a positive commandment?

[F] [Answering E's question], said Rab Zebid in the name of Rava, "It could have been a case [6b] in which it was sick on Pentecost [and therefore not acceptable for sacrifice]."

[G] {G-H rejects E-F.} Rab Ashi said, "What is the meaning of [Pappias' statement], *'And ate its offspring as peace-offerings on the Festival'*?

[H] "That which is taught on Tannaitic authority [refers to] the festival of Pentecost." {In Ashi's view, E-F is unnecessary. The offspring was too young for sacrifice on Passover, D, and it was not kept over Pentecost at all; that is when it was offered.}

[I] And the other [authority, that is, Zebid at E-F]? [He holds that] whenever [Pentecost] is referred to [in connection with] Passover, it is called Azeret. {In this view, when Pappias, C, used the term "festival," he cannot have meant Pentecost. Instead, as was originally explained, he meant Tabernacles. The offspring, accordingly, was kept over Pentecost and sacrificed at Tabernacles. E-F is required to show that this was not contrary to the rule stated at A. Since the animal was sick at Pentecost, it could not have been sacrificed then. Only for that reason could it be held over until Tabernacles without violating the rule against delaying.}

[**XXX**.A] And[83] said Rava, "Once three festivals have passed, on each additional day [that he fails to offer the sacrifice] he [again] transgresses the restriction against delaying [fulfillment of his obligation]."

[B] They objected [on the basis of T. Ar. 3:18]: **All the same are the firstling [and tithe] and all other Holy Things that one has sanctified. Once a year has passed, [even if it] did not encompass [three] festivals, or [three] festivals [have passed even if they] did not encompass a [full] year, he has violated [the precept that one] not delay [in fulfilling his obligation].**

[C] Now, as for this [passage, B]—in what way does it refute [Rava's statement, A]?

[D] Said Rab Kahana, "The one who raised the objection has done so well!

[E] "Here [is the nature of the objection]: The Tannaitic authority [cited at B] is going over negative commandments. [If he indeed agrees with Rava] let him teach [as does Rava]: on each additional day [that he fails to offer the sacrifice] he [again] transgresses [the precept that one] not delay [in fulfilling his obligation]." {Since the Tannaitic authority cited at B does not indicate this explicitly, we assume that he disagrees with Rava's statement of the law.}

[F] But [as for] the other [authority, C, who sees no contradiction between A and B, how does he view matters]?

[G] [He holds that] the Tannaitic authority [at B] is going over these things only to mark them as forbidden. He is not going over them to look for additional prohibitions!" {Therefore, even though he might accept the rule as stated by Rava, he does not explicitly indicate so in this context.}

---

[83] So the emendation in the margin of the printed edition. The body of the text lacks: And.

[**XXXI**.A] [We return to] the body [of T. Ar. 3:18, cited at unit **XXXIX**.B]: **All the same are the firstling [and tithe] and all other Holy Things that one has sanctified. Once a year has passed, [even if it] did not encompass [three] festivals, or [three] festivals [have passed even if they] did not encompass a [full] year, he has violated [the precept that one] not delay [in fulfilling his obligation].**

[B] Granted, it is possible for [three] festivals [to pass] without there having [yet] been a [full] year.

[C] But, a year's passing without there being three festivals! How is this possible?

[D] Obviously this is possible in the view of one who holds [that a person violates the law against postponing the keeping of his vows only once the festivals of an entire year have passed] in their proper sequence. {See above, unit **XVIII**. In this view, a vow made prior to Pentecost, for instance, is subject to the prohibition against delay only after five festivals have passed: Pentecost, Tabernacles, and then all three festivals in their normal yearly sequence: Passover, Pentecost, and Tabernacles. In this perspective, even after an initial year of days has passed, the three festivals that mark violation of the prohibition against delaying fulfillment of one's vows have not yet gone by.}

[E] But as for one who does not hold [that a person violates the law against postponing the keeping of his vows only once the festivals of an entire year have passed] in their proper sequence—how is it possible [for a year of days to pass without three festivals' having occurred]?

[F] Granted, in the view of Rabbi, this is possible in the case of an intercalated year.

[G] For it is taught on Tannaitic authority: [In reference to a house purchased in a walled city, Lev. 25:30 says, "If it is not redeemed within] a full year, [then the house that is in the walled city shall be made sure in perpetuity to him who bought it]."

[H] Rabbi says "One counts 365 days, that is, the number of days in the solar year."

[I] And sages say, "One counts twelve months, from day to day [yielding a lunar year of 354 days]. And if the year is intercalated [so as to contain 383 days], it is intercalated to his [that is, the seller's] advantage."

[J] In the view of Rabbi,[84] it is possible [for a year of days to pass without three festivals occurring], in a case in which he sanctified it after [the first day of] the festival of unleavened bread, since, when the end of second Adar arrives, a full year [of 365 days] will have passed, but [three] festivals will not have occurred.

[K] But in the view of rabbis [that is, sages at I], how is it possible [for a year to pass without three festivals occurring]?

[L] It is as Rab Shemayah taught on Tannaitic authority: Pentecost is sometimes on the fifth [day of the third month], sometimes on the sixth, and sometimes on the seventh.

[M] How is this so?

[N] If both of them [that is, the first two months, Nisan and Iyyar] are full, [containing 30 days, Pentecost, which always occurs on the fiftieth day from the second day of Passover, falls on the] fifth [day of Sivan, the third month].

[O] If both of them [that is, Nisan and Iyyar] are defective, [containing only 29 days, Pentecost falls on the] seventh [day of Sivan].

[P] If one of them is full and one is defective, [Pentecost falls on the] sixth [day of Sivan]. {In a year in which Pentecost falls on the fifth, the individual might sanctify an animal on the sixth. If in the following year Pentecost falls on the seventh, then, even in the view of sages at I, a full year of months will have passed and three festivals will not have occurred. We

---

[84]M and other sources lack the words "In the view of Rabbi," and begin this line: for instance.

	thus see that what is described at A is feasible within all interpretations of the prohibition against delaying.}
[Q]	Now, which Tannaitic authority disagrees with Rab Shemayah [and holds that Pentecost always falls on the same day, so that what is described at A is impossible]?
[R]	It is "Others."
[S]	For it is taught on Tannaitic authority [T. Ar. 1:11]: **Others say, "There is between one occurrence of Pentecost and another or between one New Year and another [an interval of] only four [days of the week] or, if the year was intercalated, five [days]."** {"Others" hold that full and defective months occur in strict rotation. The year has 354 days, that is, 50 full weeks and four days, and Pentecost always falls on the sixth of Sivan. An intercalated month has 29 days, that is, four weeks and a day, yielding a five day difference in the day of the week on which the holiday falls.}
[XXXII.A]	R. Zera[85] asked, "What is the law [whether or not] the prohibition against delaying applies to an heir?"
[B]	[Do we hold that] the All-Merciful stated [Dt. 23:21], "When you make a vow [to the Lord your God, you shall not be slack to pay it]"—and this one [that is, the heir] did not make the vow [and therefore is not subject to the prohibition against delaying payment]?
[C]	Or, perhaps, [we should base our answer on Dt. 12:5-6: "But you shall seek the place the Lord your God will choose out of all your tribes to put his name and make his habitation there]; thither you shall go, and thither you shall bring [your burnt-offerings and your sacrifices...]." And [based upon this verse, since] this one is obligated [to go to the place the Lord chooses, he also is obligated to bring the offering without delay].
[D]	Come and hear [which answer is correct].

---

[85]M reads: Hiyya. This appears to be a scribal error.

BAVLI ROSH HASHANAH CHAPTER ONE [6b] 111

[E] For R. Hiyya[86] taught on Tannaitic authority, "[Dt. 23:21 states, 'For the Lord your God will surely require it] of you.' This excludes the heir."

[F] {The following suggests that the expression "of you" already has been interpreted as serving a different purpose. Accordingly, it cannot mean what Hiyya says.} But this [phrase], "of you," is already needed [see above, unit **XXIII**.A-B, cited here at G]:

[G] [Dt. 23:21 states: "of you."] This refers to [T. Ar. 3:17] **gleanings, forgotten sheaves, and that which is left growing in the corner of a field.**

[H] [Hiyya can respond: One interpretation rests on Scripture's] wording, "*Imak*" [which means, of you, and is all that is needed to make sense in the current context].

[I] [The other interpretation rests on the fact that in Scripture, the full phrase is], "*Me-imak*" [literally, from of you]. {The extra preposition in the Hebrew allows the phrase to be expounded in two different ways.}

[**XXXIII**.A] R. Zera asked, "[As for] a woman—what is [the rule whether or not] she [is subject] to [the precept that one] not delay [paying an obligation to God]?

[B] "Do we say [that she is not, since] she is not obligated [in the first place] to appear [in Jerusalem on the festivals]? {See Dt. 16:16, which commands only all the males to appear.}

[C] "Or perhaps [we say she is subject to the prohibition, since] she is commanded to rejoice?" {Rejoicing implies partaking of the peace-offering, which must be done in Jerusalem. If she has to go to Jerusalem for that purpose, we might argue that she also must not delay payment of her vow.}

---

[86]M and other sources read: Hanina.

[D] Said to him[87] Abayye, "You should derive the answer from [the fact that] she is commanded to rejoice."

[E] Now, did Abayye really say this?

[F] For [to the contrary] did Abayye not say: "[As for] a woman—her husband makes her joyful"? {So the commandment that she must rejoice has nothing to do with her going to Jerusalem.}

[G] [To resolve the problem raised at E-F, we can argue that Abayye at D] spoke within the terms established by Zera.

[**XXXIV**.A] They asked them, "[As for] a firstling—from when do they count the year [within which it must be sacrificed]?"

[B] Abayye said, "From when it is born."

[C] Rab Aha bar Jacob said, "From the point at which it can be used for appeasement [that is, the eighth day]."

[D] And there is no conflict [between these two views].

[E] This view [of Aha bar Jacob] applies in the case of an unblemished animal [which can be sacrificed no earlier than the eighth day];

[F] [**7a**] [while] this view [of Abayye] applies in the case of a blemished animal [which immediately may be eaten as ordinary meat].

[G] {F's explanation of B is challenged.} Can one really consume a blemished animal [on the day it is born]?[88] {Rashi: The animal might be premature and therefore forbidden for consumption; it may not be slaughtered and consumed until the eighth day; B. Shab. 135b.}

---

[87]M lacks: to him.

[88]In M an explanatory gloss appears to have been copied into the body of the text. The words "What if it is a miscarriage?" appear here in the text. Above these words, an interlinear addition—"With what [circumstance] are we dealing?"—has been added.

[H] {G is rejected.} [Abayye speaks of] a case in which he is certain that it completed its gestational period, [so that the animal is available for consumption on the day it is born].

[XXXV.A] Our rabbis have taught on Tannaitic authority: The first day of Nisan is the new year for months, leap years, and for [use of] the heave-offering of the *sheqel* [collected in the preceding month of Adar].

[B] And some say: also for the renting of houses. {In this view, the lease on a house rented for the current year always is up on the first of Nisan, even if the renter had possessed the house for less than a full year.}

[C] "For months"—from what [verse in Scripture] do we know this?

[D] As it is written [Ex. 12:2-6]: "This month shall be for you the beginning of months;[89] it shall be the first month of the year for you.[90] Tell all of the congregation of Israel that on the tenth day of this month they shall take every man a lamb according to their fathers' houses, a lamb for a household; ... and you shall keep it until the fourteenth day of this month, when [the whole assembly of the congregation of Israel] shall kill [their lambs in the evening]."

[E] And it is written [Dt. 16:1]: "Observe the month of Abib [that is, 'first-ripening grains'], [and keep the Passover to the Lord your God]."

[F] In which month are there first-ripening grains?

[G] You must say[91] that this is Nisan [when Passover occurs], and [as Ex. 12:2-6 states] it is called "first."

---

[89]M and other manuscript sources lack the beginning of the verse.

[90]In M the following citations are abbreviated and, between each segment of the cited verse, the words "And it is written" are added.

[91]M lacks the first words of this line.

[H] But [to the contrary] might I argue that [the first day of] Iyyar [is the new year for months, A]?

[I] {This claim is unacceptable.} [For it to be the new year for months] we require [it to be a time of] first ripening grains, and [in Iyyar] there are none.

[J] But might I argue that [the first day of] Adar [in which grain begins to ripen is the new year for months, A]?

[K] {This claim too is unacceptable.} [For it to be the new year for months] we require [it to be a time of] the majority of first ripening grains, and [in Adar] this does not [occur].

[L] {K is challenged.} Now, [at Dt. 16:1 is the notion that the first month yields] the *majority of* first ripening grains written? {This is not what Dt. 16:1 says; J's claim stands.}

[M] [Arguing on different grounds:] Rather,[92] said Rab Hisda, "We know it from this [Scriptural passage: Lev. 23:39 states]: 'On the fifteenth day of the seventh month, when you have gathered in the produce of the land, [you shall keep the feast of the Lord seven days].'

[N] "In which month occurs the gathering [of the produce]?

[O] "You must say that this is Tishre.

[P] "And [Scripture] designates that [month] 'seventh.'" {Hence we know that Tishre is not the new year for months, which is "first."}

[Q] But [on the contrary] I can argue that Marheshvan [is the month of the gathering of the produce], and [in that case] what [does Lev. 23:39 mean by] "seventh"?

[R] It is seventh to Iyyar.

[S] {The following rejects Q-R.} [According to Lev. 23:39, for a month to be called "seventh"] we require [it to be a time of] gathering, and [in Marheshvan] there is none.

[T] But I can argue that [reference] is to Elul, and [in that case] what [does Lev. 23:39 mean by] "seventh"?

[U] It is seventh to Adar.

---

[92] M lacks the word: Rather.

[V] {The following rejects T-U}. [For it to be called the seventh month] we require [it to be a time of] the majority of the gathering, and [in Elul] this does not occur.

[W] {V's argument is unpersuasive.} Now, [at Dt. 16:1 is the notion that the first month yields] *the majority of* first ripening grains written?? {It is not; T-U's claim stands.}

[X] Rather, said Rabina, "We did not learn this matter [of the numbering of the months] from the Torah of Moses, our Rabbi. [Rather][93] we learned it from the words of tradition [that is, the prophetic writings or hagiographa].

[Y] "[For Zech. 1:7 states:][94] 'On the twenty-fourth day of the eleventh month, which is the month of Shevat....'"

[Z] Rabbah bar Ulla[95] said, "[We learn the numbering] from here [Es. 2:16]: 'And when Esther was taken to King Ahasuerus into his royal palace in the tenth month, which is the month of Tevet....'"

[AA] Rab Kahana said, "[We learn the numbering] from here [Zech. 7:1: 'In the fourth year of King Darius, the word of the Lord came to Zechariah] on the fourth day of the ninth month, which is Kislev.'"

[BB] Rab Aha bar Jacob said, "[We learn the numbering] from here[96] [Es. 8:9]: 'The king's secretaries were summoned at that time, in the third month, which is the month of Sivan.'"

[CC] Rab Ashi said, "[We learn the numbering] from here [Es. 3:7]: 'They cast Pur, that is the lot, before Haman day after day; and they cast it month after month till the twelfth month, which is the month of Adar.'"

---

[93] M has this word explicitly.

[94] M explicitly reads: as it is written.

[95] M reads: Rabina son of R. Ulla.

[96] The result of haplography, M lacks the following through the words "from here" at DD.

[DD] And if you wish, I can argue from here [Es. 3:7]: "In the first month, which is the month of Nisan...."

[EE] Now, what is the reason that all [of the listed authorities] did not support [A's claim, that Nisan is the first month] with this [direct statement of Es. 3:7]?

[FF] Perhaps [it is because, in the setting of Es. 3:7], what is the meaning of [the word] "first"? It was the first of [Haman's] actions. {In this reading, Es. 3:7 does not mean that Nisan is the first month at all.}

[XXXVI.A] As regards the Tannaitic authority behind our [pericope, M. R.H. 1:1B, who calls Nisan the New Year of kings and festivals, why did he not include the fact given at unit **XXXV**.A, that Nisan is the new year for months]?

[B] He was concerned with years but not with months.

[XXXVII.A] {Discussion of the Tannaitic statement introduced at **XXXV**.A continues.} [The first day of Nisan is the new year for months], leap years, [and for use of the heave-offering of the *sheqel*].

[B] How do we know that [leap years are determined] from Nisan?

[C] For [to the contrary] is it not taught on Tannaitic authority [T. San. 2:7]: **They do not intercalate the year before New Year [in Tishre],**

[D] **and if they did intercalate it, it is not deemed intercalated.**

[E] **But on account of necessity they do intercalate it immediately after New Year.**

[F] **And even so, they intercalate only Adar [that is, only a second Adar may be added].** {The determination to intercalate the year by adding a second Adar may only be made after the start of Tishre. It seems clear that Nisan, which comes after Adar but before Tishre, cannot be the new year for leap years.}

[G] [To solve this problem], said Rab Nahman bar Isaac, "[At unit **XXXV**.A] what is the meaning of 'leap year'?

[H] "It refers to the conclusion of [the period within which one may declare] a leap year,

[I] "as it is taught on Tannaitic authority [M. Ed. 7:7]: *They [that is, Joshua and Pappias] gave testimony that the year may be intercalated [through the declaration that there will be a second Adar] at any time in Adar.*

[J] *"For [authorities previously] had said, 'The year may be intercalated] only up to Purim.'"* {According to I, unit **XXXV**.A indicates that the first of Nisan marks the conclusion of the period during which a leap year may be declared. That declaration may be made only until the end of Adar.}

[K] {We now explain the reasoning of the authorities at M. Ed. 7:7, I vs. J.} What is the reasoning of the one who says that it may be intercalated only up to Purim, [J]?

[L] Insofar as a master said, "[People] inquire about the laws of Passover for thirty days prior to Passover," [if, late in first Adar, after all the inquiries had been made, authorities determined that a second Adar were to be added, delaying Passover for a month], people might wind up neglecting [the rules of] leaven. {Rather than accept the new date, people would observe Passover at the original time, within thirty days of receiving instruction regarding its rules.}

[M] But the other [side, I, which states that the year may be intercalated throughout Adar, holds that, since people] know that intercalation of the year depends upon a calculation, they reason that the rabbis have not figured it out until now. {In this view, people will not become confused. They anticipate a late determination of whether or not there will be a second Adar.}

[**XXXVIII**.A] As regards the Tannaitic authority behind our [pericope, M. R.H. 1:1B, who calls Nisan the new year of

	kings and festivals, why did he not include the fact given at unit **XXXV**.A, that Nisan is the new year for leap years]?
[B]	He was concerned with [the periods of which Nisan marks] the beginning but not [those of which Nisan marks] the end.

[**XXXIX**.A] {Discussion of the Tannaitic statement introduced at **XXXV**.A continues.} [The first day of Nisan is the new year for months, leap years], and [for use of] the heave-offering of the *sheqel*. {Reference is to the *sheqel* contributed annually by every Israelite for maintenance of the sacrificial cult. Payment was made in Adar.}

[B] How do we know this [from Scripture]?

[C] Said R. Josiah,[97] "[At Num. 28:14] Scripture said, '[Their drink offerings shall be half a *hin* of wine for a bull, a third of a *hin* for a ram, and a fourth of a *hin* for a lamb]; this is the burnt-offering of each month throughout the months of the year.'

[D] "[Through a superfluous occurrence of the word 'month'], the Torah indicates: Renew [the year] and bring an offering from the new heave-offering [of the *sheqel*].

[E] "And we learn that the 'year' [referred to here] is a year that starts with Nisan as it is written [Ex. 12:2: 'This month shall be for you the beginning of months]; it shall be the first month of the year for you.'" {We already know that this "first" month refers to Nisan.}

[F] But [contrary to E] why not learn that the year [referred to here] is a year that starts with Tishre, as it is written [Dt. 11:12: "a land that the Lord your God cares for; the eyes of the Lord your God are always upon it], from the beginning of the year [to the end of the year]."[98]

---

[97] All manuscript sources and the parallels at B. Yoma 65b and B. Meg. 29b read: Said R. Tabi said R. Josiah.

[98] M has the bracketed words explicitly.

[G] {For the reason given here, F's analogy is inappropriate.} We draw an analogy between [a reference to] "year" that includes [a mention of] "months" and a [different reference to] "year" that includes [a mention of] "months."

[H] But we do not draw an analogy between [a reference to] "year" that includes [a mention of] "months" and a [different reference to] "year" that does not include [a mention of] "months."

[XL.A] Said Rab Judah said Samuel, "[As for] communal sacrifices brought on the first of Nisan—it is a commandment to bring [them, that is, to purchase them] from new [contributions].

[B] "But if one brought them from old [contributions], he has fulfilled his obligation [and the sacrifice is valid], except that he has failed [to fulfill] a commandment."

[C] A Tannaitic statement makes the same point: [As for] communal sacrifices brought on the first of Nisan—it is a commandment to bring [them, that is, to purchase them] from new [contributions].

[D] But if one brought them from old [contributions], he has fulfilled his obligation, except that he has failed [to fulfill] a commandment.[99]

[E] And as for a private individual who contributed [sacrifices] from his own [property]—they are valid, so long as he gave them over to the community.

[F] That is obvious [and goes without saying]!

[G] {G-H argues that E is not obvious.} [In the absence of the explicit statement of E] what might one have thought?

[H] [One might have reasoned that we should] be concerned that[100] [the individual] had [7b] not intended wholeheartedly

---

[99]C-D is written in the margin of M, apparently having been dropped from the body of the text through haplography.

[100]The preceding words appear in the margin of M.

to transfer them to the community [so that, contrary to what E tells us, the sacrifices are not valid].

[I] Therefore we are informed, [that we need not be concerned whether or not the individual really meant to give the sacrifices over to the community].

[XLI.A] As regards the Tannaitic authority behind our [pericope, M. R.H. 1:1B, who calls Nisan the new year of kings and festivals, why did he not include the fact given at unit **XXXV**.A, that Nisan is the new year for the heave-offering of the *sheqel*]?

[B] Since it is taught on Tannaitic authority [at unit **XL**.D] that if one [anyway] brought [the offering from old contributions], he has fulfilled his obligation, [the authority behind M. R.H. 1:1] was uncertain [whether or not the first of Nisan should be considered new year for this purpose].

[XLII.A] {Discussion of the Tannaitic statement introduced at **XXXV**.A-B continues.} [The first day of Nisan is the new year for months, leap years, and for use of the heave-offering of the *sheqel*.] And some say: also for the renting of houses.

[B] Our rabbis have taught on Tannaitic authority:[101] One who rents a house to his fellow for a year counts twelve months from the [exact] day [of the rental] to the [same] day [in the month, twelve months later].

[C] But if he said [that the rental is], "For this year," [then] even if [the tenant] only took possession[102] on the first of Adar, as soon as the first of Nisan arrived [thirty days later], his year [of rental] is deemed completed.

[D] And even in [the view of] one who says [see above, unit **II**.E], "A single day in the year can be considered a full year," [this rule, which suggests that the minimum period of

---

[101]M reads: It is taught on Tannaitic authority.

[102]Literally: stood.

rental is thirty days, creates no problem, since] this situation is unique, insofar as a person does not go to the trouble of renting a house for less than thirty days.

[XLIII.A] Now, can I not argue that Tishre [is the new year for the renting of houses]? {If this is the case, a person who moves in on the first of Elul could be told that his tenancy is up on the first of Tishre, thirty days later.}

[B] {What is suggested at A is unacceptable.} It is taken for granted that, when a man rents a house [in Tishre], he rents it for the entire rainy season. {See. M. B.M. 8:6.}

[XLIV.A] As regards the first authority in the Tannaitic statement [cited at unit **XXXV**.A] and the Tannaitic authority behind our [pericope, M. R.H. 1:1B—why did they not state that Nisan is the new year for the renting of houses]?

[B] In Nisan too rainy weather occurs, [so that, even then, a person who rents a house for the year cannot intend only thirty days].

[XLV.A] {A-D concerns the question of which authority stands behind the law at M. R.H. 1:1C. E-G asks the same question for the law of M. R.H. 1:1B.} *The first day of Elul is the new year for tithing cattle* [M. R.H. 1:1C].

[B] Which [Tannaitic authority stands behind this statement]?

[C] It is R. Meir,

[D] as we have taught on Tannaitic authority[103] [M. Bekh. 9:5]: *R. Meir says, "On the first of Elul is the new year for tithing cattle."*

[E] *[The first day of Nisan is the new year for kings] and festivals* [M. R.H. 1:1B].

---

[103]So the marginal emendation in printed editions, as appropriate for citations of the Mishnah. The body of the text reads: for it is taught on Tannaitic authority.

[F] Which [Tannaitic authority stands behind this statement regarding festivals]?

[G] It is R. Simeon. {This is based upon T. R.H. 1:2, cited above at unit **XVIII**, where Simeon clearly understands there to be a new year for festivals.}

[H] {A-G yields a problem, set out at H-I and resolved at J-K.} Cite the following clause [at M. R.H. 1:1D]: *R. Eleazar and R. Simeon say, "[The new year for tithing cattle] is on the first day of Tishre."*[104]

[I] [Is it possible that, as A-G seems to show,] the first clause [at M. R.H. 1:1B] and the final clause [at M. R.H. 1:1D] are [the opinion of] R. Simeon, while the middle clause [at M. R.H. 1:1C] is [the opinion of] R. Meir?

[J] [To resolve this problem] said Rab Joseph, "[The authority behind the construction at M. R.H. 1:1B-D] is Rabbi [Judah the Patriarch], and he chose [the individual statements of law] according to the views of different Tannaitic authorities.

[K] "In [determining the new year for] festivals, he accepted the reasoning of R. Simeon, while, in [determining the new year for] tithing cattle, he accepted the reasoning of R. Meir."

[L] {J-K is challenged.} If this is the case, [why does he state at M. R.H. 1:1A that there are] four [new years]?

[M] There are five! {These are the first of Nisan (kings); the fifteenth of Nisan (festivals); the first of Elul (tithing cattle); the first of Tishre (years, Sabbaticals, Jubilees), the first/fifteenth of Shevat (trees).}

[N] [To solve the problem raised by L-M] said Rava, "Both parties, [Simeon and Meir], agree on four:

[O] "In the view of R. Meir there are four, excluding the [new year of] festivals, [which Simeon places on the fifteenth of Nisan].

---

[104] All manuscript sources and, apparently, Rashi and Tosafot lack H. Rabbinovicz suggests that this line is a scribal addition filling out the text on the model of E.

[P] "In the view of R. Simeon there are four, excluding the [new year of] tithing cattle." {Meir places the new year of tithing cattle on the first of Elul, as an independent new year. Simeon, M. R.H. 1:1D, dates this to the first of Tishre, so that it is not an independent new year to be counted separately.}

[Q] [Solving L-M's problem in a different manner], Rab Nahman bar Isaac said, "[M. R.H. 1:1A means that] there are four months in which there are a number of new years." {In Nahman's view, the superscription at M. R.H. 1:1A counts as one the two new year days that occur in Nisan.}

[R] They objected [to Rava and Nahman's responses, N-P and Q, based upon the following tradition]: The sixteenth of Nisan is the new year for the *omer,* [after which date new grain may be eaten; see Lev. 23:14]; the sixth of Sivan is the new year for the two loaves [that make up the meal offering of the new grain; see Lev. 23:17].

[S] [In light of this rule], in the view of Rava, [M. R.H. 1:1] should teach [that there are] *six* [new years]. {These would include the four to which Meir and Simeon concur at M. R.H. 1:1 and the additional two new years indicated by the law cited at R.}

[T] [Similarly, in light of this rule], in the view of Rab Nahman bar Isaac, [M. R.H. 1:1] should teach [that there are] *five* [new years]. {This would include the four separate months listed at M. R.H. 1:1 in which there are new years plus Sivan, indicated at R as containing a new year.}

[U] [Explaining why R-T's objection is not probative] said Rab Pappa, "[In establishing the number of new years, the authority behind M. R.H. 1:1 only] counted those that commence on the [preceding] evening; those that do not commence on the [preceding] evening, he did not count." {This excludes from consideration the two new years listed at R. The new year for the *omer* does not commence until the point during the day at which the *omer* actually is

[V] {Pappa's approach, U, is rejected, since, contrary to what Pappa suggests, M. R.H. 1:1 in fact takes account of other new years that do not start on the preceding evening.} But indeed, [as for the new year for] festivals—even though [with respect to delaying the payment of vows] it does not commence on the [preceding] evening, it is counted! {The precept that one must not delay is transgressed only after the hour at which the animal vowed actually could have been sacrificed.}

[W] {V is rejected, so that Pappa's view, U, stands.} [Contrary to V], since he has to bring [his offering to the Temple before the start of the festival and has not done so], from the beginning [of the festival, at sundown on the preceding night] he is guilty [of having transgressed]. {This is the case even though the offering, had he brought it, would not be sacrificed until the following morning.}

[X] {We have another example that appears to contradict Pappa's approach, U.} But indeed, in the case of [the new year for] Jubilee years—even though it does not start on the [preceding] evening, it is counted [at M. R.H. 1:1]! {The start of the Jubilee year is marked by the blowing of the shofar during the daytime on the Day of Atonement.}

[Y] {The Talmud now explains that, contrary to X, the Jubilee year does begin on the preceding evening. Pappa's perspective thus stands.} This is the view of R. Ishmael the son of R. Yohanan b. Beroqa, who said [see below, unit **LII**, 8b], "The Jubilee year begins on New Year." {In the view of Ishmael, the Jubilee year starts on the evening of the new year and does not depend upon the blowing of the shofar at all. Pappa's explanation of M. R.H. 1:1's statement that there are (only) four new years therefore stands.}

[Z] {A different reason that M. R.H. 1:1A includes only four new years is given.} Rab Shisha[105] the son of Rab Idi said, "[In establishing the number of new years, the authority behind M. R.H. 1:1A only] counted those that do not require some action [on the part of an individual]; those that do require some action [on the part of an individual], he did not count." {This excludes from the count at M. R.H. 1:1A the two new years listed at R. The prohibition against eating new grain or using it for offerings is lifted only at the point at which the *omer* and the two loaves actually are offered.}

[AA] {Z is challenged.} But indeed, [the new year] for festivals[106] is among those that require an action [on the part of the individual], but [even so] it is[107] counted. {The rule against delaying is transgressed only after the hour at which the animal vowed actually could have been sacrificed. Hence, we can understand this new year to depend upon the sacrificing of the morning offering.}

[BB] {AA is rejected.} [Contrary to AA, transgression of the commandment that one] not delay [fulfilling vows] occurs automatically [on the evening of the new year of festivals, without any activity on the part of an individual].

[CC] [8a] But what of [the new year for] Jubilees [which, it was argued at X, begins only when the shofar is blown on the Day of Atonement].

---

[105]M reads: Sheshet.

[106]M and all manuscripts lack the remainder of this line, reading at AA-BB: But indeed, [the new year] for festivals [is subject to the commandment that one] not delay [fulfilling vows], since [the obligation to abide by this restriction] occurs automatically. The printed edition's slight variation of wording at BB apparently is a correction necessitated by the addition of the words at AA that do not appear in the manuscripts (Rabbinovicz).

[107]Simon translates: ...and yet are not reckoned. Simon's inclusion of the word "not" is an error.

[DD] {The Talmud now explains that, contrary to CC, the beginning of the Jubilee year does not depend upon a human action.} This [explanation of M. R.H. 1:1A given at Z] follows the view of R. Ishmael the son of R. Yohanan b. Beroqa [see above, Y]. {In Ishmael's view, the Jubilee year starts on the evening of New Year and does not depend upon the blowing of the shofar on the following day.}

[EE] {A different reason that M. R.H. 1:1A includes only four new years is given.} But Rab Ashi said, "[M. R.H. 1:1A means that] there are four new years that occur on the first [days] of four months. {The new years for the *omer* and for the two loaves, which fall in the middle of the month (R), are not included.}

[FF] [Ashi's view is unacceptable, since, in his approach, to reach four new year days, we must include] the first day of Shevat, which accords with the view of the House of Shammai. {In Ashi's count, the four new year days at M. R.H. 1:1A appear to be 1) the first of Nisan (kings and festivals); 2) the first of Elul (tithing cattle); 3) the first of Tishre (years, Sabbatical years, and Jubilees); 4) the first of Shevat (trees). The problem is that this fourth new year accords only with the House of Shammai. The Hillelites, whose view represents the decided law, hold that the new year for trees is on the fifteenth of Shevat. Insofar as it suggests that the law follows the Shammaites, Ashi's approach is unacceptable.}

[GG] {Ashi's approach is explained in a way that shows it not to violate the principle that the law follows the Hillelites.} [Ashi] interprets [M. R.H. 1:1A] to mean [that] according to all parties, there are three new year days [that fall on the first of the month].

[HH] [But, whether or not] the first of Shevat [is a fourth new year day to be added to this list] is disputed by the House of Shammai and the House of Hillel.

[XLVI.A] *[The first day of Elul is the new year for tithing cattle.] R. Eleazar and R. Simeon say, "It is on the first day of Tishre"* [M. R.H. 1:1C-D].

[B] Said R. Yohanan, "Both authorities [in this dispute reached their views by] interpreting the same verse [of Scripture].

[C] "For it is stated[108] [Ps. 65:13], 'The rams have mounted the sheep,[109] the valleys deck themselves with grain, they shout and sing.'

[D] "R. Meir [the authority behind M. R.H. 1:1C (see above, unit XLV.A-D)] reasoned, 'When do the rams mount the sheep? It is at the time that the valleys deck themselves with grain. And when are the valleys decked with grain? During Adar. They conceive in Adar and give birth in Ab. [Accordingly] their new year is in Elul.'

[E] "[By contrast] R. Eleazar and R. Simeon [who hold that the new year for tithing cattle is in Tishre] say,[110] 'When do the rams mount the sheep? It is when they [that is, the stalks of grain] shout and sing. When do the stalks of grain sing? During Nisan. They conceive in Nisan and give birth in Elul. [Accordingly] their new year is in Tishre.'"

[F] {As matters have been reported, only the view of Eleazar and Simeon, E, takes into account the end of the verse: "they shout and sing."} But [for] the other [authority, Meir] this statement also appears: "...they sing...." {How does Meir make sense of this statement?}

[G] [He holds that] this refers to the ones that conceive late in the season, which occurs in Nisan.

[H] {As matters have been reported, only the view of Meir, D, takes into account the middle of the verse: "the valleys deck themselves with grain."} But [for] the other [authorities,

---

[108] Manuscripts and other sources lack: For it is stated.

[109] RSV: "the meadows clothe themselves with flocks."

[110] M reads: reason.

Eleazar and Simeon] this statement also appears: "the valleys deck themselves with grain." {How do these authorities make sense of this statement?}

[I] [They hold that] this refers to the ones that conceive early in the season, which occurs in Adar.

[J] {The following notes that the derivation of Meir's position, D and F-G, seems logical. But, Simeon and Eleazar's interpretation, E and H-I, does not make sense.} Granted that R. Meir's position [makes sense]:

[K] For it is written, "The rams have mounted the sheep." [This refers to] the time at which "the valleys deck themselves with grain." But there are also those [that conceive later, at the time at which] "they shout and sing."

[L] But for the view of R. Eleazar and R. Simeon [to be derived from Ps. 65:13], the clauses would have to be reversed:

[M] "The rams have mounted the sheep." [This refers to] the time at which "they shout and sing." But there are also those [that conceive earlier, at the time at which] "the valleys deck themselves with grain."

[N] {L-M shows that E and H-I's derivation of Simeon and Eleazar's position is unacceptable. Accordingly, Yohanan's original proposal, B, that these authorities and Meir base their views on the same verse of Scripture, is unsupported. In the following, Rava offers a different way to derive Simeon/Eleazar and Meir's contrasting views from the same verse.} Rather, said Rava, "All agree [on the interpretation of] 'the rams have mounted the sheep' [as referring to] the time at which 'the valleys deck themselves with grain.' This occurs in Adar.

[O] "Instead, they differ concerning [the interpretation of] this verse [Dt. 14:22]: 'Tithing, you shall tithe.'

[P] "Scripture speaks of two kinds of tithe: one is a tithe of cattle, and the other is a tithe of grain.

[Q] "R. Meir reasons that [Scripture thus] treats as analogous the tithe of cattle and the tithe of grain: just as, in the case of the tithe of grain, the tithe must be separated close to the time that the grain becomes liable [which occurs in Elul], so in the case of the tithe of cattle, the tithe must be separated close to the time that the cattle become liable [in Adar].

[R] "But R. Eleazar and R. Simeon reason that [Scripture] treats as analogous the tithe of cattle and the tithe of grain [in a different way]: just as, in the case of the tithe of grain, its new year occurs in Tishre, so in the case of the tithe of cattle, its new year is in Tishre."

[XLVII.A] *The first day of Tishre is the new year for the reckoning of years* [M. R.H. 1:1E].

[B] What is the purpose of this rule?

[C] Said Rab Pappa, "It is because of legal documents, as we have taught on Tannaitic authority [M. Sheb. 10:5B]: *Antedated bonds are invalid, but postdated bonds are valid.*" {Documents are dated according to the day and month in the year of the reign of a specific king. Counting all years from the first of Tishre makes it easy to determine when a legal document was created, even for people who do not know the day on which a specific king assumed the throne. See above, unit I.D, and the note there.}

[D] But [suggesting that the reason cannot be as Pappa states] thus we have taught on Tannaitic authority [M. R.H. 1:1B]: *the first day of Nisan is the new year for kings.*

[E] And we stated [above, unit I.B-C]: What is the purpose of this rule? Now, said Rab Hisda, "It is because of legal documents." {Accordingly, the new year for legal documents is Nisan, not Tishre. Pappa, C, appears to be incorrect.}

[F] There is no contradiction [between C and E]: This [statement, M. R.H. 1:1B, explained at D-E] refers to Israelite kings, [whose reign is dated to Nisan], while this statement [M. R.H. 1:1E, explained at A-C] refers to kings of other nations, [whose new year is in Tishre; see above, unit **XIII**.A-B, cited in the following].

[G] {If F is correct, then the distinction between new year for Israelite kings and for non-Israelite kings is inherent in the Mishnah. If this is the case, Hisda's statement, above at unit **XIII**.A-B, is superfluous.} What, then, of that which Rab Hisda said: "They taught [that Nisan is the new year for kings] only for the case of Israelite kings. But in the case of kings of other nations, we count [the years of their reign] from Tishre"?

[H] Did Rab Hisda intend only to tell us what the Mishnah [itself] makes explicit?

[I] No! Rab Hisda intended to teach us the significance of [verses of] Scripture. {The interpretation referred to here appears above, unit **XIII**.C-E.}

[J] {The following suggests that Hisda did not interpret M. R.H. 1:1E in accordance with the view of Pappa at all, as having to do with the new year for non-Israelite kings.} And if you wish, I can argue that Rab Hisda explained this passage in the Mishnah, [M. R.H. 1:1E, which holds that the first of Tishre is the new year for years] in accord with [the view of] R. Zera.[111]

[K] For R. Zera said, "[M. R.H. 1:1E's statement, that the first of Tishre is the new year for years, means that it is the new year for determining] annual cycles." {Simon, p. 30: This view holds that the year is comprised of four cycles, that of the vernal equinox, beginning in Nisan; that of the summer solstice, beginning in Tamuz; that of the autumn equinox, beginning in Tishre; and that of the winter solstice, beginning in Tevet.}

---

[111]M has "Eleazar" and a slightly different wording at K. A marginal correction indicates the same reading as the printed edition.

[L] And this [interpretation, K] follows the view of R. Eliezer, who said, "In Tishre, the world was created." {See below, unit **LXIII**.A, 10b.}

[**XLVIII**.A] {The following continues the theme of the preceding, offering an independent interpretation of M. R.H. 1:1E.} Rab Nahman bar Isaac said, "[M. R.H. 1:1E refers] to [the final] judgment, as it is written [Dt. 11:12, 'The eyes of the Lord your God are always upon it],[112] from the beginning of the year to the end of the year,' [which means]: 'From the beginning of the year' what will occur at the end is determined.

[B] "From what [passage in Scripture do we know that this takes place] in Tishre? For it is written [Ps. 81:3], 'Blow the trumpet at the new moon, when the moon is covered, on our feast day.'[113]

[C] "On which festival [**8b**] is the moon covered?

[D] "We must say it is New Year [in Tishre, which falls on the new moon, unlike all other festivals, which come in the middle of the month].

[E] "And [in the following verse, Ps. 81:4] it is written [regarding this festival], 'For it is a statute for Israel, an ordinance of the God of Jacob.'"

[**XLIX**.A] {The Talmud presents a thematically related interpretation of Ps. 81:4.} Our rabbis have taught on Tannaitic authority: [The verse], "For it is a statute for Israel,[114] an ordinance [*or:* (time of) judgment] of the God of Jacob"

---

[112]M and Rashi have the beginning of the citation explicitly.

[113]Cf., B. Bes. 16a, which uses this same proof to substantiate a different proposition.

[114]M and the parallel in Yalkut Tehilim add here as at unit L.B-D: [From this statement] I know only [the rule for the people of] Israel. As for the nations of the world, from what verse [do I know that it is a time of judgment for them as well]? Scripture says....

teaches that the heavenly court does not assemble [to sit] in judgment unless the earthly court has sanctified the new month. {Rashi: Only if the Israelite court has enacted the "statute" designating the new month does the heavenly court engage in the work of judgment.}

[L.A] A different Tannaitic teaching states: [Ps. 81:4 indicates]: "For it is a statute for Israel."

[B] [Based upon this verse] I know only that [the people of] Israel [will be judged].

[C] From what [Scriptural verse do I know that] the [other] nations of the world [also will be judged]?

[D] Scripture states, "an ordinance [or, time of judgment] of the God of Jacob."[115]

[E] If this is the case [that all peoples will be judged], why does Scripture need to state, "For it is a statute for Israel"? {If the nations are to be judged, it goes without saying that the Israelites also will be. The statement "For it is a statute for Israel" must teach us some additional, otherwise unknown fact.}

[F] It teaches that [the people of] Israel enter first [before God] to be judged.

[G] This accords with Rab Hisda [see below, B. R.H. 1:2 IV.A, 16a], for said Rab Hisda, "[When] the king and the community [await judgment], the king enters in first for judgment,[116] as it is said [1 Kgs. 8:59: 'May He maintain] the case of His servant [Solomon] and [then] the case of His people [Israel].'"[117]

[H] What is the reason [that the king is judged first]?

---

[115]B-D is added in the margin of M.

[116]The beginning of this line is added in the margin of M.

[117]In M this line is garbled.

BAVLI ROSH HASHANAH CHAPTER ONE [8b]   133

[I]   If you wish I can argue that[118] it is not proper for the king to remain outside [alone while the people are being judged].

[J]   And if you wish I can argue that [the king is judged] before [God has considered the community's sins and] becomes really angry.

[LI.A] *[The first day of Tishre is the new year for the reckoning of years,] for Sabbatical years* [M. R.H. 1:1E].

[B]   From what [verse of Scripture] do we know this?

[C]   As it is written [Lev. 25:4]: "But in the seventh year there shall be a sabbath of solemn rest for the land, [a sabbath to the Lord; you shall not sow your field or prune your vineyard]."

[D]   Now, one must conclude [that the meaning of the word] "year" is "a year [beginning] from Tishre," since it is written [Dt. 11:12]: "from the beginning of the year [to the end of the year]." {An analogy is drawn between the year referred to at Lev. 25:4 and that referred to at Dt. 11:12. As was shown in unit **XLVIII**, the year referred to in the latter citation begins in Tishre. We conclude that the year referred to at Lev. 25:4 also begins in Tishre.}

[E]   {D's reasoning is challenged.} Now, [following this same approach] one should conclude [that the meaning of the word] "year" is "a year [beginning] from Nisan," since it is written [Ex. 12:2: "This month shall be for you the beginning of months;] it shall be the first month of the year for you." {An analogy is drawn between the year referred to at Lev. 25:4 and that referred to at Ex. 12:2. In the latter citation, the month of Passover, Nisan, is called the beginning of the year. We should conclude that the year referred to at Lev. 25:4 also begins in Nisan.}

[F]   {For the reason given here, E's analogy is inappropriate. See unit **XXXIX**.} We draw an analogy between [a reference to]

---

[118]M introduces the following simply with the word "For."

a "year" that does not include [mention of] "months" and a [different reference to] "year" that does not include [mention of] "months." {Such an analogy is found at C-D.}

[G] But [unlike what is proposed at E], we do not draw an analogy between [a reference to] a "year" that does not include [mention of] "months" and a [different reference to] "year" that does include [mention of] "months."

[LII.A] *[The first day of Tishre is the new year for the reckoning of years, for Sabbatical years], and for Jubilees* [M. R.H. 1:1E].

[B] [Is the new year for] Jubilees [indeed] on the first of Tishre?

[C] [Rather the new year for] Jubilees is on the tenth of Tishre!

[D] [This is] as it is written [Lev. 25:9, referring to the Jubilee year: "Then you shall send abroad the loud trumpet, on the tenth day of the seventh month]; on the Day of Atonement you shall send abroad the trumpet [throughout all your land]."

[E] Who, then, [stands behind M. R.H. 1:1E, which holds that the new year for the Jubilee is the first of Tishre]?

[F] [It is] R. Ishmael the son of R. Yohanan b. Beroqa,[119] as it is taught on Tannaitic authority: [It is written, Lev. 25:10]: "And you shall consecrate the fiftieth year."

[G] What is the meaning of this [passage in] Scripture?

[H] Since it is said [Lev. 25:9], "On the Day of Atonement,"[120] it is possible [for one to think] that [the Jubilee year] is sanctified only from the Day of Atonement and onward.

[I] [Therefore] Scripture states [at Lev. 25:10]: "And you shall consecrate the fiftieth year."

[J] This teaches that [the Jubilee] is sanctified and set into effect from its [that is, the year's] inception [on the first of Tishre].

---

[119]M adds: who said, "The Jubilee commences on New Year"....

[120]M continues the citation: you shall send abroad the trumpet throughout your land.

[K] Based on this [reasoning], said R. Ishmael the son of R. Yohanan b. Beroqa, "From New Year [on the first of Tishre of the Jubilee year] through the Day of Atonement [on the tenth of Tishre] slaves are neither set free to return to their homes nor forced to serve their masters. Rather, they eat, drink, and rejoice with wreaths on their heads. Once the Day of Atonement arrived, the court sounded the trumpet, the slaves are set free to return to their homes, and the fields are returned to their [original] owners."

[L] But [as for] the rabbis [at C-D, who say that the Jubilee starts only on the tenth of Tishre—how do they interpret Lev. 25:10]?

[M] [They say it means that] one sanctifies years but not months. {See below, M. R.H. 2:7 **IV**, 24a.}

[LIII.A] A different Tannaitic teaching states: [Lev. 25:11 indicates]: "A Jubilee [shall the fiftieth year be to you]."[121]

[B] What is the point of this verse?

[C] Since it is said [Lev. 25:10], "And you shall consecrate the fiftieth year," one could think that, just as [the Jubilee] is sanctified and in effect from its [that is, the year's] inception [on the first of Tishre], so it continues to be sanctified and in effect after its [that is, the year's] conclusion.

[D] And there would be no reason to be surprised [that Scripture should hold this to be the case], for [commonly] one lengthens sanctified time by [continuing it into] secular time.[122]

[E] [In order to preclude the wrong conclusion drawn at C+D], Scripture [explicitly] states [Lev. 25:11], "A Jubilee shall the fiftieth year be to you."

---

[121]M explicitly contains the brackets continuation of the citation but then lacks B and the beginning of C, which are added between the lines with a slight variation in wording.

[122]Literally: One adds from secular [time] onto sanctified [time].

[F] [This means that] you may sanctify the fiftieth year [as the Jubilee], but you may not sanctify the fifty-first year.

[G] [9a] But [as for] the rabbis [at unit LII.C-D, who hold that the Jubilee does not start right at the beginning of Tishre—how do they interpret Lev. 25:11's statement: "A jubilee shall the fiftieth year be to you"]?

[H] [They reason]: You are to count the fiftieth year, but you are not to count the fifty-first year. {Rashi: according to the authorities of LII.C-D, Lev. 25:11 makes clear that the fiftieth year is not to be counted as the first year of the following septenary.}

[I] [And this interpretation serves] to counter [the view] of R. Judah, who said, "The fiftieth year is counted both here [as the final year of the current fifty year cycle] and here [as the first year of the coming septenary].

[J] Therefore we are informed that this is not so.[123]

[LIV.A] {The Talmud explores a secondary issue raised by the preceding unit.} And [regarding the claim, above unit LIII.D, that commonly] one lengthens sanctified time by [continuing it into] secular time—from what [verse in Scripture] do we know this?

[B] As it is taught on Tannaitic authority [see M. Sheb. 1:4: *Ex. 34:21 states: "For six days you shall work, but on the seventh day you shall cease work; even] at plowing time and harvesting time you shall cease work."*[124]

[C] R. Aqiba says,[125] *"There is no need [for Scripture] to mention plowing and harvesting of the Sabbatical year*, since, [in order expressly to prohibit this, at Lev. 25:4-5] it

---

[123]"That this is not so" is added in the margin of M.

[124]Between the lines in M is added: If this does not concern the Sabbath, apply it to the matter of the Sabbatical year.

[125]M reads: Said R. Aqiba. The body of his comment contains an explicit citation of Ex. 34:21.

already is stated: "[But in the seventh year there shall be a sabbath of solemn rest for the land, a sabbath to the Lord]; you shall not sow your field [or prune your vineyard]"

[D] *"Rather [Scripture refers to] plowing on the eve of the Sabbatical year, [the benefits of which] extend into the Sabbatical year and harvesting [the crop of] the Sabbatical year which extends into the year following the Sabbatical."*

[E] {The following continues B-C's citation of M. Sheb. 1:4. Since Ishmael disagrees with B-C's interpretation of Ex. 34:21, we will then need to ascertain his understanding of the source in Scripture of the rule that one may lengthen a period of sanctified time.} *R. Ishmael says, "[Rather Ex. 34:21 teaches that] just as plowing, [which] is a voluntary act, [is prohibited on the Sabbath], so [only that] harvesting which is voluntary [is prohibited on the Sabbath]. This excludes [from the prohibition] harvesting the first sheaf, which is a commandment [and which, therefore, is permitted even on the Sabbath]."*

[F] Now [in the view of] R. Ishmael: [as for the notion that] one lengthens sanctified time by [continuing it into] secular time—from what [verse in Scripture] do we know this?

[G] He derives it from that which is taught on Tannaitic authority: [Lev. 23:32 states]: "And you shall afflict yourselves; on the ninth [day of the month beginning at evening...you shall rest on your sabbath]."

[H] [Based on this verse] one might think [the point is literally that] the ninth [of the month is the day of affliction].

[I] Scripture [therefore] states: "Beginning at evening."

[J] If it is "at evening," one might think [that the day of affliction begins] after dark.

[K] [To preclude that wrong conclusion] Scripture states, "On the ninth [day]." {After dark it is already the tenth of the month.}

[L] How do I understand this?

[M] One begins to afflict oneself while it is still day [on the ninth].

[N] This teaches that one lengthens sanctified time by [continuing it into] secular time.

[O] [Based upon what we have seen so far] I know only [that this rule applies] at the inception [of the holy day]. From what [verse in Scripture] do I learn the rule for the conclusion of the holy day?

[P] Scripture states [Lev. 23:32: "It shall be to you a sabbath of solemn rest, and you shall afflict yourselves; on the ninth day of the month beginning at evening], from evening[126] to evening [you shall rest on your sabbath]." {Hence I know that even though the holy day is designated as being on the ninth of the month it continues through the tenth.}

[Q] [Based upon what we have seen so far] I know only [that this rule applies] to the Day of Atonement. From what [verse in Scripture] do I learn the rule for Sabbaths?

[R] Scripture states [Lev. 23:32: "It shall be to you a sabbath of solemn rest, and you shall afflict yourselves; on the ninth day of the month beginning at evening, from evening to evening] you shall rest [on your sabbath]." {Reference to the word "sabbath" indicates that the weekly Sabbath is subject to the same rule as the Day of Atonement.}

[S] From what [verse in Scripture] do I learn the rule for festivals?

[T] Scripture [Lev. 23:32] states, "[You shall rest on] your sabbath."

[U] How do I interpret this?

[V] On any occasion to which the precept of rest applies,[127] one lengthens sanctified time by [continuing it into] secular time.

---

[126]M lacks: from evening.

[127]The word for "rest" is related to the word "Sabbath." M has a slightly different wording: On any occasion on which [Scripture] states [the term] "rest"....

[LV.A] But [as for] R. Aqiba, [unit **LIV**.C-D—regarding Lev. 23:32's statement]: "And you shall afflict yourselves; on the ninth [day of the month beginning at evening]"— how does he interpret it? {Unlike Ishmael in the preceding unit, Aqiba does not require that verse to prove that one extends sanctified time into secular time. It therefore must mean something different to him.}

[B] He needs it for that which Hiyya bar Rab of Difti taught on Tannaitic authority.

[C] For Hiyya bar Rab of Difti taught on Tannaitic authority: [Lev. 23:32 states], "And you shall afflict yourselves; on the ninth day of the month beginning at evening."

[D] Now, do people fast on the ninth of the month? Do they not fast on the tenth of the month? Accordingly [it must be the case that] the passage serves to tell you [something entirely different, namely]: Someone who eats and drinks on the ninth of the month is [still] regarded by Scripture [**9b**] as if he had fasted on the ninth and the tenth."

[**LVI**.A] Our rabbis have taught on Tannaitic authority: [Lev. 25:10 states], "It is a Jubilee." [This means that it is a Jubilee] even though they did not observe the release [of fields] and even though they did not sound the horn.

[B] Might I think [that it is deemed a Jubilee] even though they did not dismiss [the slaves]?

[C] [To indicate the contrary] Scripture [at Lev. 25:10] states: "It is [a Jubilee]."[128] {The extra words "it is" limit the application of the term Jubilee to a circumstance in which the slaves are dismissed.}

[D] [A-C is] the words of R. Judah.

[E] R. Yose says, "[Lev. 25:10 states], 'It is a Jubilee.' [This means that it is a Jubilee] even though they did not observe

---

[128]Here and in the citation at G, M includes the bracketed words explicitly.

	the release [of fields] and even though they did not dismiss [the slaves].
[F]	"Might I think [that it is deemed a Jubilee] even though they did not sound the horn?
[G]	"[To prevent this wrong reasoning] Scripture [at Lev. 25:10] states: 'It is [a Jubilee].'" {In Yose's view, the words "it is" limit the application of the term Jubilee to a case in which the trumpet was sounded.}
[H]	{Yose continues, explaining his position. If the term "Jubilee" is inclusive, E, but the words "it is" are limiting, G, there is no obvious reason for him to require the sounding of the trumpet but not to require the dismissal of slaves.}[129] "And if, insofar as one Scriptural statement is inclusive and one is limiting, [you ask], 'Why do I reason that it is a Jubilee even though[130] they do not dismiss the slaves, but it is not a Jubilee unless they sound the horn'—[I can answer as follows]:
[I]	"[I reason this way] because it is possible for there to be no [opportunity] for dismissal of slaves [e.g., if no Israelite slaves exist], but it is not possible for there to be no [opportunity] to sound the horn, [since horns will always exist]. {Scripture logically could require blowing the trumpet. But, if it were to require dismissal of slaves, a situation could arise in which the Jubilee would not take place.}
[J]	"Another reason: This [sounding of the trumpet] is by the authority of a court, while this [dismissal of slaves] is not by the authority of a court." {Rashi: A court can require its agent to sound the trumpet. By contrast, since slaves are held by individuals, the court might not be able to compel

---

[129]M continues here explicitly: Said R. Yose.

[130]M adds: they do not initiate the release of debt and even though....

	their dismissal. Since dismissal of slaves cannot be guaranteed, it was not made a condition of the Jubilee year.}
[K]	What [need is there for] the additional reason, [J]? {Why does I's explanation not suffice?}
[L]	If you argue that it is impossible for there not to be one [Hebrew slave][131] somewhere in the world who can be dismissed, [such that, contrary to I, both sounding the horn and dismissal of slaves should be required]—
[M]	[I can respond that] this [sounding of the trumpet] is by the authority of a court, while this [dismissal of slaves] is not by the authority of a court. {Therefore, contrary to what you reasoned, L, dismissal of slaves is not a prerequisite of the Jubilee year.}
[N]	Granted, the position of R. Yose [E-G] makes sense, as it has been explained [H-M].
[O]	But, as for R. Judah, [A-C], what is his reasoning [in holding that the Jubilee requires the dismissal of slaves but not the sounding of the trumpet]?
[P]	[In the clause preceding the one under discussion] Scripture states [Lev. 25:10]: "And you shall proclaim liberty throughout the land [to all its inhabitants]." {The verse continues: "It is a Jubilee for you."}
[Q]	And [Judah] holds that a verse may be interpreted on the basis of what precedes it but not on the basis of what precedes that. {Judah views the limiting words "it is" as referring to the dismissal of slaves, mention of which precedes, in the statement "you shall proclaim liberty throughout the land." But he does not hold that the limitation extends to the sounding of the trumpet, mentioned at Lev. 25:9, several clauses before the words "it is."}

---

[131] M has the bracketed word "slave" explicitly.

[LVII.A] {We continue with an independent interpretation of the term "*deror*," translated "liberty" at Lev. 25:10.} All authorities concur that [the word] "*deror*" refers to freedom.

[B] What does this tell us?[132]

[C] As it is taught on Tannaitic authority: [The word] "*deror*" refers to freedom.

[D] Said R. Judah, "To what does [the word] "*deror*" refer?

[E] "[To the freedom of] one who dwells in a dwelling place [of his own choosing] and can bring goods throughout the whole country."

[LVIII.A] {We return to the issue of unit **LVI**.} Said R. Hiyya bar Abba said R. Yohanan,[133] "These are the views of R. Judah and R. Yose [recorded in unit **LVI**].

[B] "But sages say, '[Neglect of any of] the three [matters—dismissal of slaves, release of fields, and sounding of the horn]—invalidates [the Jubilee].'"

[C] [Sages have this view] because they hold that a verse is interpreted on the basis of what precedes it, on the basis of what precedes that, as well as on the basis of what follows it.

[D] {D challenges B-C and is, in turn, disputed at E.} But [following the limiting words "it is," the inclusive term] "Jubilee" is written in Scripture! {One would think that the inclusive term "Jubilee" should neutralize the limiting force of "it is" so that, contrary to sages' view, all three aspects of the Jubilee need not occur in order for the Jubilee to go into effect.}

[E] [Contrary to D] this [inclusive term indicates only that the Jubilee exists] even outside of the land [of Israel].

[F] [E seems unacceptable, since Lev. 25:10 explicitly states: "And you shall consecrate the fiftieth year, and proclaim

---

[132]In M the end of this line through the beginning of D is added in the margin.

[133]M lacks the attribution to Yohanan.

liberty] throughout the land." {This seems to indicate that the Jubilee applies only within the land of Israel.}

[G] {F is rejected.} This [reference to "in the land" indicates that] when liberty occurs in the land [of Israel], it also will occur outside of the land.

[H] When liberty does not occur in the land [of Israel], it also will not occur outside of the land.

[LIX.A] {Discussion of M. R.H. 1:1F begins.} *[The first day of Tishre is the new year for the reckoning of years, for Sabbatical years, and for Jubilees], for planting [trees and for vegetables*; M. R.H. 1:1E-F].

[B] From what verse [in Scripture] do we know this rule [regarding planting]?

[C] As it is written [Lev. 19:23: "When you come into the land and plant all kinds of trees for food, then you shall count their fruit as forbidden]; three years it shall be forbidden to you, [it must not be eaten]."

[D] And it is written [Lev. 19:24]: "And in the fourth year [all their fruit shall be holy, an offering of praise to the Lord]."[134]

[E] Now, one must conclude [that the meaning of the word] "year" is "a year [beginning] from Tishre," since it is written [Dt. 11:12]: "from the beginning of the year [to the end of the year]." {An analogy is drawn between the year referred to at Lev. 19:24 and that referred to at Dt. 11:12. As was shown in unit **XXXIX**, the year referred to in the latter citation begins in Tishre. We conclude that the year referred to at Lev. 19:24 also begins in Tishre. (See above, unit **LI**.}

[F] {E's reasoning is challenged.} Now, [following this same approach] one should conclude [that the meaning of the word] "year" is "a year [beginning] from Nisan," since it is

---

[134]M presents the entire citation at C-D continuously, without the second introductory clause found at D.

written [Ex. 12:2: "This month shall be for you the beginning of months;] it shall be the first month of the year for you." {An analogy is drawn between the year referred to at Lev. 19:24 and that referred to at Ex. 12:2. In the latter citation, the month of Passover, Nisan, is called the beginning of the year. We therefore should conclude that the year referred to at Lev. 19:24 also begins in Nisan.}

[G] {For the reason given here, F's analogy is inappropriate. See unit **XXXIX**.} We draw an analogy between [a reference to] a "year" that does not include [mention of] "months" and a [different reference to] "year" that does not include [mention of] "months." {Such an analogy is found at D-E.}

[H] But [unlike what is proposed at F], we do not draw an analogy between [a reference to] a "year" that does not include [mention of] "months" [as at Lev. 19:24] and a [different reference to] "year" that does include [mention of] "months," [as at Ex. 12:2].

[**LX**.A] Our rabbis have taught on Tannaitic authority [T. R.H. 1:8 (= T. Sheb. 2:3), referring to M. R.H. 1:1E-F's rule that the first of Tishre is the new year for planting trees]: **The same rule applies to one who plants a tree, plants a shoot, or grafts a branch onto a tree on the eve of the Sabbatical year, thirty days before the New Year: [on the first of Tishre that which was planted] is credited with a [full] year [of growth], so that it is permitted to let it continue growing during the Sabbatical year.**

[B] **[If it was planted] fewer than thirty days before the New Year, [on the first of Tishre] it is not credited with a [full] year [of growth], so that it is forbidden to let it continue growing during the Sabbatical year.**

[C] [10a] **[Even though the age of the tree is counted from the first of Tishre], the produce of such a sapling is forbidden until the fifteenth of Shevat [of the year in** which the tree's produce becomes permitted for common use].

[D] When [the tree is] *orlah* [that is, in its first three years of growth] it [remains in the status of] *orlah* [until the fifteenth of Shevat, even though the tree will have completed its third year on the preceding first of Tishre].

[E] And when [the tree is] in its fourth year [of growth] it [remains subject to the prohibitions of] the fourth year [until the fifteenth of Shevat].

[F] What is the source of these rules?

[G] Said R. Hiyya bar Abba said R. Yohanan, and some attribute it in the name of R. Yannai, "Scripture [Lev. 19:24-25] said, 'And in the fourth year [all their fruit shall be holy, an offering of praise to the Lord]. But in the fifth year [you may eat of their fruit, that they may yield more richly for you].'

[H] "[The verse suggests that] there are times that [produce grows] in [the tree's] fourth year yet still is forbidden under the restrictions of *orlah*, [which normally apply only for three years].

[I] "And there are times that [produce grows] in [the tree's] fifth year yet still is forbidden under the restrictions of the fourth year."

[J] {We return to A's claim, that thirty days of growth are counted as a full year. See above, unit II.E, 2b.} Should we reason that [A] does not accord with [the view of] R. Meir?

[K] For if it were R. Meir, he has said, "A single day in the year can be considered a full year." {This contrasts with A, which requires thirty days.}

[L] {Proving that Meir holds the position attributed to him at K:} For it is taught on Tannaitic authority: "The bullock referred to in the Torah without specification is twenty-four months and one day old"—the words of R. Meir.

[M] R. Eleazar says, "[It is] twenty-four months and thirty days old."

[N]   For R. Meir used to say, "Wherever in the Torah it says 'calf' without further specification [it is] one year old; 'young ox' [means] two years old; 'bullock' [means] three years old." {Meir thus equates twenty-four months and one day, L, with three full years, N. As K argued, he holds that a single day can be considered a year.}

[O]   {J-N's reasoning is shown to have no bearing on whether or not Meir concurs with A. See above, unit VI.D-F.} You can even argue [that] R. Meir [agrees with the rule at A].

[P]   When R. Meir stated that a single day in the year can be considered a full year, [he meant that this applies] at the conclusion of the year; but at the beginning of the year this is not the case. {A single day completes the three-year age requirement of the bullock. But a single day does not comprise a year for beginning the count of the age of a tree. In that, Meir concurs with A, requiring thirty days.}

[Q]   {The following argues that, contrary to P, it makes no difference whether the single day is at the beginning or end of the period being counted.} Said Rava, "Is [the fact that it makes no difference whether the single day is at the beginning or end of the period] not[135] an argument *a fortiori*?

[R]   "Now, if, in the case of a menstruating woman, in whose case the beginning of the [seventh] day is *not* counted as concluding [her period of purification, which ends only at nightfall on that day, even so] the end of the [first] day *is* counted as the beginning [of her period of purification, so that she begins counting in the middle of the day, and, at nightfall, is deemed to have completed a full day],

[S]   "[then, in the case of a period of] a year, in which a single day is counted [as a whole year] at the end, [**10b**] is it not logical that a single day should [also] be counted [as a full year] at the beginning?"

---

[135]M lacks this word.

BAVLI ROSH HASHANAH CHAPTER ONE [10b] 147

[T]   Then what [should we say regarding which authority stands behind the rule at A-D, which holds that thirty days count as a year]?

[U]   [It cannot be] R. Eliezer, [M, since Eliezer] requires thirty days [for that which is planted to take root] and thirty days [more, to count as the year of growth],

[V]   as we have taught on Tannaitic authority [M. Sheb. 2:6]: *"They do not plant [a tree], sink [a vine into the ground so that it emerges nearby as an independent plant], or graft [one branch to another] in the year preceding the Sabbatical within thirty days of the New Year.*

[W]   *"And if one planted [a tree], sank [a vine into the ground], or grafted [one branch to another within thirty days of the beginning of the Sabbatical year],*

[X]   *"one must uproot [that which was planted, sunk or grafted]"*—the words of R. Eliezer.[136]

[Y]   R. Judah says, "All grafting that does not take root within three days will not take root."

[Z]   R. Yose and R. Simeon say, "Within two weeks."

[AA] Now, said Rab Nahman said Rabbah bar Abbuha, "In the opinion of one [such as Eliezer, V-X] who says [the period is] thirty [days],[137] we require thirty [days for that which is planted to take root] and thirty [more to count as the year of growth].

[BB] "In the opinion of one [such as Judah, Y] who says [the period is] three [days], we require three [days for that which is planted to take root] and thirty [more to count as the year of growth].

---

[136]All manuscript sources for B. and M. lack the attribution to Eliezer, which appears to have entered printed editions as the result of a printer's error (Rabbinovicz).

[137]M has the bracketed word explicitly.

[CC] "In the opinion of one [such as Yose or Simeon, Z] who says [the period is] two weeks, we require two weeks and thirty days."

[DD] Now, in the same way, [is it possible that the rule at A-D] follows the perspective of R. Judah, [Y]?

[EE] [That is not tenable, since] he requires three and thirty [days]! {A-D refers only to thirty days.}

[FF] Rather,[138] in point of fact, [A-D follows] R. Meir.

[GG] And when it says [the plants must be in the ground] thirty [days in order to be deemed of the year prior to the sabbatical, it refers] to [the time required for the plant to] take [root]. {In Meir's view, once the plant has taken root, which requires thirty days, only a single additional day in the ground is required for it to be deemed of the preceding year. Just as the opinion attributed to him at K states, he holds that a single day counts as a full year.}

[HH] {GG's proof that Meir stands behind the rule at A-D is challenged.} If [what GG states] is the case, then [A-D] should require [the plant to have been put in the ground] thirty-one days [prior to the start of the Sabbatical year]!

[II] {HH's view is rejected.} [Meir] reasoned that the thirtieth day counts here [as the last day required for the plant to take root] and here [as the day that is deemed a year].

[LXI.A] Said R. Yohanan, "Now, both [authorities, Meir and Eliezer, derived their views by] interpreting the same verse of Scripture [Gen. 8:13]: 'In the one and six hundredth year, in the first month, the first day of the month, [the waters were dried from off the earth].'

[B] "R. Meir reasoned, 'Since only one day had passed in the year but it still was counted as a year, we learn from this[139] that a single day in the year can be considered a full year.'

---

[138]M lacks this word.

[139]M lacks: we learn from this.

[C] "But the other [that is, Eliezer, says], 'If it were written, "In the six hundred and first year....", then [the meaning] would be as you [Meir] say.

[D] "'But since it says, "In the one and six hundredth year....", [it is clear that the word] "year" [at the end of the clause only] refers to the [number] "six hundred."

[E] "'And what [in this interpretation] is the meaning of [the number] "one" [at the beginning of the clause]? It refers to the fact that it was the beginning of [year six hundred and] one.'" {But that one day was not counted as a full year.}

[LXII.A] Now, what is the [Scriptural] basis of R. Eliezer's perspective [units LX-LXI, that thirty days are considered a year]?

[B] For it is written [Gen. 8:13: "In the one and six hundredth year, in the] first [month], the first day of the month, the waters were dried from off the earth]."

[C] Since only one day had passed in the month but it still was counted as a month, we learn from this that a single day in the month can be considered a full month.

[D] And since a single day in the month can be considered a month, [we must conclude that] thirty days in a year are considered a year.

[E] For [a full] month is determined based upon its [basic constituent] unit, [that is, a day]; and [a full] year is determined based upon its [basic constituent] unit, [that is, a month].

[F] [We can] infer [from the preceding interpretations of Gen. 8:13] that both [Meir and Eliezer] reason that the world was created in Nisan.[140] {This is based upon the authorities'

---

[140]This line is lacking in the body of M and other manuscript sources. It is added in the margin of M.

agreement that "the first month, the first day of the month" refers to the first day in the new year, in Nisan.}[141]

[LXIII.A] It is taught on Tannaitic authority: R. Eliezer says, "In Tishre, the world was created; in Tishre, the patriarchs [Abraham and Jacob] were born; in Tishre, the patriarchs died; on Passover, Isaac was born; on New Year, Sarah, Rachel, and Hannah were visited; on New Year, Joseph left prison; [11a] on New Year, bondage was removed from our ancestors in Egypt; in Nisan, they were redeemed; in Tishre, they are destined to be redeemed [again]."

[B] R. Joshua says, "In Nisan, the world was created; in Nisan, the patriarchs [Abraham and Jacob] were born; in Nisan, the patriarchs died; on Passover, Isaac was born; on New Year, Sarah, Rachel, and Hannah were visited; on New Year, Joseph left prison; on New Year, bondage was removed from our ancestors in Egypt; in Nisan, they were redeemed; in Nisan, they are destined to be redeemed [again]."

[LXIV.A] {Eliezer's position, unit LXIII.A, that the world was created in Tishre, is explained.} It is taught on Tannaitic authority: R. Eliezer says, "From what [Scriptural source] do we know that the world was created in Tishre?

[B] "For it is said [Gen. 1:11]: 'And God said, "Let the earth put forth vegetation,[142] plants yielding seed, [and] fruit trees [bearing fruit in which is their seed, each according to its kind, upon the earth].'"

[C] "Which is the month in which the earth brings forth vegetation and the trees are full of fruit?

---

[141] Rashi notes that Meir and Eliezer might "equally well hold that the 'first month' here means Tishre, it being so called as the first month to the creation" (Simon, pp. 38-39, n. 6). Rashi accordingly suggests deleting this line from the text. Reflecting Rashi's judgment, in standard printings, the line is marked off by parentheses.

[142] M lacks the continuation of the citation.

BAVLI ROSH HASHANAH CHAPTER ONE [11a] 151

[D] "You must say that this refers to Tishre.
[E] "And this same period was the time of rainfall, and the rains came down and [plants] sprouted, as it says [Gen. 2:6]: 'but a mist went up from the earth [and watered the whole face of the ground].'"[143]
[F] {Joshua's position, unit **LXIII.B**, that the world was created in Nisan, is explained.} R. Joshua says, "From what [Scriptural source] do we know that the world was created in Nisan?
[G] "For it is said [Gen. 1:12]: 'The earth brought forth vegetation, plants yielding seed [according to their own kinds], and trees bearing fruit [in which is their seed, each according to its kind].'"
[H] "Which is the month in which the earth is full of vegetation and the trees bring forth fruit?
[I] "You must say that this refers to Nisan.
[J] "And the same period is the time that cattle, animals, and fowl copulate, as it says [Ps. 65:13]: 'The rams have mounted the sheep.'"[144]
[K] But the other [authority, Eliezer] must also take account of that which is written [at Gen. 1:12]: "trees bearing fruit"!
[L] [For Eliezer] this was written [to indicate] a blessing for [future] generations.
[M] But the other [authority, Joshua] must also take account of that which is written [at Gen. 1:11: "Let the earth put forth vegetation, plants yielding seed, and] fruit trees."
[N] [Joshua interprets this verse to mean that the trees were created fully matured], according to the perspective of R. Joshua b. Levi, for said R. Joshua b. Levi, "All things that were created in the beginning [during God's original acts of

---

[143] M explicitly contains the bracketed conclusion of the citation.

[144] M continues with the following clause of the verse. RSV translates: "the meadows clothe themselves with flocks, [the valleys deck themselves with grain, they shout and sing together for joy]."

	creation] were created in their [full] stature, in their full capacities,[145] and in their [full] beauty.
[O]	[We know they were created in their full beauty] since it is said [Gen. 2:4]: "Thus the heavens and the earth were finished, and all of their host (*ṣb'm*)."
[P]	Do not read [the word] *ṣb'm* [as it is written]. Rather, [read it as] *ṣbywnm* [that is, their beauty].

[LXV.A] {Eliezer's position, unit **LXIII**.A, that the patriarchs Abraham and Jacob were born in Tishre, is explained.} R. Eliezer says, "From what [verse in Scripture do we know] that the patriarchs were born in Tishre?

[B] "For it is said [1 Kgs. 8:2]: 'And all the men of Israel assembled to King Solomon at the festival in the month Ethanim, [which is the seventh month (that is, Tishre)].'

[C] "[This means they gathered in] the month in which the mighty ones (*ethanim*) of the world [the patriarchs] were born."

[D] How do you know that the word *ethan* refers to strong ones?

[E] For it is written [Num. 24:21: "And (Balaam) looked on the Kenite and took up his discourse, and said], 'Enduring [*ethan*] is your dwelling place, [and your nest is set in the rock].'"

[F] And it says[146] [Mic. 6:2]: "Hear, you mountains, the controversy of the Lord, and you enduring [*ethan*] foundations of the earth."

[G] {At Mic. 6:2, the word "*ethan*" is associated with the term "mountain." We now prove that the term "mountain" itself recalls the patriarchs. The connection proposed above at B-C between the patriarchs and the term *ethan* thus is proven.} And it says [Song 2:8]: "The voice of my beloved! Behold,

---

[145] So Simon for *yd'tn*. Literally: with their awareness. Rashi: [God] asked each thing if it wished to be created, and it said yes.

[146] Here and at G, M reads: For it is written.

	he comes, leaping upon the mountains, bounding over the hills."
[H]	"Leaping upon the mountains"—through the merit of the patriarchs.
[I]	"Bounding over the hills"—through the merit of the matriarchs.
[J]	{Joshua's position, unit **LXIII.B**, that the patriarchs Abraham and Jacob were born in Nisan, is explained.} R. Joshua says, "From what [Scriptural source do we know] that the patriarchs were born in Nisan?
[K]	"For it is said [1 Kgs. 6:1]: 'In the four hundred and eightieth year after the people of Israel came out of the land of Egypt, in the fourth year [of Solomon's reign over Israel], in the month of Ziv, [which is the second month,[147] he began to build the house of the Lord].'
[L]	"[By month of Ziv is meant] the month in which the brilliant ones [*zywtny*][148] of the world were born."
[M]	{How does Joshua interpret 1 Kgs. 8:2, which Eliezer uses to prove that the patriarchs were born in Tishre?} But thus it is written[149] [1 Kgs. 8:2: "And all the men of Israel assembled to King Solomon at the feast] in the month Ethanim, [which is the seventh month (that is, Tishre)]."

---

[147]The use of this passage to support Joshua's view is problematic, since the second month is Iyyar, not Nisan (which is the first month). Rashi, cited by Simon, p. 40, n. 5, solves the problem by stating: "sometimes the Nisan *tekufah* (vernal equinox) is late in occurring, in which case the month of Iyyar may according to solar calculation still be in Nisan." Since it is unlikely that this reasoning underlies the text before us, its actual meaning remains obscure.

[148]A play on the word "Ziv."

[149]So the marginal correction in the printed edition. The body of the printed text is clearly corrupt, reading: But the other [authority, Joshua] must also take account of that which is written.... M's slightly different reading makes the clearest sense of the passage: But R. Joshua [must] also [take account of] that which is written.... The point in all three wordings is in all events the same.

[N] [Joshua holds that] there [at 1 Kgs. 8:2 reference is to the month] that is strong in religious obligations. {Tishre, that is, contains many holidays and festivals.}

[O] But the other [authority, Eliezer, must] also [take account of] that which is written [at 1 Kgs. 6:1]: "In the month of Ziv." {Joshua uses this verse to prove that the patriarchs were born in Nisan.}

[P] [Eliezer holds that] this refers to the [month] in which there is glory for the trees.

[Q] For said Rab Judah,[150] "Anyone who goes out during the days of Nisan and sees trees in blossom should say, 'Blessed is he whose world lacks nothing and who created in it good things and nice trees[151] in which people may find enjoyment.'"

[**LXVI**.A] He [that is, Joshua, unit **LXIII**.B] who holds that [the patriarchs] were born in Nisan [holds that] they [also] died in Nisan; [and] he [that is, Eliezer, unit **LXIII**.A] who holds that [the patriarchs] were born in Tishre [holds that] they [also] died in Tishre.

[B] For it is said [Dt. 31:2]: "And [Abraham] said to them, 'I am a hundred and twenty years old this day.'"

[C] There is no need for Scripture to say, "This day." {The clause appears superfluous and therefore must have some special meaning.}

[D] Why does Scripture state, "This day"?

[E] [It means that Abraham said:] "On this day my days and years have been completed."

---

[150]M adds: said Rab. In the parallel at B. Ber. 43b, neither M nor the printed text has this additional attribution.

[151]M and other sources, including early printings of the parallel at B. Ber. 43b, lack "and nice trees," possibly a case of haplography (Rabbinovicz).

[F] This teaches you that the holy one, blessed be he, sits and completes the years of the righteous from day to day [and] from month to month,

[G] as it is written [Ex. 23:26]: "I will complete the number of your days."

[LXVII.A] "Isaac was born on Passover." {So both Joshua and Eliezer, unit **LXIII**.}

[B] From what [verse in Scripture] do we know this?

[C] As it is written[152] [Gen. 18:14]: "At the appointed time[153] I will return to you, [in the spring, and Sarah shall have a son]."[154]

[D] When was [the messenger speaking]?

[E] Should I reason that it was Passover, and [in noting his time of return] he was referring to Pentecost?

[F] {This is impossible.} Can someone give birth after [just] fifty days?

[G] Rather, [should I reason that] he was [speaking] at Pentecost and referred to Tishre?

[H] {This is impossible.} Can someone give birth even after five[155] months?

[I] Rather, [I must reason that] he was [speaking] on the festival [of Tabernacles] and referred to [his return at Passover, in] Nisan!

[J] {Even this seems impossible.} Can someone give birth after six months?

[K] [To solve the problem] it is taught on Tannaitic authority: It was a leap year, [and the pregnancy lasted seven months].

---

[152] M reads: As it is said.

[153] "Appointed time" is understood here to refer to the next festival.

[154] M explicitly has the bracketed continuation of the quote.

[155] M reads "four," presumably a scribal error.

[L] {K's proposal does not solve J's problem.} Even so, when the master [behind this tradition] deducts her days of uncleanness [as a menstruating woman], there is not enough time [between Tabernacles and Passover for her to have conceived and given birth]. {See B. B.M. 87a, which holds that, at the time of the messenger's visit, Sarah was menstruating.}

[M] Said[156] Mar Zutra, "Even one who holds that [a woman who] gives birth after nine months does not give birth after a partial month [recognizes that] one who gives birth after seven months might [even] give birth after part [of the sixth] month [has passed]. {M argues that K's reference to a seven month pregnancy encompasses a pregnancy of only six months and some number of days. The fact that, at Tabernacles, Sarah was menstruating and could not conceive until some days later does not preclude Isaac's birth at Passover, I.}

[N] "[We know that one who gives birth after seven months might give birth before the seventh month is complete, M], as it is said [1 Sam. 1:20]: 'And after a period of days [Hannah conceived and bore a son].'[157]

[O] "[Interpret this as follows:] The minimum [time deemed a] period is two, and the minimum [number of] days [referred to by the plural] is [also] two." {This seems to suggest that Hannah gave birth several days into a month, not after a number of full months.}

[LXVIII.A] "On New Year, Sarah, Rachel, and Hannah were visited." {So both Joshua and Eliezer, unit **LXIII**.}

[B] From what verse [in Scripture] do we know this?

---

[156]M introduces this line: Rather.

[157]M explicitly has the bracketed continuation of the quote.

BAVLI ROSH HASHANAH CHAPTER ONE [11a] 157

[C] Said R. Eleazar,[158] "It is derived from an analogy [between the appearance of the term] 'visiting' [at 1 Sam. 2:21 and the appearance of the term] 'visiting' [at Gen. 21:1].

[D] "It [further] is derived from an analogy [between the appearance of the term] 'remembering' [at Gen. 30:22 and the appearance of the term] 'remembering' [at 1 Sam. 1:19]."[159]

[E] {The specific verses concerning "remembering" follow.} It is written concerning Rachel [Gen. 30:22]: "Then God remembered Rachel."

[F] And it is written concerning Hannah [1 Sam. 1:19: "And Elkanah knew Hannah his wife], and the Lord remembered her."

[G] Now, [these mentions of] "remembering" are analogous to [the use of the term] "remembering" in conjunction with New Year.

[H] For it is written [Lev. 23:24: "On the first day of the month, you shall observe] a day of solemn rest, a *memorial* proclaimed with the blast of trumpets." {We learn from Lev. 23:24 that "remembering" has to do with New Year. The remembering that took place in the cases of Rachel, E, and Hannah, F, therefore must have taken place on New Year, just as A claims.}

[I] {I-K proves that the cases of Hannah and Rachel, E-H, are analogous to that of Sarah. We know this because the term "visiting," which occurs in Hannah's case, also appears in reference to Sarah.} [There is an analogy between the appearance of the term] 'visiting' [at 1 Sam. 2:21 and the appearance of the term] 'visiting' [again at Gen. 21:1]:

---

[158]M lacks the attribution.

[159]M repeats this line twice.

[J]   It is written concerning Hannah [1 Sam. 2:21]: "And the Lord visited Hannah, [and she conceived and bore three sons and two daughters]."

[K]   And it is written concerning Sarah [Gen. 21:1]: "The Lord visited Sarah."

[LXIX.A] "On New Year, Joseph left prison." {So both Joshua and Eliezer, unit **LXIII**.}

[B]   From what verse [in Scripture] do we know this?

[C]   It is written [Ps. 81:3-5]: "Blow the trumpet at the new moon, when the moon is covered,[160] on our feast day.[161] For it is a statute for Israel, [an ordinance of the God of Jacob]. [11b] He made it a decree in Joseph, when he went out [over the land of Egypt]." {The clause "when he went out" is taken to refer to Joseph's release from prison. The proof further depends upon unit **XLVIII** (above, 8a, end = B. Bes. 16a), which notes that New Year is the only festival that occurs on the new moon, the others coming in the middle of the month. The passage accordingly is read to refer to Joseph's release from prison on New Year.}

[LXX.A] "On New Year, bondage was removed from our ancestors in Egypt." {So both Joshua and Eliezer, unit **LXIII**.}

[B]   It[162] is written here [Ex. 6:6: "I am the Lord], and I will bring you out from under the burdens of the Egyptians."

[C]   And it is written there [Ps. 81:6, in reference to Joseph]: "I relieved your shoulder of the burden." {Ps. 81:6, the continuation of the passage cited in the preceding unit,

---

[160] Heb.: *KSH*. RSV: at the full moon.

[161] M adds here and before the beginning of the coming biblical sentence: And it is written.... Additionally, M explicitly contains the final bracketed clause of this line.

[162] M and other sources begin this line: From what [verse] do we know this? It is derived from an analogy [between the two appearances of the term] "burden."

suggests that "burdens" are removed on New Year. The release from bondage, described by Ex. 6:6 as a removal of "burdens," must also have taken place on New Year.}

[LXXI.A] "In Nisan, they were redeemed." {So both Joshua and Eliezer, unit **LXIII**.}
[B] This is as is known.

[LXXII.A] "In Tishre, they are destined to be redeemed [again]." {So Eliezer in unit **LXVIII**.A.}
[B] [This][163] is derived from an analogy [between the appearance of the term] "trumpet" [at Ps. 81:3 and the appearance of the term] "trumpet" [again at Is. 27:13].
[C] Here it is written [Ps. 81:3, in reference to New Year, in Tishre]: "Blow the trumpet at the new moon."
[D] And there it is written [Is. 27:13, in reference to the final redemption]: "And on that day a great trumpet will be blown."
[E] R. Joshua says [unit **LXVIII**.B], "In Nisan they were redeemed [from Egypt], and in Nisan they are destined to be redeemed [again]."
[F] From what verse [in Scripture] do we know this?
[G] Scripture [at Ex. 12:42] says [regarding Passover], "It was a night of watching."
[H] [This means it was] a night that was continually watched for [root: *SMR*] since the six days of creation. {In this regard, Passover and the final redemption are similar. The latter, like the former, will occur in Nisan.}
[I] But [as for] the other [that is, Eliezer, A, who holds that the final redemption will occur in Tishre, how does he interpret Ex. 12:42]?
[J] [He says it refers to] a night under continuous protection [root: *ŠMR*] against damaging demons.

---

[163]M introduces this line: From what [verse] do we know this?

160 BAVLI ROSH HASHANAH CHAPTER ONE [11b]

[LXXIII.A] [In taking the positions attributed to them at unit **LXIII** and explained at unit **LXXII**, Eliezer and Joshua] are consistent with views they hold elsewhere.

[B] For it is taught on Tannaitic authority: [Gen. 7:11 states]: "In the six hundredth year of Noah's life, in the second month, on the seventeenth day of the month, [on that day all the fountains of the great deep burst forth, and the windows of the heavens were opened]."

[C] R. Joshua says, "That day was the seventeenth of Iyyar,[164] the day on which the constellation Draco[165] sets by day and the fountains [begin to] dry up [that is, the rainy season ends].

[D] "But because [human beings] changed [i.e., perverted] their ways,[166] the holy one, blessed be he, changed on them the order of creation and made the constellation Draco rise by day, and took two stars from Draco,[167] and brought a flood upon the world."

[E] R. Eliezer says, "That day was the seventeenth of Marheshvan, the day on which the constellation Draco rises by day and the fountains [begin to] fill [that is, the rains begin].

[F] [**12a**] "But because [human beings] changed [that is, perverted] their ways, the holy one, blessed be he, changed on them the order of creation and made the constellation

---

[164]M reverses the words "Iyyar" and "Marheshvan" here and at D.

[165]So Jastrow, p. 633, s.v., *kymh*. Jastrow explicitly rejects the notion, reflected in Simon's translation, that reference is to Pleiades.

[166]M lacks the preceding, beginning the line simply: But. This may be the result of haplography.

[167]M reads: Kimah. Jastrow associates this constellation with Draco. See note 165.

Draco rise by day, and took two stars [from Draco], and brought a flood upon the world."[168]

[G] Granted [that the view of] R. Joshua, [that the flood began in Iyyar, makes sense].

[H] For this is why it is written [at Gen. 7:11: "In the] second [month]." {This is within Scripture's understanding that Nisan [= Abib] is the first month. The flood thus began in Iyyar, the second month.}

[I] But, in [the view of] R. Eliezer, what [is the meaning of] "second"?

[J] [Eliezer holds that it means] second to [the month containing the day of] judgment [that is, Tishre]. {In Eliezer's view, the flood thus occurred in Marheshvan, the month after Tishre.}

[K] Granted [that the view of] R. Joshua, [that the flood began in Iyyar, makes sense].

[L] For [in this view God did] change [the order of creation]. {At the point at which the dry season normally begins, God started the flood.}

[M] But in [the view of] R. Eliezer, what did [God] change? {This is a question because, in Eliezer's view, it already was the rainy season. The following responds by suggesting that, in Eliezer's view, God made the rains boil.}

[N] [Eliezer's position] accords with the view of Rab Hisda, for Rab Hisda said, "With boiling liquid they sinned, and with boiling liquid they were judged."

[O] "With boiling liquid they sinned"—through [sexual] transgression.

[P] "And with boiling liquid they were judged"—[this is as follows]:

---

[168]Simon, p. 43, n. 1: "There seems to be some confusion in the text here. To make it astronomically correct we should read (with Seder Olam) in the dictum of R. Joshua 'When Pleiades *rises* at daybreak,' and in the dictum of R. Eliezer, '*sets* at daybreak'."

[Q] Here it is written [Gen. 8:1, referring to the flood]: "And the waters abated."

[R] And there it is written [Es. 7:10]: "Then the anger [lit: heat] of the king abated." {By analogy to Es. 7:10, that which "abates," including the water of the flood, Gen. 8:1, was hot.}

[LXXIV.A] Our rabbis have taught on Tannaitic authority: The sages of Israel date [the calendar from] the flood, in accordance with the view of R. Eliezer, but [date the four] annual cycles according to the view of R. Joshua. {See above, unit **XLVII**.K, 8a. They deem Tishre to mark the new year for years but hold that the world was created in Nisan.}

[B] The sages of other peoples date even the flood in accordance with the view of R. Joshua, [holding that new year for years is in Nisan].

[LXXV.A] *[The first day of Tishre is the new year for the reckoning of years, for Sabbatical years, and for Jubilees, for planting trees] and for vegetables* [M. R.H. 1:1E-F].

[B] It is taught on Tannaitic authority: [The first of Tishre is the new year] for vegetables, tithes, and vows. {See T. R.H. 1:7, which explicitly states that the first of Tishre marks the new year for tithes and vows.}

[C] "For vegetables"[169]—what is the meaning [of this rule]?

[D] [If reference is to the separation of] tithes from vegetables, [the point is the same as is made by the inclusion here of the term] "tithes." {The point in either case would be that vegetables picked prior to the first of Tishre may not be designated tithes on behalf of vegetables picked after the first of Tishre, or *vice versa*. Since the term "vegetables" here

---

[169]M lacks the introductory citation.

	must have a distinctive meaning, it cannot refer to the rules for the separation of tithes.}
[E]	{Contrary to D, both terms in fact concern tithes. Even so, each makes a distinctive point.} [By mentioning "vegetables," the list at B first] teaches on Tannaitic authority [the rule for a tithe imposed] by the rabbis. And [then, by referring to "tithes" in general] it teaches [the rule for tithes imposed] by Scripture.
[F]	[If this indeed is the meaning], it should refer first to [the tithes imposed by] Scripture! {The fact that it does not suggests that E's interpretation is incorrect.}
[G]	{Rejecting F, the reason the Rabbinic rule appears first is explained.} Since he [who taught B particularly] liked this [Rabbinic rule], he placed it first!
[H]	{We see that in order completely to clarify the rule for designating new produce as tithes on behalf of old produce, it was necessary to mention both terms, "tithes" and "vegetables."} [This being the case, as for] our Tannaitic authority [behind M. R.H. 1:1F—why did he only mention "vegetables"]?
[I]	He taught the Rabbinic rule [to make the point that], all the more so [this same rule, prohibiting designating produce picked prior to the first of Tishre as tithes for produce picked after that date, applies to tithes imposed by] Scripture.
[J]	{F's explanation of B remains problematic.} [If the term "tithes" at B in fact refers only to the tithe imposed by Scripture, but not to tithes enacted by Rabbinic authorities, B's author] should have mentioned "tithe" [in the singular]. {The fact that he says "tithes" in the plural suggests that, contrary to the distinction drawn at F, the term refers both to biblical and Rabbinic tithes.}
[K]	[His point was that] the same rule applies to the tithe of cattle and to the tithe of grain, [both of which are imposed by Scripture].

[L] {The same challenge applies to B's use of the term "vegetables" in the plural. If the term in fact refers only to the tithe imposed by the rabbis, but not to that enacted by Scripture, B's author] should have mentioned "vegetable" [in the singular].

[M] [The reference is in the plural since] there are two types of vegetables,

[N] as we have taught on Tannaitic authority [M. Ma. 1:5:[170] *At what point after the harvest must tithes be removed from produce?] ... Green vegetables which are [normally] tied in bunches—after he ties [them]. But if he does not tie them, [tithes need not be removed] until the vessel [into which he places the picked greens] is filled.*

[LXXVI.A] Our rabbis have taught on Tannaitic authority [T. R.H. 1:9]: **[If] one picked vegetables on the eve of the new year before sunset and went back and picked [more] [12b] after sunset, they do not designate heave-offering or tithes from this [batch] on behalf of that [other] batch,** since they do not designate that which is new as heave-offering and tithes on behalf of that which is old, and [do] not [designate that which is] old [as heave-offering and tithes] on behalf of that which is new.

[B] **If it was the second year of the Sabbatical cycle and the third year was beginning, [that which was picked before New Year], in the second year, [is subject to the separation of]** first tithe and **second tithe; [that which was picked after New Year], in the third year, [is subject to the separation of]** first tithe and **poor-man's tithe.**

[C] What is the [Scriptural] foundation of these rules?

[D] Said R. Joshua b. Levi, "[Dt. 26:12 states]: 'When you have finished paying all the tithe of your produce in the third year, which is the year of the tithe....'

---

[170]Translation: Jaffee.

[E]	"[This suggests that in the third] year [one separates] only one [of the two] tithe[s separated in the first and second years of the Sabbatical cycle]."
[F]	How should he do it?
[G]	[Does he designate] first tithe and poor man's tithe, but second tithe is omitted?
[H]	Or [is it the case that] first tithe also is omitted [so that only one tithe is designated at all]?[171]
[I]	[To prove that first tithe is not omitted] Scripture states [Num. 18:26]: "Moreover you shall speak to the Levites and say to them, 'When you take from the people of Israel the tithe[172] that I have given you from them for your inheritance, [then you shall present an offering from it to the Lord, a tithe of the tithe].'"
[J]	Scripture equates [first tithe] with an inheritance.
[K]	Just as an inheritance is never interrupted, so first tithe is not interrupted.
[L]	{D-I recurs with a different Scriptural proof text.} A Tannaitic statement makes the same point:[173]
[M]	[Dt. 26:12 states]: "When you have finished paying all the tithe [of your produce in the third year]...."[174]
[N]	[This suggests that in the third] year [one separates] only one [of the two] tithe[s separated in the first and second years of the Sabbatical cycle].
[O]	How should he do it?
[P]	[Does he designate] first tithe and poor man's tithe, but second tithe is omitted?

---

[171]M lacks this line, a case of haplography (Rabbinovicz).

[172]M lacks the conclusion to the citation.

[173]So M and the marginal correction in printed editions. The body of the text reads: The other [master] teaches on Tannaitic authority.

[174]M explicitly includes the bracketed conclusion of the citation.

[Q] Or is it possible that first tithe also is omitted [so that only one tithe is designated at all]?

[R] "Scripture states [Dt. 14:29]: 'And the Levite shall come [... and eat and be filled].'

[S] "[This means that] each time he comes, [even in the third year], you must give him [his tithe]"—the words of R. Judah.[175]

[T] R. Eliezer b. Jacob says, "We do not need [to appeal to the text cited by Judah at R].

[U] "For [at Num. 18:26] it says, 'Moreover you shall speak to the Levites and say to them,[176] "When you take from the people of Israel the tithe that I have given you from them for your inheritance, [then you shall present an offering from it to the Lord, a tithe of the tithe].""

[V] "Scripture equates [first tithe] with an inheritance.

[W] "Just as an inheritance is never interrupted, so first tithe is not interrupted."

[LXXVII.A] And for vows.... {See above, unit LXXV.B, and T. R.H. 1:7, which cites M. R.H. 1:1E-F and adds that the first of Tishre also is the new year for tithes and for vows.}

[B] Our rabbis have taught on Tannaitic authority [T. R.H. 1:10, with variations]: **One who took a vow not to derive benefit from his fellow for a year reckons [as the period of prohibition] twelve month from the day [of the vow] to the [same] day [a year later].**

[C] **But if he said, "[The vow is for] this year," [then] even if he took it only on the twenty-ninth of Elul, once the first of Tishre arrived, his year is up.**

[D] [This applies] even [in the opinion] of one who says, "A single day in the year cannot be counted as a [full] year."

---

[175]M lacks the attribution.

[176]M lacks the conclusion of the citation.

BAVLI ROSH HASHANAH CHAPTER ONE [12b] 167

[E]   [The reason that all deem the period of the vow to be up is that] he undertook [the vow] to degrade himself, and, lo, he already has degraded himself.

[F]   {Why, for this purpose, is the first of Tishre considered the new year?} But why not say [that for vows] Nisan [is the new year]?

[G]   In the case of vows, follow people's normal usage! {People generally refer to Tishre as the beginning of the new year.}

[LXXVIII.A] There we have taught on Tannaitic authority: [M. Ma. 1:3, referring to the point at which produce becomes subject to tithes]: *fenugreek—when the seeds [are able to] sprout; grain and olives—when they reach a third [of their mature growth].*[177]

[B]   What is referred to by [the phrase] *when the seeds [are able to] sprout*?

[C]   [This means][178] from the point at which it sprouts [sufficiently to be used] for seed.

[D]   *Grain and olives—when they reach a third [of their mature growth]*—What is the meaning of these rules?

[E]   Said Rab Assi[179] said R. Yohanan, though some teach this in the name of R. Yose the Galilean, "Scripture said [Dt. 31:10: 'And Moses commanded them], "At the end of every seven years,[180] at the time of the year of release, at the festival of Tabernacles, [when all Israel comes to appear before the Lord your God at the place which he will choose, you shall read this law before all Israel in their hearing]."'

[F]   "What is [the reference to] 'the year of release' doing here in association with 'the festival of Tabernacles'? [Since we are

---

[177]Translation: Jaffee.

[178]M introduces this line with an attribution to Assi.

[179]M reads: Ami.

[180]M lacks the first and last clauses of the citation found in P.

	speaking of events to take place 'at the end of every seven years,' this feast of Tabernacles will be in] the eighth year!
[G]	{We must conclude that the reference to "the festival of Tabernacles" has nothing to do with the reading of the law.} "Rather, it is to teach you: [as for] all grain that reaches a third of its growth in the seventh year prior to New Year—in the eighth year, [when you harvest it], you treat it according to the rules for the Sabbatical year."
[H]	Said R. Zera to Rab Assi,[181] [13a] "But perhaps [this refers even to a case in which the produce] has not begun to ripen at all. But [even so] the Merciful has said, '[In the eighth year, when it has ripened and is harvested], treat it as subject to the rules of the Sabbatical year until the festival of Tabernacles.'"
[I]	Do not even think that, for it is written [Ex. 23:16: "You shall keep] the feast of ingathering at the end of the year, [when you gather in from the field the fruit of your labor]."
[J]	What [is the meaning of the term] "ingathering"?
[K]	Might I say it refers to the festival that comes at the time of the harvest?
[L]	This [already is indicated by] that which is written [in the continuation of the verse]: "When you gather in [from the field the fruit of your labor]."[182] {Hence the term "ingathering" must have some different meaning.}
[M]	Rather, what [is the meaning of] "ingathering"?
[N]	Harvesting. {Simon: The implication is that what is harvested at this time of year is deemed to be of the same, not the following, year.}
[O]	But the rabbis were certain that all grain that is harvested at the festival [of Tabernacles] certainly had reached a third [of its growth] by New Year;

---

[181]M reads: Said to him R. Zera.

[182]M explicitly has the bracketed conclusion of the citation.

[P] and indeed [Ex. 23:16] refers to it [with the words] "at the end of the year."

[**LXXIX**.A] {O-P of the preceding unit is challenged.} Said R. Jeremiah to R. Zera, "Were the rabbis [indeed] certain [that a distinction could be made] between [that which had reached] a third [of its growth] and [that which had] not [reached] a third [of its growth, so that one could be assigned to one year of the cycle and the other to a different year]?"

[B] [Zera] said to him, "Have I not told you not to place yourself outside of the established law?

[C] "All measures established by the sages are comparable to this [that is, all reflect very slight distinctions].

[D] "[To remove uncleanness] one immerses in forty *seahs* of water; in forty *seahs* less one *qortab*, one may not immerse. An egg's volume [of food] has the capacity to convey uncleanness of foods; an egg's volume less [the volume of] a sesame seed[183] does not have the capacity to convey uncleanness of foods. [A piece of cloth] three-by-three handbreadths [in size] has the capacity to contract uncleanness by reason of a sitting or lying person afflicted with a flux [see Lev. 15]; [a piece of cloth] three-by-three handbreadths less a [single] thread does not have the capacity to contract uncleanness by reason of a sitting or lying person afflicted with a flux."[184]

[E] {Jeremiah now brings evidence that the distinction between produce that has not reached a third of its growth and that which has reached a third of its growth in fact is legitimate and workable as a way of determining whether or not the produce is subject to Israelite agricultural law.} Jeremiah reversed [himself and] said, "That which I said is of no weight.

---

[183]Instead of "sesame seed," M reads: a little bit

[184]See B. Men. 103b and Neusner, *Menahot*, p. 143.

170   BAVLI ROSH HASHANAH CHAPTER ONE [13a]

[F] "For the associates asked Rab Kahana: [As for] the first sheaf (*omer*) that the Israelites offered upon their entry into the land [of Israel]—where did they [get it so as to] offer it?

[G] "If you say it grew in the possession of the gentile [inhabitants of the land, this would be impossible, since] the Merciful [at Lev. 23:10] said: '[When you come into the land that I give you and reap its harvest, you shall bring to the priest the sheaf of the first fruits of] your harvest.'

[H] "[This reference to 'your harvest' means that the sheaf may] not [come] from the harvest of gentiles."

[I] {Since we so far are unable to determine where the sheaf offered upon the Israelites' entry into the land came from, the following question seems appropriate:} How do you know that [upon their entry] they offered [a first sheaf at all]? Perhaps they did not offer it!

[J] Do not [even] imagine [such a thing], for it is written [Josh. 5:11]: "And they ate of the produce of the land, on the day after the Passover, [on that very day, unleavened cakes and parched grain]."

[K] [The text states that] on the day after the Passover they ate [the produce of the land]. At first they did not eat [this produce. This suggests that] they offered the first sheaf and [only] then went and ate [the land's produce].

[L] {Since, contrary to I, it is clear that, upon entry into the land, the Israelites did offer the first sheaf, we return to the question the associates posed at F.} [As for the first sheaf that the Israelites offered upon their entry into the land of Israel]—where did they [get it so as to] offer it?[185]

[M] [Kahana] said to them[186] [that is, the associates, F], "All that had not reached a third [of its growth] in the possession of gentiles [was appropriate for the first sheaf]." {Produce that

---

[185]M and other manuscript sources read: from what [verse in Scripture do we know] that they offered it?

[186]A scribal error (Rabbinovicz), M lacks: [Kahana] said to them.

	reached a third of its growth in Israelite hands was deemed Israelite-grain and was used as the first sheaf.}
[N]	{M is challenged.} But perhaps [one should think that the grain] had grown and it was not certain [whether or not it had reached a third of its growth in gentile hands]. {If this is the case, M's solution to L's question is unworkable.}
[O]	This is not so. [Since, after Passover, they ate the food of the land] they indeed were certain [that what they had offered as the first sheaf had not reached a third of its growth in gentile hands].
[P]	Here too [in the case of the grain harvested at Tabernacles, above, unit **LXXVIII.G**], they are certain [of when the produce reaches a third of its growth].
[Q]	{M again is challenged.} But perhaps [at the point at which the Israelites entered the land, the grain that eventually would be used for the first sheaf] had not [started to] grow at all. {In this argument, only grain that grew entirely in Israelite hands was used as the first sheaf.}
[R]	[If matters are as Q suggests, one can argue] however [that] in the case [of grain] that had [upon the Israelites' entry into the land already] reached a quarter[187] [of its total growth], whether it had reached a third of its growth or still was at less than a third was unclear to them, [so that such grain was not used for the first sheaf at all].
[S]	Do not [even] imagine [such a thing], for it is written [Josh. 4:19]: "The people came up out of the Jordan on the tenth day of the month."
[T]	Now, if you think that [upon their entry into the land, the grain that was to become the first sheaf] had not [yet started to] grow at all—in five days could it [grow and] become ripe, [so as to be ready for offering immediately after Passover]? {This clearly is impossible. Hence we must

---

[187]M and other sources add "or a sixth," as is found in the printed edition below at U.

conclude that the grain used for the first sheaf was growing under gentile ownership prior to the Israelites' entry into the land, and that, beginning with produce that had reached a quarter of its growth, the people were able to distinguish the point at which it achieved a third of its growth and could be used for the offering.}

[U] {T's response to R leaves open another possible challenge to M.} But [even as for] that which had grown a fourth or a sixth[188] [at the time of the Israelites' entry into the land]—can it complete its ripening in five days?

[V] [To respond to U's argument] what can you say?

[W] It is written [concerning the land of Israel, Dan. 11:16], "The land of the gazelle."[189] {The land is understood to be like a gazelle in being swift to bring its produce to ripeness; see B. Ket. 112a.}

[X] In this matter too, it is written, "The land of the gazelle."

[**LXXX**.A] {We return to unit **LXXVIII**.M-P's claim that, at Ex. 23:16, the word "ingathering" means "harvest," and serves to support the rabbis' rule regarding the significance of produce's reaching a third of its mature growth.} [Responding to that interpretation] R. Hanina objected, "But how can you say that this 'ingathering' is the 'harvest'?

[B] "For [indicating a contrary meaning] it is written [Dt. 16:13: 'You shall keep the feast of Tabernacles seven days], when you make your ingathering from your threshing floor and your wine press.'

[C] "And [explaining this verse] a master said, '[By using the word "ingathering"] Scripture speaks of what is left on the threshing floor and of the dregs of the wine press.'" {See B. Suk. 12a. The point is that these things are appropriate roofing material for a booth used on Tabernacles. The term

---

[188]So Jastrow, p. 315, s.v. *dnq'*. Cf., Simon: a fifth. M lacks: a forth or a sixth.

[189]RSV: the glorious land.

"ingathering" thus refers to a period much later than the harvest and cannot be used to support the rabbis' understanding of the significance of produces' reaching a third of its mature growth.}

[D] Said R. Zera, "We had a firm proposition in hand, but R. Hanina came and threw an ax at it!"

[E] Rather, from what verse [in Scripture] do we know [the rule about the third of produce's growth]?

[F] As it is taught on Tannaitic authority: R. Jonathan b. Joseph says, "[Lev. 25:21 states: 'I will command my blessing upon you in the sixth year], so that [it] will bring forth fruit for three years.' {The produce of the sixth year, that is, will suffice to feed the people in the sixth, seventh, and eighth years of the Sabbatical cycle, until the produce that begins to grow after the Sabbatical year is ripe and available for consumption, in the ninth year.}

[G] [13b] "Do not read [the verse as it actually is written]: 'for three years.'

[H] "Rather, [by adding one letter, read it as though it said]: 'for a third.'" {In this reading, the point of the verse is that produce is deemed ripe when it has reached a third of its mature growth.}

[I] {The Talmud now argues that Lev. 25:21 is not available for the interpretation given at H.} But, do we not need this verse to [express] its literal meaning, [that the sixth year will provide enough food for three years]?

[J] {I's problem is resolved by locating a different verse that expresses what Lev. 25:21 literally says.} A different verse [Lev. 25:22] states: "When you sow in the eighth year, you will be eating old produce. Until the ninth year, [when its produce comes in, you shall eat the old]."[190] {Like Lev. 25:21, Lev. 25:22 indicates that the produce of the sixth year will last three years. Lev. 25:21 therefore can be used to

---

[190]M contains the bracketed conclusion of the verse explicitly.

[LXXXI.A] There we have taught on Tannaitic authority [M. Sheb. 2:7: *After their harvest] rice, durra, millet, and sesame that took root before New Year [of any year in the Sabbatical cycle] are tithed according to the [rules that apply to produce of the] previous year [in which they were planted].*

[B] *And [if they were planted in the sixth year], they are permitted during the Sabbatical year.* {Even though these items are picked during the Sabbatical, they are subject to the rules of the sixth year, in which they took root. This is just as A states.}

[C] *But if [they did] not [take root before New Year, but during the Sabbatical year itself], they are forbidden during the Sabbatical year [under the Sabbatical restrictions, as we would expect].*

[D] *And [in a case such as is described at C], they are tithed according to the [rule that applies to produce of the] year following [the one in which they were planted].* {They are tithed, that is to say, according to the rule for the year in which they take root, just as the preceding rules already have indicated.}

[E] Said Rabbah, "The rabbis state that [the tithing year for fruit of] a tree is determined by when it blossoms; [the tithing year for] grain and olives is determined by when they reach a third [of their growth; the tithing year for] vegetables is determined by when they are picked.

[F] "As for these [foods listed at A]: to which [of the types indicated at E] did the rabbis deem them comparable?"

[G] Rabbah went ahead and [answering his own question] said, "Since [the items listed at A] are prepared by being husked, [in determining when they become subject to tithes] the rabbis followed the point at which they take root." {Simon:

[H] [Arguing that, for purposes of separating tithes, the old and new produce need not be kept distinct at all], said to him Abayye, "But let him [simply] pile [all of the harvest] on his threshing floor, so that, as a result, he separates from the new produce as tithes for the new and from the old produce as tithes for the old. {A mixture containing old and new produce may be designated heave-offering and tithes on behalf of the rest of the produce on the threshing floor, which comparably contains old and new produce.}

Otherwise it would be impossible to keep old and new produce separate for purposes of the removal of tithes.}

[I] "For [indicating the validity of this procedure] is it not taught on Tannaitic authority [T. Sheb. 2:5]: **R. Yose b. Kiper said in the name of R. Simeon Shezuri,** '[As for] Egyptian beans that one sowed for seed, a portion of which took root prior to New Year and a portion of which took root after New Year—they may not separate heave-offering and tithes from this portion for that portion, since they do not separate heave-offering and tithes from that which is new on behalf of that which is old or from that which is old on behalf of that which is new [see M. Ter. 1:5].

[J] "'What should he do?

[K] **"'He gathers his crop [which includes the produce of the two different years] on [the threshing floor] and, as a result, separates heave-offering and tithes from the new produce in it as tithes for the new and from the old produce in it as tithes for the old.'"**

[L] [Rabbah] said to him [that is, to Abayye, "To explain the position of the rabbis] you cite Simeon Shezuri!! [That is illogical since] R. Simeon Shezuri reasons that [complete] mixing [occurs, so that what is separated as heave-offering and tithes is exactly the same as the produce on behalf of which it is separated].

[M] "But the rabbis reason that [complete] mixing does not [occur, so that the procedure described at H+I-K is unacceptable]."

[N] Said R. Isaac bar Nahmani said Samuel, "The decided law follows [the view of] R. Yose b. Kiper, who spoke in the name of R. Simeon Shezuri."

[O] R. Zera objected, "But did Samuel really say this?

[P] "Rather, thus said Samuel, '[Completing] mixing does not occur except [in the cases] of wine or oil.'"

[Q] {Zera, O-P, incorrectly represents Samuel's view.} [Zera] forgot the following, which Samuel said: "In all cases [the year for tithing] follows [the point at which] the produce is ripened." {Samuel thus agrees with Simeon Shezuri that Egyptian beans that rooted before and after new year may be tithed together. But his reasoning is different from that of Simeon Shezuri, who holds that this may be done *despite* the fact that the mixture contains beans subject to the rules of different years of the Sabbatical cycle. Samuel, by contrast, deems the beans all to be subject to the same law in the first place. While Samuel agrees with Simeon Shezuri about the law, his statement therefore cannot be used to support Simeon's legal premise regarding mixtures.}

[R] {The problem now is to explain the need for all the statements attributed to Samuel: N, P, and Q.} [14a] Now, [each of these three statements] is necessary [in order fully to express Samuel's view].

[S] For if we were taught [only as at N, that, in Samuel's view] the decided law follows [the perspective of] R. Simeon Shezuri, we would have thought it is because [Samuel] reasons that [complete] mixing occurs.

[T] Therefore we are instructed [at P that in Samuel's view] in all [cases complete] mixing does not occur.

[U] And if we were taught [only as at P, that in Samuel's view] in all [cases complete] mixing does not occur, we would have thought that he concurs with rabbis, [M, who say that combinations of produce never are treated as completely mixed].

[V] Therefore we must be instructed, [N, that in Samuel's view] the decided law follows [the perspective of] R. Simeon Shezuri, [who, as we know from L, holds that we can depend upon mixing].

[W] And if we had taught [only] these two [rules at N and P], we would have thought that the positions of Samuel are contradictory. {The contradiction would be evidenced in Samuel's statements that, on the one hand, mixing cannot be relied on, but that, on the other, the law follows Simeon Shezuri, which suggests that mixing can be relied on.}

[X] Therefore we must be informed, [Q, that], "In all cases [the year for tithing] follows [the point at which] the produce is ripened." {On the basis of this statement, we understand why Samuel holds that the law follows Simeon Shezuri, as explained at Q.}

[Y] Now, if we were taught [only as at Q, that] in all cases [the year for tithing] follows [the point at which] the produce is ripened, we would have thought [that, in Samuel's view, this applies] even [in the case of] produce and olives.

[Z] Therefore we must be instructed, [N, that in Samuel's view] the decided law follows [the perspective of] R. Simeon Shezuri even in the case in which he disagrees.

[AA] Now, [it appears as though] we need be taught [only] these two rules, [Q and N, stating that, in Samuel's view, the law follows the position of Simeon Shezuri and that produce is tithed according to the year in which it ripens].

[BB] [As for the rule which states], "In all [cases complete] mixing does not occur"—why do I need it? {The rules expressed at N and Q seem to make this statement unnecessary.}

[CC] It [is needed to] instruct us that, in the case of wine and oil, [complete] mixing does occur.

[LXXXII.A] It is taught on Tannaitic authority: R. Yose the Galilean says, "[Dt. 16:13 states: 'You shall keep the feast of Tabernacles seven days], when you make your ingathering from your threshing floor and your wine press.'

[B] "[This suggests that] just as [the produce on] the threshing floor and [in] the wine press, which is distinguished by having grown as a result of the waters [that is, rains and irrigation] of the past year, is tithed [according to the rules that applied] in that [same] past year,

[C] "so every kind [of produce] that grows as a result of the waters of the past year is tithed [according to the rules that applied] in that past year.

[D] "This excludes [from this rule] vegetables, which grow from the water of the coming year [after the one in which they are planted] and which are tithed [according to the rules that apply] in that [same] coming year."

[E] R. Aqiba says, "[Dt. 16:13 states: 'You shall keep the feast of Tabernacles seven days], when you make your ingathering from your threshing floor and your wine press.'

[F] "[This suggests that] just as [the produce on] the threshing floor and [in] the wine press, which is distinguished by having grown as a result of the rains[191] [but not irrigation] of the past year, is tithed [according to the rules that applied] in that [same] past year,

[G] "so every kind [of produce] that grows as a result of the rains [of the past year] is tithed [according to the rules that applied] in that past year.

[H] "This excludes [from this rule] vegetables, which grow from all the water [that is, rain and irrigation] and which are tithed [according to the rules that apply] in the coming year."

[I] In what case is there a practical difference between these [two views]?

---

[191]So Rashi. Literally: most water.

[J] Said R. Abbahu,[192] "They differ concerning the rule for seedless onions and Egyptian beans.

[K] "For we have taught on Tannaitic authority [M. Sheb. 2:9]: *Seedless onions and Egyptian beans that one deprived of water thirty days before New Year are tithed according to the [rule that applies to produce of the] previous year.*

[L] "*And [if they were planted in the sixth year of the Sabbatical cycle] they are permitted during the Sabbatical year.* {This follows from the fact that they are treated as produce of the preceding, sixth year.}

[M] "*But if [one did] not [deprive them of water within thirty days of New Year of the Sabbatical year], they are forbidden during the Sabbatical year.*

[N] "*And [if they were watered close to New Year in any year of the Sabbatical cycle other than the sixth], they are tithed according to the [rule that applies to produce of the] following year.*" {The way in which this passage responds to the question posed at I depends upon our understanding of the significance of "depriving the produce of water." Simon, pp. 51-52, cites two possibilities proposed by Rashi: "According to one opinion, if these vegetables have been kept without water for the last thirty days of the outgoing year, then R. Jose would hold that they must have been nurtured by the rain water of that year, and so are to be tithed for that year; whereas R. Aqiba would hold that their growth is due in part to irrigation, and so they would be tithed for the next year; and the Mishnah quoted follows R. Jose. The other opinion is that as they have not been irrigated for thirty days, it is R. Aqiba and not R. Jose who would hold that they have been nurtured by the rain of the outgoing year, and the Mishnah therefore follows R. Aqiba.}

---

[192]M lacks the attribution.

[**LXXXIII**.A] *The first day of Shevat is the new year for trees, [in accord with the opinion of the House of Shammai. The House of Hillel say, "On the fifteenth day of that month (is the new year for trees);"* M. R.H. 1:1G-H].

[B] What is the reason [that the month of Shevat marks the new year for trees, such that produce that formed prior to Shevat may not be used as heave-offering or tithes on behalf of produce that forms after Shevat, or *vice versa*]?

[C] Said R. Eleazar said R. Oshaia, "It is because [by then] most of the year's rain has fallen, but the greater part of the cycle [of the winter solstice] is still to come." {On the division of the year into four cycles, see above, unit **XLVII**.K, 8a.}

[D] What does this mean?

[E] It means this: Even though the greater part of the cycle is still to come, since most of the year's rain has fallen [we deem the fruit that has already formed to belong to the previous year].[193] {The fruit formed as a result of the previous year's rain. Even though it continues to grow and is picked after Shevat, it may not be tithed together with other fruit that will take shape after Shevat. That other fruit, which will depend upon the next cycle of rain, is deemed part of a distinct crop.}

[**LXXXIV**.A] {The Shammaites, M. R.H. 1:1G, hold that the first of Shevat is the new year for trees; the Hillelites hold that the new year for trees occurs on the fifteenth of that month.} Our rabbis have taught on Tannaitic authority: An incident occurred concerning R. Aqiba, who picked a citron on the first of Shevat[194] and treated it [as subject] to two tithes,

[B] [**14b**] one which followed the teaching of the House of Shammai [M. R.H. 1:1G] and the other following the

---

[193]M reverses the clauses here. The meaning is the same.

[194]Prior to being corrected, M read: on the eve of the fifteenth of Shevat, before the sun had set.

teaching of the House of Hillel [M. R.H. 1:1H]. {Aqiba separated poor tithe, required by the Shammaites for the third year, as well as second tithe, required by the Hillelites for the second year.}

[C] {C-I is interjected and is taken up in the following unit.} [Rejecting B] R. Yose bar Judah says, "[In separating two tithes, Aqiba] did not follow the practices required by [the distinct perspectives of] the House of Shammai and the House of Hillel.

[D] "Rather, he followed the practices required by [the distinct perspectives of] Rabban Gamaliel and R. Eliezer.

[E] "For we have taught on Tannaitic authority [M. Bik. 2:6]: *A citron [tree] is like a tree in three ways and like a vegetable in one way.*

[F] "*It is like a tree in three ways: [regarding the laws of] orlah, the Fourth [Year], and the Sabbatical [year].*

[G] "*And [it is like] a vegetable [in one way]:*

[H] "'*that it is tithed in accordance with the point at which it is picked'—the words of Rabban Gamaliel.*

[I] "R. Eliezer says, 'It is like a tree in every way, [so that its tithing year follows the point at which it blossoms].'" {Yose bar Judah explains Aqiba's actions as follows: Following the view of Gamaliel, H, he separated poor tithe, which applies in the third year, in which the citron was picked; in line with the perspective of Eliezer, he also separated second tithe, always separated in the second year, in which the tree blossomed.}

[J] {The appropriateness of Aqiba's actions, described at A-B, is questioned.} But [as a matter of principle] do we [in fact] follow two stringencies?[195] {That is, should Aqiba have accepted the burden of two tithes, following both the Hillelite and Shammaite views?}

---

[195]M lacks: stringencies.

[K] For [to the contrary] it is taught on Tannaitic authority [T. Ed. 2:3, with variations]: **The decided law follows the opinion of the House of Hillel. But one who wishes to follow the position of the House of Shammai may do so, [and one who wishes to follow] the opinion of the House of Hillel may do so.**

[L] **But [one who follows] the lenient positions of the House of Shammai and the lenient positions of the House of Hillel is evil.**

[M] **And [as for one who follows] the stringent positions of the House of Shammai and the stringent positions of the House of Hillel[196]—concerning him Scripture states [Eccles. 2:14]: "The fool walks in darkness."**

[N] **Rather, if [the person acts] in accord with the House of Shammai, [let him follow] both their lenient and strict rulings; [and] if [the person acts] in accord with the House of Hillel, [let him follow] both their lenient and strict rulings.**

[O] {The following explains that Aqiba did not contradict the principle outlined at K-N.[197] Aqiba, rather, followed two different understandings of the Hillelite perspective.} R. Aqiba was in doubt [regarding the Hillelites' position], and he did not know if the House of Hillel said[198] [that the new year for trees is on] the first of Shevat or on the fifteenth of

---

[196]In place of "the House of Shammai and the stringent positions of the House of Hillel," M reads simply: both.

[197]What Aqiba is accused of doing in fact is somewhat different from what is prohibited by K-N. Aqiba is accused of following the positions of two different authorities on a single issue. K-N prohibits picking a single view based simply upon the leniency or stringency of the opinion.

[198]So the marginal correction in P, which reads the verb in the plural as is normal for the subject "House of Hillel." Manuscripts, Venice, other early printings, and the parallel at B. Erub. 7a have the passive participle. The point is the same.

Shevat.[199] {Aqiba wished simply to abide by the ruling of the House of Hillel. Since he did not know for certain what the Hillelite position was, he followed both views he thought they might hold. But he did not violate the principle outlined at K-O by following both the Hillelites' and Shammaites' opinions.}

[LXXXV.A] {We now evaluate the interpretation of Aqiba's actions at unit **LXXXIV**.C-I.} R. Yose bar Judah says, "[In separating two tithes, Aqiba] did not follow the practices required by [the distinct perspectives of] the House of Shammai and the House of Hillel. Rather, he followed the practices required by [the distinct perspectives of] Rabban Gamaliel and R. Eliezer [at M. Bik. 2:6]."

[B] {At issue is whether Yose bar Judah's statement completely explains what Aqiba did.} [Since the citron was picked] on the first of Shevat, [would Yose bar Judah not hold that, in separating tithes required for the third year, Aqiba] followed the perspective of the House of Shammai? {In tithing the citron for the third year, Aqiba clearly followed Gamaliel's view, that the citron is subject to tithing according to the year in which it is picked. But it further should be clear that Aqiba interpreted Gamaliel's view in conjunction with that of the Shammaites. They hold that the new year for trees is on the first of Shevat, so that the citron Aqiba picked in fact was picked in the third year. In the Hillelite perspective, which holds that the new year for trees is on the fifteenth of Shevat, even if tithed according to when it is picked, this citron would be treated as second year produce.}

[C] [Rejecting B] said R. Hanina, and some say it was R. Hanania,[200] "In this [case] we deal with a citron tree that

---

[199]M and the parallel at B. Erub. 7a add: so he followed the stringent position in both cases.

[200]M reads: Rab Hananiah.

blossomed [in the second year] before [the preceding] fifteenth [of Shevat], and the same principle would have been at issue [even if Aqiba had picked the fruit] earlier [than the first of the following Shevat]. But the way the story is told is how it actually happened." {Aqiba's picking of the fruit on the first of Shevat is irrelevant to the principle at issue here. Contrary to B, Aqiba accepted the Hillelite view, that the new year for trees is on the fifteenth of Shevat. In the case of a citron that blossomed prior to the fifteenth of Shevat, he tithed it according to the rules for the second year, in which it blossomed (= Eliezer) and according to the procedure for the third year, in which the produce was picked (= Gamaliel).}

[D] Rabina said, "Combine [the two versions of the case, C and unit **LXXXIV**.A, into one] and teach [that Aqiba did] not [pick the produce] on the first of Shevat but, rather, on the fifteenth of Shevat, and that he did not follow the practices required by [the distinct perspectives of] the House of Shammai and the House of Hillel, but, rather, he followed the practices required by Rabban Gamaliel and R. Eliezer. {The tree blossomed before the fifteenth of Shevat in one year and the fruit was picked after the fifteenth of Shevat of the following year. In this circumstance, in the views of both Houses, the produce began growing in the second year and was picked in the third year. The issue disputed by the Houses, of the exact date on which the new year for trees begins, therefore was irrelevant here. Of concern only was whether the produce is to be tithed in accordance with when the tree blossomed—here, the second year—or in line with when the fruit was picked—here the third year. Relying on the perspectives of both Gamaliel and Eliezer, Aqiba followed both possibilities.}

[LXXXVI.A] Said Rabbah bar Rab Huna, "Insofar as Rabban Gamaliel said [that], like a vegetable, a citron is tithed according to when it is picked, [he further should hold that, like a vegetable] its new year is on [the first of] Tishre. {See M. R.H. 1:1F.}

[B] They objected [citing T. R.H. 1:9]: R. Simeon b. Eleazar says,[201] "**[If] one picked a citron on the eve of the fifteenth of Shevat before sunset and then went and picked another one after sunset, they do not separate heave-offering and tithes from this one [gathered before sunset] on behalf of that one [gathered after sunset, or** *vice versa*], since they do not separate have-offering or tithes from new produce on behalf of old produce or from old produce on behalf of new produce.

[C] "**If it was third year [of the Sabbatical cycle] and the fourth year was beginning, that which was [picked in] the third year [is subject to]** first tithe and **poor tithe, [and that which was picked in] the fourth year [is subject to]** first tithe and **second tithe.**"

[D] {We now see how T. R.H. 1:9 disproves A's proposition.} **[15a]** Who teaches that [the tithing year of a citron] follows [the point at which it is] picked?

[E] Rabban Gamaliel. {See unit **LXXXIV**.H, which cites M. Bik. 2:6. Since this is his view, Gamaliel apparently stands behind T. R.H. 1:9, just cited, which comparably deems the citron to be subject to tithing according to the point at which it is picked.}

[F] But [contrary to A, at T. R.H. 1:9] he teaches [explicitly that the citron's new year is] Shevat!

[G] {B-F proves that A's contention is untenable. A new suggestion is made regarding what A should say.} Rather, if [A] was said [at all], thus it was phrased:

---

[201]The attribution, lacking in sources for the Tosefta, is added in the margin of M.

[H] Said Rabbah bar Rab Huna, "Even though Rabban Gamaliel said [that], like a vegetable, a citron [is tithed][202] according to when it is picked, [he holds that, like other trees] its new year is in Shevat." {See M. R.H. 1:1G.}

[LXXXVII.A] Why in the former statement [above, unit **LXXVI**, 12a, which cites the beginning of T. R.H. 1:9] do we learn on Tannaitic authority [of a case in which] it was the second year [of the Sabbatical cycle] and the third year began, whereas, in the current instance [unit **LXXXVI**, 14b, which cites the conclusion of T. R.H. 1:9] we learn on Tannaitic authority [of a case in which] it was the third year [of the Sabbatical cycle] and the fourth year began?

[B] [In this way] we incidentally are taught an [additional] rule, that handling is hard on a citron tree, and since everyone handles it during the Sabbatical year [during which, like all trees, it is deemed common property], it does not produce fruit until the third year [after blossoming].

[LXXXVIII.A] R. Yohanan asked R. Yannai, "[As for] the citron tree—when is its new year?

[B] [Yannai] said to him, "Shevat."

[C] [Yohanan questioned further, "By 'Shevat' do you mean] Shevat of the [calendar of] months, or Shevat of the cycle [of four yearly periods]." {See above, unit **XLVII**.K, 8a. The year is perceived as comprised of four cycles: the vernal equinox, beginning in Nisan; the summer solstice, beginning in Tamuz; the autumn equinox, beginning in Tishre; and the winter solstice, beginning in Tevet. Shevat of the cycle refers to the period beginning thirty days from the winter solstice, in the cycle of Tevet.}

[D] [Yannai] said to him, "[Shevat] of the [calendar of] months."

---

[202]M has the bracketed words explicitly.

[LXXXIX.A] Rava asked Rab Nahman, and some say R. Yohanan [asked] R. Yannai, "[As for] a leap year—what is the rule? {Simon, p. 55, following Rashi: "Do we make the New Year in Shevat which comes next to Tebeth, or in First Adar, which takes the place of Shevat in this year?"}

[B] [Nahman] said to him, "Follow [the rule for] ordinary years, [observing this new year in Shevat]."

[XC.A] Said Rabbah,[203] "A citron [that blossomed] in the sixth year [of the Sabbatical cycle] that continued growing in the Sabbatical year is exempt from tithing and is exempt from removal. {Insofar as it is picked during the Sabbatical year, the citron is treated as Sabbatical produce, exempt from tithes. But since it blossomed prior to the Sabbatical year, it is not treated entirely like Sabbatical produce. Even after other produce of its type ceases to be available in the fields freely to all people, individuals need not remove from storage in their homes citrons of the Sabbatical year that they have stocked for themselves.}

[B] "[And a citron that blossomed] in the Sabbatical year that continued growing in the eighth year is exempt from tithing but is subject to removal." {We treat this citron as totally subject to the Sabbatical restrictions.}

[C] Said to him Abayye, "[Your] final clause [at B] creates no problem, for it imposes a stringency. {B treats the citron as tithed in accordance with when it blossomed. This creates a stringency, insofar as it renders the citron subject to all of the Sabbatical restrictions.}

[D] "But [your] first clause [at A surely creates a problem, for it states], 'It is exempt from removal.'

[E] "Why [is this the case]?"

---

[203]M reads: Rava. In light of the participation in this discussion of Hamnuna, unit **XCI**, Rabbinovicz suggests that the reading of the printed edition, "Rabbah," is likely correct.

[F] [Rabbah can respond: The reason is that] we say, "Follow blossoming as the deciding factor [in determining to what year the citron belongs]." {Since the blossom appeared in the sixth year, the fruit is not subject to the Sabbatical restriction of removal.}

[G] {Since in a different regard the citron referred to at A is subject to the Sabbatical law, F does not solve D's problem.} [Abayye can reply to Rabbah:] If this is the case [that we determine the citron's year by when the tree blossomed, in A's case, contrary to what you say] it should be subject to tithes!

[H] [Rabbah] said to him, "Everyone handles it during the Sabbatical year, yet you say it should be subject to tithes!" {Even though these citrons, growing in the fields during the Sabbatical year, are not Sabbatical produce and in fact remain the private possession of the fields' owners, people treat them like Sabbatical food, available for everyone's consumption. As a result, the citrons are deemed in the category of abandoned property, which, like Sabbatical produce, is exempt from tithes.}

[XCI.A] {Hamnuna presents a different approach to the issue of the preceding unit.} But Rab Hamnuna said, "[A citron[204] that blossomed] in the sixth year [of the Sabbatical cycle] that continued growing in the Sabbatical year in all regards is treated as produce of the sixth year.

[B] "[And a citron that blossomed] in the Sabbatical year that continued growing in the eighth year in all regards is treated as produce of the Sabbatical year."

[C] They objected: R. Simeon b. Judah says in the name of R. Simeon,[205] "A citron [that blossomed] in the sixth year [of the Sabbatical cycle] that continued growing in the

---

[204]M explicitly includes: A citron.

[205]M adds: b. Yohai. It is the same authority either way.

Sabbatical year is exempt from tithing and is exempt from removal,

[D] "for nothing exists that is subject to tithes that did not grow in [a period of] liability and was not picked in [a period of] liability. {The citrons referred to here are exempt, since the Sabbatical year is not a period of liability to tithes.}

[E] "And a citron [that blossomed] in the Sabbatical year that continued growing in the eighth year is exempt from tithing and [also] is exempt to removal,

[F] "for nothing exists that is subject to removal that did not grow in the Sabbatical year and get picked in the Sabbatical year." {The citrons referred to here are exempt, since they were picked after the Sabbatical year.}

[XCII.A] {The approaches of the several cited authorities are now compared and explained.} The first part [of Simeon's statement, unit **XCI.C**] contradicts the position of Rab Hamnuna [unit **XCI.A**]. {Simeon states that a citron that blossoms in the sixth year and continues growing in the seventh is exempt from tithing. This is contrary to Hamnuna, who says that such fruit is treated in all ways as produce of the sixth year and therefore is subject to tithes.}

[B] [And] the concluding part [of Simeon's statement, unit **XCI.E**] contradicts both the position of Rabbah[206] [unit **XC.A**] and that of Rab Hamnuna [unit **XCI.B**]. {Simeon holds that a citron that blossoms in the Sabbatical year and continues growing in the eighth year is exempt from removal. Both Rabbah and Hamnuna hold that, like Sabbatical produce, this citron is subject to removal.}

[C] {The reason for these disagreements is as follows:} There is [a dispute among] Tannaitic authorities [regarding whether, to determine if the citron is subject to the Sabbatical restrictions, we follow the point of blossoming or picking].

---

[206]M reads: Rava. See note 203.

[D] For it is taught on Tannaitic authority [T. Sheb. 4:21]: **Said R. Yose, "Abtolemos testified[207] in the name of five elders that a citron is subject to [the separation of] tithes [required] in the year in which it is picked.**

[E] **"But in Usha, our rabbis voted and ruled[208] [that its liability] both for tithing and [in regard to the restrictions of] the Sabbatical year follows the point at which it is picked."**

[F] [E refers to] the Sabbatical year. Why is this brought up? {On the surface, there is no need to mention the Sabbatical year, since, as D assumes, liability to its restrictions should be determined in the same way as liability to all other tithing rules.}

[G] [15b] [You can understand the reference to the Sabbatical year by proposing that the statement at D] is defective.

[H] Now, here is how [the statement at D-E] should be taught on Tannaitic authority: **"A citron is subject to [the separation of] tithes [required] in the year in which it is picked** and is subject to [the restrictions of] the Sabbatical year according to when it blossomed. {The appended statement accounts for Rabbah and Hamnuna's view, that a citron that blossoms in the Sabbatical year but is picked in the eighth year is subject to removal. Rashi: Unlike Rabbah, however, Hamnuna reads Abtolemos' view to hold that, while for tithes, picking is decisive, a citron picked in the Sabbatical year is exempt, since people treat it as common property.}

[I] **"But in Usha, our rabbis voted and ruled [that its liability] both for tithing and [in regard to the restrictions of] the Sabbatical year follows the point at which it is picked."**[209]

---

[207]M reads: R. Yose b. Abtolemos testified.

[208]Literally: said. M reads: determined.

[209]M reads: follows the point at which it takes shape.

[XCIII.A] {The following disputes the proposition of H of the preceding unit, that we distinguish the determining factor for tithing from that for the restrictions of the Sabbatical year.} It is taught on Amoraic authority: R. Yohanan and Resh Laqish, the two of them, say, "A citron of the sixth year that continued growing in the Sabbatical year in all regards [is treated as produce of the] sixth year."

[B] [Elaborating on A] when Rabin came [from the land of Israel] he said: "R. Yohanan [says], 'A citron of the sixth year that continued growing in the Sabbatical year—even though [at the end of the sixth year it was only as big] as an olive and [in the Sabbatical year] it became as big as a loaf— [it is treated as produce of the sixth year, such that, by eating it without tithing, people] are guilty [for violating the restrictions against eating] untithed produce.'"

[XCIV.A] Our rabbis have taught on Tannaitic authority: A tree the fruit of which blossomed prior to the fifteenth of Shevat is tithed according to [the rules for] the prior year [in which it blossomed]. {This is the case even though it is picked in the new year, after the fifteenth of Shevat.}

[B] [A tree that blossomed] after the fifteenth of Shevat is tithed according to [the rules for] the coming year, [that is, again, the year in which it blossomed and, in this case, is picked].

[C] Said R. Nehemiah, "In what circumstance does this apply?

[D] "In the case of a tree that produces two broods a year."

[E] {The following is interjected, explaining the use of the term "brood," which normally applies to birds.} "Two broods"— does this [wording] make sense to you? Rather [to make himself clear, Nehemiah] should say, "[Trees that produce fruit] like two broods." {Reference is to the fact that, like eggs, all of which do not hatch at once, the fruit on the tree ripens over a period of time.}

[F]   [Nehemiah continues], "But [in the case of] a tree that produces only one brood, such as dates, olives, and figs, even though the fruit blossomed prior to the fifteenth of Shevat, it is tithed [according to the procedure] for the coming year, [in which the fruit ripens and is picked]." {In the case of such trees, the year for tithing follows the point at which the produce is picked.}

[XCV.A] Said R. Yohanan, "In respect to the carob tree, the people followed [the law] as expressed by R. Nehemiah [in the preceding unit].

[B]   Resh Laqish objected to [this statement of] R. Yohanan [by citing M. Sheb. 5:1: *As for] white figs [that appear in the Seventh Year]—their [period of being subject to the restrictions of the] Sabbatical year is the second year [of the new Sabbatical cycle], because they take three years to ripen fully.* {This indicates that, contrary to Nehemiah's view, even fruit that ripens all at once is tithed according to the year in which the blossoms appeared, not when it is picked.}

[C]   [Unable to respond, Yohanan] was silent.

[D]   Said R. Abba the Priest to R. Yose the Priest, "Why was he silent?

[E]   "He should have responded,[210] '[Your refutation is irrelevant, since] I have told you [the view of] R. Nehemiah, while you have replied [with the view of the anonymous] rabbis, [who stand behind M. Sheb. 5:1].'"

[F]   [E's retort would have been unacceptable] since [Resh Laqish] would have said to him, "Have you rejected [the majority view of] the rabbis and followed [the practice of] R. Nehemiah?"

[G]   {Another possible response of Yohanan to Resh Laqish is suggested.} Then let him respond, "[Your answer to me, B, is irrelevant since, whereas] I informed you of [the people's

---

[210]Literally: said.

actual] practice, you told [me of] the [legal] prohibition!" {At A Yohanan did nothing more than to indicate how the people carry out the law. This is quite a separate matter from what Resh Laqish brings up at B, which is the true nature of the law.}

[H] [G's retort would have been unacceptable] since [Resh Laqish] would have said to him, "Where a [legal] prohibition exists, [simply] because [the people have a different] practice, do we allow it?"

[I] {Another possible response of Yohanan to Resh Laqish is suggested.} Then let him respond, "[Your answer to me, B, is irrelevant since, whereas] I spoke [only] about [the people's practice in] tithing carobs, which is a Rabbinical [requirement in the first place], you spoke of the laws for the Sabbatical year, which derive from Scripture.

[J] {We see from I that Resh Laqish's point, B, is completely off-base.} Rather,[211] [with this fact in mind] said R. Abba the Priest, "I would be surprised if Resh Laqish responded to this statement [of Yohanan, A, at all]!"

[K] [Abba's comment, J, is odd, for how can he question] whether [or not Resh Laqish] responded [to Yohanan's statement]. Indeed, [we are told explicitly, B, that] he responded!

[L] Rather [to correct the problem] phrase[212] [Abba's comment as follows: "I would be interested to know] whether Yohanan [did not reply to Resh Laqish's challenge, C, because he] accepted [the validity of Resh Laqish's point] or [because, for the reason given at I, he] did not accept [the validity of Resh Laqish's statement at all and believed it undeserving of a response]."

---

[211]M lacks: Rather. Later in this line, it lacks: the Priest.

[212]M lacks this word.

1:2

[A] **[16a]** *At four seasons [of the year] the world is judged:*
[B] *(1) at Passover through grain;*
[C] *(2) at Pentecost through the fruit of the tree;*
[D] *(3) at New Year all who enter the world[213] pass before Him like troops,*
[E] *since it is said [Ps. 33:15]: "He who fashions the hearts of them and who considers all their works;"*
[F] *(4) and on the festival [of Tabernacles] they are judged through water.*

Only unit **I** is exegetical in a narrow sense, discussing through which grain—that of the previous year or that of the following year—people experience God's judgment at Passover (M. R.H. 1:2B). The remainder of this long Talmudic composite discusses in general terms God's judging of the people. When does judgment actually occur (units **II-III+IV**), how can people move God to a favorable judgment (units **V-X+XI-XV**), what will happen to the truly wicked, the thoroughly righteous, and those in the middle (units **XVI-XIX**), and, finally, once God's judgment has been sealed, will repentance move him to revoke the punishment?

Units **V-X** concern the ways in which people can move God towards a favorable judgment. Daily prayers for the sick and ailing are appropriate, unit **V**, since, as units **II-III** indicate, God judges people day-by-day. Unit **VI** explains that the offering of the *omer* at Passover (M. R.H. 1:2B) and the water libation at Tabernacles (M. R.H. 1:2F) move God to favorable judgments, signified by his providing the people with sufficient grain and water. Units **VII-X** develop this same theme in a discussion of the sounding of the ram's horn, which, the Talmud says, moves God to a positive judgment of the people by recalling the binding of Isaac.

---

[213]"All who enter the world" is added in the margin of M.

The theme of how people can affect their judgment continues at units **XI-XIII**. Having discussed appropriate rituals in the preceding units, we turn now to personal behaviors and attitudes. God judges people based upon their actual behaviors up to the time of judgment (unit **XI**). Testing God or hoping to bring a bad judgment upon another person leads to a negative review by God (unit **XII**). By contrast, acts of charity, supplication of God, changing one's name, or improving one's character cancel a person's judgment (unit **XIII**). Units **XIV-XV** conclude these materials by ruling that, on festivals, people must pay respect to their teachers and purify themselves. These requirements appear to be discussed here because they are understood to be additional methods through which people can assure a positive judgment.

Unit **XVI** introduces the concept of God's ledger books, in which, on New Year, he records his judgment of each individual. God's three books correspond to three types of people (units **XVI-XIX**), the thoroughly good, the thoroughly evil, and those in the middle. After detailing the way in which people of each type are treated, the Talmud turns to a central question: once God has rendered judgment, will repentance move him to change the verdict (units **XX-XXXV**)? The Talmud argues that, in the case of a community as a whole, God's judgment never is final. Communal repentance always moves God to revoke the punishment. Individuals, by contrast, are subject to a different rule. An individual's act of repentance is efficacious only until God's judgment has been sealed, on the Day of Atonement. For individuals, accordingly, the ten days between the New Year, when God first enters his judgment against a person, and the Day of Atonement, when the judgment is finalized, have a particular importance. During this period in particular people must repent and change their ways.

The final pericope (unit **XXXVI**) turns to M. R.H. 1:2D, explaining how the people are brought before God for judgment.

[I.A]   [At M. R.H. 1:2B] which grain is meant?

[B] Shall I assume that it is grain that [at Passover] already exists [ready to be harvested, having been sown the preceding fall]?

[C] [This is unacceptable since, if reference is to the standing crop, as for] all of those hardships [the grain underwent that reduced the yield]—when were they suffered? {A poor harvest at the current Passover cannot result from God's judging of the world at that same time. This poor crop necessarily reflects an earlier judging of the world.}

[D] [M. R.H. 1:2B thus means that, through] grain that will be sown [in the coming fall, God's judgment, which took place at Passover, is actualized].

[E] {C-D is challenged.} [D] suggests that only one judgment is passed [that has an impact on grain].

[F] But [to the contrary] thus it is taught on Tannaitic authority: A calamity or misfortune that affects the grain prior to Passover [results from a] judgment from the preceding [Passover; if the incident occurs] after Passover, [it results from a] judgment [to be enacted] on the coming Passover. {M. R.H. 1:2B might refer to grain already growing at Passover. This grain would have been subject to a judgment passed the preceding Passover.}

[G] {F's Tannaitic teaching continues with a parallel example.} A man who experiences a calamity or misfortune prior to the Day of Atonement [suffers as a result of a] judgment from the preceding [Day of Atonement; if the incident occurred] after the Day of Atonement, [it results from a] judgment [to be enacted] on the coming [Day of Atonement].

[H] [Making explicit the implication of F-G][214] said Rava, "Learn from this that two judgments apply [to the same produce, one from the preceding year, one from the coming year]."

[I] [Responding to this notion] said Abayye, "Therefore, if a man sees that a [normally] slow-growing [kind of] seed is

---

[214]M introduces the line: Rather.

doing well [indicating a positive judgment on the preceding Passover], he should go ahead [quickly] and plant fast-growing seed, so that, before the time of the coming judgment, it may get a good start."

[II.A] Which authority [stands behind] the Mishnaic passage [at M. R.H. 1:2]?

[B] It is neither R. Meir, R. Judah, R. Yose, nor R. Nathan.

[C] For it is taught on Tannaitic authority [T. R.H. 1:13]: "**All are judged on New Year, and the decree is sealed on the Day of Atonement**"—the words of R. Meir. {This clearly disagrees with M. R.H. 1:2, which speaks of judgment's taking place at four different points in the year.}

[D] **R. Judah says, "All are judged on the New Year, and the decree of each and every one of them is sealed in its own time:**

[E] *"at Passover through grain, at Pentecost through fruit of the tree, and on the festival [of Tabernacles] they are judged through water* [M. R.H. 1:2B-C+F]. {Judah also disagrees with M. R.H. 1:2, which does not distinguish between the time of judgment and the point at which the individual's fate is sealed.}

[F] "**And** humans are judged on New Year and **their decree is sealed on the Day of Atonement.**"

[G] **R. Yose says,**[215] "**Humans are judged every single day, as it says** [Job 7:17-18, 'What is man that you did make so much of him and did set your mind upon him], **did visit him every morning?**'"

[H] R. Nathan says, "Humans are continually[216] judged, as it says [Job 7:17-18, 'What is man that you did make so much of him and did set your mind upon him, did visit him every

---

[215]All of F and G through this point are added in the margin of M. These words apparently dropped out of the text through haplography.

[216]Literally: every hour.

morning] and test him every moment?'" {Yose and Nathan disagree with M. R.H. 1:2's notion that there are only four times of judgment.}

[I] Now, if you say that, in all events, R. Judah [stands behind M. R.H. 1:2] and that, when [the Mishnah] speaks of [seasons of judgment it refers to] the final judgment [whereas Judah is giving a separate rule for intermediate acts of judgment]—

[J] in this [interpretation] the [different perspectives of M. R.H. 1:2 and Judah's statement, F, regarding the rule for] humans [still poses] a difficulty. {Rashi: M. R.H. 1:2D refers only to people's being judged on New Year, whereas Judah states that their judgment is completed on the Day of Atonement.}

[K] Said Rava, "The Tannaitic authority [who phrased the Mishnaic passage at M. R.H. 1:2D] was of the House of R. Ishmael.[217]

[L] "For the House of R. Ishmael teaches on Tannaitic authority: *At four seasons of the year the world is judged: at Passover through grain; at Pentecost through fruit of the tree; on the festival [of Tabernacles] they are judged*[218] *through water* [M. R.H. 1:2B-C+F]. *And humans are judged on New Year, and their decree is sealed on the Day of Atonement.*

[M] "And when the Mishnah [at M. R.H. 1:2D] speaks [of humanity's being judged at New Year, it refers only to] the beginning of [the act of] judgment." {According to L-M, M. R.H. 1:2D's point is exactly the same as that of Judah, cited above at F. Judgment begins at New Year, but the decree is sealed on the Day of Atonement. Contrary to B, Judah concurs with M. R.H. 1:2.}

---

[217]Here and at L, M reads: Samuel.

[218]M lacks: they are judged.

[III.A] Said Rab Hisda, "What is the basis in Scripture for [the position of] R. Yose [in unit II.G, that humans are judged every single day]?

[B] {The question seems unnecessary, since Yose explicitly indicates his Scriptural proof.} The reason is as is stated [through the citation of Job 7:17-18: "What is man that you did make so much of him and did set your mind upon him], did visit him every morning?"

[C] {Contrary to B, A refers to an issue that is not explicit at unit II.G.} [Through the question at A] here is what we meant to ask: Why [did Yose] not phrase the Scriptural basis [for his view using the same words of the verse] as R. Nathan [at unit II.H]? {Both authorities hold that humans are continually judged. Why do they not argue this claim on the basis of the same words of Scripture?}

[D] {To answer C's question, we focus upon the different significance of the clause "test him every moment," which serves as Nathan's proof, and the clause "did visit him every morning," which Yose cites.} [In Yose's view] "testing" [which is referred to in the clause cited by Nathan] only suggests scrutiny! {Yose rejects the notion that the clause cited by Nathan refers to judgment at all. To prove his point he used a different clause.}

[E] {D's explanation is rejected.} But "visiting" [referred to in the clause cited by Yose] also suggests nothing more than scrutiny! {D has not explained why Yose does not cite the same verse as Nathan.}

[F] {Since it does not explain *why* Yose cites a different verse from Nathan, the following does not in fact answer the question at hand. It simply provides an additional verse that proves that people constantly are judged.} Rather said Rab Hisda, "The Scriptural foundation of R. Yose's view derives[219] from here [1 Kgs. 8:59: 'Let these words of mine,

---

[219]M has the attribution but lacks the rest of the line to this point.

with which I have made supplication before the Lord, be near to the Lord our God day and night], to do the judgment of his servant and the judgment of his people[220] Israel, as each day requires.'"

[IV.A] And said Rab Hisda,[221] "[When] the king and the community [await judgment], the king enters in first for judgment, as it is said [1 Kgs. 8:59: '...to do] the judgment of his servant [Solomon] and [then] the judgment of his people Israel.'"

[B] What is the reason [that the king is judged first]?

[C] If you wish I can argue that[222] it is not proper for the king to remain outside [alone while the people are being judged].

[D] And if you wish I can argue that [the king is judged] before [God has heard the community's sins and] become really angry.

[V.A] Said Rab Joseph,[223] "Whose authority are we following when, these days, we [daily] pray for the sick and the ailing?"

[B] Whose authority? That of R. Yose, [who, we have seen, holds that judgment occurs every day].

[C] But if you wish, I [even] can reason: Indeed, [it is done] according to [the authority of] the rabbis, [M. R.H. 1:2, who hold that people are judged only at New Year].

[D] And [in accepting this view of the rabbis, we interpret their statement] according to [the perspective of] R. Isaac.

[E] For said R. Isaac, "Crying out [that is, supplication] is good for a person whether it occurs prior to or after the [actual] passing of final judgment." {Remembering the sick in daily

---

[220]M lacks the conclusion of the citation.

[221]See above M. R.H. 1:1 L.G-J, 8b.

[222]M introduces the line simply: For.

[223]M and the parallel at B. Ned. 49a read: Rava.

prayers is worthwhile even though judgment already was passed on the preceding New Year.}

[VI.A] It is taught on Tannaitic authority [see T. R.H. 1:12 and T. Suk. 3:18]: Said R. Judah in the name of R. Aqiba, "Why does the Torah state [that the Israelites must] offer the *omer* at [the time of] Passover? Because Passover is the season of [the harvest of] grain.

[B] "The holy one, blessed be he, said, 'Offer before me an *omer* at [the time of] Passover so that the grain in the fields might be blessed for you.'

[C] "And why does the Torah state [that the Israelites must] offer two loaves at Pentecost? Because Pentecost is the season for fruit of the tree. {Simon, p. 60: "The connection between the loaves and fruit lies in the fact that first fruits were not brought to the Temple before Pentecost."}

[D] "The holy one, blessed be he, said, 'Offer before me two loaves at Pentecost so that the fruit of the trees might be blessed for you.'

[E] "And why does the Torah state [that the Israelites must] pour out a water libation at the festival [of Tabernacles]?[224]

[F] "Said the holy one, blessed be he, 'Pour out a water libation before me at the festival [of Tabernacles] so that the rains of the year will be blessed for you.'

[G] "[The holy one further said],[225] 'Also, say before me on New Year [the Scriptural passages concerning][226] sovereignty, remembrance, and [the blowing of] the ram's horn:

[H] "'Sovereignty—so that you will proclaim me king over you.

---

[224]To render the passage parallel to the previous materials, Rif and Rosh add: For the festival [of Tabernacles] is the time of the yearly rains.

[225]M and other sources have the bracketed words explicitly.

[226]M lacks the conclusion of this line, possibly a case of haplography.

[I] "'Remembrance—so that memory of you may rise favorably before me.

[J] "'And through what [will that memory be made to rise]? Through the ram's horn.'"

[VII.A] Said R. Abbahu, "Why do we blow a ram's horn?

[B] "Said the holy one, blessed be he, 'Blow a ram's horn before me[227] so that I will remember in your favor the binding of Isaac, the son of Abraham, and will credit [that act] to you, as though you bound yourselves [before me, willing to offer yourselves as a sacrifice].'"

[VIII.A] And said R. Isaac, "Why do we sound [the ram's horn] on New Year?" {The Hebrew verb used here for "sound" refers specifically to the blowing of the sound called "Tekiah."}

[B] [How can you ask], "Why do we sound [it]?"

[C] {This is obvious.} The merciful told us to sound [it]! {Ps. 81:3 reads: "Sound the trumpet at the new moon, at the full moon, on our feast day."}

[D] Rather [Isaac's question, A, intends to ask], "Why do we blow the Teruah sound?" {We might suppose that this sound is not encompassed by the reference to the Tekiah at Ps. 81:3.}

[E] {Again the question appears obvious.} [How can you ask], "Why do we blow the Teruah sound?"

[F] [It is because] the merciful said [Lev. 23:24: "Say to the people of Israel, 'In the seventh month, on the first day of the month, you shall observe a day of solemn rest], a memorial proclaimed with the blast [*Teruah*] of trumpets.'"[228]

[G] Rather [Isaac's question, A, intends to ask], "Why do they sound the Tekiah and blow the Teruah sitting [**16b**] and

---

[227]M lacks the beginning of this line, the result of haplography.

[228]M and most exegetical sources lack E-F.

[then] sound the Tekiah and blow the Teruah standing?"[229] {On this practice, see Y. R.H. 3:8.}

[H] It is to confuse Satan.[230]

[IX.A] {The theme of the preceding is developed.} And R. Isaac said, "[As for] any year at the beginning of which they do not sound the Tekiah—at the end of it evil will occur.

[B] "What is the reason?

[C] "For they have not confused Satan."

[X.A] And said R. Isaac, "[As for] any year that is poor at the beginning—at its end it becomes rich.

[B] "As it says [in Scripture][231] [Dt. 11:12]: 'From the beginning of the year [to the end of the year].'

[C] "[The phrase 'From the beginning'] is written [without the Hebrew letter *aleph*, so as also to spell] 'from poverty.'

[D] "[The verse then concludes], 'to the end'—[this signifies] a conclusion that is[232] an end." {Simon: "Apparently there is an allusion here to the verse, *'for the latter end of man is peace'*. Ps. XXXVII."}

[XI.A] And said R. Isaac, "A person is judged only on the basis of his actions up to that time,[233] as it is said [Gen. 21:17: 'The angel of God called to Hagar from heaven, and said to her, "What troubles you, Hagar? Fear not], for God has heard the voice of the lad as he is.""'"

---

[229]M lacks the middle of this line, a case of haplography.

[230]Simon: the Accuser.

[231]M introduces this line: What is the basis [in Scripture]? As it is written.... M explicitly includes the conclusion of the citation, found here in brackets.

[232]M and other sources read: a year that has....

[233]"Up to that time" is added in the margin of M.

[XII.A] And said R. Isaac, "Three things call to mind a person's iniquities.

[B] "These are they: a shaky wall, testing of prayer, and requesting [divine] judgment upon one's fellow." {By walking by a teetering wall, the individual tempts fate. "Testing prayer" refers to experimenting to see if prayer produces the desired effect. The third item is explained in the following.}

[C] For said R. Abin,[234] "Whoever requests [divine] judgment on his fellow—he is punished first, as it says [Gen. 16:5]: 'And Sarai said to Abram, "May the wrong done to me be on you!"' {Sarah thus called for divine judgment of Abraham.}

[D] "And [proving that, as a result, she herself was judged first] it is written [after that, Gen. 23:2]: 'And Abraham went in to mourn for Sarah and to weep for her.'"

[XIII.A] And said R. Isaac, "Four things cancel a person's judgment.

[B] "And these are they: charity, crying out [in supplication], change of name, and change of deeds.

[C] "Charity—as it is written [Prov. 10:2: 'Treasures gained by wickedness do not profit], but righteousness delivers from death.'

[D] "Crying out [in supplication]—as it is written [Ps. 107:6]: 'And they cried out to the Lord in their trouble, and he delivered them from their distress.'

[E] "Change of name—as it is written [Gen. 17:15: 'And God said to Abraham],[235] "As for Sarai your wife, you shall not call her name Sarai, but Sarah shall be her name.'" And

---

[234] As indicated in the marginal note in the printed edition, Alfasi to the parallel at B. B.Q. 93a reads: Rab Hanan. This same reading is found in M, Rif, Rosh, and many other manuscript and exegetical sources.

[235] Here and later in the line, M has the bracketed words explicitly.

	[after this statement] it is written [Gen. 17:16]: 'I will bless her, and moreover I will give you a son by her.'
[F]	"Change of deeds—as it is written [Jon. 3:10]: 'When God saw what they did, [how they turned from their evil way....' And [after this statement, in the continuation of the verse] it is written:²³⁶ 'God repented of the evil that he had said he would do to them, and he did not do it].'"
[G]	And some say also [that] changing location [cancels a person's judgment].
[H]	For it is written [Gen. 12:1]: "Now the Lord said to Abram, 'Go from your country [and your kindred and your father's house to the land I will show you].'" And it continues [Gen. 12:2]: "'And I will make of you a great nation, [and I will bless you and make your name great, so that you will be a blessing].'"
[I]	But [as for] the other [that is, Isaac, A—why does he not include in his list changing location]?
[J]	{Isaac rejects H's claim that Gen. 12:1-2 proves that changing location alters a person's fate.} [Isaac holds that, contrary to H's interpretation] here [in the case of Abraham] the merit of [being in] the land of Israel benefited him. {Abraham's becoming great was not related to the simple fact that he had changed locations but, rather, resulted from his going in particular to the land of Israel.}

[XIV.A] And said R. Isaac, "A person is obligated to pay respect to his master [that is, teacher] on [each] festival,

[B] "as it says [2 Kgs. 4:22-23, referring to the story of Elisha and the Shunamite woman: 'Then she called to her husband and said, "Send me one of the servants and one of the asses, that I may quickly go to the man of God and come back again." And he said],²³⁷ "Why will you go to him today? It

---

²³⁶M presents the entire verse, without the interjected: And...it is written.

²³⁷M explicitly includes the final three bracketed words.

is neither the New Moon nor Sabbath.'" {As Simon, p. 62, notes, "Sabbath" here is used as a generic term for all holy days.}

[C] "From [this there is an obvious] inference that on the New Moon and Sabbath one should go."

[XV.A] And said R. Isaac, "A person is obligated to purify himself on [each] festival,

[B] "as it says [Lev. 11:8, referring to swine]: 'and their carcasses you shall not touch—[they are unclean to you].'" {This is explained in the following.}

[C] That which is taught on Tannaitic authority makes the same point—[Lev. 11:8 states]: "And their carcasses you shall not touch—[they are unclean to you]."

[D] Is it logical [to assume] that [at Lev. 11:8 ordinary] Israelites are cautioned regarding touching carcasses?

[E] [Clearly this is not the case, since] Scripture states [elsewhere, Lev. 21:1: "And the Lord said to Moses], 'Speak to the priests, the sons of Aaron, [and say to them that none of them shall defile himself for the dead among his people].'"

[F] The sons of Aaron[238] are cautioned [against contact with a corpse]; the people of Israel are not cautioned.

[G] Now, is there not an argument *a minori ad majus*?

[H] If in the case of the severe uncleanness [of a human corpse, Lev. 21:1], priests are cautioned, but Israelites are not cautioned,

[I] [then, in the case of] the minimal uncleanness [of an animal carcass, Lev. 11:8], all the more so [are priests, but not Israelites, cautioned]!

[J] {H-I proves that Lev. 11:8 cannot mean what it seems to say, that ordinary Israelites may not touch an animal carcass.} What then [is the meaning of that which] Scripture states [Lev. 11:8]: "And their carcasses you shall not touch"?

---

[238]M reads: Priests.

[K]   [The verse applies] on a festival. {This is as Isaac claimed, A, that on festivals Israelites must remain pure.}

[XVI.A]   Said R. Kruspedai said R. Yohanan, "Three books are opened [by God] on the New Year: one for the thoroughly wicked, one for the thoroughly righteous, and one for middling [people].

[B]   "The thoroughly righteous immediately are inscribed and sealed for [continued] life.

[C]   "The thoroughly wicked immediately are inscribed and sealed for death.

[D]   "Middling [people] are left hanging from New Year until the Day of Atonement.

[E]   "[If] they [are found to have] merit, they are inscribed for life.

[F]   "[If] they [are found] not [to have] merit, they are inscribed for death."

[G]   Said R. Abin,[239] "What is the Scriptural [foundation for this]?

[H]   "[Ps. 69:28 states]:[240] 'Let them be blotted out of the book of the living. Let them not be inscribed among the righteous.'

[I]   "'Let them be blotted out of the book'—this refers to the book of the thoroughly wicked.[241]

[J]   "'[... of the] living'—this refers to the book of the[242] righteous.

[K]   "'Let them not be inscribed among the righteous'—this refers to the book of middling [people]."

[L]   Rab Nahman bar Isaac said, "[A-F may be proven] from here [Ex. 32:32, referring to Moses' entreating of God to forgive

---

[239] M reads: Zera. Other sources read: Abbahu.

[240] M reads explicitly: It is written.

[241] M and other sources lack: this refers to the book of the thoroughly wicked.

[242] Here and at N, M adds: thoroughly.

the people's sin: 'So Moses returned to the Lord and said, "...But now, if you will, forgive their sin]. But if not, blot me, I pray, from your book that you have written.'"

[M] "'Blot me, I pray'—this refers to the book of the [thoroughly] wicked.[243]

[N] "'From your book'—this refers to the book of the righteous.

[O] "'That you have written'—this refers to the book of middling [people]."

[XVII.A] It has been taught on Tannaitic authority [see T. San. 13:3]: The House of Shammai say, "[There will be] three groups on the Day of Judgment [when the dead will rise]: one [comprised] of the thoroughly righteous, one [comprised] of the thoroughly wicked, and one of middling [people].

[B] "The thoroughly righteous immediately are inscribed and sealed for eternal life.[244]

[C] "The thoroughly wicked immediately are inscribed and sealed for Gehenna.[245]

[D] "[We know B and C to be the case] as it is said [Dan. 12:2]: 'And many of those who sleep in the dust of the earth shall awake, some to eternal life and some to shame and everlasting contempt.'

[E] "Middling [people] go down to Gehenna [17a], scream [in prayer],[246] and rise [again],

[F] "as it is said [Zech. 13:9]: 'And I will put this third into the fire and refine them as one refines silver and test them as

---

[243] M and other sources lack this line.

[244] M and other sources read: for life of the world to come.

[245] M reads: death.

[246] So Jastrow, p. 1298, s.v., *ṢPṢP*. Simon, p. 64: squeal.

gold is tested.²⁴⁷ They will call on my name, and I will answer them.'

[G] "And concerning this group, Hannah said [1 Sam. 2:6]: 'The Lord kills and brings to life. He brings down to Sheol and raises up.'"

[H] {The Hillelites reject the notion that the middling group initially is sent to Gehenna.} The House of Hillel say, "But [contrary to what the Shammaites hold, God] who abounds in mercy leans towards [a judgment of] mercy.

[I] "And concerning them [that is, the middling group] David said [Ps. 116:1]: 'I love the Lord, because he has heard my voice [and my supplications].'

[J] "And [further] concerning them David stated²⁴⁸ the whole passage [that begins, Ps. 116:6: 'The Lord preserves the simple]; when I was brought low, he saved me.'"

[XVIII.A] Israelite wrongdoers [who sin] with their body and gentile wrongdoers [who sin] with their body go down to Gehenna and are judged [i.e., punished] there for twelve months.

[B] After twelve months their body is consumed [in fire], their soul is burned, and a wind scatters them²⁴⁹ under the feet of the righteous.

[C] [This is] as it says [Mal. 4:3]: "And you shall tread down the wicked, for they will be ashes under the soles of your feet [on the day when I act, says the Lord of hosts]."

[D] But²⁵⁰ the sectarians, the informers, and heretics, who denied the Torah, who denied the resurrection of the dead, who separated themselves from the ways of the community, who

---

²⁴⁷M lacks the conclusion of the citation.

²⁴⁸M and other manuscripts read: was stated.

²⁴⁹M adds: and they are made dust.

²⁵⁰M as well as all other manuscripts and early printings add: the apostates.

	tyrannized the land of the living, and who sinned and caused many others to sin—such as Jeroboam son of Nebat and his associates[251]—[these individuals] go down to Gehenna and are judged there for generations.
[E]	[This is] as it says [Is. 66:24]: "And they shall go forth and look on the dead bodies of the men who have rebelled against me. [For their worm shall not die, their fire shall not be quenched, and they shall be an abhorrence to all flesh]."
[F]	Gehenna will be consumed [by fire], but they will not be consumed,
[G]	as it says [Ps. 49:14]: "And their form shall waste away; Sheol shall be their habitation."
[H]	Now, [as for] all of this [punishment]—why? {The reason, I-J, appears to be that those listed at D caused the destruction of the Jerusalem Temple. But because the Scriptural citation at I is not to the point, the weight of the proof is not entirely clear.}
[I]	Because they place their hands on the habitation, as it says [Ps. 49:14: "Death shall be their shepherd; straight to the grave they descend, and their form shall waste away; Sheol shall be] their habitation."[252]
[J]	And [the term] "habitation" refers only to the Temple sanctuary, as it says [1 Kgs. 8:13, concerning Solomon's completion of the Temple]: "I have built you an exalted habitation, [a place for you to dwell for ever]."[253]
[K]	And concerning those [listed at D] Hannah said [1 Sam. 2:10]: "The adversaries of the Lord shall be broken to pieces."

---

[251]See 1 Kgs. 11:26ff.

[252]Disregarding the Hebrew text, in order to make sense of the proof, Simon renders the verse: "That there be no habitation for Him."

[253]M explicitly contains the bracketed conclusion of the citation.

[L]   Said R. Isaac bar Abin,[254] "Now, their faces shall look like the sides of a pot [that is, black and charred]."

[M]   And said Rava, "And these are the most handsome of the people of Mehoza, and they shall be called, 'sons of Gehenna.'"[255]

[XIX.A]   Said a master:[256] [At unit **XVII**.H] the House of Hillel say, "But [God] who abounds in mercy leans towards [a judgment of] mercy."

[B]   Now, [suggesting the contrary], thus it is written [Zech. 13:9, taken at unit **XVII**.F to refer to middling people]: "And I will put this third into the fire."

[C]   {The Talmud explains that Zech. 13:9 does not disprove the Hillelites' contention.} There [in the Hillelites' statement, quoted at A, we speak of] Israelite wrongdoers [who sin] with their body.

[D]   {C seems unacceptable.} [How can the Hillelites' statement that God leans towards mercy refer to] Israelite wrongdoers [who sin] with their body?[257]

[E]   For, indeed, you have said that they have no remedy [but are doomed]. {Unit **XVIII**.A-B states that, after twelve months in Gehenna, such people's bodies are consumed in fire, their souls are burned, and a wind scatters them under the feet of the righteous.}

---

[254]M lacks: bar Abin.

[255]Simon, p. 65, n. 9, suggests accepting M's reading of K-M, which he renders: "Of them (of the intermediate class) Hannah said *The Lord killeth and maketh alive, he bringeth down to the grave and bringeth up*". R. Isaac b. Abin said, And their faces (that is, of the intermediate class) shall (on rising from Gehinnom) be black like the sides of the pot. Raba added, And yet (despite this disfigurement) they shall be more beautiful than the most handsome men of Mahuza who shall be called the sons of Gehinnom."

[256]M and other manuscript sources lack: Said a master.

[257]M lacks this line. The meaning of the passage is not altered.

[F] {E is not accurate.} They have no remedy [only]²⁵⁸ when their wrongdoings are more numerous [than their good deeds].

[G] Here [in the Hillelites' pronouncement we speak of people who have]²⁵⁹ an equal number of wrongdoings and merits, but whose wrongdoings include those of Israelite wrongdoers [who sin] with their body.

[H] Their [judgment] will not be fulfilled until [they experience what is described in Zech. 13:9]: "And I will put this third into the fire."

[I] But if [we speak of people who are] not [in the category of Israelite wrongdoers who sin with their body, they are subject to the principle]: "But [God] who abounds in mercy leans towards [a judgment of] mercy."

[J] And concerning them said David [Ps. 116:1]: "I love the Lord, because he has heard [my voice and my supplications]."²⁶⁰

[K] Rava explained, "What is the meaning of that which is written [Ps. 116:1]: 'I love the Lord, because he has heard [my voice and my supplications]'?

[L] "The community of Israel stated in the presence of the holy one, blessed be he: 'Master of the world!²⁶¹ When am I beloved before you? When you hear the voice of my supplication.'

[M] {The community of Israel continues its statement, as reported by Rava:} "'[Ps. 116:6 states]: "When I was made poor,²⁶² he saved me." Even though I am poor in [the

---

²⁵⁸M lacks the beginning of this line.

²⁵⁹M explicitly reads: we speak of.

²⁶⁰M explicitly contains the bracketed conclusion of the citation.

²⁶¹In the following, M refers to God in the third person.

²⁶²Normally translated: brought low.

observance of] commandments, it pleases [God] to save me.'"

[XX.A] {Unit **XVIII** is explicated.} [As for] "wrongdoers of Israel [who sin] with their body"—who are they?

[B] Said Rab,²⁶³ "[Reference is to] a cranium that does not put on a phylactery."

[C] [As for] "gentile wrongdoers [who sin] with their body"—[who are they]?²⁶⁴

[D] Said Rab, "[People who erred] through [sexual] impropriety."

[E] [Unit **XVIII**.D refers to those] "who tyrannized the land of the living."

[F] Said Rab Hisda, "This is a leader of the community who spreads excessive fear upon the community other than for the purpose of [promoting the demands of God in] heaven."

[G] Said R. Judah said Rab, "Every leader of the community who spreads excessive fear upon the community other than for the purpose of [promoting the demands of God in] heaven will never have²⁶⁵ a son who is a disciple of a sage.

[H] "[We know this to be the case] as it is said [Job 37:24]: 'Therefore people fear him. He shall not see any who are wise of heart.'

[XXI.A] {We again explicate unit **XVII**.H.} The House of Hillel say, "But [God] who abounds in mercy leans towards [a judgment of] mercy."

[B] How does [God] act?

---

²⁶³M lacks the attribution, possibly a scribal error (Rabbinovicz).

²⁶⁴M has the bracketed words explicitly.

²⁶⁵Literally: see.

[C]   R. Eleazar[266] says, "He presses down on it." {Rashi: God presses down on the side of the balance-scale representing merit],

[D]   "as it is said [Mic. 7:19]: 'He will again have compassion upon us. He will push down our iniquities.'"[267]

[E]   R. Yose bar Hanina[268] said, "He raises [the side of the balance-scale representing wrongdoings],

[F]   "as it is said [Mic. 7:18: 'Who is a God like you], raising[269] iniquity and passing over transgression.'"

[G]   It is taught on Tannaitic authority in the house of R. Ishmael: He passes over the first transgression [of each type], and this is [God's] attribute [of mercy].

[H]   Said Rava, "But the transgression itself is not erased, so that, if there [turns out to] be a majority of transgressions, [God] considers it with the others."

[XXII.A] Rava said, "[As for] anyone who passes over his right [to exact punishment against another], they pass over all of his transgressions,

[B]   "as it says [Mic. 7:18: 'Who is a God like you], pardoning iniquity and passing over transgression.'[270]

[C]   "For whom does [God] pardon iniquity? For the one who pardons transgression [in others]."

[D]   {A-C's theory is illustrated.} Rab Huna the son of Rab Joshua was ill. Rab Pappa entered to ask about him. He saw that he was in his final illness.

---

[266]So M. P: Eliezer.

[267]The verse continues: under foot.

[268]M reads simply: R. Hanina.

[269]Normally translated: pardoning. M and other sources lack the beginning of this line, through this word.

[270]M has the continuation of the citation: ...for the remnant of his inheritance? He does not retain his anger forever because he delights in steadfast love.

[E]	[Pappa therefore] said to those [present], "Prepare a [burial] shroud for him!"
[F]	In the end [however, Huna] recovered. Rab Pappa[271] was embarrassed to see him.
[G]	They said to him, "[When you were ill] what did you see?"[272]
[H]	[Huna] said to them, "Indeed, it was as [Pappa thought], but the holy one, blessed be he, said to them [that is, to the heavenly court], 'Since [Huna] did not assert his rights [against others], do not assert [yourselves] against him,'
[I]	"as it says [Mic. 7:18]:[273] 'Pardoning iniquity and passing over transgression.'
[J]	"For whom does [God] pardon iniquity? For the one who pardons transgression [in others]."

[XXIII.A]	{We continue with an unrelated analysis of the continuation of Mic. 7:18.} "[Who is a God like you, pardoning iniquity and passing over transgression] for the remnant of his inheritance?"
[B]	Said R. Aha bar Hanina,[274] "[This is like] a fat tail that has a thorn in it.
[C]	"[God passes over transgression] 'for the remnant of his inheritance,' but not for all [the people] of his inheritance!"
[D]	{The Talmud responds that matters are not so bad as B-C suggests.} [17b] [The verse means that God passes over the transgression of] whoever makes himself as though he were a remnant [by humbling himself and behaving like the righteous (Rashi)].

---

[271]M lacks: R. Pappa.

[272]M and all other manuscripts lack this entire line

[273]M has the beginning of the verse: Who is a God like you?

[274]M lacks the attribution.

[**XXIV**.A] Rab Huna pointed out an [apparent] inconsistency [within a single biblical verse]:

[B] "It is written [Ps. 145:17]: 'The Lord is just in all his ways.'

[C] "And [in the continuation of the same verse] it is written,[275] 'and kind in all his doings.'" {Huna suggests that it is impossible to be just and kind at the same time.}

[D] {There is no contradiction.} [The point is that] at first [God is] "just" and, at the end, [he is] "kind."

[**XXV**.A] R. Eleazar pointed out an [apparent] inconsistency:

[B] "It is written [Ps. 62:12]: 'And to you, Lord, belongs kindness.'

[C] "And [in the continuation of the same verse] it is written, 'For you requite a man according to his deeds.' {How can God be kind and, at the same time, judge a man according to his deeds?}

[D] At first—"For you requite a man according to his deeds." And, at the end—"And to you, Lord, belongs kindness."

[**XXVI**.A] Ilpi, and some say[276] Ilpa, pointed out an [apparent] inconsistency:

[B] "It is written [Ex. 34:6]: 'and abounding in kindness.'

[C] "And [in the continuation of the same verse] it is written, 'and truth.' {How can God be kind and, at the same time, judge a man according to the truth?}

[D] At first—"and truth." And, at the end—"and abounding in kindness."

[**XXVII**.A] {The Talmud presents an unrelated interpretation of the beginning of Ex. 34:6.} "The Lord passed before him and proclaimed...."

---

[275]Here and at **XXV**.C, M lacks the beginning of the line, presenting the verse of Scripture continuously.

[276]M inserts the honorific: R.

[B]	Said R. Yohanan, "Had Scripture not stated this [explicitly] we would not be able to claim it.

[C]	"[This verse] teaches that the holy one, blessed be he, wrapped himself [in his prayer shawl] like the representative of the community [who leads the prayer service] and showed Moses[277] the order of the prayers.

[D]	"[God] said to him, 'Whenever [the people of] Israel sin, they should perform before me this order [of worship], and I shall forgive them.'"[278]

[XXVIII.A]	{We continue the interpretation of the passage at Ex. 34:6-7.} "The Lord, the Lord"—[this means]: "I am he before a person sins, and I am he[279] after a person sins and repents."

[B]	"A God merciful and gracious"[280]—said Rab Judah,[281] "A covenant has been made through the thirteen attributes [enumerated in these verses], so that [the people of Israel] will not return empty handed [upon reciting them].

[C]	"[This is] as it says [Ex. 34:10]: 'Behold, I make a covenant.'"[282]

[XXIX.A]	Said R. Yohanan, "Great is [the power of] repentance, which obliterates a person's final judgment.

[B]	"[This is] as it says [Is. 6:10]: 'Make the heart of this people fat and their ears heavy and shut their eyes, lest they see with

---

[277]M adds "our rabbi" and then lacks the conclusion of the line.

[278]M concludes the sentence: their sins.

[279]M lacks the conclusion of the line, a scribal error.

[280]M and other manuscripts continue with the rest of the verse: "slow to anger, and abounding in steadfast love and faithfulness."

[281]M lacks: Judah.

[282]M continues with the conclusion of the verse: "Before all your people I will do marvels."

	their eyes[283] and hear with their ears and understand with their hearts and repent and be healed.'" {If people repent, they will be healed, meaning that a negative judgment will be reversed. This is as A claims.}
[C]	[Suggesting that the verse at B does not prove Yohanan's claim] said Rab Pappa to Abayye, "But perhaps [Is. 6:10's notion that if people repent they will be healed applies only] before the final decree [is made]?" {In this view, contrary to Yohanan, repentance does not have the power to obliterate an already finalized judgment.}
[D]	[Rejecting C, Abayye] said to him, "[At Is. 6:10] 'and[284] be healed' is written.
[E]	"Which thing [leads the individual to] require healing? Let us say [it is] the final decree!" {Hence the power of repentance is as Yohanan, A, said.}
[F]	{Yohanan's view of the power of repentance again is challenged.} They objected: "[We know a teaching that states that if a wrongdoer] repented in the meantime [that is, between New Year and the Day of Atonement, his transgressions] are forgiven.
[G]	"If he did not repent in the meantime, even if he brought [as sacrifices] all of the rams of Nebayot, he will not be forgiven." {The efficacy of repentance is restricted to a specific period. Repentance does not have the power Yohanan ascribes to it.}
[H]	There is not contradiction [between the teaching cited at F-G and Yohanan's statement, A].
[I]	This [latter statement, at F-G, refers] to an individual. This [former statement, at A, refers] to a community.
[J]	{Yohanan's view of the power of repentance again is challenged, J-S.} They objected [on the following grounds:

---

[283]M lacks the conclusion of the verse.

[284]M reads: turn and

Referring to the land of Israel, Dt. 11:12 states]: "The eyes of the Lord your God are always upon it"[285]—[which means] sometimes for good and sometimes for evil.

[K] "Sometimes for good"—how so?

[L] Lo, if at New Year [the people of] Israel were [in the category of people who are] thoroughly evil, so that insubstantial rains were decreed for them, [but], in the end, they turned [and changed their ways]—

[M] [for God] to supply additional [rain] is impossible, since the judgment already has been decreed.

[N] Rather, the holy one, blessed be he, brings down [the rain] at the proper time, upon the land that requires it, entirely according to [the needs of the particular plot of] land. {But the amount of rain, previously decreed, does not change.}

[O] "Sometimes for evil"—how so?

[P] Lo, if at New Year [the people of] Israel were [in the category of people who are] thoroughly righteous, so that substantial rains were decreed for them, [but], in the end, they turned [and changed their ways]—

[Q] [for God] to supply less rain is impossible, since the judgment already has been decreed.

[R] Rather, the holy one, blessed be he, brings down [the rain] at the wrong time, upon land that does not require it. {The previously decreed quantity of rain does not change. But the rain is made to fall in areas in which it is wasted.}

[S] {Based upon the material at J-R, the objection to Yohanan's view, A, is as follows:} [If, as Yohanan claims, in response to repentance, the decree will be rescinded], for [the case of individuals who changed their ways to the] good, at least, let the judgment be rescinded so as to increase for them [the quantity of rain]! {The fact that the quantity of rain is not

---

[285]M has the conclusion of the verse: "from the beginning of the year to the end of the year."

increased proves that repentance does not have the power Yohanan ascribes to it.}

[T] {S's argument is rejected.} There[286] [in the case of a decree regarding the quantity of rain] it is different, since it is possible to [solve the problem by doing] that [which is described at N]. {In this case actually altering the decree is not necessary and therefore is not done. This reflects the special nature of the circumstance, not a limitation of the power Yohanan attributes to repentance.}

[U] Come and learn [a further challenge to Yohanan's position, A]:

[V] [Ps. 107:23-31 states:] "Some went down to the sea in ships, doing business on the great waters. They saw the deeds of the Lord, [his wondrous works in the deep]. For he commanded and raised the stormy wind, which lifted up the waves of the sea. [They mounted up to heaven, they went down to the depths. Their courage melted away in their evil plight]. They reeled and staggered like drunken men [and were at their wits' end]. Then they cried to the Lord in their trouble, [and he delivered them from their distress. He made the storm be still, and the waves of the sea were hushed. Then they were glad because they had quiet, and he brought them to their desired haven]. Let them thank the Lord for his steadfast love, [for his wonderful works to the sons of men]!"[287]

[W] [The holy one, blessed be he][288] made them signs corresponding to the "buts" and "onlys" in the Torah, so as to teach you [that if] they cried [in supplication to the Lord] prior to the passing of [their] final judgment, they were answered. {Reference is to an inverted Hebrew letter

---

[286] M reads: Here.

[287] M includes the bracketed sections of the verse explicitly.

[288] M has the bracketed words explicitly.

("nun") that appears in the Masoretic text before a number of the verses of this psalm.}

[X] But if they cried[289] [to the Lord] after [their] final judgment was passed, they were not answered. {Repentance does not have the unmitigated power Yohanan ascribes to it.}

[Y] {V-X's challenge to Yohanan's understanding of the power of repentance is rejected.} Here too the people are treated as individuals! {We already know, F-I, that for individuals, repentance is not invariably efficacious. Yohanan's view applies only to the case of a community. V-X does not disprove Yohanan's theory.}

[XXX.A] {The conclusion of the following formally and topically unrelated story makes the same point that appears in the prior unit: for individuals, forgiveness is possible only until final judgment has been passed.} Come and learn:

[B] Valeria, the proselyte, questioned Rabban Gamaliel:[290] "It is written in your Torah [at Dt. 10:17: 'For the Lord your God is God of gods and Lord of lords...], who does not lift his countenance[291] [and takes no bribe].'

[C] "But [by contrast, at Num. 6:26] it is written: 'May the Lord lift up his countenance upon you, [and give you peace.]'" {These passages appear contradictory.}

[D] R. Yose the Priest joined her and said, "I will tell you a parable illustrating the matter:[292]

[E] "[This is] as in [the case of] a man who lent his associate a *maneh* and, in the presence of the king, established a time [for repayment]. And [the borrower] swore to him on the life of the king [that he would repay the loan].

---

[289]In M, the first words of this line are implicit.

[290]M lacks: Rabban Gamaliel.

[291]RSV: who is not partial.

[292]So Simon. Literally: what the thing is like.

[F] "The time came, and he did not repay it. He [therefore] went to make peace with the king.

[G] "But [the king]²⁹³ said to him, '[For] the insult done to me, I forgive you. Go and make peace with your associate [who lent you the money].'

[H] "So too [is the distinction between the verses quoted at B and C]:

[I] "Here [at Num. 6:26, which refers to God's lifting his countenance in forgiveness, reference is] to transgressions that are between a person and the omnipresent.

[J] "[But] here [at Dt. 10:17, which states that God does not lift his countenance in forgiveness, reference is] to transgressions that are between one person and another."²⁹⁴

[K] [This explanation was accepted] until R. Aqiba came and taught: [**18a**] "This [at Num. 6:26, which refers to God's lifting his countenance in forgiveness, applies] prior to the passing of the final judgment.

[L] "[But] this [at Dt. 10:17, which states that God does not lift his countenance in forgiveness, applies] after the passing of the final judgment."

[M] {The following rejects Aqiba's notion that forgiveness ever is impossible, returning instead to the notion with which the previous unit ends, that different rules apply to individuals and communities.} Here too we are dealing with an individual! {We know from unit **XXIX**.F-I that, for individuals, repentance is efficacious only up to the point of the final judgment. But in the case of a community that repents, God will forgive at any time.}

[**XXXI**.A] {The Talmud now examines the larger question of God's handling of the final judgment of an individual.} Now, [the rule for] the final judgment of an individual [is under dispute

---

²⁹³M has the bracketed term explicitly.

²⁹⁴M and other sources reverse the order of I and J.

	by] Tannaitic authorities.[295] {Meir, B-I, holds that whether or not final judgment has been passed has no impact on the effectiveness of the individual's repentance. Eleazar, J, disagrees.}
[B]	For it is taught on Tannaitic authority: R. Meir used to say, "[As for] two [men] who took to bed with the same illness,
[C]	"and so [in the case of] two men who ascended the scaffold to be punished for the same offense—
[D]	"this one leaves [bed alive], while this [other] one does not leave [the bed alive],
[E]	"this one escapes [death], while this [other] one does not escape [death].
[F]	"Why did this one leave [bed alive], while this [other] one did not leave [the bed alive], this one escape [death], while this [other] one did not escape [death]?
[G]	"[In each case] this one [who was saved] prayed and [his prayer] was answered, while this [other] one [who was not saved] prayed, but [his prayer] was not answered.
[H]	"Why was this one answered while this [other] one was not answered?[296]
[I]	"This one offered a sincere[297] prayer and [therefore] was answered, while this [other] one did not offer a sincere prayer and [therefore] was not answered."
[J]	[Disagreeing] R. Eleazar[298] said, "Here [in the case of the individual who was saved] it was prior to the passing of the final judgment; here [in the case of the individual who was not saved] it was after the passing of the final judgment."

---

[295]M and other manuscripts reads: Now, [as to the rule for] the final judgment of an individual—[we return to] the substance of this issue. It is [under dispute by] Tannaitic authorities.

[296]M lacks this line.

[297]Literally: "complete," or "perfect."

[298]M reads: Eliezer.

[K] [Agreeing with Meir], R. Isaac said "Crying out [that is, supplication] is good for a person whether it occurs prior to or after the [actual] passing of final judgment." {See above, B. R.H. 1:2 V.E, 16a.}

[XXXII.A] {The Talmud now examines the larger question of God's handling of the final judgment of a community.} Now, can the final judgment of a community indeed be revoked [once it has been passed]?

[B] Now [two verses contradict each other regarding this, for][299] thus it is written in one text [Jer. 4:14: "Jerusalem], wash your heart from wickedness, [that you may be saved];"

[C] while [in a different place] it is written [Jer. 2:22]: "'Though you wash yourself with lye and use much soap, the stain of your guilt is still before me,' [says the Lord God]."

[D] Indeed, does this [verse, cited at B] not pertain prior to passing of the final judgment, while this [verse, cited at C] applies after the passing of the final judgment? {If this is so, then in the case of the community repentance is efficacious only prior to the passing of the final judgment.}

[E] {Rejecting D's explanation:} No! Both [statements] apply after passing of the final judgment.

[F] But [even so] there is no contradiction:[300]

[G] This [verse, cited at C, which denies the efficacy of supplication] pertains to a final judgment accompanied by an oath, while this [verse, cited at B, which assumes that repentance works] applies to a final judgment that is not accompanied by an oath.

[H] This accords with [the view of] Rab Samuel bar Imi, for said Rab Samuel bar Imi, and some say, said Rab Samuel bar Nahmani, said R. Yohanan, "From what passage in Scripture

---

[299] M has the bracketed words explicitly here and in the verse that follows.

[300] M lacks this line.

	do we know that a final judgment accompanied by an oath never is revoked?
[I]	"[This is] as it is said [1 Sam. 3:14]: 'Therefore I swear to the house of Eli that the iniquity of Eli's house shall not be expiated by sacrifice or offering [for ever].'"
[J]	{Rava argues that I does not prove H's contention that a final judgment accompanied by an oath under no circumstances is revoked.} Said Rava, "[1 Sam. 3:14 means nothing more than that] through sacrifice or offering [the transgression of the house of Eli] will not be atoned.
[K]	"But it will be atoned through [study of] Torah."
[L]	Abayye said, "Through sacrifice or offering [the transgression of the house of Eli] will not be atoned. But it will be atoned through Torah and acts of loving kindness."[301]
[M]	Rabbah[302] and Abayye were of the house of Eli.
[N]	Rabbah, who engaged in [study of] Torah, lived forty years.
[O]	Abayye, who engaged in [study of] Torah and acts of loving kindness, lived sixty years.
[XXXIII.A]	{The following story develops the reference to the house of Eli and the efficacy of Torah study.} Our rabbis have taught on Tannaitic authority: There once was a family in Jerusalem whose [members] would die at the age of eighteen years. They came and informed Rabban Yohanan b. Zakkai.
[B]	He said to them, "Perhaps you are of the house of Eli?
[C]	"For concerning them it is written [1 Sam 2:33]: 'And all the increase of your house shall die [as young] men.'[303]

---

[301]M lacks this line, a case of haplography.

[302]So Tosafot, whose emendation appears in the printed text. Other sources have "Rava," who was not a priest.

[303]RSV: "and all the increase of your house shall die *by the sword of* men."

[D]	"Go and engage [yourselves in study of] Torah that you might live!"

[E]	They went and engaged in [study of] Torah and [as a result] they lived [to an old age].

[F]	And [thereafter people] referred to this [family] as the family of Rabban[304] Yohanan, after his name.

[XXXIV.A]	{We return to the rules for the final judgment of a community.} Said Rab Samuel bar Inia in the name of Rab, "From what [verse in Scripture] do we know that the final judgment of a community is never sealed?"

[B]	{A's underlying claim is rejected.} Never sealed?[305]

[C]	But [indicating the contrary] thus it is written [Jer. 2:22: "'Though you wash yourself with lye and use much soap], the stain of your guilt is still before me,' [says the Lord God]."

[D]	{In light of C, to uphold A's larger point, we must rephrase Samuel's question as follows:} Rather [how do we know that] even after [the judgment of a community][306] is sealed, it can be revoked?

[E]	For it says [Dt. 4:7: "For what great nation is there that has a god so near to it] as the Lord our God [is to us], whenever we call upon him?" {The fact that God listens "whenever we call" proves that the community's judgment is never final.}

[F]	But [to the contrary, suggesting that God is not always available] it is written [Is. 55:6]: "Seek the Lord while he may be found, [call upon him while he is near]."

[G]	That [verse] applies to an individual, [whose final judgment, we already know, cannot be changed], while here [at E] reference is to a community.

---

[304]M lacks: Rabban.

[305]M lacks this line.

[306]M has these and the preceding bracketed words explicitly.

[**XXXV**.A] {This unit develops the notion of F-G in the preceding materials, that individuals must call upon God while he may be found.} As for an individual—when [should he call upon God so as to alter his sentence]?

[B] Said[307] Rabbah bar Abbuha, "During the ten days between New Year and the Day of Atonement."

[C] {We have additional evidence for the significance of the ten days between New Year and the Day of Atonement.} [1 Sam. 25:38 states]:[308] "And about ten days later the Lord smote Nabal."

[D] Ten days? What is their significance? {That is, why was Nabal allowed ten days before his final judgment was imposed?}

[E] Said Rab Judah said Rab, "[The ten days of respite] correspond to the ten meals Nabal gave to David's servants." {See 1 Sam. 25:5-8.}

[F] Said[309] Rab Nahman said Rabbah bar Abbuha, "These were the ten days between New Year and the Day of Atonement."

[**XXXVI**.A] *At the New Year all who enter the world pass before Him like troops* [M. R.H. 1:2D].

[B] What is the meaning of [the term "Benei Maron," translated here] "*like troops*"?

[C] Here [in Babylonia] it was translated "like sheep."

[D] Resh Laqish said, "[It refers to the fact that people pass before God] as [though they were going through] the pass of Beth Maron." {Reference apparently is to a narrow pass, through which people would need to walk single-file.}

[E] Said Rab Judah said Samuel, "[They pass in review] like the troops of the house of David."

---

[307]M and all manuscripts read: Said Rab Nahman said Rabbah bar Abbuha.

[308]M adds: As it is stated.

[309]M lacks this word

[F] Said Rabbah bar bar Hannah said R. Yohanan,[310] "[Even though individuals pass by God single-file] still, all of them are examined [together], with a single glance."

[G] Said Rab Nahman bar Isaac, "Indeed we also have learned this on Tannaitic authority: [Ps. 33:14-15 reads: 'From where he sits enthroned he looks out upon all the inhabitants of the earth], he who fashions together the hearts of them all, who observes all their deeds.'

[H] "What does this mean?

[I] "Shall I reason it means that [God] created everyone on earth and unites their hearts together?

[J] "But [that is impossible, since] we see that it is not the case. {People on earth are not united.}

[K] "Rather, does it not mean the following?—The creator sees [into] their hearts together and observes all their deeds."

1:3

[A] *On the occasion of six new moons messengers go forth:*

[B] *(1) at Nisan, because of Passover; (2) at Ab, because of the fast; (3) at Elul, because of the New Year; (4) at Tishre, because of the determination of the set feasts; (5) at Kislev, because of Hanukkah; and (6) at Adar, because of Purim.*

[C] *And when the Temple stood, they would go forth also at Iyyar, because of the lesser Passover [observed by those unclean for the first Passover].*

Before the calendar was fixed in the mid third century C.E., the beginning of the new month was determined by the appearance of the new moon in the land of Israel. This information then needed to be conveyed to Jewish communities in Babylonia, so that they could correct their calendar to the actual appearance of the new moon. The speedy transmittal of this information, by special messengers, was particularly important in months that contained festivals or

---

[310] M lacks the attribution to Yohanan.

other special days. These would be observed on the correct day only if word arrived from the land of Israel indicating when the new month had actually begun.

Units **I-II** explain that messengers were sent forth in Ab but not in other months containing fast days because of the special status of the fast of the ninth of Ab. This explanation of M. R.H. 1:3B(2) introduces a sizable sub-unit on the Scroll of Fasting, which lists dates on which joyous events occurred in the Second Temple period and on which fasting subsequently was prohibited. At issue for the Talmud is whether or not the destruction of the Second Temple had overridden the prohibitions, so that fasting would now be permitted on dates discussed in the scroll. Units **III-VI** provide talmudic arguments that the destruction of the Temple did not change things. The Scroll remains in effect; fasting still is prohibited on the days it lists. Unit **VII** presents a Tannaitic dispute on the same issue.

Units **VIII** and **IX+X-XII** explain the use of messengers in Tishre and discuss the special problem presented by second Adar, the thirteenth month of an embolismic year, added to maintain the correspondence between the lunar and solar calendars. Analysis of the items listed M. R.H. 1:3B concludes the Talmud's directly exegetical interests. Now it takes up general issues regarding the determination of the calendar. Units **XIII-XV** concern the practice of adding an extra day to Elul to prevent New Year or the Day of Atonement from falling on a Sunday, thereby creating a Sabbath-festival sequence. Amoraic authorities dispute why one might want to prevent such a sequence in the first place and discuss whether or not, to accomplish this purpose, witnesses to the appearance of the new moon may be forced to alter their testimony.

Samuel's claim, unit **XVI**, to have fixed the calendar for the diaspora is rejected. Abba suggests that Samuel does not have the knowledge necessary to accomplish this task. The claim that the calendar has not been fixed introduces discussions of the nature of the appearance of the new moon (units **XVII-XVIII**), details regarding how the calendar in the diaspora is corrected when it turns out that an extra day must be added to a month already in progress (unit **XIX**), and examples of how specific rabbis responded to the possibility that, in the diasopra, the Day of Atonement could wind up being observed on the wrong day (units **XX-XXIV**). These materials conclude (unit **XXV**) with a brief discussion of the intercalation of the year and a review of the method by which sailors at sea should determine when the new month begins (unit **XXVI**).

[I.A] {Why were messengers sent out only on the occasions listed at M. R.H. 1:3?} Now, [messengers] should also go forth at Tamuz [the seventeenth of which is a fast day] and Tevet [the tenth of which is a fast day]!

[B] [**18b**] For, [indicating that these months contain fasts], said Rab Hanna bar Biznah said R. Simeon the Pious, "What is written [Zech. 8:19]? 'Thus says the Lord of hosts: "The fast of the fourth month, the fast of the fifth, the fast of the seventh, and the fast of the tenth shall be to the house of Judah [seasons of] joy and gladness [and cheerful feasts].""'"311

[C] {The following points out an inconsistency in the verse. In context, the point seems to be that, since the referenced days are not always fasts, messengers need not be sent out to announce their month.} [God] called them "fasts," and he called them "[seasons of] joy and gladness."

[D] {How can they be both fasts and times of joy?}312 In times of peace they shall be [seasons of] joy and gladness. [If] there is no peace, [they are] fasts.

[E] [Offering a different explanation] said Rab Pappa, "This is the meaning: In times of peace they shall be [seasons of] joy and gladness.

[F] "[If] there is [a period of] persecution decreed by the government,313 [they are] fasts.

311M has the bracketed conclusion of the verse explicitly.

312All manuscripts add: Rather, is [the following] not what it means?

313M and Ritba introduce this line: If there is no peace and there is persecution....

[G] "[If] there is not [a period of] persecution decreed by the government but also not peace,[314] those who so desire fast, and those who [do not] wish [to fast] do not fast."

[H] {Pappa's notion that these are optional fasts is rejected through reference to a different fast day which, on his theory, should be optional, but which, everyone agrees, is incumbent upon the entire community.} If it is the case [as Pappa states, that the fasts in Tamuz and Tevet are optional], then the [fast of the] ninth of Ab also [should be optional]. {The same circumstances described at E-G apply on the ninth of Ab. Since that fast is not optional, it is clear that, contrary to Pappa, the fasts of Tevet and Tamuz likewise are not optional. The question of why messengers do not go forth to announce these months stands.}

[I] {Pappa responds to H's criticism by arguing that the comparison with the ninth of Ab is inappropriate.} Said Rab Pappa, "The case of the ninth of Ab is different,[315] since many misfortunes occurred on that date.

[J] "For a master said [M. Ta. 4:6]: *On the ninth of Ab [the decree was made against our forefathers that they should not enter the land], the Temple was destroyed the first and second time, Betar was taken, and the city [of Jerusalem] was plowed up [after the war of Hadrian]*."

[II.A] It is taught on Tannaitic authority: Said R. Simeon [b. Yohai], "R. Aqiba expounded four verses, but I do not interpret [them] like him."[316]

[B] {In B-L, Simeon reports one of Aqiba's interpretations:} "[In reference to Zech. 8:19, cited above, unit I.B, Aqiba said],

---

[314]M and Ritba read: If there is no peace but there is not persecution....

[315]The beginning of the quotation is added in the margin of M.

[316]See T. Sot. 6:6ff., which lists the other interpretations in which Simeon differed. In error, M reads: and I interpret them like him.

[C] "'The fast of the fourth [month]'—this is the ninth[317] of Tamuz, on which [the wall of] the city [of Jerusalem] was breached,

[C] "'as it says [Jer. 52:5-7: "So the city was besieged until the eleventh year of King Zedekiah.] On the ninth day of the fourth month the famine was so severe in the city that there was no food for the people of the land.[318] Then a breach was made in [the wall of] the city."[319]

[D] "'Now, why is it called the fourth [month]? It is the fourth [in the sequence] of months.'"

[E] {Simeon's report of Aqiba's interpretation of Zech. 8:19 continues:} "'"The fast of the fifth [month]"—this is the ninth of Ab, on which the house of our God was burned.

[F] "'Now, why is it called the fifth? It is the fifth [in the sequence] of months.'"

[G] {Simeon's report of Aqiba's interpretation of Zech. 8:19 continues:} "'"The fast of the seventh [month]"—this is the third of Tishre, on which Gedaliah the son of Ahikam was killed. And who killed him? Ishmael the son of Netaniah killed him.[320]

---

[317]T. Sot. 6:10, M, and other sources read: seventeenth.

[318]M and others add here: And it is written.

[319]M's text here is garbled. Rabbinovicz suggests that an addition, found in two manuscript sources, should read: And it is taught on Tannaitic authority: The first time, it was on the ninth of the month; the second time, it was the seventeenth of the month.

[320]M lacks: killed him. See Jer. 41:1-2: "In the seventh month, Ishmael the son of Netaniah, son of Elishama, of the royal family, one of the chief officers of the king, came with ten men to Gedaliah the son of Ahikam, at Mizpah. As they ate bread together there at Mizpah, Ishmael the son of Nethaniah and the ten men with him rose up and struck down Gedaliah the son of Ahikam, son of Shaphan, with the sword and killed him, whom the king of Babylon had appointed governor in the land."

[H] "'[The fact that there is a fast on this day] teaches you that the death of the righteous is given equal weight as the burning of the house of our God.

[I] "'Now, why is it called the seventh? It is the seventh [in the sequence] of months.'"

[J] {Simeon's report of Aqiba's interpretation of Zech. 8:19 continues:} "'"The fast of the tenth [month]"—this is the tenth of Tevet, on which the king of Babylon laid siege to Jerusalem,

[K] "'as it says [Ezek. 24:1-2]: "The word of the Lord came to me in the ninth year, in the tenth month, on the tenth day of the month: 'Son of man, write down the name of this day, this very day. The king of Babylon has laid siege to Jerusalem [this very day].'"

[L] "'Now, why is it called the tenth? It is the tenth [in the sequence] of months.'"

[M] {Simeon now indicates his disagreement with Aqiba:} "But [if the meaning is as Aqiba claims] would it not have been appropriate [at Zech. 8:19] to list [this fast] first, [insofar as it commemorates the event that occurred first]?[321]

[N] "Now, why [in Aqiba's interpretation] is it written about here [as the last referenced fast in Zech. 8:19]?

[O] "In order to place the months in their correct order [even though, chronologically, this makes no sense]."

[P] {Simeon continues:} "But I do not interpret [matters] thus.

[Q] "Rather [in my view] 'the fast of the tenth'—this is the fifth of Tevet, on which the news reached the diaspora that the city [of Jerusalem] had fallen,

[R] "as it says [Ezek. 33:21]: 'In the twelfth year of our exile, in the tenth month, on the fifth day of the month, a man who had escaped from Jerusalem came to me and said, "The city has fallen."'

---

[321]M and other sources lack L-M.

- [S] "And they treated the day of the report as comparable to the day of the actual burning [of the city].[322]
- [T] "Now, my interpretation is more likely than his [that is, Aqiba's].
- [U] "For I say [that the verse speaks] of the first [misfortune] first and of the last, last,
- [V] "while he says [that the verse speaks] of the first [misfortune] last and of the last [misfortune] first.
- [V] "Thus, while he [only] orders them according to the months [in which the fasts occur], I [also] order them according to the [chronology of the] events."[323]

- [III.A] It was stated on Amoraic authority: Rab and R. Hanina say, "[As a result of the destruction of the Temple] the Scroll of Fasting has been nullified." {Fasting and mourning no longer are precluded on the days enumerated in the scroll, which recalls miraculous or joyous days in Israelite history.}[324]
- [B] R. Yohanan and R. Joshua b. Levi say,[325] "The Scroll of Fasting has not been nullified."
- [C] {Each of the positions at A-B is now explained.} Rab and R. Hanina say, "[As a result of the destruction of the Temple] the Scroll of Fasting has been nullified"—

---

[322]M and other sources lack this line.

[323]M adds: and according to the months. The meaning is the same.

[324]Reference is to a chronicle that lists thirty-five dates on which the people of Israel experienced or witnessed miraculous or joyous events. These days were celebrated as feasts, on which public fasting was forbidden. The events described range chronologically from pre-Maccabean times through shortly after the destruction of the First Temple. B. Shab. 13b as well as the final lines of the document itself variously describe the authorship of the scroll. While the exact dating is under dispute, the Scroll of Fasting clearly took shape by the end of the first century C.E.

[325]Here and at G, M reverses the order of the names.

[D] This is what is meant [interpreting the four fast days listed at Zech. 8:19]:

[E] In times of peace they shall be [seasons of] joy and gladness [on which fasting is prohibited. If] there is no peace, [these occasions are] fasts. {See unit I.D.}

[F] And so here [in the case of the days listed in the Scroll of Fasting]. {After the destruction there is no peace. Fasting now is permitted on the listed days. The prohibition against fasting no longer is in affect.}

[G] R. Yohanan and R. Joshua b. Levi say, "The Scroll of Fasting has not been nullified."

[H] [G's authorities hold this position because they argue that] those [four days listed at Zech. 8:19] are the [only] ones that the Merciful made dependent upon the construction of the Temple. {When the Temple is rebuilt, the days listed by Zechariah will be feasts; until then, they are fast days.}

[I] But these [other days listed in the Scroll of Fasting] remain as they were. {They mark special events in Israelite history and, on them, fasting is prohibited.}

[IV.A] {Here and in the following units, the Talmud presents a series of challenges to the view that the Scroll of Fasting has been nullified.} Objected Rab Kahana [to the view of Rab and Hanina, unit III.C-F, citing T. Ta. 2:5], "**Once, in Lud, they enacted a fast on Hanukkah, and [contrary to the rules for a fast day] R. Eliezer went down [there] and bathed, and R. Joshua [who was there] cut his hair. And R. Joshua said to them**[326] **[that is, to the residents of the city], "Go and fast [in penitence] for having fasted [on a day listed in the Scroll of Fasting]!"** {The two Rabbinic authorities reject the notion that, even after the destruction, a public fast could be held on a day listed in the Scroll of

---

[326] So M, T. Ta. 2:5, and all other citations of this passage. P reads: And they said to them.

Fasting. Contrary to Rab and Hanina, the Scroll remains in affect.}

[B] [Rejecting A] said Rab Joseph, "The case of Hanukkah is different, since [celebrating it] is a religious obligation." {The requirement to kindle Hanukkah lights is deemed comparable to religious obligations listed in the Torah. Hanukkah thus differs from the other days listed in the Scroll of Fasting, which are not deemed to be on scriptural authority. Eliezer and Joshua's contention that one may not fast on Hanukkah, A, therefore cannot be used to argue that, in their view, the Scroll of Fasting remains in affect and that fasting is prohibited on all of the dates it lists. The view of Rab and Hanina, unit III.C-F, stands.}

[C] {Abayye now challenges Joseph's notion that Hanukkah is in the category of a religious obligation derived from the Torah.} Said to him Abayye, "[In response to the destruction of the Temple Hanukkah] should be abolished and the religious obligation with it!" {Abayye holds that Hanukkah is on Rabbinic authority and therefore can be abolished. The fact that Eliezer and Joshua did not allow this to occur proves the point argued at A. The Scroll of Fasting remains in affect. Joseph, B, has not proven that A's example is irrelevant.}

[D] [Offering a different argument that A does not suggest the rule for all of the days listed in the Scroll of Fasting] said Rab Joseph, "Hanukkah is different, since the miracle is well known." {For this reason the prohibition against fasting on Hanukkah cannot be annulled. But, since this same consideration does not apply to the other days listed in the Scroll of Fasting, celebration of those days as feasts remain in effect. The Scroll has not been annulled.}

[V.A] {Aha bar Huna provides a different historical occurrence that suggests that the Scroll of Fasting has not been nullified.} Objected Rab Aha bar Huna [to the view of Rab and Hanina, unit III.C-F, that the Scroll of Fasting has been nullified: "The Scroll of Fasting reads], 'On the third of Tishre the [practice of] mentioning [God's name] in legal documents was abolished.'

[B] {The passage cited at A is explained:} "For the Syrian[327] government decreed that [the Israelites] could not speak [lit., mention by mouth] the name of [God in] heaven.

[C] "But when the Hasmonean kingdom grew strong and defeated them [that is, the Syrians], they ordained that [Israelites] should mention the name of heaven even[328] in legal documents.

[D] "And thus [people] would write: 'In the such-and-such year of [the reign of] Yohanan the high priest of the almighty God....'

[E] "But when sages heard about this practice, they said, '[This must be abolished since], in the future, this one [i.e., the borrower] will repay the debt, and the legal document [recording the loan, containing God's name] will wind up lying in the garbage heap, [which would be sacrilege].'

[F] "So [sages] annulled [the practice of including God's name in legal documents], but [in all events] they designated [that day] a feast [on which fasting would be prohibited].

[G] "Now, if you imagine that they annulled the Scroll of Fasting—[is it feasible that] former [prohibitions against fasting, listed in the Scroll] were annulled, while later [dates on which fasting was to be prohibited, as at F] were added?" {This is unreasonable. It is clear that, contrary to Rab and Hanina, the Scroll of Fasting has not been nullified. Both prior and later feast days are in effect. This is what Yohanan and Joshua b. Levi, unit III.G, argue.}

---

[327]Literally: Greek. M and others read: evil.

[328]M lacks this word.

[H] {At H-I, the Talmud rejects Aha bar Huna's argument, explaining that, despite his argument at G, the Scroll of Fasting may have been nullified.} In this case [described at A-F] with what [situation] are we dealing?

[I] [The designation, F, of the third of Tishre as a feast occurred] while the Temple stood. {In this view, G's argument is not probative. The later date on which fasting is prohibited was added while the earlier dates remained in effect. The designation of a new feast while the Temple stood, that is, teaches nothing about whether or not the Scroll of Fasting continued to be in effect after the Temple was destroyed. At G, Aha bar Huna, by contrast, presumably holds that the new day on which fasting is banned was decreed, F, after the destruction of the Temple. Only in this understanding does G's argument make sense.}

[J] {H-I is rejected through the argument that, while the Temple stood, the third of Tishre would not be designated as a feast responding to the lifting of the Syrian decree. The impact of this is to uphold Aha bar Huna's understanding, that the prohibition against fasting on the third of Tishre was added after the destruction of the Temple. This suggests that, as G argues, following the destruction, the Scroll of Fasting remains in effect.} [19a] But [if, as H-I claims, we speak of the period while the Temple stood], explain [the designation of the third of Tishre to be a feast, F, as recognizing] that Gedaliah son of Ahikam was killed on that day. {See above unit II.G. Rashi: As we know from Zech. 8:19, during the time of the Temple, fast days were called periods of joy and gladness and feasts. In this view, the prohibition against fasting referred to at F must have occurred after the destruction. G's reasoning is upheld, with the implication that, even after the destruction, the Scroll of Fasting is in effect.}

[K] {At K-L, I is upheld, rejecting G+J's proof that the Scroll of Fasting remains in effect. Even if, as J claims, the third of

Tishre recognizes the killing of Gedaliah, a biblical event, and even if the Scroll of Fasting had been nullified, sages might, after the destruction, have imposed a ban against fasting on that day.} Said Rab,[329] "[Its designation as a feast day] was needed only to render forbidden [fasting] on the preceding [day].

[L] "Further, [regarding] the preceding day, you can explain its [designation as a feast] on the grounds that it is the day after the New Moon [on which day, too, fasting would be prohibited]." {The weight of this is to suggest that, after the destruction, despite the fact that the Scroll of Fasting was nullified and previous feast days canceled, a new day on which fasting is banned might have been declared, so as to prevent fasting on the day before, or after, a biblical feast. G's argument thus is shown to be unacceptable. We have no proof that, after the destruction, the Scroll of Fasting remains in effect.}

[M] {K-L depends upon the fact that prohibitions against fasting on certain days are extended to encompass the surrounding days. M now argues that the prohibition against fasting on a New Moon or biblical feast is not subject to such an extension. This means that the designation of the third of Tishre as a feast can have nothing to do with the attempt to preclude fasting on the previous day. Instead, as G and J reason, the sages' actions, described at F, comprised the designation of an entirely new feast day, with the implication that the prior feast days, listed in the Scroll of Fasting, had not been nullified.} [K-L is unacceptable, since observance of] the New Moon [referred to at L] is [derived] from Scripture, and that which [derives] from Scripture requires no extension.

[N] [This is] as it is taught on Tannaitic authority: Those days that are listed in the Scroll of Fasting—[along with] both [the

---

[329]M reads: Rava.

[O] [But as for] Sabbaths and festival days—these are forbidden [for fasting], but [the days] before and after them are permitted [for fasting].

[P] What factor distinguishes [days listed in the Scroll of Fasting, N, from Sabbaths and festivals, O]?

[Q] These [festivals and Sabbaths, mentioned at O, derive from] Scripture, and that which [derives] from Scripture requires no extension. {People are cognizant of the significance of these days and therefore do not fast on them, even if they intend to fast on the preceding or following day.}

[R] [But] these [days listed in the Scroll of Fasting, N, derive from] the words of the scribes, and that which [derives] from the words of the scribes requires extension.

[S] {M-R has negated L's argument, referring specifically to the New Moon. K's reasoning is rejected here.} Then explain [the prohibition against fasting on the second of Tishre] as resulting from the fact that it is the day before the day on which Gedaliah son of Ahikam was killed. {The implication of this argument is explained above at L.}

[T] {S's reasoning is unacceptable for the reason already given at M. The sort of extension assumed at K+S does not apply in the case of the killing of Gedaliah.} Said Rab Ashi, "[The killing of] Gedaliah son of Ahikam [is recorded in] tradition [that is, the later prophets],

[U] "and they deemed [that which derives from] tradition to be comparable to [that which derives from] Scripture, [so as not to require extension]." {The designation of the third of Tishre as a feast day was, as E-G argued, an entirely new occurrence, responding to the lifting of the ban against mentioning God's name. G's argument thus has been upheld,

[day] before and [the day] after them—are forbidden [for fasting]. {The period during which fasting is prohibited is extended to lessen the likelihood that an individual will fast on the feast day itself.}

that after the destruction of the Temple, the Scroll of Fasting was not nullified.)

[VI.A] {Tovi bar Mattenah provides another argument against the claim that the Scroll of Fasting has been nullified.} Objected Rab Tovi bar Mattenah [to the view of Rab and Hanina, unit III.C-F, that the Scroll of Fasting has been nullified, "[The Scroll of Fasting reads], 'On the twenty-eighth of that [month, that is, Adar], good news came to the Jews, that they need not separate themselves from [practice of] the law.'

[B] "For the government had decreed[330] that they may not involve themselves with [study and practice of] Torah, that they may not circumcise their sons, and that they must profane the Sabbath.

[C] "What did Judah b. Shammua and his associates do?

[D] "They went and took council with a certain matron with whom all of the notables of Rome[331] were familiar.

[D] "She said to them, 'Tonight, come and cry [to the Roman government] for help!'"

[E] "That night they went and cried out: 'In [the eyes of God in] heaven, are we not your brothers? And are we not all the children of a single father? And are we not all the children of a single mother?[332]

[F] "'How are we different from every other people and language, that you enact harsh decrees upon us?'

[G] "Now, as a result [the government] annulled those [decrees], and [as for] that same day—they designated it a feast.

[H] "Now, if you imagine that the Scroll of Fasting was annulled—[is it feasible that] former [prohibitions against

---

[330]M and others read: For the evil government had decreed a persecution of [the people of] Israel....

[331]The result of censorship, some late printings have: the city.

[332]M lacks the final sentence here.

[I] {fasting, listed in the Scroll] were annulled, while later [dates on which fasting was to be prohibited] were added?" {This cannot be the case. It is clear that, contrary to Rab and Hanina, unit III.C-F, the Scroll of Fasting has not been nullified. Both prior and later feast days are in effect.}
{The Talmud continues, responding to a possible criticism parallel to that found at unit V.H-I, that what is reported at A-H took place while the Temple stood and therefore has no implications for whether or not the Scroll of Fasting later was annulled.} And if you suggest that here too, [as in the case described in unit V, the incident took place] while the Temple stood, [this would not be acceptable since], in fact, Judah b. Shammua was a student of R. Meir, and R. Meir lived after [the destruction of the Temple]!

[J] [We know that Judah b. Shammua was Meir's student] as we have taught on Tannaitic authority:[333] [As for] a glass vessel in which they made holes and into which they [subsequently] poured lead [in order to seal the openings]—said Rabban Simeon b. Gamaliel,[334] "Judah b. Shammua declares it unclean[335] in the name of R. Meir. [**19b**] But sages declare it clean." {The important point is the proof that Judah b. Shammua lived later than Meir, whom he cites. This means that H's argument stands. Even after the destruction of the Temple, the Scroll of Fasting remains in effect.}

---

[333] The marginal gloss in the printed edition suggesting reading: For it is taught on Tannaitic authority.

[334] In P, a marginal gloss states that some authorities read: Simeon b. Eliezer.

[335] The vessel is deemed repaired and *susceptible to* uncleanness, as it was prior to the creation of the holes. Alternatively, if the vessel was actually unclean before the holes were made, the presence of the holes rendered it useless and, hence, clean. The point may be that, now that it is repaired, it is deemed again to be unclean.

BAVLI ROSH HASHANAH CHAPTER ONE [19b] 243

[VII.A] {The Talmud proposes a new perspective on unit III's issue of whether or not, after the destruction of the Temple, the Scroll of Fasting was nullified.} This [issue, disputed at unit III by Amoraic authorities, is disputed by] Tannaitic authorities.

[B] For it is taught on Tannaitic authority: "[On] those days recorded in the Scroll of Fasting—whether during the period in which the Temple exists or in the period in which the Temple does not exist—[people] are forbidden [from fasting]"—the words of R. Meir.

[C] R. Yose says, "During the period in which the Temple exists, [people] are forbidden [from fasting], since [each listed day is a time of] joy for them.

[D] "[But] when the Temple does not exist, they are permitted [to fast on days listed in the Scroll of Fasting], since it is a time of mourning for them."

[E] And there is a decided law that [holds that the restrictions against fasting on days listed in the Scroll of Fasting] have been annulled,

[F] and there is a decided law that [states that the restrictions against fasting on days listed in the Scroll of Fasting] have not been annulled.

[G] This is a problem, [for one] decided law contradicts the [other] decided law!

[H] There is no problem.

[I] This [law, F, that the Scroll of Fasting remains in effect] applies in [the case of] Hanukkah and Purim, [on which days fasting is prohibited].

[J] This [law, E, that the Scroll of Fasting has been annulled] applies to all other days [listed in the Scroll, on which fasting now is permitted].

[VIII.A] *[On the occasion of six new moons messengers go forth: ...] (3) at Elul, because of the New Year; (4) and at Tishre, because of the determination of the set feasts* [M. R.H. 1:3B].

[B] Since [messengers] go forth [to announce the new month] of Elul, [as for] Tishre—why do they [need to do this again]?

[C] Now, if you say it is lest Elul has been intercalated [through the addition of a thirtieth day, so that, if they do not receive special notification, the Diaspora communities will begin Tishre a day early and celebrate the Day of Atonement and Tabernacles[336] on the wrong dates—this reasoning would be unacceptable].

[D] For thus said R. Hinena bar Kahana[337] said Rab, "From the time of Ezra and onward, we have not found [a case in which] Elul has been intercalated."

[E] {At E-F, the Talmud argues that D does not prove the point made at C.} [D reports nothing more than that] "we have not found [a case in which Elul has been intercalated]." This is because, [in all those years, intercalating Elul] was not necessary.

[F] But if doing so were necessary, they would intercalate that [month]! {Accordingly, the reason is as introduced at C. Messengers go out at Elul and again at Tishre lest Elul was intercalated.}

[G] [The Talmud now rejects E-F's argument, claiming that, as D suggests, under no circumstance could Elul be intercalated, so as to cause the Diaspora to celebrate New Year on the wrong day.} But this [that is, intercalating Elul] would spoil New Year, [by causing it to be observed on the wrong day]! {In G's view, B-C has not correctly explained why messengers go out for Tishre as well as Elul.}

---

[336] As noted at G, the New Year holiday itself in all events would be celebrated incorrectly, since the messenger would not arrive until after it had been observed, beginning a day early.

[337] M reads: Rab Hinena.

BAVLI ROSH HASHANAH CHAPTER ONE [19b] 245

[H] {The Talmud responds that, while G is correct that intercalating Elul will cause the New Year to be celebrated on the wrong day, this does not preclude carrying out just such an intercalation.} It is better that New Year be spoiled [through being celebrated on the wrong day] and that all the other appointed times not be spoiled! {The reason suggested—and rejected—at C is shown to be correct. Messengers go out at Tishre so that, should Elul have been intercalated, the Day of Atonement and Tabernacles can be celebrated on the correct days.}

[I] [That H is in fact the reason] also is indicated by that which is taught on Tannaitic authority [at M. R.H. 1:3B itself, which states: *On the occasion of six new moons messengers go forth: ...*] *at Tishre, because of the determination of the set feasts.*

[J] Learn from this [that matters are as H states].

[IX.A] [*On the occasion of six new moons messengers go forth: ...*] *(5) at Kislev, because of Hanukkah; and (6) at Adar, because of Purim* [M. R.H. 1:3B].

[B] But [the notion that] if the year is intercalated, [messengers] go forth also at Second Adar, because of Purim, is not taught [at M. R.H. 1:3B].

[C] [The absence of this rule is accounted for by the fact that] the Mishnaic passage does not accord with [the view of] Rabbi [Judah the Patriarch].

[D] For it is taught on Tannaitic authority [see T. R.H. 1:14]: Rabbi says, "If the year has been intercalated, [messengers] go forth also at Second Adar, because of Purim."

[E] Should I reason that the following is the basis of the dispute [between Rabbi, D, who holds that messengers go forth to announce Second Adar, and the anonymous rule in the Mishnah, A, explained at B, which holds that they do not]?

[F] For the master [that is, the anonymous authority at M. R.H. 1:3] reasons that all the religious obligations that apply in

	Second [Adar] apply [as well] in First [Adar]. {In this view, the correct dating of the days of Second Adar is unimportant, and therefore messengers need not be sent. All pertinent obligations already were observed in First Adar.}
[G]	But the [other] master [that is, Rabbi, D] reasons that all of the religious obligations that apply in Second [Adar] do not apply in First [Adar].[338] {In this view, what happens in Second Adar really matters. Messengers must be sent to assure that people correctly count the dates of that month.}
[H]	{F-G's explanation of the dispute is rejected.} No, [F-G is unacceptable]! In fact, both [disputants] reason that all of the religious obligations that apply in Second [Adar] do not [also] apply in First [Adar].
[I]	But [instead] they differ concerning the intercalation of the year.
[J]	For it is taught on Tannaitic authority: How many [days are added in] the intercalation of a year? {Rashi: How long is *First* Adar?}
[K]	Thirty days.
[L]	Rabban Simeon b. Gamaliel says, "A month [that is, twenty-nine days]."
[M]	What is special about [its being] thirty [days,[339] such that the one who holds that view, assumed to be the anonymous authority at M. R.H. 1:3, does not require messengers to go forth to announce the beginning of Second Adar]?
[N]	[Since it is thirty days, people naturally] know [on what day First Adar ends and Second Adar begins]! {Therefore, messengers are not necessary.}
[O]	[N does not explain matters, since, if First Adar is] a month [as Simeon b. Gamaliel says, L, people] also will know

---

[338] M reverses the order of F and G.

[339] M has this word explicitly.

	[when Second Adar begins, a month always comprising twenty-nine days]!
[P]	[Explaining that O is not the case] said Rab Pappa, "The one who said [that the intercalated period is] a month [holds that, in adding a month, if] it wants [the court may add] a month [of twenty-nine days, or if] it wants [the court may add] thirty [days]." {This being the case, in the view of one who says that the intercalated period is a month, the people will not automatically know when Second Adar begins. This explains why, in such a person's view, messengers must be sent.}
[X.A]	R. Joshua b. Levi testified in the name of the holy community of Jerusalem, regarding the two [months of] Adar, that they sanctify them on the day on which they are intercalated. {Reference is to the thirtieth day of the month, added when the month is intercalated. The point here is that, when either First or Second Adar is intercalated, the thirtieth day is celebrated as the New Moon festival of the coming month.}
[B]	This is to say that we treat [the month of Adar] as defective [that is, containing only twenty-nine days, but] we do not treat it as full [that is, containing thirty days].[340] {This is true insofar as the extra, thirtieth day is treated as the first day of the following month.}
[C]	[This serves] to reject that which Rab Nahman bar Hisda explained, [for explained Rab Nahman bar Hisda],[341] "Testified R. Simai in the names of Haggai, Zechariah, and Malachi concerning the two Adars, that if they desired to make them both full, they make [them both full; to make] them both defective, [they make them both defective; to make] one full and one defective, [they likewise do so].

---

[340] In M, the clauses are reversed.

[341] The bracketed material appears in M and the margin of P.

[D] "And this was their practice in the Diaspora."

[E] But in the name of our Rabbi, they said, "Always,[342] one is full and the other is defective.

[F] "[This applies] unless it becomes known to you [through the arrival of messengers] that the New Moon [of Second Adar] has been set at its proper time [that is, on the thirtieth day of First Adar]."

[XI.A] {Discussion of whether the months of Adar consistently are full or defective continues.} They sent [from the land of Israel] to Mar Uqba [saying], "The [month of] Adar that precedes Nisan always is defective."

[B] Objected Rab Nahman, "[We know that *in order to present testimony] of the [beginning] of two months they profane the Sabbath [by traveling beyond the Sabbath limit in order to notify the court of the appearance of the new moon]: for Nisan and for Tishre* [M. R.H. 1:4A-B].

[C] "If you say, 'Granted, sometimes [Adar] is full and sometimes it is defective'—for this reason they [would need to] profane [the Sabbath so as to deliver information about the actual sighting of the new moon, needed to establish the beginning of the month].

[D] [20a] "But if [as at A] you say that [Adar] is always defective, why would [those who sight the moon need to travel beyond the Sabbath limit to report their finding, which would] profane [the Sabbath]?" {This would be unnecessary insofar as the beginning of the new month has been fixed and is known without the actual sighting.}

[E] {Responding to D:} [Even though the beginning of the new month is fixed, the sighting overrides the Sabbath] because it is a religious obligation to sanctify [the new month] on the basis of an [actual] sighting. {This applies even if the

---

[342]The result of a scribal error (Rabbinovicz), M lacks the words: they said, Always.

sighting is not strictly necessary. Nahman's objection to A therefore is unacceptable. Despite the fact that the messengers may profane the Sabbath, we can accept the claim that the month of Adar before Nisan always is defective.}

[F] {A different version of Nahman's statement follows. In this version, Nahman supports A's claim that the month of Adar prior to Nisan always is defective.} There are those who report [Nahman's statement as follows]: Said Rab Nahman, "[In support of A's claim that Adar before Nisan always is defective], we also teach on Tannaitic authority [M. R.H. 1:4A-B: *In order to present testimony] of the [beginning] of two months they profane the Sabbath [by traveling beyond the Sabbath limit in order to notify the court of the appearance of the new moon]: for Nisan and for Tishre.*

[G] "If you say, 'Granted, [Adar] is always defective'—for this reason they [would need to] profane [the Sabbath], since it is a religious obligation to sanctify [the new month] on the basis of an [actual] sighting.

[H] "But, if you say, 'Sometimes [Adar] is full and sometimes it is defective'—why would [those who sight the moon need to travel beyond the Sabbath limit to report their finding, which would] profane [the Sabbath]?

[I] "[In the situation described at H, instead of profaning the Sabbath], let us intercalate [the month] now, [making it a full month, in which the Sabbath is the thirtieth day], and sanctify [the new month] tomorrow, [on the thirty-first day, when messengers can come without profaning the Sabbath]!"

[J] {This time, Nahman's argument in support of A is rejected.} In the case in which the thirtieth day [of Adar] falls on the Sabbath, that [which is described at I] is exactly what we do. {The month is intercalated and treated as full, something which A does not allow.}

[K] Here[343] [in the situation described at B and F, which Nahman says proves that Adar before Nisan always is defective] with what circumstance do we deal?

[L] [It is a case][344] in which the thirty-first day [of the month] falls on the Sabbath. {Since this is the longest the month can be, messengers who report sighting the new moon cannot wait until after the Sabbath.}

[M] [And, in this case, we allow the messengers to profane the Sabbath even though we know that the new month must now begin], because it is a religious obligation to sanctify [the new month] on the basis of an [actual] sighting.

[XII.A] {We have another objection to the rule at unit XI.A, that a month of Adar that precedes Nisan always is defective.} Objected Rab Kahana, "When the Temple existed, they profaned [the Sabbath] for all [of the months, not just Nisan and Tishre, as reported in the preceding unit],

[B] "because of the [need correctly to] set the sacrifice [for the New Moon].

[C] "[We must conclude that] since, in the case of all [the other months, the reason for allowing profanation of the Sabbath was] not because it is a religious obligation to sanctify [the new month] on the basis of an [actual] sighting, so in the case of Nisan and Tishre [the reason for allowing profanation of the Sabbath was] not because it is a religious obligation to sanctify [the new month] on the basis of an [actual] sighting.

[D] "If you say, 'Granted, sometimes [Adar] is full and sometimes it is defective'—for this reason they [would need to] profane [the Sabbath so as to deliver information about the actual sighting of the new moon, needed to establish the beginning of the month].

---

[343] M reads: Rather, here....

[344] M adds: such as.

[E] "But if you say that [Adar] is always defective, why would [those who sight the moon need to travel beyond the Sabbath limit to report their finding, which would] profane [the Sabbath]?" {This would be unnecessary insofar as the beginning of the new month has been fixed and is known without the actual sighting.}

[F] This is a [valid] objection!

[XIII.A] When Ulla came [to Babylonia from the land of Israel] he said, "They have intercalated Elul." {Rabbinical authorities added an extra day to Elul to prevent a festival in Tishre from falling on a Sunday, consecutively with the Sabbath.}

[B] Said Ulla, "Do the Associates in Babylonia know[345] what a good thing we [in the land of Israel] have done for them?"

[C] What is the good thing?

[D] Ulla said, "It is because of vegetables." {Vegetables required for a Sabbath-festival sequence must be picked on Friday. By the time they are consumed on the festival, they are undesirable. By preventing a Sabbath-festival sequence, the authorities of the land of Israel assured that people could have freshly picked food for holiday consumption.}

[E] [Offering a different explanation of the advantage of intercalating Elul] R. Aha bar Hanina[346] said, "It is because of the [unburied] dead." {In the case of a Sabbath-festival sequence, a corpse that is unburied at the onset of the Sabbath cannot be buried until the conclusion of the festival. Preventing a Sabbath-festival sequence assures that a corpse not remain unburied for more than the period of the Sabbath or festival alone.}

[F] What is the practical difference between these [two different understandings of the advantage of intercalating Elul to prevent a Sabbath-festival sequence during Tishre]?

---

[345]M lacks the end of this line, a case of haplography.

[346]M reads simply: R. Hananiah.

[G] The practical difference between them is [apparent in the case of] a Day of Atonement that, [were Elul not intercalated, would] fall immediately after the Sabbath.[347]

[H] [In such a case] the one [that is, Aha bar Hanina] who says [that we intercalate Elul] on account of the [unburied] dead [would hold that] we [go ahead and] intercalate [so that the dead not remain unburied for two days].

[I] But [in the circumstance described at G, as for] the one [that is, Ulla] who says [that we intercalate Elul] on account of vegetables—[we must ask]: For when do we need [the vegetables]? For the evening [after the conclusion of the fast on the Day of Atonement].

[J] [This being the case, in Ulla's reasoning, in this instance, Elul should not be intercalated, since] in the evening[348] one can take the trouble to bring [fresh vegetables].

[K] {G+H-J is rejected.} But [even] in the view of the one [that is, Ulla] who states that [Elul is intercalated] on account of [the desire to make available fresh] vegetables, [in an instance such as is described at G] let them intercalate [it anyway], on account of [the need to bury] the dead! {Contrary to H-J, even in the case defined at G, both Ulla and Aha bar Hanina can hold that Elul should be intercalated.}

[L] {G-J has failed to find a practical difference between the views assigned to Ulla and Aha bar Hanina regarding why Elul is intercalated. The following attempts again to answer the question.} The practical difference between them is [apparent in the case of] a festival that falls consecutively with the Sabbath, whether falling [immediately] before or after it.

---

[347]In error, instead of "immediately after the Sabbath," M reads: on the first of the week. In Hebrew, this is a difference of only two letters ("b'hd" instead of "'ḥr").

[348]M lacks: in the evening.

BAVLI ROSH HASHANAH CHAPTER ONE [20a] 253

[M] [In this instance] the one [that is, Ulla] who says [that we intercalate Elul] on account of vegetables holds that we should intercalate [Elul on account of vegetables].

[N] But [in the view of] the one [that is, Aha bar Hanina] who says [that we intercalate Elul] on account of the [unburied] dead—[Elul should not be intercalated, since] it is possible for [other] people [that is, non-Jews, to see to the corpse].

[O] {L-N is rejected.} But [even] in the view of the one [that is, Aha bar Hanina] who states that [Elul is intercalated] on account of [the need to bury] the dead, [in an instance such as is described at L] let them intercalate [it anyway], on account of [the desire to make available fresh] vegetables! {Contrary to N, even in the case defined at L, both Ulla and Aha bar Hanina can hold that Elul should be intercalated.}

[P] {We find that in no case can Aha bar Hanina concede that the need for fresh vegetables is a reason to intercalate Elul and prevent a Sabbath-festival sequence from occurring.} [Vegetables] can be [improved] by [being placed in] warm water.

[Q] {The preceding identified two distinct advantages to intercalating Elul to prevent a Sabbath-festival sequence from occurring, so that the dead not remain unburied (Aha b. Hanina) or so that fresh vegetables are available (Ulla). We turn now to a secondary question raised by B.} If this is the case [that the reasons are as Ulla and Aha indicate] why [is the intercalation of Elul a] particularly [good thing] for us [in Babylonia]?

[R] Even for them [in the land of Israel it should be seen as advantageous]!

[S] {Distinguish between the situation in the land of Israel and in Babylonia as follows:} As for us [in Babylonia], the world is oppressively [hot, so that keeping vegetables or corpses over the Sabbath-festival sequence is a serious concern].

[T]   As for them [in the land of Israel], the world is not oppressively [hot, so that keeping vegetables or corpses over the Sabbath-festival sequence is not a concern at all].

[XIV.A] {The preceding unit assumes that a month can be intercalated so as to prevent the occurrence of a Sabbath-festival sequence.} Is this [really] so?

[B]   But [to the contrary] so taught Rabbah bar Samuel on Tannaitic authority: Is it logical that, just as the year is intercalated [through the addition of an extra month] because of a special need [other than that of keeping the calendar in adjustment], so a month may be intercalated because of a special need?

[C]   "[Indicating that we do not do this] Scripture states [Ex. 12:2, referring to the month of the Exodus]: 'This month shall be for you the beginning of months.'

[D]   "[The meaning of the verse is that, when you] see [a moon that appears] like 'this' [one, referred to in the verse], you must sanctify [it]." {In this view, one may not take into account human needs at all.}

[E]   Said Rava, "There is no contradiction [between the view of the preceding unit and that of D].

[F]   "This [passage, unit XIII, refers] to intercalating the month, [while] this one [refers to] sanctifying it,

[G]   "and here is the larger point: Is it logical that, just as they intercalate the year[349] out of a special need, so they sanctify a month according to a special need?

[H]   "[To show that this is not the case] Scripture states [Ex. 12:2]: 'This month shall be for you [the beginning of months,' meaning: when you] see [a moon that appears] like 'this' [one, referred to in the verse], you must sanctify [it]."

---

[349]M, the printed edition, and some other sources adds: and the month. Rashi proposes reading the entire question as follows: Is it logical that, just as they intercalate out of a special need, so they sanctify according to a special need?

[I] "And this accords with that which R. Joshua b. Levi said: 'They intimidate the witnesses [to withhold the fact that they saw] a new moon that appeared in its [normal] time, [on the thirtieth day], so that [the month] may be intercalated.

[J] "'But they do not intimidate the witnesses [into reporting that they saw] a new moon that [in fact] did not appear in its [normal] time, so that [the month may be] sanctified [on the thirtieth when, in fact, it should be intercalated].'"

[K] Is this really so?

[L] But [indicating the contrary] R. Judah the Prince[350] sent to R. Ami [saying]: "Know that during all of the days[351] of R. Yohanan, he would teach us [that] they intimidate witnesses [into reporting that they saw] a new moon that [in fact] did not appear in its [normal] time, so that [the month may be] sanctified [on the thirtieth instead of being intercalated].

[M] "Even though they did not see it, they may say, 'We saw it.'"

[N] Said Abayye, "There is no contradiction [between the rule attributed to Yohanan, K, and that phrased by Joshua b. Levi, J].

[O] "This [rule of Yohanan, which states that the month may be sanctified early] applies in the case of Nisan and Tishre.

[P] "This [other rule, which precludes sanctifying the month early] applies to all other months."

[Q] Rava said, "That which Rabbah bar Samuel taught on Tannaitic authority, [B-D, that intercalation of the year or month never takes into account special circumstances] accords with [the view cited in the name of] 'Others.'

[R] "For it is taught on Tannaitic authority [T. Ar. 1:11]: **Others say, 'There is between one occurrence of Pentecost and another or between one New Year and another [an interval of] four [days of the week] or, if the year was interca-**

---

[350]Reference is to the grandson of "Rabbi."

[351]M reads: years.

lated, five [days].'" {"Others" hold that full and defective months occur in strict rotation. The year accordingly has 354 days, that is, 50 full weeks and four days, and Pentecost always falls on the sixth of Sivan. An intercalated month has 29 days, that is, four weeks and a day, yielding a five day difference in the day of the week on which the holiday falls. See Simon, pp. 21-22, nn. 12-13, and above, M. R.H. 1:1 **XXXI**.S, 6b.}

[XV.A] Rab Dimi of Nehardea taught the opposite on Tannaitic authority: "They intimidate witnesses [into reporting that they saw] a new moon that [in fact] did not appear in its [normal] time, so that [the month may be] sanctified [on the thirtieth instead of being intercalated]. {This is the view of Yohanan, unit **XIV**.L.}

[B] "They do not intimidate the witnesses [to cause them to withhold the fact that they saw] a new moon that appeared in its [normal time, on the thirtieth day], so that [the month] may be intercalated. {This is the opposite of the view of Joshua b. Levi, unit **XIV**.J.}

[C] "What is the reason [for this view]?

[D] [20b] "In this instance [B, in which the witnesses were forced not to report what they saw], the lie would be apparent, [since other people can report that they saw the new moon].

[E] [But] in this instance [A, if the witnesses are forced to report what they did not see], the lie would not be apparent, [since it could not be proven that they did not see it (Rashi)]."

[XVI.A] Said Samuel, "I am able to set [the calendar] for [use by] the entire diaspora. {Rashi: Samuel knew the stages of the moon well enough to determine the lengths of the months without use of witnesses.}

[B] Said Abba, the father of[352] R. Simlai, to Samuel, "Does the master know [the meaning of] this [following] statement, which is taught on Tannaitic authority in [the document known as] 'The Secret of Intercalation'?[353]

[C] "'[What is the implication of whether the new moon] is born before midday[354] or after midday?'"

[D] [Samuel] said to him, "No."[355]

[E] [Abba] said to him [that is, Samuel], "Since the master [that is, you] does not know this, there must [also] be other things that the master do not know!" {The implication is that Samuel is not fit to set the calendar as described at A.}

[F] When R. Zera went [to the land of Israel] he sent back to them [in Babylonia this explanation of the question cited at C: "In order to proclaim the new moon on the thirtieth of the month] there must be a full night and day of the new moon, [without any appearance of the old moon].

[G] "And that which Abba, the father of R. Simlai, said[356] [means]: They calculate [the new moon's] birth.

[H] "If it was born prior to midday, it is known that it will appear close to sunset.

[I] "If it was not born before midday, it is known that it will not appear close to sunset."

[J] What is the practical application of this [fact]?

---

[352] Here and at G, M lacks "the father of," a scribal error resulting from the similarity of this term to the name "Abba," which precedes (Rabbinovicz).

[353] Rashi: Reference is to a collection of enigmatic statements on the calendar.

[354] So Rashi, Simon, and as required by G-H. The term usually refers to midnight.

[355] M reads: I do not know.

[356] M and others add: in the presence of R. Samuel.

[K] Said Rab Ashi,[357] "[It can be used] to rebut the witnesses [who claim to have seen the new moon at a point at which it could not yet have appeared]."

[XVII.A] Said R. Zera said Rab Nahman, "[At the time of the new moon] the moon is covered [and invisible] for twenty four hours.

[B] "In our situation [in Babylonia] six [of these hours are attributable] to the old moon and eighteen [are attributable] to the new [moon]. {Rashi: This means that, in Babylonia, the moon cannot be seen until eighteen hours after its birth.}

[C] "In your situation [in the land of Israel], six [of these hours are attributable] to the [new [moon] and eighteen [are attributable] to the old moon." {Rashi: This means that, in the land of Israel, the moon can be seen six hours after its birth.}

[D] What is the practical application of this [fact]?

[E] Said Rab Ashi, "[It can be used] to rebut the witnesses [who claim to have seen the new moon at a point at which it could not yet have appeared]."

[XVIII.A] Said a master [unit XVI.F: "In order to proclaim the new moon on the thirtieth of the month] there must be a full night and day of the new moon, [without any appearance of the old moon]."

[B] From what verse do we know this? {At issue is why the period of invisibility of the old moon must begin in the evening.}

[C] R. Yohanan said, "[Referring to the Day of Atonement, Lev. 23:32 states]:[358] 'from evening to evening....'" {We thus know that festivals run from evening to evening.}

---

[357]M lacks the attribution.

[358]M explicitly reads: Scripture states.

[D] Resh Laqish said, "[Ex. 12:18 states: 'In the first month, on the fourteenth day of the month at evening, you shall eat unleavened bread] until the twenty-first day of the month at evening.'" {We see from this verse too that festivals run from evening to evening.}

[E] What is the practical difference between these [two different understandings of the Scriptural proof for A]?

[F] Abayye said, "The meaning [attributed to the verse] by those who interpret distinguishes them." {That is, there is no practical difference at all.}

[G] [Disagreeing] Rava said, "[Their view of the status of the hours up to] midnight distinguishes them." {Rashi: Yohanan holds that for judging the appearance of the moon, as in the case of the Day of Atonement, "night" begins in the evening. If the old moon was seen early in the evening, the next day cannot begin the new month. Resh Laqish, by contrast, holds that for purposes of sighting the new moon, "night" commences with midnight, just as for the requirement to eat unleavened bread on Passover. In this view, even if the old moon is visible in the hours before midnight, the next day can begin the new month.

[XIX.A] {The problem in the rather elliptical materials that follow is how to determine the calendar in the diaspora when no direct evidence is available regarding the actual appearance of the new moon in the land of Israel.} Said R. Zera said Rab Nahman,[359] "[In] every case of doubt [for which we retroactively determine to intercalate a month by adding a day] we throw it forward [that is, make the following day the added one].

[B] "This is to say that [in the case of Passover and Tabernacles] we observe the fifteenth and the sixteenth [as the festivals]. We do not observe the fourteenth [as the festival]." {Simon,

---

[359]M lacks the attribution to Nahman.

[C] But should we not also observe the fourteenth [as part of the festival], lest both Ab and Elul[360] were made short [months, of only twenty-nine days]? {Simon: "And in this case, what we suppose to have been the twenty-ninth day of Adar or of Elul would really have been the first of Nisan or Tishre."}

[D] [21a] [C is not the case, since] two [consecutive] short months have a voice [that is, are generally known, so that no special action need be taken]. {Simon, citing Rashi: "Tebeth and Tamuz are always, according to the principles of fixed calendar, defective, and if Shevat which follows Tebeth, Ab and Tamuz were also to be defective, it would have become known to the Diaspora before the advent of the festivals."}

[XX.A] {We refer to a case in which, in Babylonia, it was not known that, in the land of Israel, the preceding month had been intercalated through the addition of a day.} Levi reached Babylonia on [what the people in Babylonia held to be] the eleventh of Tishre.

[B] He said,[361] "How tasty is the food of the Babylonians on that which, in the West, is the great day [of the fast of the Day of Atonement]!"

[C] [The people] said to him, "Testify [that today in fact is the tenth, and then we will observe it too as the Day of Atonement]!"

---

[360]M, Rashi, and other exegetical sources read: Shevat.

[361]M and other sources add: to them.

citing Rashi, explains: "I.e., that we reckon fifteen days from the thirtieth day, and also from the thirty-first day of the previous Adar or Elul, out of doubt, but in no case from the twenty-ninth. This dictum would seem to be superfluous, as in no circumstances was the New Moon proclaimed on the twenty-ninth day of the preceding New Moon."}

[D] He said to them, "[I cannot give testimony, since] I did not hear directly from the court [the statement], 'It is sanctified [as the New Moon].'"³⁶²

[XXI.A] Decreed R. Yohanan: "In any place to which messengers [announcing the new month] of Nisan can arrive [prior to Passover], but to which messengers [announcing the new month] of Tishre cannot arrive [in time for Tabernacles], you must [in all events] observe two days [both of Passover and Tabernacles]. {In the case of Tishre, because of New Year and the Day of Atonement, the messengers lose three travel days and hence do not get as far as they do when they travel to announce Nisan.}

[B] "[The inclusion of Passover as a two day observance in] Nisan is a preventative measure because of Tishre. {That is, if people observed the initial festival of Passover for only one day, they might, by analogy, come as well to observe Tabernacles for only a single day.}

[XXII.A] {A specific case is reviewed involving the rule of the preceding unit.} R. Aibo bar³⁶³ Nagri and R. Hiyya bar Abba reached a certain place to which messengers [announcing the new month] of Nisan can arrive [prior to Passover], but to which messengers [announcing the new month] of Tishre cannot arrive [in time for Tabernacles].

[B] Now [even though the residents] observed only a single day [of the initial festival of Passover, these rabbis] didn't say a word to them [about their wrong practice].

---

³⁶²M reads: It is intercalated. M, Cracow, and other sources add at this point (in M's version): R. Aibo bar Nagri and R. Hiyya bar Abba reached Babylonia on [what the people in Babylonia held to be] the eleventh of Tishre. [The people] said to him, "Testify [that today in fact is the tenth, and then we will observe it too as the Day of Atonement]!" They said, "[I cannot give testimony, since] I did not hear directly from the court [the statement], 'It is intercalated."

³⁶³M reads: ben.

[C] R. Yohanan heard [about this] and became angry.

[D] He said to them, "Did I not tell you [that] in any place to which messengers [announcing the new month] of Nisan can arrive [prior to Passover], but to which messengers [announcing the new month] of Tishre cannot arrive [in time for Tabernacles], people must [in all events] observe two days [of Passover], as a preventative measure because of Tishre?" {No response is given.}

[XXIII.A] {We turn to the issue of observance of the fast of the Day of Atonement. The problem is that, in Babylonia, the correct day of the observance may not be known.} Rava normally sat and fasted two days [on the Day of Atonement]. {This was because he would not know whether or not, in Jerusalem, the preceding month, Elul, had been intercalated through the addition of a thirtieth day. Hence he treated both the tenth and eleventh of Tishre as the Day of Atonement.}

[B] On one occasion [things] were found to be in accord with his [practice]. {That is, it turned out that Elul had been intercalated. Rava's additional fast had fallen on the actual Day of Atonement.}

[XXIV.A] {The theme of the preceding unit continues.} [Once] Rab Nahman[364] sat fasting for the entire Day of Atonement.

[B] In the evening [when he was ready to conclude the fast] a certain man arrived [from the land of Israel] and said to him, "Tomorrow[365] is the Great Day [that is, the Day of Atonement] in the West!"

[C] [Nahman] said to him, "Where are you from?"

[D] [The man] said to him, "From Damharia."

[E] [Nahman] said to him, "Blood will be his [that is, your] destiny." {This is a play on words, with the letters of this

---

[364]M adds: bar Isaac.

[365]M and others read, "Now," and lack "in the West" at the end of the line.

phrase spelling "Damharia." Rashi: Nahman means that the man will be responsible for Nahman's death, insofar as his arrival means that Nahman will have to continue fasting for a second day.}

[F] [Nahman] invoked on himself [the verse, Lam. 4:19]: "Our pursuers were swifter [than the vultures in the heavens]."[366]

[XXV.A] Rab Huna bar Abin sent to Rava[367] [saying], "When you see that the cycle of Tevet[368] continues until the sixteenth of Nisan, intercalate that year and don't scruple about doing so,

[B] "as it is written [Dt. 16:1]: 'Observe the month [ḥodesh] of Abib.'[369]

[C] "[This means]: Observe Abib of the cycle [that is, the day on which the vernal equinox begins] so that it falls in the new part [ḥodesh] of Nisan."

[XXVI.A] Said Rab Nahman to those going out to sea, "[As for] you who do not know how to fix [the beginning of] the month—

[B] "when you see the moonlight completing [its appearance] by day, remove the leaven [in your possession, to prepare for Passover]."

[C] When does the [moonlight] complete [its appearance by day]?

[D] On the fifteenth [of the month]!

[E] [Nahman' system seems unworkable, since] we must remove the leaven on the fourteenth!

[F] {C-E's criticism does not apply.} Since [out at sea] the [whole] world is revealed to them, [they can see the

---

[366] The bracketed conclusion of the verse appears explicitly in M.

[367] A scribal error (Rabbinovicz), M reads: Rab.

[368] See above unit 1:1 **XLVII.K**, 8a.

[369] M adds the continuation of the verse: and keep the Passover.

moonlight] complete [its appearance by day even] on the fourteenth.

1:4

[A] [21b] *[In order to present testimony] of the [beginning] of two months they profane the Sabbath [by traveling beyond the Sabbath limit in order to notify the court of the appearance of the new moon]:*

[B] *for Nisan and for Tishre.*

[C] *For on these occasions the messengers go forth to Syria.*

[D] *And on them they determine the set feasts.*

[E] *And when the Temple stood, they profane the Sabbath [by traveling beyond the Sabbath limit in order to notify the court of the appearance of the new moon] on the occasion of all of the [months],*

[F] *because of the [need] to determine [the correct day for] the offering [marking the beginning of the new month].*

In Nisan and Tishre it is particularly important that the messengers alert the diaspora communities of the correct date. This is so that Passover (in Nisan) and Tabernacles (in Tishre) may be correctly observed. To assure that the messengers have the time needed to make the trip, those who see the new moon in these months must go immediately to testify to the court Jerusalem. To get quickly to Jerusalem, they even may violate the usual restrictions upon travel on the Sabbath (A-D). When the Temple stood (E-F), the need to offer the special sacrifice for the new month provided reason for witnesses of the new moon to violate the Sabbath restrictions in the other months as well. After the destruction, no immediate need for these witnesses' testimony remained, and the practice of violating the Sabbath restrictions was ended.

Unit I coordinates the rules of M. R.H. 1:3A and 1:4A. In months other than Nisan and Tishre, the messengers go forth based on the word of the witnesses alone, even before the court has officially sanctified the new month. In Nisan and Tishre, by contrast, they wait for the court's action. In those months, it is important for the witnesses to get to Jerusalem as quickly as possible. Unit II provides the scriptural foundation for allowing these witnesses to violate the restrictions of the Sabbath. Unit III discusses M. R.H. 1:4E-F, attributing to Yohanan b. Zakkai the decision to cease allowing witnesses to violate the prohibition against Sabbath-travel in months other than Nisan and Tishre.

[I.A] {The issue here concerns whether or not messengers are sent only for the same two months for which witnesses may profane the Sabbath.} *[In order to present testimony] of the [beginning] of two months [they profane the Sabbath;* M. R.H. 1:4A]—

[B] But [is it really the case that for] more [months than these messengers do] not [go forth]?

[C] But [M. R.H. 1:3A] contrasts with that [notion]: *On the occasion of six new moons messengers go forth....*

[D] Said Abayye, "This is what is meant [by M. R.H. 1:3A and 1:4A]:

[E] "For all [the other months] messengers go forth while it is still evening [on the thirty-first day, since it is certain that the court will proclaim this the New Moon].

[F] "[But] in the case of Nisan and Tishre, [the messengers wait] until they hear directly from the court, 'It is sanctified.'" {This might occur at anytime during the following day.}

[G] That which is taught on Tannaitic authority makes the same point.

[H] For all [the other months messengers][370] go forth while it is still evening.

[I] [But] in the case of Nisan and Tishre, [the messengers wait] until they hear directly from the court, "It is sanctified."

---

[370]M explicitly reads: messengers.

[II.A] Our rabbis have taught on Tannaitic authority: From what [verse do we know] that [only in order to present testimony of the beginning] of these [two months] may they profane the Sabbath?

[B] Scripture states [Lev. 23:4]: "These are the appointed feasts of the Lord, [the holy convocations],[371] which you shall proclaim at the time appointed for them."

[C] Is it logical that, just as they profane [the Sabbath[372] on their account] up to the point at which they are sanctified, so they may profane [the Sabbath on their account] until they are declared [through notification of the people in the diaspora]?

[D] Scripture states: "which you shall proclaim"[373]—this means that, in order to proclaim them you [that is, witnesses who saw the new moon] may profane [the Sabbath];

[E] but you may not profane [the Sabbath] in order to declare them [to the communities in the diaspora].

[III.A] *And when the Temple stood, they profane the Sabbath [by traveling beyond the Sabbath limit in order to notify the court of the appearance of the new moon] on the occasion of all of the [months], because of the [need] to determine [the correct day for] the offering [marking the beginning of the new month*; M. R.H. 1:4E-F].

[B] Our rabbis have taught on Tannaitic authority: At first they would profane [the Sabbath] on account of all of them.

[C] Once the Temple was destroyed, Rabban Yohanan b. Zakkai said to them, "Now, is there an offering [that needs to be brought, for which we must have immediate knowledge of the new moon]?"

---

[371] M and other manuscripts have the bracketed words explicitly.

[372] Here and in the following, M reads "the Sabbath" explicitly.

[373] M adds the continuation of the verse: "at the time appointed for them."

[D] They ordained that they would not profane [the Sabbath] except for Nisan and Tishre alone.

1:5

[A] *Whether [the new moon] appeared clearly or did not appear clearly,*
[B] *they violate the [prohibitions of] the Sabbath on its account.*
[C] *R. Yose says, "If it appeared[374] clearly, they do not violate the prohibitions of the Sabbath on its account."*

1:6

[A] *It once occurred: More than forty pairs [of witnesses] passed [on their way to Jerusalem].*
[B] *But R. Aqiba kept them back at Lud.*
[C] *Rabban Gamaliel sent to him [saying], "If you keep back so many [people], you will turn out to make them err in the future."*

Yose, M. R.H. 1:5C, disagrees with the anonymous law and holds that when the new moon appears clearly, witnesses may not violate the Sabbath in order to go to Jerusalem to testify. Since such a moon will likely have been seen by the court itself, the testimony is unnecessary and there is reason to violate the Sabbath. Aqiba, M. R.H. 1:6A-B, follows Yose's same theory. Only one pair of witnesses is needed by the court; there is no reason for the others to be allowed to violate the restrictions of the Sabbath. Gamaliel, M. R.H. 1:6C, allows such witnesses to go anyway. He is concerned that, on a future occasion when witnesses are needed, they will all choose to stay home on the assumption that, as in the past, others preceded them so that they are not needed.

Unit **I** explains from Scripture the meaning of the term "clearly" at M. R.H. 1:5A. Unit **II** seems topically out of place. Perhaps it is here because, at J-L, it highlights the need to make judgments based upon the testimony of witnesses, which is the

---

[374]M reads: did not appear.

concern at M. R.H. 1:6. But this is only a guess. Unit **III** claims that, contrary to M. R.H. 1:6B, it was not Aqiba who held the witnesses back at Lud.

[I.A] How do we know that [the word] *alil* [translated at M. R.H. 1:5A as "clearly" in fact] means "clearly"?

[B] Said R. Abbahu, "Scripture states [Ps. 12:6]: 'The promises of the Lord are promises that are pure, silver refined in clear view [*alil*]³⁷⁵ on the ground, purified seven times.'"

[II.A] Rab and Samuel [disagreed regarding the meaning of the following texts]:

[B] One [of them] said,³⁷⁶ "Fifty gates of understanding were created in the world, and all of them were given to Moses, except for one,

[C] "as it says [Ps. 8:5]: 'Yet you have made him little less than God.' {Hence Moses did not pass through one "gate of understanding."}

[D] "[And suggesting Moses' unique greatness, Eccles. 12:10 reads]: 'The Preacher sought to find pleasing words.'

[E] "[This means that] the Preacher sought to be like Moses. ³⁷⁷

[F] "A heavenly voice went out and said to him [citing Eccles. 12:10]: 'And uprightly he wrote words of truth.'

[G] "[But regarding Moses it says, Dt. 34:10]: 'And since then, there has not arisen a prophet in Israel like Moses.'" {We see that, however he might have tried, F, Solomon ("the Preacher") could not become comparable to Moses.}

---

³⁷⁵RSV: "...silver *refined in a furnace* on the ground...."

³⁷⁶Not seeing the interpretation at B-C as subject to dispute, M and the parallel at B. Ned. 38a read: For the two of them say.

³⁷⁷At D-E, M reads: Rab and Samuel—One of them said, "Solomon sought to be like Moses, our Rabbi, as it is stated, 'The Preacher sought to find pleasing words.'"

[H]	But the other says, "[Dt. 34:10 means that] among the prophets there has not arisen [another person like Moses].
[I]	"[But][378] among the kings there has arisen [another individual such as Moses].
[J]	"Rather, how do I explain [Eccles. 12:10, cited at D to prove that Solomon did not succeed at achieving the level of Moses' knowledge]: 'The Preacher sought to find pleasing words'?
[K]	"[This means that] the preacher wished to pass judgments from his heart,[379] that is, without [relying upon] witnesses or [requiring there to have been] prior warning [as a precondition without which punishment would not be imposed].
[L]	"[As a result of this] a heavenly voice went out and said to him [citing Eccles. 12:10]: 'And uprightly he wrote words of truth.' [To 'write words of truth' you must follow Dt. 19:15, which states]: 'Only on the evidence of two witnesses, [or of three witnesses, shall a charge be sustained].'"[380]
[III.A]	[22a] *It once occurred: More than forty pairs [of witnesses] passed [on their way to Jerusalem]. But R. Aqiba kept them back...* [M. R.H. 1:6A-B].
[B]	It is taught on Tannaitic authority: Said R. Judah, "Heaven forbid that R. Aqiba kept them back.
[C]	"Rather, Shizpar, head[381] of Geder, kept them back.
[D]	"And Rabban Gamaliel sent, and they removed him from his [position of] greatness."

---

[378]M has this word explicitly.

[379]"From his heart" is lacking in M.

[380]M has the bracketed conclusion of the verse explicitly.

[381]Jastrow, p. 1545, s.v., *šzpr*: magistrate.

1:7

[A] *A father and his son who saw the new moon should go [to give testimony].*

[B] *It is not that they join together with one another [to provide adequate testimony],*

[C] *but so that, if one of them should turn out to be invalid [as a witness], the other may join with someone else [to make up the requisite number of witnesses].*

[D] *R. Simeon says, "A father and his son, and all relatives, are valid to give testimony about the new moon."*

[E] *Said R. Yose, "It once occurred: Tobiah, the physician, saw the new moon in Jerusalem—he, his son, and his freed slave.*

[F] *"And the priests accepted him and his son [as witnesses to the new moon], but they invalidated the testimony of his slave.*

[G] *"But when they came before the court, they accepted his [testimony] and that of his slave, but they invalidated that of his son."*

The issue concerns whether or not close relatives may serve as the two independent witnesses required to provide the court with evidence regarding the appearance of the new moon. Unit **I** locates in Scripture the foundations for the opposing answers given by Simeon, M. R.H. 1:7D, and the anonymous authorities of M. R.H. 1:7A-C. Units **II-III** question which view represents the decided law. Hanan bar Rava's claim that the law accords with Simeon is rejected, unit **II**. In unit **III** that same claim, now said to originate with Samuel, goes unchallenged.

[I.A] Said R. Levi, "What is the basis [in Scripture] for [the view of] R. Simeon, [M. R.H. 1:7D]?

[B] "As it is written [Ex. 12:1-2]: 'The Lord said to Moses and Aaron in the land of Egypt, "This month shall be for you [the

	beginning of months. It shall be the first month of the year for you]."³⁸²
[C]	"[This implies that] this testimony [regarding the sighting of the new moon] shall be valid [when given] by you, [even though you are relatives]."
[D]	But the rabbis [that is, the anonymous authorities at M. R.H. 1:7A-C, who disallow testimony from close relatives—how do they interpret Ex. 12:1-2]?
[E]	[They hold it implies only that] this testimony [regarding the sighting of the new moon] shall be give to you. {The authorities of M. R.H. 1:7A-C interpret Ex. 12:1-2 to mean only that communal leaders are to receive testimony regarding the sighting of the new moon. But, contrary to Simeon, they do not hold that the verse teaches anything regarding accepting testimony from close relatives.}
[II.A]	*Said R. Yose, "It once occurred: Tobiah, the physician, [saw the new moon in Jerusalem—he, his son, and his freed slave;* M. R.H. 1:7E].
[B]	Said Rab Hanan bar Rava,³⁸³ "The decided law accords with [the position of] R. Simeon, [M. R.H. 1:7D, which accepts testimony of relatives]."
[C]	Said Rab Huna³⁸⁴ to Rab Hanan bar Rava, "[We have the view of] R. Yose and the incident [he reports, M. R.H. 1:7E-G, which shows that the court itself rejected the testimony of close relatives], yet you say that the decided law accords with [the position of] R. Simeon!" {Since Simeon's view appears to be a minority position, it cannot represent the law.}

---

³⁸²M has the bracketed conclusion of the verse explicitly.

³⁸³M, other manuscripts, and Ritba add: said Rab.

³⁸⁴In place of "Rab Huna," M reads: Rava. This is an error (Rabbinovicz).

[D] [Hanan bar Rava] said to him,[385] "But many times I stated in the presence of Rab [that] the decided law accords with [the position of] R. Simeon, and he didn't say a word to me!"

[E] [Huna] said to him, "[In Rab's presence] how did you recite the Tannaitic tradition [reporting the statements of Simeon and Yose, M. R.H. 1:7D+E-G]?"

[F] [In reciting the Mishnaic passage, Hanan bar Rava] said to him the reverse[386] [of how M. R.H. 1:7D+E-G reads]. {Hanan placed the name of Yose at M. R.H. 1:7D, accepting the testimony of relatives, and cited that of Simeon with M. R.H. 1:7E-G, the incident that shows that the court rejected the testimony of relatives.}

[G] [Huna] said to him "[Only] for this reason [that you reported the tradition incorrectly] did Rab not [discern your mistake and] say a word to [correct] your [view that the decided law accords with the view of Simeon]."

[III.A] {We have an independent statement that the law follows Simeon.} Said Tabi the son of Mari Tabi said Mar Uqba said Samuel,[387] "The decided law accords with [the position of] R. Simeon, [M. R.H. 1:7D, which accepts testimony of relatives]."

---

[385]M lacks the beginning of this line.

[386]Simon, p. 92, translates this as direct discourse: "He [R. Hanan] replied [I repeated it to him with the names] reversed." While the formulary pattern found here ("He said to him") generally introduces direct discourse, it seems unlikely that the point is that Hanan knowingly reversed the names, which is what Simon's translation proposes. More likely is that, in response to Huna's question, E, Hanan, F, recited M. R.H. 1:7 as he knew it. Huna, G, then informs him that he has the tradition wrong and that only for this reason did Rab accept Hanan's judgment that the law follows Simeon.

[387]In place of "said Samuel," M repeats the words: the son of Mari Tabi. This is a scribal error.

1:8

[A] *These [individuals] are invalid [to testify about the appearance of the new moon]:*

[B] *(1) he who plays with dice, (2) they who lend on interest, (3) they who race pigeons, (4) they who trade in produce of the Seventh Year, (5) and slaves.*

[C] *This is the governing principle: Any evidence that a woman is not valid [to offer], also they are not valid [to offer].*

The preceding theme of who may offer evidence is developed. The Talmud's one unit rephrases what already is implicit in the Mishnah.

[I.A] {The implication of M. R.H. 1:8C is made explicit.} Thus any evidence that a woman is valid [to offer], also they are valid [to offer].[388]

[B] Said Rab Ashi,[389] "This is to say that a person who, by their [that is, Rabbinical] standards, is a robber [and hence in the same category as the first four individuals listed at M. R.H. 1:8B] is valid to offer testimony [normally allowed] of a woman."

1:9

[A] *He who saw the new moon but cannot go [on his own to testify]—they bring him along on an ass, even in a palanquin.*

[B] *And if there is an ambush set up against them, they take staves in hand.*

[C] *And if it was a long trip, they take food in hand.*

[D] *For: On account of a journey [requiring travel] for a night and a day they violate [the prohibitions of] the Sabbath and go forth to give testimony about the new moon,*

---

[388] In place of this line, M cites M. R.H. 1:8A and the second half of M. R.H. 1:8C.

[389] M and other manuscripts read: Menashi.

[E] *since it is said [Lev. 23:4]: "These are the set feasts of the Lord, [even holy convocations], which you shall proclaim in their appointed season."*

The chapter concludes by emphasizing the obligation that witnesses of the new moon take all steps necessary to appear before the court. In this way they assure that, as Scripture requires, festivals and holy convocations may be declared at the correct time (M. R.H. 1:9E). The Gemara does not comment on this passage.[390]

---

[390]M concludes the chapter "Our rabbis have taught on Tannaitic authority" followed by a complete citation of M. R.H. 1:9. Rabbinovicz suggests that this is a scribal addition intended to compensate for the absence of any passages of Gemara on this Mishnaic pericope.

CHAPTER TWO

ROSH HASHANAH CHAPTER TWO

2:1

[A] [22a] *If [the people in Jerusalem] are not going to recognize him, [the people of his own town] send another with him to give evidence about him.*

[B] *At first they would accept testimony concerning the new moon from everybody.*

[C] *Once the minim[1] had spoiled matters, they made the rule that they should accept testimony only from those who are recognized.*

The court must establish that those who testify concerning the appearance of the new moon are trustworthy. Units **I-II** propose that for this purpose, the court must hear from two witnesses who attest to the honesty of the ones who actually saw the new moon. Unit **III** by contrast rejects the Mishnah's notion entirely. It presents a Tannaitic statement that holds that all testimony regarding the new moon is accepted and that additional witnesses need not attest to the character of a person who reports seeing the new moon. Ignoring that proposition, unit **IV** details the circumstances referred to at M. R.H. 2:1B-C, when, according to the Talmud, sectarians hired witnesses to mislead the court.

[I.A] [At M. R.H. 2:1A] what is the meaning of "another"?

[B] [Presumably it means] one [other individual who can testify regarding the identity of the actual witness].

[C] {B's proposal seems unacceptable.} [22b] But is [the word of] one [person] trusted [to state that the witness of the new moon may be believed]?

---

[1] So M, other manuscripts, and all early printings. P: Boethusuans.

[D] But [to the contrary] it is taught on Tannaitic authority: There was an incident in which [a witness of the new moon] came [to the court in Jerusalem], and his witnesses [came] with him to give testimony regarding the one [who actually saw the new moon]. {The fact that several individuals were brought to attest to the character of the one who saw the new moon proves that B's interpretation of M. R.H. 2:1A is incorrect.}

[E] [Offering a different explanation] said R. Pappa, "What is the meaning of 'another'?

[F] "[It means] 'another pair [of individuals].'" {These two people can attest to the character of the two people who are required as witnesses of the new moon.}

[G] This [interpretation suggested by Pappa at F] also makes sense [based upon the actual wording of M. R.H. 2:1]:

[H] For if you [reject Pappa's explanation and] do not say this, [then, in the phrase at M. R.H. 2:1A]: *If they [in Jerusalem] are not going to recognize that one...*—what is the meaning of [the word] "that one"?

[I] Should I say that "that one"[2] [refers to] one [person]?

[J] But [that is impossible, since] is [the word of] one [person] trusted [to give evidence of the appearance of the new moon]?

[K] {The fact that one witness may not give evidence for the new moon is proven by Ps. 81:5.} [At Ps. 81:4 the word], "judgment" is written regarding it [that is, the testimony for the new moon]. {Ps. 81:3-4 reads: "Blow the trumpet at the new moon, at the full moon, on our feast day. For it is a statute for Israel, a judgment of the God of Jacob." J-K's point is that any "judgment" requires two witnesses.}

[L] Rather [contrary to what is proposed at I, at M. R.H. 2:1A, the word] "that one" [means] "that *pair* [of witnesses]."

---

[2]M lacks the beginning of this line. There is no difference in meaning.

[M] Comparably, what is the meaning of "another"?³
[N] [It means] "another pair."

[II.A] {The concern of the preceding unit is developed.} But [in this instance] is [the testimony of] one [individual, regarding the character of the witness] not trusted?

[B] But [to the contrary] it is taught on Tannaitic authority [T. R.H. 1:16]: **It once occurred: R. Nehorai went with a witness to give testimony concerning him on the Sabbath at Usha.**

[C] {For the reason given here, B's description proves nothing.} I can say that another witness was with R. Nehorai, and [the fact that] they do not mention him is because of respect for R. Nehorai. {That is, the other individual would not be mentioned with, and therefore put on the same footing as, Nehorai.}

[D] [Explaining exactly what happened in the incident reported at B] Rab Ashi said, "[In the case of] R. Nehorai,⁴ a different witness [already] was at Usha, and R. Nehorai went to join with him [to present the required testimony of two individuals]."

[E] {The point of what is reported at B accordingly is not clear.} If that is so [that there was another witness], what does [the story] mean to teach?

[F] [Had the incident not been recounted] what might you have thought?

[G] In a case of doubt [regarding a witness to the new moon], they do not profane the Sabbath.

[H] So we are informed, [that even in a case of doubt, one may profane the Sabbath, as Nehorai is represented as doing, B].

---

³Here and at N, in place of "another," M reads: one.

⁴M lacks: R. Nehorai.

[III.A] When Ulla came [to Babylonia] he said, "[On such-and-so day] they sanctified the [new] moon in the west[5] [that is, in the land of Israel]." {Contrary to what is proposed in the preceding units, Ulla's testimony was accepted despite the fact that other individuals were not with him to attest to his character.}

[B] Said Rab Kahana, "[To ascertain the law] we do not require [this story about] Ulla,[6] for he is a great person who [obviously] is believed.

[C] "Rather, even[7] an ordinary person is also believed [to give testimony about the new moon]!

[D] "What is the reason?[8]

[E] "[In regards to] anything that eventually will become known [through other sources], people do not lie."

[F] A Tannaitic statement makes the same point: [If] someone comes from[9] the [other] end of the world [so as not to be known to anyone] and says, "A court has sanctified the [new] month," he is believed.

[IV.A] *At first they would accept testimony concerning the new moon from everybody. [Once the minim had spoiled matters, they made the rule that they should accept testimony only from those who are recognized;* M. R.H. 2:1B-C].

[B] Our rabbis have taught on Tannaitic authority: How did the *minim*[10] spoil matters?

---

[5]M and other manuscripts lack: in the West.

[6]M lacks "Ulla" and "who is believed," at the end of the line.

[7]M lacks this word.

[8]M lacks this line. It introduces E with the word: For.

[9]So the emendation of Meiri. The printed text reads: at.

[10]So M. Here, at C, and at I, P reads: Boethusuans.

[C] {See T. R.H. 1:15:} Once the *minim* wished to lead the sages into error. They hired two people for 400 *zuz*, one of our [group], and one of theirs [that is, a sectarian].

[D] **The one who was of their [group] testified and departed.**

[E] Ours [came in]. They said to him, "Tell [us] how you saw the moon."

[F] He said to them, **"I was going up the ascent of Adumim,[11] and I saw it crouching between two rocks, its head looking like a calf, and its ears looking like a lamb, and its horns looking like a deer, and its tail lying between its[12] thighs. I saw it, I was astonished, and I fell backwards.**

[G] "And if you do not believe me, lo, two hundred *zuz* are tied up in my purse [as a surety]!"

[H] They said to him, "Who forced you into this [act of deceit]?

[I] **He said to them, "I heard that the *minim* wished to lead the sages into error.** I said, I shall go myself and inform them,[13] lest untrustworthy people come and [in fact] mislead the sages!"

[J] **They said to him, "The two hundred *zuz* are given to you as a gift. But the one who hired you will be laid out on the post [for flogging]."**

[K] At that exact moment, *they made the rule that they should accept testimony only from those who are recognized* [M. R.H. 2:1C].

2:2

[A] *At first they would kindle flares.*

---

[11] See Josh. 15:7.

[12] M adds: two.

[13] M reads: sages. The rest of this line is missing from the text of M and is added in the margin.

[B]   *Once the Samaritans had spoiled matters, they made the rule that messengers would go forth.*

2:3

[A]   *How did they kindle flares?*

[B]   *They bring long cedar wood sticks, reeds, oleaster wood, and flax tow.*

[C]   *And one binds them together with a rope.*

[D]   *And he goes up to the top of the hill and lights them.*

[E]   *And he waves them to and fro and up and down, until he sees his fellow doing the same on the next hilltop, and so with the third hilltop [and beyond].*

2:4

[A]   *And beginning at what place did they kindle flares?*

[B]   *From the Mount of Olives [they gave the signal] to Sarteba, from Sarteba to Agrippina, from Agrippina to Hauran, from Hauran to Bet Baltin.*

[C]   *But they did not move from Bet Baltin.*

[D]   *Rather [from that vantage point] one waves them to and fro, up and down, until he would see the whole Exile[14] before him lit up like a bonfire.*

Unit **I** explains from Scripture the use of the term for "flare" at M. R.H. 2:2-4. Unit **II** questions when these flares were lit, whether to mark the beginning of full months, defective months, or, perhaps, both. This is a concern because of the need to determine how to mark a new month that begins on a Friday night, when flares cannot be lit. M. R.H. 2:3B's list of the types of wood used in the flares introduces a discussion of types of cedar, unit **III**. Unit **IV**, on a method of farming coral from the ocean bottom, appears here because of unit **III**'s reference to a type of wood called coral.

Unit **V** returns to the general theme of unit **III**, asserting that God is destined to restore the trees of Jerusalem destroyed by

---

[14]M reads: so that the entire Exile would see [it].

gentiles. Use of the term "wilderness" to refer to Jerusalem leads the Talmud in unit **VI** to present a statement about the futility, or, in an alternative version, the value, of teaching Torah where there are no students. This in turn introduces a discussion (unit **VII**) of the value to the community of rabbinic scholars, who serve as a means of atonement for sin.

Units **VIII-XI** explain M. R.H. 2:4. The Talmud identifies the places referred to in the Mishnah, indicates how the Exile was "lit up like a bonfire," and discusses the distances between the specific points at which flares were lit.

[I.A][15] How [do we know that the word translated here as] "flares," conveys the meaning "burning"?[16]

[B] As it is written [2 Sam. 5:21: "And the Philistines left their idols there], and David and his men carried them away." {The word "carried" in this verse has the same root as the word translated as "flares."}

[C] Now, we translate [this verse into Aramaic as follows]: "And David burned them [that is, the idols]." {The implication is that the root translated as "flare" indeed signifies burning.}

[II.A] Our rabbis have taught on Tannaitic authority [see T. R.H. 1:17]: They kindle flares only for a month that came at its [proper] time, in order to sanctify it.

[B] And when are they kindled?

[C] On the day of its intercalation.

[D] This is to say that for defective [months containing only twenty-nine days], we do it [that is, kindle flares].

[E] [But] for full [months containing thirty days], we do not do it.

[F] What is the reason for this?

---

[15]This unit is lacking in all manuscripts, suggesting (Rabbinovicz) that it is a late addition.

[16]The Hebrew term connotes "raising up."

[G] Said R. Zera, "It is a precautionary measure [enacted] because of [the case of] the new moon [of a] defective [month] that falls on the eve of the Sabbath.

[H] "[In such an instance] when do we do [it, that is, light the flares]?

[I] "At the end of the Sabbath.[17] {Even though the new month began with Friday evening, because of the prohibition against kindling on the Sabbath, the flares are not lit until Saturday night.}

[J] "Now, if you say that we do the same [that is, kindle flares] for full [months], [23a] people will be led into error.

[K] "[For, if flares were lit both for defective and full months, when flares are seen on a Saturday night people will become confused and] will say, '[Perhaps] this was actually a defective [month], and the reason that they did not do [it, that is, kindle the flares] yesterday [on Friday night] is because doing so was not possible. Or perhaps it [actually] is a full [month], and they did [it, that is, kindled the flares on Saturday night] at the correct time.'" {Zera claims that because of this possible confusion, flares never are kindled for a full month. As a result, if flares are lit on a Saturday night, the thirtieth of the month, people will know that the month actually was defective and ended on the twenty-ninth.}

[L] {Zera's argument, that because of the potential confusion flares are kindled only for defective months, is rejected.} But [despite the problem raised by Zera] let us do [it, that is, kindle flares] for both full and defective [months]!

---

[17] All manuscripts lack H-I.

[M] And when the new moon[18] falls on Sabbath's eve, let them [simply] not do anything [that is, in this instance, no flares are kindled either on Friday or Saturday night].

[N] Now, [in this approach], since they did not do [it, that is, light flares] at the conclusion of the Sabbath, even though they do [it] for a full [month], people will know that it was a defective month [which ended Friday night, at which time flares could not be kindled].

[O] {L-N's approach is rejected.} Even in this approach people will be led into error!

[P] They will say, "This[19] was a full month, but the reason that they did not do [it, that is, kindle flares] is that they were [somehow] prevented.[20]

[Q] {A new solution is offered to the problem posed by Zera.} Then they should do [it, that is, kindle flares] for full [months] but not do [it] at all for defective [months]!

[R] [Explaining why this is not acceptable] said Abayye, "[They do not do this] so as not to prevent the people from working for two days." {People did not work on the celebration of the new moon. If flares were used only to announce a full month, then, because of doubt, people always would have to cease work to celebrate the thirtieth day, which, in the case of a defective month, is the day of the new moon. Then, if the month turned out to be full, they would have to continue without working to celebrate the actual new moon, on the thirty-first day.}

---

[18]M adds: after a defective month.

[19]M adds: was a defective month, and the reason that they did not do it yesterday is that it was impossible. Or perhaps it....

[20]Rashi, cited by Simon, p. 98: Those who light the flares might have become drunk through drinking too much wine on the Sabbath.

[III.A] *How did they kindle flares? They bring long cedar wood sticks, [reeds, oleaster wood, and flax tow;* M. R.H. 2:3A-B].

[B] Said Rab Judah, "There are four kinds of cedar: cedar, qetros, oleaster, and cypress.

[C] Qetros?[21]

[D] Said Rab Idra,[22] "Those of the house of R. Shila say [it is] *mabliga*.[23]

[E] "But [others] say it is *gulmish*."

[F] This disputes [the perspective of] Rabbah bar Rab Huna, for said Rabbah bar Rab Huna, "They say in the house of Rab,[24] 'There are ten kinds of cedar, as it is said [Is. 41:19]: "I will plant in the wilderness cedar [*erez*], the acacia tree [*shittah*], the myrtle [*hadas*], and oleaster [*eṣ shemen*]. I will set in the desert the cypress [*berosh*], teak [*tidhar*], and the pine [*teashur*] together."

[G] "'Erez' [means] cedar, "shittah" [means] pine, "hadas" [means] myrtle, "eṣ shemen" [means] balsam, "berosh" [means] cypress," "tidhar" [means] *shaga*, "teashur" [means] *shurbina*.'"

[H] But are these not only seven [kinds of cedar]?

[I] When R. Dimi came [from the land of Israel], he said, "They added to them:[25] *alonim, almonim, almogim.*

---

[21] M and other sources read: What is meant by "Qetros"?

[22] M, in error, records the name as: Adda Idra

[23] See Jastrow, p. 379, s.v. *zblygh*.

[24] M lacks the preceding clause. The clause appears in the manuscript and printed edition of the parallel at B. B.B. 80b but is absent at B. Ta. 25b. At B. Suk. 37a it appears in the printed edition but not in M.

[25] M adds: another three, and these are they.

[J]   "'Alonim' are pistachio trees; 'almonim' are oaks; 'almogim' are corals."

[K]   Others say, "[They added] *aronim, armonim, almogim*.

[L]   "'Aronim' are ore, 'armonim' are plane trees, 'almogim' are corals."[26]

[IV.A]   [Is. 33:21 states: "But there the Lord in majesty will be for us a place of broad rivers and streams], where no galley with oars can go, [nor stately ship can pass]."

[B]   Said Rab,[27] "This [refers to] a great, fast-sailing vessel."[28]

[C]   [Add following M:] "Why is it built? To raise corals."

[D]   How is this done?

[E]   They bring six thousand men for twelve months.[29]

[F]   But some say: [It is] twelve-thousand men for six months of a year.

[G]   And they load it [that is, the boat] with sand until it sinks.[30]

[H]   Then a diver goes down and ties [one end of] a rope of flax to the coral and ties [the other end] to the boat.

[I]   Then they remove the sand and throw it outside [the boat], and when [the boat] rises [the coral] is detached [from the bottom] and brought up [to the surface].

[J]   And they exchange one [weight in coral] for two [of that same weight in] silver.

---

[26]M lacks K-L. The material appears in M in the parallel at B. B.B. 80b, suggesting that it dropped out of the manuscript here through haplography.

[27]M and other sources read: Said R. Judah said Rab.

[28]See Jastrow, p. 150, s.v. *bwrny*: "*Liburnian* (ship), a light fast-sailing vessel."

[29]Literally: for a twelve month year.

[30]M adds: to the earth.

[K] There are three ports [at which coral can be collected], two belonging to the Romans,[31] and one belonging to the Persians.

[L] From that belonging to the Romans coral is brought up.

[M] From that belonging to the Persians pearls are brought up,

[N] and it is called the port of Mashmahig.

[V.A] Said R. Yohanan, "Each and every[32] acacia tree that gentiles took from Jerusalem the holy one, blessed be he, is destined to restore,

[B] "as it is said [Is. 41:19]: 'I will put in the wilderness the cedar, the acacia....'

[C] "Now, [the term] 'wilderness' means nothing other than 'Jerusalem,'

[D] "as it is said [Is. 64:10]: 'Zion has become a wilderness, [Jerusalem a desolation].'"

[VI.A] And said R. Yohanan, "Anyone who studies Torah but does not teach it [to others] is like a myrtle in the wilderness [which is wasted, since no one can enjoy it]."

[B] There are those who say: Anyone who studies Torah and teaches it [to others] in a place in which there are no other scholars is like a myrtle in the wilderness, which is precious.[33]

---

[31] So M. P: Armae, referring to the land of the Syrians.

[32] M lacks: and every.

[33] At A-B, M is garbled. It reads: Anyone who studies Torah and teaches it in a place in which there are no students of sages is like a myrtle in the wilderness, which is not appreciated. And there are those who say: Anyone who studies and teaches—said R. Yohanan—that he is appreciated.

[VII.A] And said R. Yohanan, "Woe to the nations of idol-worshippers,[34] for they have no remedy [to atone for their sins],

[B] "as it is said [Is. 60:17]: 'Instead of bronze I will bring gold; and instead of iron I will bring silver; instead of wood, bronze; instead of stones, iron.'

[C] "[But, as for the idol worshippers] instead of R. Aqiba and his associates, what can they bring?

[D] "And concerning them [that is, the idol worshippers, Scripture] says [Joel 3:21]: 'I shall cleanse [them of other transgressions, but] their blood I shall not cleanse.[35]

[VIII.A] *And beginning at what place did they kindle flares? [From the Mount of Olives (they gave the signal) to Sarteba, from Sarteba to Agrippina, from Agrippina to Hauran, from Hauran to Bet Baltin]. But [they did not move] from Bet Baltin* [M. R.H. 2:4A-C].

[B] What is Bet Baltin?

[C] Said Rab, [**23b**] "This [name] refers to Biram."

[IX.A] [At M. R.H. 2:4D] what is [meant by the term] "Exile"?

[B] Said Rab Joseph,[36] "This refers to Pumpedita."

[X.A] [At M. R.H. 2:4D] what is [meant by *"lit up] like a bonfire"*?

[B] A Tannaitic authority [said]: Everyone [in Pumpedita] takes a torch in his hand and goes up to his roof [to spread the news]."

---

[34]M, other manuscripts, and all early printings read simply: nations of the world. The words "idol-worshippers" were added by the censor in the Silia printing.

[35]RSV: "I will avenge their blood, and I will not clear the guilty, [for the Lord dwells in Zion]."

[36]M lacks the attribution entirely. In L, the attribution is to Abayye.

[C]   It is taught on Tannaitic authority: R. Simeon b. Eleazar says, "[This] also [was done in] Harim, Kiyyar, Geder,[37] and their neighboring [towns]."

[D]   There are those who say [that these places] are between [the locations mentioned at M. R.H. 2:4, and, hence, are in the land of Israel].

[E]   [And][38] there are those who say [that these places] are on the other side of the land of Israel.

[F]   [In E's understanding] one authority [e.g., M. R.H. 2:4] considers this side [of the land of Israel], while [the other] authority [e.g., Simeon b. Eleazar, C] considers the other side of the land of Israel.

[XI.A] [Referring to the locales listed at M. R.H. 2:4] said R. Yohanan, "Between each [place and the next] were eight parasangs."

[B]   How much distance was there [in all from the Mount of Olives to Bet Baltin]?

[C]   Thirty two [parasangs].

[D]   But, lo, now there is a greater [distance]!

[E]   Said Abayye, "[This is because] the [direct] roads have been closed,

[F]   "as it is written [Hos. 2:6]: 'Therefore I will hedge up her way with thorns [and I will build a wall against her, so that she cannot find her paths].'"[39]

---

[37]M reads: Haritz and Biyyar.

[38]M and other manuscripts have the bracketed word explicitly and add: there is a dispute.

[39]M has the bracketed conclusion of the verse explicitly.

[G] Rab Nahman bar Isaac said, "[We know the direct roads have been closed] from this [verse], as it is written[40] [Lam. 3:9: 'He has blocked my ways with hewn stones, he has made] my paths crooked.'"

2:5

[A] *There was a large courtyard in Jerusalem, called Bet Ya'azeq, to which all the witnesses gather.*

[B] *And the court examines them there.*

[C] *Now they prepare big meals for them, so that they should make it a habit to come.*

[D] *At first, [having come on the Sabbath and therefore having no permitted area of Sabbath travel], they did not move from there the whole day.*

[E] *Rabban Gamaliel the elder[41] ordained that they may move about for two thousand cubits in every direction.*

[F] *And [this rule applies] not only to these,[42] but also (1) a midwife who comes to assist, and one who comes to save [people] (2) from a fire, (3) from a siege, (4) from [drowning in] a river, (5) or from the debris of a collapsed [house]—*

[G] *lo, [having completed their task], these are in the status of the townsfolk, and they have the right to move about for two thousand cubits in all directions.*

The Talmud's one unit concerns the character of the courtyard in which witnesses to the new moon gathered and were questioned, M.

---

[40]M lacks "as it is written" but explicitly has the first clause of Lam. 3:9, shown here in brackets.

[41]M and Mishnah manuscript Napoli lack: the elder. In the citation of this pericope at B. Erub. 45a, however, the term appears in both the printed edition and in M.

[42]M and all manuscripts add: they said. The term is found in the printed edition at B. Erub. 45a.

R.H. 2:5A. The question whether the place was elegant and inviting or roughly built and used primarily as a location for rigorous questioning remains undecided.

[I.A] They asked them: "[At M. R.H. 2:5A] do we teach on Tannaitic authority [that the name is] *Bet Ya'azeq* [as in the Mishnaic text before us] or do we teach on Tannaitic authority [that the name actually is] *Bet Yazeq*? {The issue, detailed in the following, is whether the name refers to an elegant place, which people would enjoy, or a place in which people were questioned rigorously.}

[B] [The answer is that] we teach on Tannaitic authority *Bet Ya'azeq*

[C] This is parlance that refers to elegance,

[D] as it is written [Is. 5:2]: "He ringed it around [*ya'azeqhu*] and cleared it of stones." {So Rashi, followed by Simon, p. 101, who understands the name "Bet Ya'azeq" to refer to a stone fence around the courtyard. The Aramaic root means "ring."}

[E] Or perhaps [in fact] we teach on Tannaitic authority *Bet Yazeq*.

[F] This is parlance that refers to grief,

[G] as it is written [Jer. 40:1: "The word that came to Jeremiah from the Lord after Nebuzaradan, the captain of the guard, had let him go from Ramah], when he took him bound in chains [*azyqym*] [along with all the captives of Jerusalem and Judah who were being exiled to Babylon]."

[H] Said Abayye, "Come and learn [from M. R.H. 2:5C that B-D is correct]: *Now, they prepare big meals for them, so that they should make it a habit to come.*"

[I] {Abayye's proof is rejected as inconclusive.} Perhaps they treated them both ways, [kindly and with rigor]! {The question of which interpretation is correct is left unresolved.}

2:6

[A] *How do they examine the witnesses?*

[B] *The pair that makes its appearance first they examine first.*

[C] *They bring in the elder of them and say to him, "Tell [us]!*[43] *How did you see the moon? Was it facing the sun or turned away from it? Was it to the north or to the south? How high was it, and in which direction was it leaning? And how broad was it?"*

[D] *If he said, "It was facing the sun," he has said nothing at all.*

[E] *Afterwards they would bring in the second party*[44] *and examine him.*

[F] *If their testimony coincided, their testimony was confirmed.*

[G] *And [in the case of] all the other pairs of witnesses, they ask the main points,*

[H] *not because they needed their [evidence], but so that they should not go out disappointed,*

[I] *so that they would make it a habit of coming [in the future].*

The Talmud's interests here are narrowly exegetical. Units **I-II** explain the questions asked by the court (M. R.H. 2:6C) and indicate the reason that certain responses disqualify the witnesses (M. R.H. 2:6D). Unit **III** concerns the acceptable range of difference between the testimony of two witnesses. Units **IV-V** note that the witness must have clearly seen the new moon in the sky. Testimony is not accepted from a witness who saw a reflected image or who caught only a momentary glimpse of the moon.

[I.A] [At M. R.H. 2:6C the meaning of] *facing the sun* is the same as [the meaning of] *to the north*; [the meaning of] *turned away*

---

[43] M and other manuscripts of B. lack: Tell us.

[44] M lacks the conclusion of this line.

from it is the same as [the meaning of] *to the south*.⁴⁵ {Why are these apparently duplicative questions asked?}

[B]⁴⁶ [Explaining that the questions are not redundant] said Abayye, "[It means], 'Is the concavity of the moon in front of [that is, turned towards] the sun or behind [that is, turned away from] the sun?'

[C] "If [the witness] said [that the concavity of the moon is] in front of [that is, turned towards] the sun, he has said nothing at all.

[D] "For said R. Yohanan, 'What is written [at Job 25:2]? "Dominion and fear are with God. He makes peace in his high heaven." {Proof of Abayye's statement, C, lies in the explanation of how God "makes peace in his high heaven," which follows.}

[E] "'The sun never saw the concavity of the moon, nor the concavity of a rainbow.

[F] "'[It never sees] the concavity of the moon, so that [the moon] will not feel humiliated.

[G] "'[The sun never sees] the concavity of a rainbow⁴⁷ so that those who worship the sun will not say, "[The sun] is [**24a**] shooting arrows!"'"

---

⁴⁵Simon, p. 102, n. 6, explains: "The new moon can be seen only about sunset, close to the sun, when the sun is traveling towards the north. We should therefore naturally take 'in front of the sun', to mean 'to the north of the sun', and 'behind the sun' to mean 'to the south of the sun'."

⁴⁶M adds: You have spoken of its concavity? Rabbinovicz proposes reading with other manuscripts and the Cracow edition: [We speak] on Tannaitic authority of its concavity.

⁴⁷M lacks all of F and the beginning of this line through this word, the result of haplography.

[II.A] *How high was it, and in which direction was it leaning?* [M. R.H. 2:6C].⁴⁸

[B] One Tannaitic authority [taught: "If the witness says that it was leaning], 'To the north,' his words are accepted.

[C] "[But if he says that it was leaning], 'To the south,' he has said nothing at all."

[D] But the opposite has been taught on Tannaitic authority⁴⁹ [T. R.H. 1:17, with the order of the sentences reversed: **If he said, "It was leaning] to the south," his words are accepted. [If he said, "It was leaning] to the north," his statement is null.**

[E] There⁵⁰ is no contradiction [between D and B-C]!

[F] This [statement at D] applies during the sunny season, and this [statement at B-C] applies during the rainy season. {Simon, p. 103, n. 3, explains: "The new moon always appears due west. Hence, in the summer months when the sun sets in the north-west it is south of the sun, and similarly in the winter months north of the sun."}

[III.A] Our⁵¹ rabbis have taught on Tannaitic authority [T. R.H. 1:17: **If] one [of them] says, "[I saw it] two ox-loads⁵² high," and one says, "Three," their testimony is accepted.**

---

⁴⁸ M lacks this line.

⁴⁹M and other manuscripts lack the continuation of this line.

⁵⁰In M and other sources, this line is introduced with the attribution: Said Abayye.

⁵¹In M, this line is introduced with a citation of M. R.H. 2:5C: *How high was it?*

⁵²Alternatively, ox-goads. See Jastrow, p. 837, s.v. *mrd'* and *mrd't*. Simon, p. 103, has "ox-load." A correction, p. 175, suggests "ox-goad."

[B]   **[If] one [of them] says, "Three," and one of them says, "Five,"** their testimony is null, but [what each states may be used to] join together with other testimony [to comprise the two witnesses needed to confirm the sighting].[53]

[IV.A] Our rabbis have taught on Tannaitic authority [cf., T. R.H. 1:17: If they say], "We saw it [reflected] in the water," "We saw it reflected in a mirror," [or] "We saw it through the clouds,"[54] they are not allowed to testify concerning it.[55]

[B]   [If they say], "We saw half of it [reflected] in the water," "We saw half of it through the clouds," [or] "We saw half of it reflected in a mirror," they are not allowed to testify concerning it.

[C]   {The need explicitly to state B is evaluated.} Now, [insofar as in a case in which the individual saw] all of it [through clouds or reflected in water or a mirror] you said, [A, that his testimony is] not [allowed], need we [even] ask [whether or not the testimony is permitted in an instance in which the individual saw *only*] half of it [in these manners]? {The answer seems obvious that the testimony will be excluded. It appears, therefore, that, contrary to B, the issue need not even be considered.}

[D]   {The need for B is explained. C's reading of matters, clarified by the italicized *only* at C, is unacceptable.} Rather,[56] here is the point of what is said [at B]: [If he said that he saw] "Half of it [reflected] in the water [and] half of it in the sky," [or] "Half of it through the clouds [and] half of it

---

[53]T. R.H. 1:17 reads: they do not join together with one another, but one of them may join together with other [witnesses]. The point is the same.

[54]Probably as a result of haplography, M lacks: We saw it through clouds.

[55]Here, at B, and in the following unit, M lacks: concerning it.

[56]In place of the word "Rather," M and other manuscripts read: Said Abayye.

in the sky,' [or] "Half of it reflected in a mirror [and] half of it in the sky,"⁵⁷ [despite the fact that they appropriately saw half of the moon] they are not allowed to testify [concerning it].

[V.A] Our rabbis have taught on Tannaitic authority: [If the witnesses say], "We saw it [once but a moment later] could not see it again," they are not allowed to testify concerning it.

[B] {How can A be the case?} For the whole period are they [required] continually to see it?

[C] Said Abayye, "This is the point of what is said [at A: If witnesses said], 'We saw it of ourselves [that is, by chance], and [looked] back with the express intention of it seeing it [again], but [at that time] we did not see it,' they are not allowed to testify concerning it.

[D] "What is the reason?

[E] "One can say: They simply saw a globe-shaped cloud [and not the new moon at all]."

2:7

[A] *The head of the court says, "It is sanctified."*

[B] *And all the people respond*⁵⁸ *after him, "It is sanctified. It is sanctified."*

[C] *Whether it appears in the expected time or does not appear in the expected time, they sanctify it.*

[D] *R. Eleazar*⁵⁹ *b. R. Sadoq says, "If it did not appear in its expected time, they do not sanctify it, for Heaven has already declared it sanctified."*

---

⁵⁷The result of haplography, M lacks: Half of it reflected in a mirror [and] half of it in the sky.

⁵⁸Here and at unit II.A, M reads: say.

⁵⁹M and texts of the Mishnah read: Eliezer. Eleazar, as found in P, is correct.

The Talmud again is concerned with narrowly exegetical issues. Units **I-III** provide the scriptural foundations for the actions described at M. R.H. 2:7A-B. Unit **IV** records a Tannaitic statement that disagrees with the position of Eleazar b. Sadoq, M. R.H. 2:7D. Unit **V** argues that the decided law concurs with Eleazar b. Sadoq's view.

[I.A] *The head of the court [says, "It is sanctified;"* M. R.H. 2:7A].

[B] What [verse in Scripture stands behind] these words?

[C] Said R. Hiyya bar Gamda said R. Yose b. Saul, said Rabbi, "Scripture states [Lev. 23:44]: 'Moses declared the appointed festivals of the Lord.'

[D] "From this [verse we deduce] that the head of the court [playing a role parallel to that of Moses] says, 'It is sanctified.'"

[II.A] *And all the people respond after him, "It is sanctified. It is sanctified"* [M. R.H. 2:7B].

[B] From where [in Scripture] do we [learn this]?

[C] Said Rab Pappa,[60] "Scripture states [Lev. 23:4: 'These are the appointed feasts of the Lord, the holy convocations], which [you] shall proclaim.' {The cited verse concludes with the direct object *'wtm*, meaning "them," and rendered in English by the relative pronoun "which." In the Hebrew original, the bracketed "you" is implicit, required by the second person, plural verb, "shall proclaim."}

[D][61] "[Instead of *'wtm*] read [the verse as though the word were] *'tm*, [meaning 'you']." {Pappa wishes to read the verse as stating explicitly that "you" (that is, Israelites) shall proclaim the appointed feasts. This is what M. R.H. 2:7B requires.}

---

[60]M lacks the attribution.

[61]In M, this line appears garbled. Cf., Rabbinovicz.

[E] [Offering a different scriptural basis for M. R.H. 2:7B] Rab Nahman bar Isaac said, "[Lev. 23:2 states: 'As for] these, they are my appointed feasts.' {Nahman focuses upon the redundant appearance of two second person plural pronouns. The second "they" seems superfluous and therefore must have a special significance, indicated at F.}

[F] "[This means that] 'they' [i.e., the Israelites] shall say, '[These are] my seasons.'"

[III.A] [And all the people respond after him], "It is sanctified. It is sanctified" [M. R.H. 2:7B].

[B] Why [must they say it] twice?

[C] As it is written [Lev. 23:2: "The appointed feasts of the Lord, which you shall proclaim as] holy convocations."[62] {The word "convocations" derives from the root meaning "to proclaim." The word's appearance here in the plural is taken to mean that the people must make their proclamation twice (the smallest plural).}

[IV.A] R. Eleazar b. R. Sadoq says, "If it did not appear in its expected time, they do not sanctify it, [for Heaven has already declared it sanctified;" M. R.H. 2:7D].[63]

[B] It is taught on Tannaitic authority: [Contrary to Eleazar b. Sadoq] Polemo says, "[If it did appear] in its expected time, they do not sanctify it, [but if it did] not [appear] in its expected time, they do sanctify it."

[C] R. Eleazar b. R. Simeon[64] says, "Whether this way or that, they do not sanctify it,

---

[62]M adds: [This plural signifies] two times.

[63]M lacks this line.

[64]M and L (where the text is corrected) lack: b. R. Simeon. Early printings have "b. R. Sadoq," a printer's error.

[D] "for it is said [Lev. 25:10]: 'And you shall sanctify the fiftieth year.'

[E] "[This means that] years you must sanctify, but you do not sanctify months."

[V.A] Said Rab Judah said Samuel, "The decided law follows [the opinion of] R. Eleazar b. R. Sadoq [at M. R.H. 2:7D]."

[B] Said Abayye, "We also have taught [this] on Tannaitic authority [M. R.H. 3:1A-B: *If] the court and all the Israelites saw [the new moon on the thirtieth day], the witnesses having been examined, but they had no chance to say, 'It is sanctified,' before it [actually] got dark, lo, this [month coming to an end] is an intercalated month, [and a thirty-first day is added].*

[C] "[The passage is explicit that the month is] intercalated, not sanctified [through an act of the court]!" {This is as Eleazar b. Sadoq, M. R.H. 2:7D, states. They only sanctify the new moon at the expected time.}

[D] {Abayye's reasoning, B-C, is rejected through the contention that the case he cites is subject to special considerations and that the issue raised by Eleazar b. Sadoq in fact is irrelevant to it.} [In the case cited at B, the Mishnah] needed [explicitly to indicate that the month is] intercalated.

[E] You might have thought, "Since the court and all [the people of] Israel saw it, the matter has become known, so that [the new month in all events should be proclaimed and the past month] should not be intercalated.

[F] Therefore we are informed [that even in such circumstances, the new month cannot be proclaimed on the thirtieth day accept through a declaration of the court]. {Contrary to Abayye, B-C, since this case is subject to a special consideration, it cannot be used to support the point made by Eleazar b. Sadoq, that the new moon is sanctified only when it appears at its proper time.}

2:8a

[A] *A picture of the shapes of the moon did Rabban Gamaliel have on a tablet and on the wall of his upper room,[65] which he would show ordinary folk, saying, "Did you see it like this or like that?"*

The Talmud is concerned with the permissibility of making images of heavenly bodies or other beings that minister to God. The result here is to propose that the making of certain images is permitted. This is the case 1) so long as they will be used in public places where there can be no suspicion of idol-worship or 2) as in the case of Gamaliel's pictures of the moon, if they are to be used for instructional purposes.

[I.A][66] Now is this [that is, making a picture of the shapes of the moon] permitted?

[B] But [suggesting the contrary] has it not been written [Ex. 20:23]: "You shall not make with me [gods of silver," meaning], you shall not make anything that looks like my attendants?

[C] [Rejecting B] said Abayye, "The Torah only has prohibited [making images of those][67] attendants that it is possible to reproduce in facsimile."

[D] This is as it has been taught on Tannaitic authority: A person may not make a house in the form of the Temple, a covered porch in the form of the [Temple] court, a courtyard[68] like the

---

[65]M and other sources have a different ordering of clauses here: in his attic, on a tablet on the wall. The meaning is the same.

[66]The translation of the Talmudic materials pertinent to M. R.H. 2:8a is based upon Neusner's rendering of the parallel passage at B. A.Z. 43a-b.

[67]M has the bracketed words explicitly.

[68]M lacks this word, apparently a scribal error.

[Temple] courtyard, a table like the [Temple's] table, [or] a candelabrum like the [Temple's] candelabrum.

[E] But he may make [**24b**] [a candelabrum] that has five, six, or eight [branches], but he may not make one with seven, even though it is of metals other than the ones [used in the Temple].

[F] R. Yose bar Judah says, "Even one of wood he may not make, because that is how the kings of the House of the Hasmoneans made it [Rashi: when they first recaptured the Temple]."

[G] They said to him, "Is there any proof from that [precedent]? It was made of metal staves plated with tin.[69] When they got rich, they made one of silver. When they got still richer, they made one of gold."

[II.A] {We return to Abayye's claim at C in the preceding unit.} But [regarding] those attendants that one cannot reproduce in facsimile—is it really permitted [to make images of them]?

[B] But [indicating the contrary] it has been taught on Tannaitic authority: [Ex. 20:23 states]: "You shall not make with me," [meaning], you may not make anything that looks like my attendants who serve before me in the heights.

[C] Said Abayye, "The Torah has prohibited only the making of images of the four faces together." {Reference is to the image described at Ezek. 1:10.}

[D] Then, from this [we should conclude that] the face of a man by itself is permitted!

[E] [If this is the case] why has it been taught on Tannaitic authority: All faces may be [reproduced] except the human face?

---

[69]In place of "plated with tin," M reads, "plated [that is, covered] with wood," a difference of one letter. M's reading may be authentic, reflecting Yose bar Judah's statement at F, that the candelabrum of the House of the Hasmoneans was made of wood (Rabbinovicz).

[F] Said Rab Huna the son of Rab Idi,[70] "From the lesson of Abayye I have learned: [The verse] 'You shall not make with me....' [is to be read[71] as though the vowels yielded], 'You shall not make me.' {Since humankind was created in God's likeness, pictures of people's faces, like images of God, may not be produced.}

[III.A] But is it really permitted [to make images of] the other attendants?

[B] But [indicating the contrary] it has been taught on Tannaitic authority: [Ex. 20:23 states]: "You shall not make with me,"[72] [meaning], you may not make anything that looks like my attendants, who serve before me in the heights, such as Ophannim, Seraphim, the holy Hayyot, and the ministering angels.

[C] Said Abayye, "The Torah has prohibited only [making images of][73] the attendants who are at the highest level."

[D] But is it really permitted [to make images of] the attendants at the lower level?

[E] [For indicating the contrary] thus it has been taught on Tannaitic authority: [Ex. 20:4 states: "You shall not make for yourself a graven image, or any likeness of anything] that is in heaven [above, or that is in the earth beneath...]."

[F] [The words "in heaven" serve] to encompass [under the prohibition] the sun, moon, stars, and planets.

---

[70]B. A.Z. 43b reads: Judah b. R. Joshua. In place of "Idi," M reads, "Ashi," thus referring to an individual unknown elsewhere in the Rabbinic literature.

[71]M and other sources have "is to be read" explicitly.

[72]M lacks the citation.

[73]M has the bracketed words explicitly.

[G] [The word] "above" [serves] to encompass the ministering angels.

[H] {The Talmud now argues that the statement at E-G does not disprove Abayye's point, C.} That Tannaitic statement [E-G] refers [to the prohibition against making such images in order] to serve them. {But the statement does not preclude making such images if they are not to be worshipped.}

[I] {If the point is as H claims, E-G's statement would be obvious and therefore need not be said at all.} If [it refers only to a case in which the individual wishes] to serve them, then [in such a case, making the image] even of a tiny worm also [is prohibited]! {As interpreted by H, E-G would be obvious and need not have been said. E-G must therefore mean what it says on the surface, that in no circumstance may an image be made of anything in heaven.}

[J] Quite true, [as shown by the continuation of the interpretation of the same verse], for it has been taught on Tannaitic authority: [Ex. 20:4 states: "You shall not make for yourself a graven image, or any likeness of anything that is in heaven above, or] that is in the earth [beneath]."

[K] [The words "in the earth" serve] to encompass [under the prohibition that which is in the] mountains, hills, seas, rivers, streams, and valleys.

[L] [The word] "beneath" [serves] to encompass a tiny worm.

[IV.A] But is it [indeed] permitted simply to make them [without worshipping them]?

[B] But [indicating the contrary] it has been taught on Tannaitic authority: [Ex. 20:23 states]: "You shall not make with me," [meaning], you shall not make anything that looks like my attendants, who serve before me,[74] such as the sun, moon, stars, and planets.

[C] {In light of B, why was what Gamaliel did, M. R.H. 2:8A, permitted?} [The case involving] Rabban Gamaliel was exceptional, because other people had made the charts for him.

[D] But, lo, there is the case of Rab Judah, for whom others made [a ring with a design on it], and yet said Samuel to Rab Judah, "Smartass,[75] put out the eyes!" {Contrary to C, the fact that others made the image does not render it permitted to possess it.}

[E] There [in the case of the ring, even though others made it, it had to be defaced because][76] the signet [was cut] in relief, and [the prohibition] was on account of suspicion [that the item might be used for idolatry],

[F] as it has been taught on Tannaitic authority [see T. A.Z. 5:2]: A ring, the signet of which is cut in relief, is forbidden for wearing but permitted for use as a seal; [a ring], the signet of which is incised, is permitted for wearing but forbidden for use as a seal.

[G] But do we [in fact] take into account the suspicion [that an object may be worshipped]?

[H] [Indicating the contrary], lo, there is [the case of] the synagogue that moved and settled[77] in Nehardea, in which a

---

[74]In place of the following words through the end of this line, M, the parallel at B. A.Z. 43b, and other sources read simply: on high.

[75]So Neusner. Literally: "sharp-toothed," meaning "clever."

[76]All manuscripts have "because" explicitly.

[77]So Neusner, following Simon.

statue of a man was situated,[78] and Rab, Samuel,[79] the father of Samuel, and Levi went in there to pray, and they did not take account of the suspicion [that the object might be worshipped].

[I] [A case involving] the public is exceptional, [since there would be no worshipping of idols in an Israelite community].

[J] But, lo, the case of Rabban Gamaliel involves only an individual! {Hence, by I's standard, Gamaliel should have been prohibited.}

[K] Since he was patriarch, the public was constantly in his presence.

[L] And[80] if you prefer, I shall say, the chart was in sections. {Since it was not a complete likeness, it was permitted.}

[M] And if you prefer, I shall say, he made it for instructional purposes.

[N] For[81] it his written [Dt. 18:9: "When you come into the land that the Lord your God gives you], you shall not learn to do [the abominable practices of those nations]."

[O] [The implication is that] you may learn in order to understand and to teach.

2:8b

[B] *It once occurred: Two witnesses came and said, "We saw it at dawn [on the morning of the twenty-ninth] in the east* [25a] *and at eve in the west."*

[C] *Said R. Yohanan b. Nuri, "They are false witnesses."*

---

[78] M and the parallel at B. A.Z. 43b read: in which they erected the statue of a man.

[79] All manuscripts, the parallel at B. A.Z. 43b, and other sources lack: Rab, Samuel.

[80] So M. P lacks: And.

[81] So M. P reads: And.

[D] *[But] when they came to Yavneh, Rabban Gamaliel accepted their [testimony, assuming they erred at dawn].*

[E] *And furthermore two came along and said, "We saw it at its proper time, but on the night of its intercalation it did not appear."*

[F] *And Rabban Gamaliel accepted their testimony.*

[G] *Said R. Dosa b. Harkinas, "They are false witnesses.*

[H] *"How can they testify that a woman has given birth, when, on the very next day, her stomach is still up there between her teeth!?"*

[I] *Said to him R. Joshua, "I can see your point."*

2:9

[A] *Rabban Gamaliel sent to him [saying], "I decree that you come to me with your staff and purse on the Day of Atonement as you reckon it."* {At issue is the start of Tishre. Since he rejects the witnesses' testimony, Joshua would place the Day of Atonement a day later than would Gamaliel.}

[B] *R. Aqiba went [to Joshua] and found him troubled.*

[C] *[Aqiba] said to him, "I can provide grounds for showing that everything that Rabban Gamaliel has done is validly done, since it says [Lev. 23:4]: 'These are the set feasts of the Lord, even holy convocations, which you shall proclaim.' [This means that] whether they are in their proper time or not in their proper time, I have no set feasts but these [that you shall proclaim; vs. M. R.H. 2:7D]."*

[D] *[Joshua] came along to R. Dosa b. Harkinas.*

[E] *[Dosa] said to him, "Now if we are going to take issue with the court of Rabban Gamaliel, we have to take issue with every single court that has come into being from the time of Moses to the present day,*

[F] *"since it says [Ex. 24:9]: 'Then went up Moses and Aaron, Nadab and Abihu, and seventy of the elders of Israel.'*

[G] *"Now why have the names of the elders not been given? To teach that every group of three [elders] who came into being as a court of Israel—lo, they are equivalent to the court of Moses himself."*

[H] *[Joshua] took his staff with his purse in his hand[82] and went along to Yavneh, to Rabban Gamaliel, on the Day of Atonement as determined in accord with his [that is, Joshua's] reckoning.*

[I] *Rabban Gamaliel stood up and kissed him on his head and said to him,[83] "Come in peace, my master and my disciple—*

[J] *"My master in wisdom, and my disciple in accepting my rulings."*

Gamaliel's idiosyncratic views regarding the appearance of the new moon leads him to declare the start of Tishre a day earlier than other authorities. The result is a disagreement between him and Joshua regarding when the Day of Atonement should be observed. Asserting his power as patriarch, Gamaliel requires Joshua publicly to show his acceptance of Gamaliel's position.

The Talmud provides the reason Gamaliel accepted witnesses that other authorities rejected (unit **I**). Then it concentrates on the idea that the decision of the court regarding the calendar is binding, whether or not it is empirically correct (units **II+III-IV**). The point, parallel to M. R.H. 2:9B, is that the power to sanctify the month and to determine when the festivals will occur has been placed by God in the hands of the court, whose decision is final. Unit **V** presents a general discussion regarding the authority of the court in each generation. Unit **VI** concludes the chapter by describing in detail what happened in the meeting between Joshua and Gamaliel, M. R.H. 2:9I-J.

---

[82]M lacks: in his hand.

[83]M lacks: to him.

[I.A] {Why Gamaliel accepted the testimony described at M. R.H. 2:8B is explained.} It is taught on Tannaitic authority: Said Rabban Gamaliel to sages, "Thus I have received from the house of my father's father: Sometimes [the moon] comes by a long [course] and sometimes it comes by a short course." {The quick movement described at M. R.H. 2:8B is possible.}

[B] Said R. Yohanan, "What is the foundation in Scripture for [the view of] the house of Rabbi [a descendent of Gamaliel, who follows Gamaliel's view in this matter]?

[C] "As it is written [Ps. 104:19]: 'You have made the moon to mark the seasons. The sun knows its time for setting.'

[D] "[This indicates that] it is the sun that knows [the time of] its setting. The moon does not know [the time of its setting, that is, its speed varies]."

[II.A] R. Hiyya saw the [old] moon in the early morning of the twenty-ninth [of the month].[84] {This meant that the new moon could not appear for at least twenty-four hours.}

[B] He picked up a stone [and] threw it at it [that is, at the moon].

[C] He said, "This evening, we wish to sanctify you, but you are still here! Go hide [yourself]!"[85] {Rashi: The court wished to declare the next day to be New Year, so that the Day of Atonement would not fall on a Sunday. If the moon immediately disappeared, the court could accomplish this purpose by forcing witnesses on the next day to say that they saw the new moon.}

---

[84] M adds: of Elul.

[85] M lacks the word "Go," reading instead: [The moon] hid. The Cracow printing makes the same point. It presents this line as it appears in P but then adds: [The moon] went and hid.

[D] Said Rabbi[86] to R. Hiyya, "Go to Ein Tab [where the court meets to sanctify the new moon] and [despite what you saw] sanctify the month!

[E] "And [once you have done this let me know by] sending me the coded [message]: 'David, the king of Israel, is alive and well.'" {See Ps. 89:36-37, referring to David: "His line shall endure forever, his throne as long as the sun before me. Like the moon it shall be established for ever; it shall stand firm while the skies endure."}

[III.A] Our rabbis have taught on Tannaitic authority: Once the sky was filled[87] with clouds and an image like that of the moon was seen on the twenty-ninth[88] of the month.

[B] The people reckoned that it was the new moon, and the court wished to sanctify it.

[C] Said to them Rabban Gamaliel, "Thus I have learned from the house of my father's father: the reappearance of the moon takes place after no less than twenty-nine and a half days, two-thirds of an hour, and seventy-three parts [of an hour]. {It is clear that the new moon cannot appear on the twenty-ninth day itself.}

[D] Now, on that same day, the mother of Ben Zaza died, and Rabban Gamaliel delivered a grand eulogy about her,

[E] not that she was deserving of this, but so that the people would know that the court had not sanctified the month. {Eulogies were not delivered on the new moon, which was treated as a festival.}

[IV.A] *R. Aqiba went [to Joshua] and found him troubled* [M. R.H. 2:9B].

---

[86] In error, M adds: Zera.

[87] Literally: knotted.

[88] M reads: twenty-seventh.

[B] They asked them, "Who was troubled? Was R. Aqiba troubled or was R. Joshua troubled?"

[C] Come and learn [the answer from the following], which is taught on Tannaitic authority: R. Aqiba went and found R. Joshua troubled.

[D] [Aqiba] said to him, "Rabbi, why are you troubled?

[E] [Joshua] said to him,[89] "Aqiba, it would be better for a person to fall [sick] to bed for twelve months rather than have this decree [to report to Gamaliel on the day he reckons as the Day of Atonement] placed upon him."

[F] [Aqiba] said to him, "Rabbi, permit me to tell you something I learned!"

[G] [Joshua] said to him, "Speak."

[H] [Aqiba] said to him, "Lo, it says[90] [in Scripture, at Lev. 22:31,[91] Lev. 23:2,[92] and Lev. 23:4],[93] 'you', 'you,' 'you'—three times [meaning that] 'you' [are responsible for fixing the festivals].

[I] "Even if [you err] inadvertently, 'you' [have validly fixed the festival]; even if [you err] deliberately, 'you' [have validly fixed the festival]; even if you are misled [by the witness, 'you' have validly fixed the festival]."

[J] [Joshua] said to him, "Aqiba, you have comforted me, [indeed] you have comforted me!"

---

[89] Some editions continue with the word "Rabbi."

[90] M lacks the preceding three words.

[91] In each of the cited verses, the direct object "them" or "which" (*'wtm*) is read as "you" (*'tm*). Lev. 22:31 reads: "So you shall keep my commandments and do *them*."

[92] "The appointed feasts of the Lord, *which* you shall proclaim as holy convocations, my appointed feasts, are these."

[93] "These are the appointed feasts of the Lord, the holy convocations, *which* you shall proclaim at the time appointed for them."

[V.A] *[Joshua] came along to R. Dosa b. Harkinas* [M. R.H. 2:9D]. {The following refers to Ex. 24:9, cited at M. R.H. 2:9F: "Then went up Moses and Aaron, Nadab and Abihu, and seventy of the elders of Israel."}

[B] Our rabbis have taught on Tannaitic authority [see T. R.H. 1:18]: *Now why have the names of the elders not been given* [M. R.H. 2:9G]?

[C] So that no person can say, "Is So-and-So like Moses and[94] Aaron? Is So-and-So like Nadab and Abihu? Is So-and-So like Eldad and Medad?

[D] And it says [1 Sam. 12:6]: "And Samuel said to the people, 'The Lord [is witness], who appointed Moses and Aaron.'"

[E] And it says [1 Sam. 12:11]: "And the Lord sent Jerubaal and Bedan,[95] and Jephthah, and Samuel."

[F] [As for the name] "Jerubaal"—this [refers to] Gideon.

[G] And why is he called Jerubaal? For he contended against Baal.

[H] [As for the name] "Bedan"—this [refers to] Samson.

[I] And why is he called Bedan? For he was from [the tribe of] Dan.

[J] [The name] Jephthah is as it states [that is, it refers to Jephthah].

[K] [25b] And [Scripture further] says [Ps. 99:6]: "Moses and Aaron were among his priests. Samuel also was among those who called on his name."[96]

---

[94]M lacks: Moses and. Rabbinovicz prefers M's reading, since it is unimaginable that someone could be expected to compare to Moses.

[95]So Hebrew texts of 1 Samuel. Following the Greek and Syriac translations, RSV translates: Barak.

[96]M has the continuation of the verse: They cried to the Lord, and he answered them.

[L] Scripture balances three of the least valuable people of the world against three of the most valuable people of the world, so as to teach you:

[M] Jerubaal was to his generation as Moses was to his generation.

[N] Bedan was to his generation as Aaron was to his generation.

[O] Jephthah was to his generation as Samuel was to his generation,

[P] to teach you that even the least of the least valuable people, if he is named a leader of the community, lo, he is equivalent to the mightiest of the mighty.

[Q] And [indicating this, Scripture] states [Dt. 17:9, regarding the adjudication of legal issues]: "And you shall come to the Levitical priests or to the judge who is in office in those days."

[R] Now, could you think that a person can go to a judge who is not active in his [own day]? {Since this clearly is impossible, the verse clearly must teach something different.}

[S] [Rather, the verse means that] you may go only to the judge who is active in your day.[97] {The point, substantiated in the following, is that one must willingly accept the judgment of the current court.}

[T] And [Scripture] states [Eccles. 7:10]: "Say not, 'Why were the former days better than these?'"

[VI.A] *[Joshua] took his staff with his purse in his hand [and went along to Yavneh, to Rabban Gamaliel, on the Day of Atonement as determined in accord with Joshua's reckoning; M. R.H. 2:9H].*

---

[97]M and many other sources lack this line, apparently the result of haplography.

[B] Our rabbis have taught on Tannaitic authority: When [Gamaliel] saw him [that is, Joshua], he stood from his chair and kissed him on the head.

[C] *He said to him, "Come in peace, my master and my disciple!*[98] [M. R.H. 2:9I].

[D] "'My master'—for you taught me Torah in public.

[E] "'My disciple'—for I enacted an edict[99] against you, and you accepted it like a disciple.

[F] "Happy[100] is the generation in which the greater heed the lesser.

[G] "All the more so [in which] the lesser [heed] the greater!"

[H] {G is questioned.} [Why would Gamaliel say], "All the more so [a generation in which the lesser heed the greater has reason for joy]"?

[I] [This is no reason for special joy, since] it is [simply the lesser's] obligation [to heed the greater]!

[J] Rather [the point is this]: Since the greater heed the lesser, the lesser apply this responsibility all the more so to themselves [and heed those who are greater than themselves].

---

[98]In M, this line is garbled, the result of dittography.

[99]M lacks this word.

[100]M introduces this line: He said to him.

CHAPTER THREE

ROSH HASHANAH CHAPTER THREE

3:1

[A] [25b] *[If] the court and all [the people of] Israel saw [the new moon on the thirtieth day, and] witnesses were examined [on the thirtieth day], but they had no chance to say, "It is sanctified," before it got dark [marking the beginning of the thirty-first day],*

[B] *lo, this [month coming to an end] is an intercalated month [so that the new month is marked on the thirty-first day].*

[C] *[If] the court alone saw it, let two of them get up and give testimony before the rest of them,*

[D] *and [then] they should say, "It is sanctified, it is sanctified."*

[E] *[If] three of them saw it, and they comprise the [entire] court, let two of them arise, and let them seat some of their colleagues with the remaining judge, and give testimony before them, so they may say, "It is sanctified, it is sanctified."*

[F] *For an individual is not regarded as trustworthy by himself [to pronounce the sanctification of the month].*

As we saw in the preceding chapter, determination of the start of the new month depends upon the actions of the court, without regard for when the new moon actually appeared. Even though the court has solid evidence that the thirtieth should be celebrated as the beginning of the new month, if it does not sanctify the month before the conclusion of that day, an extra day is added, and the thirty-first marks the beginning of the new month (M. R.H. 3:1A-B). This point, that the action of the court and not the appearance of the new moon is determinative, is made explicit at unit I, which notes that the rule applies even though everyone saw the new moon on the thirtieth. Unit II continues the interpretation of this passage, arguing that the clauses at M. R.H. 3:1A are disjunctive. The rule applies either to a case in which the court and all the people saw the new moon or to one in which witnesses saw it and were examined. The Talmud learns from this that if the general public and members of the court saw the new moon, additional witnesses are not required at all. Unit **III** argues from this same clause that even though the hearing is in progress and witnesses already have been examined, the matter may not be completed at night. The rule for hearings on the new moon differs from the handling of commercial cases, in which, once the evidence has been heard, a decision may be reached at night.

While M. R.H. 3:1C-F is introduced as a counterpart to M. R.H. 3:1A ("If the court and all the people saw the new moon" vs. "If the court alone saw the new moon"), the issue at M. R.H. 3:1C-F in fact is separate. A member of the court may not serve simultaneously as a witness. Judges who wish to testify on the appearance of the new moon must relinquish their seat on the panel reviewing the matter. Continuing the Talmud's clause-by-clause interpretation of this pericope, unit **IV** asks why, if the entire court saw the new moon, testimony is required at all. Contrary to what is implicit in the Mishnah, the Talmud responds that this is the case only if, at the time of the sighting, the court was not in session. But if it were daylight and the court were in session when the sighting occurred, no witnesses would be needed. Unit **V** applies the same mode of questioning to M. R.H. 3:1E, arguing that a determination regarding the new month may not be made by a single judge acting alone. Unit **VI** asks a broader question about the propriety of allowing people who witnessed an event to serve as judges concerning that same event. The matter is subject to a Tannaitic dispute, with Aqiba holding that, especially in capital cases, a person who saw what occurred may not serve as a judge.

[I.A] Why is it taught on Tannaitic authority [M. R.H. 3:1A: *If] the court and all [the people of] Israel saw [the new moon]....*? {The rule at M. R.H. 3:1A-B seems obvious and need not be stated.}

BAVLI ROSH HASHANAH CHAPTER THREE [25b] 315

[B] [Contrary to A, this rule] is needed!

[C] [If this rule were not explicitly stated] you might have thought that, since *the court and all [the people of] Israel saw it*, it has become general knowledge.

[D] [This being the case, the same day should be declared the new moon, and the preceding month] should not be intercalated [though the addition of an extra day]!

[E] Therefore [at M. R.H. 3:1A-B] we are informed [that the contrary applies]. {Even if the witnesses were examined and everyone saw that the new moon appeared, so long as the declaration "It is sanctified" has not been made, the preceding month must be intercalated.}

[II.A] Now, since it is taught on Tannaitic authority [M. R.H. 3:1A, that] *the court and all [the people of] Israel saw [the new moon]*, why do I need [the additional fact that] *the witnesses were examined*? {Since all the people saw the new moon, why are witnesses required at all?}

[B] Here is how [M. R.H. 3:1A-B] should be understood: *[If the court and all the people of Israel saw the new moon on the thirtieth day], or [if] the witnesses were examined, but they had no chance to say, "It is sanctified," before it [actually] got dark, lo, this [month coming to an end] is an intercalated month.*

[III.A] Now, since it is taught on Tannaitic authority [M. R.H. 3:1A-B: *they had no chance to say, "It is sanctified"] before it [actually] got dark, lo, this [month coming to an end] is an intercalated month*,[1] why should I have taught on Tannaitic authority about the examination of the witnesses at all? {Since the declaration "It is sanctified" was not made prior to when it got dark, whether or not the witnesses were examined is

---

[1] All manuscripts lack the beginning of this line up to this point as well as the words "the examination of the witnesses" in the following.

[B]   [Contrary to A, the fact of the witnesses being examined]² is needed!

[C]   [If the fact that witnesses were examined was not explicitly stated at M. R.H. 3:1A-B] you might have thought that the examination of the witnesses is comparable to the beginning of a law-suit and that the statement "It is sanctified, it is sanctified" is comparable to the conclusion of the law-suit.

[D]   And [in this theory, you might have argued that, in a case in which witnesses already had been examined] one should sanctify [the new moon even] at night, [after it has gotten dark].

[E]   [One might draw this conclusion since this is] an approach that does apply in the case of commercial law,³

[F]   as we have taught on Tannaitic authority [M. San. 4:1]: *In commercial cases they try the case by day and [if necessary] complete it at night.*

[G]   [On this basis, one might have thought that] here too [in the case of the new moon, when witnesses already have been examined, to complete "the case"] they sanctify it at night.

[H]   Therefore we are informed [by M. R.H. 3:1A-B, that this is not the law].

[I]   {H is challenged.} But can I not say that here too [the rule about completing the case at night applies]?

[J]   {I is rejected.} Said Scripture [Ps. 81:4]: "For it is a statute for Israel, a judgment of the God of Jacob."

[K]   Under what circumstances is it called a "statue"?⁴

[L]   At the conclusion of the act of judging.

---

²M introduces this line: Rather.

³Simon: money-suits.

⁴M lacks J-K, a case of haplography.

[M] Now [at Ps. 81:4] the merciful calls it a "judgment." {That is, a statue and judgment, in the sense of a legal proceeding or "case," are equated.}

[N] [This means that] just as a judgment [must take place] by day, so here [the conclusion of the legal case concerning the declaration of the new moon must take place] by day.

[IV.A] {The Talmud continues its clause-by-clause evaluation of M. R.H. 3:1.} *[If] the court [alone] saw it, let two of them get up and give testimony before the rest of them* [M. R.H. 3:1C].

[B] But[5] why? {Since the entire court saw the new moon, why is testimony required at all?}

[C] [Surely, contrary to what is indicated by the Mishnah's rule] hearing [about what occurred] should not be given greater weight than [actually] seeing it [oneself]!

[D] [Explaining M. R.H. 3:1C's point] said R. Zera, "[The Mishnaic rule applies in a case] such as when they saw it at night." {Rashi: In such an instance, when the court sits the following day, witnesses are necessary to report what was seen the previous night. The point seems to be that, since the court was not in session when the evidence was seen, it must, while in session, rely upon testimony.}

[V.A] *[If] three of them saw it, and they comprise the [entire] court, let two of them arise, and let them seat some of their colleagues with the remaining judge* [M. R.H. 3:1E].

[B] Why? {Since the entire court saw the new moon, why is testimony required at all?}

[C] Here too [contrary to what is indicated by the Mishnah's rule] hearing [about what occurred] should not be given greater weight than [actually] seeing it [oneself]!

---

[5] M lacks this word.

[D] And if you say, here too, it is a case such as when they saw it at night, [then] this [case, at M. R.H. 3:1E] would be the same as that [case, at M. R.H. 3:1C-D]. {Since the Mishnah does not contain such redundancies, the point at M. R.H. 3:1E must be different.}

[E] [The phrasing of matters as it stands at M. R.H. 3:1E] was necessary in order to set up the conclusion [of the law, at M. R.H. 3:1F, that is]: *For an individual is not regarded as trustworthy by himself [to pronounce the sanctification of the month].*

[F] [For, if this were not stated] you might have thought: Since, as we have taught on Tannaitic authority[6] [M. San. 4:1]: *Commercial cases are to be tried by a court of three judges, but if the judge was recognized by the community as an expert, he may judge all by himself—*

[G] here too, the sanctification [of the month] may be done by an individual.

[H] Therefore we are informed [by M. R.H. 3:1E-F, that this is not the case].

[I] {H is challenged.} But can I not say that here too [the case may be completed by a single judge who is an expert]?

[J] {No!} You can find no expert [recognized by] the community of Israel greater than Moses, our rabbi.

[K] Yet [even so] the holy one, blessed be he,[7] said to him, "[Do not sanctify the new month] unless Aaron is at your side,"

[L] as it is written [Ex. 12:1-2]: "The Lord said to Moses and Aaron in the land of Egypt, 'This month shall be for you [the beginning of months].'"[8]

---

[6] A marginal note in the printed edition suggests reading: as it is taught on Tannaitic authority. That reading recognizes the fact that what follows is only in part a citation of the Mishnah.

[7] M, which has a slightly different wording at J-K, refers to God as: the Merciful.

[8] M has the bracketed conclusion of the verse explicitly.

[VI.A] [M. R.H. 3:1C-D and E] suggest that one who is [able to act as] a witness may be designated a judge.

[B] [Since it suggests this] I can argue that the Mishnaic passage does not accord with [the view of] R. Aqiba [reported below at D].

[C] For it is taught on Tannaitic authority: "[Members of] a Sanhedrin that saw someone kill someone else—[26a] some of them serve as witnesses, and some of them serve as judges," the words of R. Tarfon.

[D] R. Aqiba says, "All of them are witnesses, and a witness cannot serve as a judge."

[E] [Contrary to B-D] one might even argue [that] R. Aqiba [concurs with the rules of M. R.H. 3:1C-D and E].

[F] Up to this point, [we can assume that] R. Aqiba did not state [the position given] there [at D, precluding a witness from acting as a judge] except for capital cases,

[G] for which the merciful said [Num. 35:24-25]: "Then the congregation shall judge [between the man slayer and the avenger of blood...], and the congregation shall rescue [the man slayer from the hand of the avenger of blood]."

[H] {Scripture requires that those who judge be willing to rescue the man slayer from the avenger.} But [Aqiba holds that] once one has seen that [the accused] killed a person, [that witness] will not find in him any merit [so as to be willing to rescue him, as required by law]. {For this reason, in capital cases, Aqiba does not allow a witness to act as judge.}

[I] But here [in the case of the sanctification of the new moon] even R. Aqiba concurs [with M. R.H. 3:1, that witnesses may act as judges].

3:2

[A] *All shofars are valid, except for that of a cow,*

[B] *because it is a horn.*

[C] *Said R. Yose, "But are not all shofars called horns,*

[D] *"as it is said [Josh. 6:5], 'And when they make a long blast with the ram's horn, [as soon as you hear the sound of the shofar,[9] then all the people shall shout with a great shout]'?"* {*The term "horn" thus is equated with the word "shofar."*}

The issue of what horns are permitted for use as a shofar concerns units I-V. Through reference to Scripture, the Talmud discerns the distinction between the horn of a cow and that of other animals and suggests the grounds for the disagreement between Yose and anonymous sages, M. R.H. 3:2A-B vs. C-D. Unit V contributes to this endeavor by providing a story in which Aqiba, during his travels, happens to learn the meaning of a word crucial to an earlier argument. Having presented this story, the Talmud, at units VI-IX, recalls a long series of similar incidents, in which Aqiba or other rabbis happened to hear in common usage a word found in the Mishnah or in Scripture but the meaning of which they had not known.

[I.A] Correctly has R. Yose stated[10] [matters, at M. R.H. 3:2C, holding that all shofars are called horns].

[B] But, [as for] the rabbis, [who stand behind the anonymous rule of M. R.H. 3:2A-B—what can they say to support their position]?

[C] [They can argue that] all shofars are called "shofar" and are called "horn."

[D] [But] that of a cow is called "horn" but is not called "shofar."

[E] [This is] as it is written [Dt. 33:17]: "His firstling ox has majesty, and his horns are the horns of a wild ox." {The horns of a ox, deemed to be in the same category as a cow, are called by the word "horn" not "shofar."}

[F] And R. Yose? {How can he respond to C-E?}

[G] He will say that [the horns of] a cow are also called "shofar."

---

[9]M explicitly has the bracketed continuation of the verse through this point.

[10]M adds: to our rabbis.

[H]	[This is] as it is written [Ps. 69:31]: "This will please the Lord more than an ox-bullock [with horns and hoofs]. {The following plays upon the fact that, in Hebrew, the word "ox" is *shor* and "bullock" is *par*, the masculine form of *parah*, that is, "cow."}
[I]	If ox [is meant], why [does it also say] bullock?
[J]	If bullock [is meant], why [does it also say] ox? {Clearly, the text cannot mean literally "ox-bullock".}
[K]	Rather, what [is meant here]?
[L]	[The words] "ox-bullock" [*shor-par*] refer to [the word] "shofar."
[M]	And [as for] the rabbis? {How do they interpret Ps. 69:31?}
[N]	[They interpret it] like Rab Mattenah, for said Rab Mattenah, "What is [meant by] 'ox-bullock'?
[O]	"[It is an ox] that is as big as a bullock."[11]
[P]	Ulla said, "The explanation of the rabbis is like that of Rab Hisda.
[Q]	"For said Rab Hisda, 'Why does the high priest not enter the inner most area [that is, the holy-of-holies] to worship there [on the Day of Atonement] wearing golden clothing?[12]
[R]	"'It is because the accuser cannot be made the defender.'" {Gold is reminiscent of the golden calf and so acts as accuser of the people of Israel. The high priest and his worship, including his garments, serve to defend the people. Gold, the accuser, can have no role in that. Ulla's point is that, comparably, a cow's horn, reminiscent of the golden calf, cannot serve as a shofar, the blowing of which defends the people of Israel.}
[S]	But [can the accuser in fact] not [serve as defender]?

---

[11] Simon, p. 116, n. 7: "The name *shor* could be applied only to the animal at birth; the name *par* not till it entered its third year."

[12] The garments are linen, Lev. 16:4 and 23.

[T] For, indicating the contrary, there is the blood of the calf. {The calf, reminiscent of the Golden Calf, can be seen as an accuser. Even so its blood is sprinkled by the high priest on the Day of Atonement.}

[U] {For the reason given here, the case of blood is different.} Since it has been changed [and no longer is in the form of the calf], it is deemed changed [and, unlike the calf from which it is derived, is not an agent of accusation].

[V] {We have a second example that challenges R.} But there is also the ark, with its mercy-seat, and the cherub. {These agents of atonement are made with gold, Ex. 25.}

[W] {R's concern is not at issue for the ark, mercy-seat, and cherub.} [So that these items need not serve as defenders at all] we say that a sinner may not bring an offering.

[X] {Again challenging R:} But there is the spoon and censer [made of gold and used by the high priest in the holy-of-holies; see, e.g., Lev. 16:12].

[Y] [To avoid the problem posed by R] we say a sinner should not adorn himself [with these things].

[Z] {Again challenging R:} But there is the golden clothing used by the high priest outside [of the holy-of-holies]!

[AA] [Only] concerning [that which occurs] in the inner areas [of the Temple] did we say [that R applies].

[BB] {In light of AA, we can return to the question of the use of the cow's horn and suggest that, contrary to R, it should not be excluded.} [Now, as for] a shofar, it similarly is used outside [and not in the inner most areas of the sanctuary].

[CC] {The case of the shofar is different.} Insofar as [a shofar] is meant to encourage remembering, it is as though [it were used] inside [the sanctuary]. {As R argued, it therefore cannot derive from an animal that would represent an accusation against the people.}

BAVLI ROSH HASHANAH CHAPTER THREE [26a]   323

[II.A] {The Talmud reflects upon BB-CC's explanation for the exclusion of the cow's horn, which argues that, as in other instances, "the accuser may not be made the defender." The problem is that M. R.H. 3:2B explains on different grounds the exclusion of the cow's horn from use as a shofar.} But [contrary to what is proposed above], lo, the Tannaitic authority [at M. R.H. 3:2B] teaches [that a cow's horn may not be used as a shofar] *because it is a horn*. {Since the Mishnah states explicitly that this is the reason, the Talmudic explanation, concluded above at BB-CC, cannot be correct.}

[B] {A incorrectly evaluates the Mishnaic authority's point.} [Contrary to what A proposes, the Tannaitic authority] stated [only] one [possible reason].

[C] But [he is able to] state yet another [reason]:

[D] [One reason for the exclusion of the cow's horn is] that an accuser may not be made the defender.

[E] But another [reason is] *because it is a horn* [as M. R.H. 3:2B states].

[III.A] {Again we reflect upon unit I's explanation for the exclusion of the cow's horn.} Now, [as for] R. Yose, [M. R.H. 3:2C, who permits use of the cow's horn as a shofar—how does he respond to the claim that a cow's horn may not be used because an accuser may not be made the defender]?

[B] He can say to you: "That which you say, that an accuser may not be made the defender, applies only in the inner areas [of the Temple].

[C] "But [as for] a shofar, [it is used] outside [and therefore should be permitted to be made from a cow's horn].

[D] "And [as for] your statement [M. R.H. 3:2B, that the cow's horn is excluded] *because it is a horn*—[that objection is of no weight, since] all shofars likewise are called 'horn.'"

[IV.A] Abayye said, "The rabbis' reason [for excluding a cow's horn from use as a shofar, M. R.H. 3:2A-B, is that] the merciful

	said [that is, required] a [single]¹³ shofar, but not two or three shofars,
[B]	"and that [horn] of a cow, insofar as it is comprised of layer upon layer, appears to be two or three shofars."
[C]	{A-B is challenged based upon the fact that M. R.H. 3:2B explains on different grounds the exclusion of the cow's horn from use as a shofar.} But [contrary to what Abayye proposes], lo, the Tannaitic authority [at M. R.H. 3:2B] teaches [that a cow's horn may not be used as a shofar] *because it is a horn*. {Since the Mishnah states explicitly that this is the reason, Abayye's explanation, A-B, cannot be correct.}
[D]	{C incorrectly evaluates the Mishnaic authority's point.} [Contrary to what C proposes, the Tannaitic authority] stated [only] one [possible reason].
[E]	But [he is able to] state yet another [reason]:
[F]	[One reason for the exclusion of the cow's horn is] that the merciful said [that is, required] a single shofar, but not two or three shofars.
[G]	But another [reason is] *because it is a horn* [as M. R.H. 3:2B states].
[H]	Now, [as for] R. Yose, [M. R.H. 3:2C, who permits use of the cow's horn as a shofar—how does he respond to the claim that a cow's horn may not be used because it appears to be more than a single horn]?
[I]	He can say: "Insofar as you have said that the merciful said [that is, required] one [shofar] and not two or three shofars¹⁴—since [the layers of the cow's horn] are [tightly] joined to one another, it is [treated as] a single [shofar, so as to be permitted].

---

¹³M has this word explicitly.

¹⁴M lacks: and not two or three shofars.

[J] "And [as for] your statement [M. R.H. 3:2B, that the cow's horn is excluded] *because it is a horn*—[that objection is of no weight, since] all shofars likewise[15] are called 'horn.'"

[V.A] How do we know that the term *yovel* [found at Josh. 6:5 and rendered at M. R.H. 3:2D as "ram"] actually means "ram"?

[B] [We know this] for it is taught on Tannaitic authority: Said R. Aqiba, "When I went to Arabia, [I heard that] they called a ram [by the term] '*yovel*.'"

[C] And said R. Aqiba, "When I went to Gallia, they called a menstruant [by the term] '*galmuda*.'"

[D] What is [the meaning of] "*galmuda*"? This one is set apart [*gamul da*] from her husband.

[E] And said R. Aqiba, "When I went to Africa,[16] they called a *maah* [that is, a coin, by the term] '*keshitah*.'"

[F] What is the practical significance of this [fact]?

[G] [It is important] for the interpretation [of Gen. 33:19: "And from the sons of Hamor, Shechem's father, he bought for] a hundred *keshitah* [the piece of land on which he had pitched his tent]."

[H] In Scripture [it refers to] a hundred *danqi*.[17]

[VI.A] {The theme of the preceding continues.} Said Rabbi,[18] "When I went to sea-ports, they called 'selling' [*mekirah*] [by the term] '*kirah*.'"

[B] What is the practical significance of this [fact]?

---

[15]M lacks this word.

[16]Alternatively, Phrygia, in Asia Minor. See Jastrow, pp. 108-109, s.v., 'pryqy.

[17]A small Persian coin, valued at a sixth of a dinar. See Jastrow, p. 315, s.v., *dnq'*. In M this line is garbled and corrected.

[18]In place of the attribution, M reads: It is taught on Tannaitic authority. L has: It is taught on Tannaitic authority: Said Rabbi.... Cracow's text is like that of L, except that there the attribution is to Aqiba.

[C] [It is important] for the interpretation [of Gen. 50:5, Joseph's citation of a statement made by Jacob: "In my tomb][19] which I bought (root: *KRH*)[20] for myself [in the land of Canaan,[21] there shall you bury me]."

[VII.A] {The theme of the preceding continues.} Said R. Simeon b. Laqish, "When I went to the district of Kennesrin, they called a bride '*ninfe*' and a cock '*sekvi*.'

[B] A bride, "*ninfe*"?

[C] What is the basis for this in Scripture?

[D] [Ps. 48:2, referring to Mt. Zion, states]: "beautiful in elevation (*yph nwp*), the joy of all the earth." {The term "beautiful in elevation is deemed related to the word "*ninfe*," and hence to describe a bride.}

[E] And a cock, "*sekvi*"?

[F] Said Rab Judah said Rab, and some say,[22] R. Joshua b. Levi, "What is the basis for this in Scripture?

[G] "[Job 38:36 says]: 'Who has put wisdom in the *tuhot*[23] or given understanding to the *sekvi*?[24]

[H] "'Who has put wisdom in the *tuhot*'—these are the kidneys.[25]

[I] "'Or given understanding to the *sekvi*'—this is the cock."

[VIII.A] {This is a slight variation on the theme of the preceding.} Levi happened to be in a certain place. A man came before him [and] told him [26b] a certain person is a *qaba'an*.

---

[19]M has the bracketed beginning of the verse explicitly.

[20]RSV and others: hewed out.

[21]M has the bracketed conclusion of the verse up to this point explicitly.

[22]So M and most sources. P reads: if you wish, I can say.

[23]Normally: clouds.

[24]Normally: mists.

[25]M adds: For a master said, "Kidneys give wise counsel."

[B] [Levi] did not know what he was telling him, [since he did not understand the term *"qaba'an"*].

[C] He came to ask [in] the house of study.

[D] They[26] said to him, "He told you [the man is] a robber,

[E] "as it is written [Mal. 3:8]: 'Will man rob [*KB'*] God?'"[27]

[F] Said Rava from Barnish to Rab Ashi, "If I had been there [and had not understood the word], I would have asked him. 'Where did he *qaba'* you,[28] of what did he *qaba'* you, why did he *qaba'* you,"[29] and from what he said, I would have found out [the meaning of the term]."

[G] But the other [that is, Levi, had not done this since] he thought the person was referring to a forbidden matter [that Levi was not meant to understand].[30]

[IX.A] {The theme of the preceding continues.} The rabbis did not know the meaning of the term *serugin* [which occurs at M. Meg. 2:2, describing a permitted manner of reading the Scroll of Esther].

[B] They[31] heard a handmaid of the house of Rabbi, who saw the rabbis entering a few at a time, say to them, "For how long are you going to keep coming in *serugin*?"

[C] The rabbis did not know the meaning of the term *haluglaot* [referred to, e.g., at M. Sheb. 9:1].

---

[26]So M, early printings, and the marginal correction in P. The body of P has the verb in the singular.

[27]M has the continuation of the verse: Yet you are robbing me.

[28]M lacks the preceding clause.

[29]Some sources lack the preceding clause.

[30]This line is added in the margin of M.

[31]M and manuscripts and editions introduce this line: One day. In the following lines, in place of the phrase "of the house of Rabbi," M reads simply: of Rabbi.

[D] One day they heard a handmaid of the house of Rabbi, who saw a certain man scattering[32] purslane.
[E] She said to him, "For how long will you scatter[33] *haluglaot*."
[F] The rabbis did not know the meaning of [the first word in Prov. 4:8]: "*salsalah* and it will exalt you."
[G] One day they heard a handmaid of the house of Rabbi, who said to a man who was curling his hair, "For how long will you *salsel* your hair?"
[H] The rabbis did not know the meaning of [the two related words in Is. 14:23]: "And I will *ta'ta'* with the *mata'te'* of destruction."
[I] One day they heard a handmaid of the house of Rabbi, who said to her counterpart, "Take this *ta'tita'* [broom] and sweep the house."
[J] The rabbis did not know the meaning of [a word in Ps. 55:22]: "Cast your *yehab* on the Lord,[34] and he will sustain you."
[K] Said Rabbah bar bar Hannah, "One day I was traveling with a certain Arab.[35]
[L] "I was carrying a load, and he said to me, 'Lift up your *yehab* and place it on [one of] the camels.'"

3:3

[A] *The shofar for the New Year derives from an antelope.*
[B] *It is straight,*
[C] *and its mouth is overlaid with gold.*
[D] *And at the sides [of the one who blew the shofar] are two [who blow] trumpets.*

---

[32]Simon, for *mbdr*: peeling.

[33]Simon, for *mpzr*: peel.

[34]M lacks the remainder of the biblical citation.

[35]See Jastrow, p. 531, s.v., *tyy'*, "*traveler,* esp. Arabian caravan merchant."

[E] *The shofar [is sounded] for a long note, and the trumpets [are sounded] for a short note,*

[F] *for the [religious] obligations of the day apply to the shofar.*

3:4

[A] *And [the shofars used] on fast days derive from rams.*

[B] *They are curved,*

[C] *and their mouth is overlaid with silver.*

[D] *And in the middle [of those who blew the shofar] are two [who sound] trumpets.*

[E] *The shofar [is sounded] for a short note, and the trumpets [are sounded] for a long note,*

[F] *for the [religious] obligations of that day apply to the trumpets.*

3:5

[A] *The [proclamation of the] year of Jubilee is equivalent to the New Year in regard to the sounding of the shofar and to the blessings.*

[B] *R. Judah says, "On the New Year they sound the rams' horn, and at the Jubilee Year they sound antelopes' horns."*

Unit **I** adds a third position to the dispute between the Mishnah's anonymous authorities and Judah, M. R.H. 3:5B. Levi holds that on New Year and the Jubilee a curved shofar is used, while on fast days, a straight one is sounded. Unit **II** offers explanations for the divergent views regarding this matter of Judah and the Mishnah's anonymous statements. With these general issues out of the way, the Talmud begins a line-by-line evaluation of the pericopae before us. Unit **III** cites T. R.H. 2:4, claiming that it clarifies M. R.H. 3:3C. Units **IV-VII** turn to M. R.H. 3:3D, explaining how the shofar and horns are to be used together. Unit **VIII** explains why the shofar used for fast days, M. R.H. 3:4A-C, differs from that used on New Year, M. R.H. 3:3A-C. Unit **IX** points out that the procedures described in the Mishnah, using shofars and other horns together, applied only in the Temple. Outside of the Temple, a ram's horn alone is sounded. Unit **X** concerns M. R.H. 3:5A: in what ways are

New Year and the proclamation of the Jubilee in fact similar or different?

[I.A] Said R. Levi, "The [religious] obligation of the New Year and the Day of Atonement is [carried out] with curved [shofars], while that of the rest of the year is [carried out] with straight [shofars]."

[B] But [suggesting the contrary] thus we have taught on Tannaitic authority [M. R.H. 3:3A-B]: *The shofar for the New Year derives from an antelope. It is straight.* {By contrast, Levi, A, says it is curved.}

[C] That which [Levi] said accords with this Tannaitic master, as it is taught on Tannaitic authority:[36] *R. Judah says, "On the New Year they would blow a ram's [horn] that was curved, while [for purposes of proclaiming] the year of the Jubilee [they used] an*[37] *antelope's [horn]."*

[D] {Challenging C:} Now, [if C correctly reports Judah's view, then, instead of stating matters in his own words, Levi, A, would simply have] said, "The decided law accords with [the view of] R. Judah [M. R.H. 3:5B]."

[E] {D's reasoning is rejected.} [Levi did not do that since], if you said that the decided law accords with [the view of] R. Judah, one would believe that you concur with [the view of] R. Judah[38] for [the case] of the [proclamation of the] Jubilee as well.

---

[36]M, all other manuscripts, Rif, and other sources phrase the preceding differently: That which [Levi] said accords with [the view of] R. Judah. For we have taught on Tannaitic authority....

[37]M adds: straight.

[38]M and other manuscripts have simply: him.

[F]	Therefore we are informed [that Levi concurs with Judah about the horn used on New Year but not about that used for proclaiming the year of the Jubilee].³⁹

[II.A] {The Talmud now evaluates the dispute between Judah, unit I.C, and the anonymous authority at M. R.H. 3:3A-B and 3:4A-B.} Concerning what do they disagree?

[B] One master [Judah] reasons that on the New Year, the more a man curves his mind, the more effective [is his prayer].

[C] But on the Day of Atonement, the more the person makes his thinking straight-forward, the more effective [is his prayer].

[D] But [the other] master reasons [M. R.H. 3:3A-B] that on the New Year the more the person makes his thinking straight-forward, the more effective [is his prayer].

[E] But on fast days [M. R.H. 3:3A-B], the more a man curves his mind, the more effective [is his prayer]. ⁴⁰

[III.A] [27a] *And its mouth is overlaid with gold* [M. R.H. 3:3C, referring to the shofar used for the New Year].

[B] But [suggesting the contrary] thus we have taught on Tannaitic authority [T. R.H. 2:4: **If] one overlaid it with gold at a place the mouth touches, it is invalid.**

[C] [If it is overlaid with gold] at a place the mouth does not touch, it is valid.

[D] [Resolving the contradiction] said Abayye,⁴¹ "That which we taught on Tannaitic authority in the Mishnah we also taught in reference to a place the mouth does not touch."

---

³⁹M has the bracketed words explicitly.

⁴⁰At B-E, the text of M and other sources, including Rashi and Tosafot, suggests that the dispute concerns New Year alone. These sources read simply: One master reasons that the more a man curves his mind, the more preferable it is. And one master reasons that the more a man makes his thinking straight-forward, the more preferable it is.

⁴¹M reads: Rava. Other sources have: Pappa.

[IV.A] *And [on New Year] at the sides [of the one who blew the shofar] are two [who blow] trumpets* [M. R.H. 3:3D].

[B] Now [this seems unacceptable, since] can two sounds be [distinctly] heard [at once]? {The affect of playing the shofar and trumpets together is that the shofar will not be heard. This would result in a violation of the religious obligation to hear the shofar.}

[C] And [to indicate that, as B states, two distinct sounds cannot be heard at the same time] thus it is taught on Tannaitic authority: [The word] "Remember" [in the fourth commandment as recorded at Ex. 20:8] and [the word] "Observe" [in the fourth commandment as recorded at Dt. 5:12] were stated in a single act of speech,

[D] which [is something] the [human] mouth cannot pronounce and the ear cannot hear.

[E] {In light of B-D, the issue is how the shofar, played along with the trumpets, could be heard. That question is answered here.} For this reason, one plays a long note on the shofar.

[V.A] {The implication of the preceding unit is stated.} This is to say that if one hears the end of the blast but not the beginning of the blast, he has fulfilled [his obligation to hear the shofar].

[B] And it goes without saying [that if he heard] the beginning of the blast but not the end of the blast, he has fulfilled [his obligation].

[VI.A] {The following independent construction explains M. R.H. 4:9. As my interpolated comment at D indicates, however, in context, it serves to refute the preceding unit.}[42] Come and

---

[42]This is made clear in the phrasing of A in all manuscripts. In place of the words "Come and learn," manuscripts read: Has he really fulfilled [his obligation]? But [indicating the contrary] we have taught on Tannaitic authority [M. R.H. 4:9]....

learn [M. R.H. 4:9: *If] one sounded the first Tekiah-blast [of the set of three] and then sustained the second blast for twice as long, he [still] has credit only for one.* {That is, he cannot count the sustained blast half for the first set and half for a later set.}

[B] Why [does he get credit for only one]?

[C] [Rather] you should [deem the blast to] be divided into two parts [so as to allow credit for two separate blasts]!

[D] [This cannot be done, since] we do not divide a single blast. {The implication is that what unit V.A-B describes comparably should not be permitted. Since a blast is indivisible, in order to fulfill one's obligation to hear the shofar, he must hear all of it.}

[VII.A] {We have another independent unit, of unclear relationship to the preceding.} Come and learn [M. R.H. 3:7]: *He who sounds the shofar into a cistern, cellar, or large jar—if he heard the sound of the shofar, he has fulfilled his obligation.*

[B] *But if he heard the sound of the echo, he has not fulfilled his obligation.*

[C] Why?

[D] [To the contrary] let him [be deemed] to have fulfilled his obligation [by having heard] the beginning of the blast, before it became mixed up with the sound [of the echo]!

[E] Rather [what D proposes is impossible, since] two voices coming from a single person cannot be distinguished. {The point seems to be to reject D's notion that one ever can distinguish the sound of the shofar from that of the echo.}[43]

---

[43] The terms of the argument, however, are quite different from those of D, which does not propose that one can distinguish between the two different sounds when they are heard at the same time. The incongruity becomes clearer in the following, where the issue shifts entirely from that raised by unit V (to which Simon argues that the present material continues to relate) to the question raised by unit IV, concerning how one can hear the shofar distinctly from the trumpets played at the same time (M. R.H. 3:3D).

[F]   [But two voices] coming from two people can be distinguished. {Contrary to unit **IV**, M. R.H. 3:3D presents no problem.}

[G]   {F is challenged.} Indeed, coming from two people can [separate sounds] be distinguished?

[H]   But [suggesting the contrary] thus it is taught on Tannaitic authority [T. Meg. 3:20]: **In [the public reading of] the Torah [in the synagogue] one person reads and one translates [into Aramaic].**

[I]   **But [one should not read while two translate,[44] nor should two read while one translates], nor should two read while two translate.** {I implies that when two people talk at the same time, neither voice can be distinguished. As a result, the person who hears does not fulfill the obligation to hear the reading of the Torah. Contrary to F, it is unclear how what is described at M. R.H. 3:3D can be allowed.}

[J]   {I is rejected as dissimilar to the case at M. R.H. 3:3D.} But [contrary to I, the issue of M. R.H. 3:3D] resembles only the conclusion [of the text cited at H-I (and not found at T. Meg. 3:20)]: For the [public recitation of the] Hallel and the Scroll [of Esther], even ten [people] may read [together].[45]

[K]   I can argue[46] that, since [these liturgical passages] are beloved, [people] pay attention [and are able to distinguish individual voices].[47]

---

[44]The parallel at B. Meg. 21b has this first clause but lacks the remainder of the line.

[45]M, other manuscripts, and the parallel at B. Meg. 21a, add: and ten act as expounders.

[46]M reads: What is the reason?

[47]For the bracketed words, M has explicitly: and hear [the individual voices].

[L] Here too [in the case of the shofar sounded along with trumpets, M. R.H. 3:3D], since [the sound of the shofar] is beloved, [people] pay attention and [distinctly] hear [the sound of the shofar].[48]

[M] Then [contrary to the reason given at unit IV.E] why does one play a long note [on the shofar]?

[N] To make known that *the [religious] obligations of the day apply to the shofar* [M. R.H. 3:3F].

[VIII.A] *And [the shofars used] on fast days derive from rams. They are curved, and their mouth is overlaid with silver* [M. R.H. 3:4A-C].

[B] What is distinctive there[49] [in the case of the shofar used for New Year, M. R.H. 3:3C, such that] gold [is used]?

[C] And what is distinctive here [in the case of the shofar used for fast days such that] silver [is used]?

[D] If you wish I can explain that [for] all public assemblies silver [is used],

[E] as it is written [Num. 10:2]: "Make two silver trumpets; [of hammered work you shall make them, and you shall use them for summoning the congregation and for breaking camp]."

[F] And if you wish I can explain that the Torah took pity upon the wealth of [the people of] Israel, [allowing the use of silver to spare expense].

[G] {F is challenged.} [If that is the case] there too [in the case of the shofar used for New Year] it should be made with silver!

[H] Despite this consideration [raised at F+G], the honor due the holiday took precedence, [so that gold was prescribed].

[IX.A] Rab Pappa bar Samuel intended to do things as [described] in the Mishnah [that is, using both a shofar and trumpets].

---

[48] This line is added in the margin of L.

[49] At B-C, M reverses the words "here" and "there."

[B] Said to him Rava,[50] "They gave that instruction[51] only for the sanctuary."

[C] That which is taught on Tannaitic authority makes the same point: For what [circumstance] were these things [at M. R.H. 3:3-5] said?

[D] For the sanctuary.

[E] But outside of the Temple,[52] in a situation in which [one uses] trumpets [e.g., on fast days], there is no shofar.

[F] [And] in a situation in which [one uses] a shofar [e.g., for New Year and to proclaim the start of the Jubilee], there are no trumpets.[53]

[G] And thus did R. Halafta direct [the community to act] in Sepphoris,

[H] and R. Hanania[54] b. Teradion in Sikni. {From the continuation of the passage, it appears that, like Pappa bar Samuel, A, Halafta and Hanania wished to use both trumpets and a shofar outside of the Temple.}

[I] And when this matter came[55] before the sages, they said, "They do not follow this practice [of using trumpets and a shofar] except at the Eastern Gate and on the Temple Mount alone."

[J] Said Rava, and some say R. Joshua b. Levi, "What is the [foundation] in Scripture [for this rule]?

---

[50]M reads: Rabbah. "Rava" is preferable (Rabbinovicz), appearing as well in the parallels at B. B.Q. 84a and B. B.M. 60b and 109b.

[51]Literally: said.

[52]Literally: in the border areas.

[53]At E-F, in M and other manuscripts, the terms "shofar" and "trumpets" are reversed.

[54]M reads: Hanina.

[55]M reads: and when they came.

[K] "As it is written[56] [Ps. 98:6]: 'With trumpets and the sound of the horn make a joyful noise in the presence of the King, the Lord!'

[L] "[The verse indicates that] 'in the presence of the King, the Lord' [that is, in the Temple itself] we require trumpets and the sound of the shofar.

[M] "But anywhere else, no!"

[X.A] *The [proclamation of the] year of Jubilee is equivalent to the New Year in regard to the sounding of the shofar and to the blessings* [M. R.H. 3:5A].

[B] Said Rab Samuel bar Isaac, "Nowadays, in accordance with [the view of] which [authority] do we state the prayer [on New Year]: 'Today is the beginning of your works, the commemoration of the first day'?

[C] In accordance with [the view of] which [authority]?

[D] In accordance with [the view of] R. Eliezer, who said, "In Tishre, the world was created." {See above B. R.H. 1:1 **XLVII**.L, 8a, and B. R.H. 1:1 **LXIII**.A, 10b.}

[E] Objected Rab Ena[57] [to the premise of M. R.H. 3:5A, which states: *"The proclamation of] the year of Jubilee is equivalent to the New Year in regard to the sounding of the shofar and to the blessings.*

[F] "But [this clearly is not the case],[58] since we have [the statement], 'Today is the beginning of your works, the commemoration of the first day' which applies on the New Year but does not apply in the Jubilee." {Apparently the blessings used on New Year are not the same as those used for the proclamation of the Jubilee.}

---

[56]M and other manuscripts lack: As it is written.

[57]M reads: Huna.

[58]M adds: since he said, "In Tishre, the world was created."

[G] {E-F misses the point:} When [the statement at M. R.H. 3:5A] was taught on Tannaitic authority, [it was taught] in reference to all other aspects [of New Year and the Jubilee].

[H] Rab Shisha[59] the son of Rab Idi teaches [the preceding discussion] as follows:

[I] Said Rab Samuel bar Isaac, "That which we have taught on Tannaitic authority [M. R.H. 3:5A: *The proclamation of] the year of Jubilee is equivalent to the New Year in regard to the sounding of the shofar and to the blessings*—in accordance with which [authority is this stated]?

[J] "It is not in accordance with [the view of] R. Eliezer.

[K] "For if [one were to claim that it is] R. Eliezer, [that would not make sense], since he said, 'In Tishre, the world was created.'"

[L] {The Talmud explains the fallacy of the premise that Eliezer stands behind M. R.H. 3:5A.} Lo, we have [the statement, which Eliezer will accept], "Today is the beginning of your works, the commemoration of the first day,'[60] which applies on the New Year but does not apply in the Jubilee. {Eliezer, who accepts this statement, cannot stand behind M. R.H. 3:5A, which holds that the blessings for New Year and the proclamation of the Jubilee are the same.}

[M] {Contrary to J-L, Eliezer in fact can stand behind M. R.H. 3:5A, so long as that passage is properly understood.} When [the statement at M. R.H. 3:5A] was taught on Tannaitic authority, [it was taught] in reference to all other aspects [of New Year and the Jubilee].

3:6

[A] *A shofar that cracked and that they stuck together is invalid.*

---

[59]M reads: Sheshet.

[60]M lacks: the commemoration of the first day.

[B] *[If] one stuck together the shreds of shofars,[61] [the shofar constructed in that way] is invalid.*

[C] *[27b] [If] it was perforated and one filled up the hole—*

[D] *if [the filled hole] affects the sound of the shofar, it is invalid.*

[E] *But if not, it is valid.*

3:7

[A] *He who sounds the shofar into a cistern, cellar, or large jar—*

[B] *if he heard the sound of the shofar, he has fulfilled his obligation.*

[C] *But if he heard the sound of the echo, he has not fulfilled his obligation.*

[D] *And so too:[62] He who was going along behind a synagogue,*

[E] *or whose house[63] was near a synagogue,*

[F] *and who heard the sound of the shofar*

[G] *or the sound of [the reading of] the Scroll [of Esther]—*

[H] *if he directed his heart [thereby intending to carry out his obligation], he has fulfilled his obligation.*

[I] *But if not, he has not fulfilled his obligation.*

[J] *Even though this one heard and that one [also] heard, [only one of them has fulfilled his obligation, for] this one directed his heart, and that one did not direct his heart [to what he heard].*

At units **I-V**, Toseftan and Amoraic materials supplement M. R.H. 3:6. Of concern are the proper ways of preparing a shofar for use and the methods by which, if the instrument is damaged, it may be repaired so as to remain valid for ritual use. Units **VI-VII** explain the circumstances under which the rule of M. R.H. 3:7A-C applies. This leads, at units **VIII-X**, to a review of the issue discussed above

---

[61]M has this word in the singular.

[62]M lacks: And so too.

[63]M and other manuscripts lack the word "house," reading simply: or who was near....

at B. R.H. 3:3-5 **V-VI**, concerning whether or not a blast of the shofar is divisible. The Talmud deemed it not to be, such that one who properly hears only part of the blast is not held to have fulfilled his obligation to hear the shofar.

Units **XI-XIII** take up a concern not directly introduced by the Mishnaic passages before us, the determination of what animal horns may be used as a shofar. Unit **XI** considers the use of horns from sacrificial animals. The Talmud argues that this is appropriate or not, depending upon whether the restriction against trespass applies to the particular sacrifice. Unit **XII** presents the rule for animals used in idolatry or taken from a city placed under a ban of destruction. Unit **XIII** develops the theme in a general way, discussing cases in which one has vowed to receive no benefit either from the particular shofar or from the person who sounds it.

Beginning at unit **XIV** the Talmud takes up the issue of M. R.H. 3:7, regarding the need for one who wishes to fulfill a religious obligation to formulate the intention to do so. Central here is the perspective of Rava, unit **XV**, that intention is not required. This view is challenged through a series of counter-examples (units **XVI-XVIII**) and ultimately is successfully overturned by Shaman b. Abba, unit **XIX**. At unit **XX**, Rava himself is made to revise his original statement. While continuing to hold that the fulfillment of religious obligations in general does not require intention, he agrees that, in the matter discussed by Shaman, intention in fact is necessary. Units **XXI-XXII** return us to the rule for the hearing of the shofar in particular, proposing that, to fulfill this obligation, the one who hears as well as the one who sounds the shofar must formulate appropriate intention.

[I.A] Our rabbis have taught on Tannaitic authority[64] [T. R.H. 2:4: **If a shofar was] long and one cut it down, it is valid.**

---

[64]M lacks the introductory formula, beginning instead with a citation of M. R.H. 3:6A.

[B] [If] one shaved it down, and left it as thin as its coating, it is valid.

[C] **[If] one overlaid it with gold at the place the mouth touches, [or if one added to it any amount at all, even of the same substance], it is invalid.**

[D] [If one overlaid it] at a place the mouth does not touch, it is valid.

[E] [If] one overlaid it with gold on the inside, it is invalid.

[F] [If one did so] on the outside—if the sound is altered from the way it had been, it is invalid.

[G] But if not, it is valid.

[H] [M. R.H. 3:6C-E: *If] it was perforated and one filled up the hole—*

[I] *if [the filled hole] affects the sound of the shofar, it is invalid.*

[J] *But if not, it is valid.*

[K] **[If] one placed [one] shofar inside [another] shofar [and sounded them]**[65]**—**

[L] **If he heard the sound [made by] the inner one, he has fulfilled [the obligation to hear the shofar].**

[M] **But if he heard the sound of the outer one, he has not fulfilled [his obligation].**[66]

[II.A] Our rabbis have taught on Tannaitic authority [T. R.H. 2:4: **If] one shaved it down, whether inside or outside, it is valid.**

[B] [If] one shaved it down, and left it as thin as its coating, it is valid.

---

[65] The bracketed words appear explicitly in M and other sources.

[66] This line is added in the margin of M. It apparently was dropped from the body of the text through haplography.

[C] [If] one set [one] shofar inside [another] shofar [and sounded them][67]—

[D] if he heard the sound[68] [made by] the inner one, he has fulfilled [the obligation to hear the shofar].

[E] But if he heard the sound of the outer one, he has not fulfilled [his obligation].

[III.A] [If] he [softened the shofar and] turned it inside out and sounded it, he has not fulfilled [his obligation].

[B] Said Rab Pappa,[69] "Do not say [that this applies] simply if he turned it inside out like a coat.

[C] "Rather, if he broadened the narrow part and narrowed the broad part [it is not valid].

[D] "What is the basis [in Scripture for this]?

[E] "It accords with [the view of] Rab Mattenah, for said Rab Mattenah, '[Lev. 25:9 says], "Then you shall carry[70] [the loud trumpet on the tenth day of the seventh month]."

[F] "'[This means that] we require [the shofar to be] in the form in which it is carried [by the ram].'"

[IV.A] *[If] one stuck together the shreds of shofars, [the shofar constructed in that way] is invalid* [M. R.H. 3:6B].

[B] Our rabbis have taught on Tannaitic authority[71] [see T. R.H. 2:4: **If] one added to it in any amount,** whether of the

---

[67]The bracketed words are found explicitly in M and other sources.

[68]Here and at E, M lacks the word: sound.

[69]M lacks the name: Pappa.

[70]In context the term means: make heard. RSV: send abroad.

[71]M and other sources lack the introductory formula. Rabbinovicz argues that the manuscript reading is correct, and that rather than a Mishnah citation (A) followed by a separate comment (B), A-B comprises a unitary Tannaitic statement.

	same substance or of some different substance, **it is invalid.**[72]
[C]	***[If] it was perforated and one filled up the hole*** [M. R.H. 3:6C], whether with the same substance or with some different substance, it is invalid.
[D]	R. Nathan says, "[If it is] with the same substance, it is valid;[73]
[E]	"[but] with some different substance, it is invalid."
[F]	{The Tannaitic citation at B-E is interrupted with a gloss on Nathan's statement, D.} "[If it is] with the same substance, it is valid"—
[G]	Said R. Yohanan, "But this applies [only] if the majority [of the original shofar] remains."
[H]	From this [statement of Yohanan] we can derive the rule that, [if it is] with some different substance [that one fills the hole], then even though the majority [of the original shofar] remains, it is invalid.
[I]	There are those who teach [Yohanan's gloss] in reference to the latter part [of Nathan's statement, E: "but] with some different substance, it is invalid."
[J]	Said R. Yohanan, "But this applies [only] if the majority [of the original shofar] is removed."
[K]	From this [statement of Yohanan] we can derive the rule that, [if it is] with the same substance [that one fills the hole], then

---

[72]For the interpolated words (which are not in boldface), through the end of the line, the body of M reads: and they taught: [if it is] of its same substance, it is valid; [if it is] not of its same substance, it is invalid. A marginal emendation essentially indicates the reading found as well in P and other sources: and they taught: whether it is of its same (valid) or some different substance, it is invalid. In this correction, the appearance of the word "valid" (marked here by parenthesis) is an error.

[73]This first line of Nathan's statement is lacking in P, the Venice printing, and some commentators. It appears to have dropped from the text through haplography.

	even though the majority [of the original shofar] is removed, it is valid.
[L]	{We continue the Tannaitic passage begun at B-E.} [If] one overlaid it with gold on the inside, it is invalid.
[M]	[If one did so] on the outside—if the sound is altered from the way it had been, it is invalid.
[N]	But if not, it is valid.
[O]	[If] it was split open lengthwise, is it invalid.
[P]	[If it was split] along its breadth—
[Q]	if enough of it remains to make a blast, it is valid.
[R]	But if not, it is invalid.
[S]	[T. R.H. 2:4, with variations:] Now, **what is the [minimum] measure** [that yields a proper] blast?
[T]	Rabban Simeon b. Gamaliel explained:[74] "**Sufficiently large so that a person can hold it in his hand** and see [a part of it sticking out] on either side."
[U]	If its sound is thin, thick, or coarse,[75] it [in all events] is valid,
[V]	since all sounds made by a shofar are valid.

[V.A]	They sent to the father of Samuel [this rule: If] one pierced it and [anyway] used it for the [required] blast, he has fulfilled [his religious obligation].
[B]	This is obvious [and goes without saying, since] all [shofars] are pierced. {Without the hole, no sound can be produced.}
[C]	[To explain that A is not obvious] said Rab Ashi, "[This applies even if] he pierced the bony projection [over which the horn grows on the animal]. {That bone normally is entirely removed in the production of a shofar.}
[D]	"[Had A's rule not been taught] what might you have thought?

---

[74] M has: Rabban Simeon b. Gamaliel says.

[75] Follow Aruch and Rashi to B. Hul. 36a, and read: *srwd*. Sources for B. R.H. read: *srwr* ("knotted").

[E] "[Even though the bone] is of the same category [as the material comprising the horn itself], it interposes [between the mouth and the horn so that, if it is not entirely removed, the shofar is invalid].

[F] "Therefore we are informed [by the rule at A, that if the bone is pierced but not removed, the shofar is valid]."

[VI.A] *He who sounds the shofar into a cistern, cellar, [or large jar...; M. R.H. 3:7A].*

[B] Said Rab Huna,[76] "They did not teach [this rule to apply] except to those who are standing on the edge of the cistern. {Such people have fulfilled their obligation only if they hear the sound of the shofar itself, not an echo.}

[C] "But those who are standing in the cistern [itself, and who hear the shofar being blown into the cistern], have fulfilled [the obligation of hearing the shofar]." {Such people are assumed to have heard the shofar, not the echo.}

[D] That which is taught on Tannaitic authority makes the same point: *He who sounds the shofar into a cistern or cellar* has fulfilled his [religious] obligation.

[E] But [indicating the contrary] we have taught on Tannaitic authority [M. R.H. 3:7C]: *he has not fulfilled his obligation!* {M. R.H. 3:7C applies this statement to the case in which the individual heard the echo, not the shofar itself. That fact is ignored here.}

[F] Accordingly, [you] cannot [interpret this statement, at E, out of its larger context].

[G] [Rather] you must interpret it following [the perspective of] Rab Huna, [distinguishing between individuals who are at the edge of the cistern, who have not fulfilled their obligation (E), and those who are in the cistern, who have fulfilled their obligation (D)].

---

[76]Rosh reads: Judah.

[H] [Contrary to the solution offered at F-G], some view the statements [at D vs. E] as in opposition [to each other]:

[I] We have taught on Tannaitic authority [M. R.H. 3:7A+C]: *He who sounds the shofar into a cistern or cellar has not fulfilled his obligation.*

[J] But [to the contrary], it is taught on Tannaitic authority: [He who sounds the shofar into a cistern or cellar] has fulfilled his [religious] obligation.

[K] [Resolving the contradiction raised at H-J] said Rab Huna, "There is no contradiction!

[L] "This [statement, I] applies to those who are standing on the edge of the cistern,

[M] "while this [statement, J] applies to those who are standing in the cistern [itself]."

[VII.A] Said Rabbah,[77] [28a] "[If] one heard part of the blast while in the cistern and [having stepped out heard] part of the blast on the edge of the cistern, he has fulfilled [his obligation].

[B] "[If one heard] part of the blast prior to dawn and part of the blast after dawn, he has not fulfilled [his obligation]."

[C] Said to him Abayye, "What is the difference [between the two cases]?

[D] "[Do you claim the difference to be that] there [in the situation described at B] we require the entire blast[78] [to be heard in a period of time in which] one is obligated [to hear the shofar], and [this condition is] not [met]?

[E] "[That argument fails, since I can respond that] here too [in the case described at A] we require the entire blast [to be heard] as one is obligated, but [this condition is] not [met]!" {At A, as at B, half of the blast that the individual hears

---

[77] Here and in the following, M, other manuscripts, Rosh, Rashi, and others read: Rava.

[78] Here and at E, M lacks the word: blast.

cannot be counted towards the fulfillment of the obligation, lest he heard an echo, not the shofar itself. Abayye's question, C, stands: why is the rule at A different from that of B?}

[F] Now what? {Simon: Are the two cases really parallel? An explanation of Rabbah's perspective follows.}

[G] [Distinguishing the cases is the fact that] there [at B] it is night, which is not a time of obligation [to hear the shofar] at all. {That which the individual hears therefore cannot fulfill his obligation.}

[H] [But] here [at A, we deal with] a cistern, in which those who stand are obligated[79] [to hear the shofar]. {Since, at A, both before and after the individual stepped out of the cistern, the obligation to hear the shofar existed, and the shofar was heard, we deem the individual to have fulfilled the obligation. This is different from the case at B, where the beginning of the blast was heard when there was no obligation at all.}

[VIII.A] {Here and in unit IX, Rabbah's statement at A-B of the preceding unit is judged in light of the issue raised above, at B. R.H. 3:3-5 V-VI, 27a, concerning whether or not a blast of the shofar is divisible.} This is to say that Rabbah reasons that [if] one hears[80] the end of the blast but not the beginning of the blast, he has fulfilled [his obligation to hear the shofar].

[B] And it goes without saying [that if he heard] the beginning of the blast but not the end of the blast, he has fulfilled [his obligation].

[IX.A] {The following independent construction explains M. R.H. 4:9. As my interpolated comment at D indicates, however, in context, it serves to refute Rabbah's position in the preceding

---

[79]M lacks: a cistern, in which those who stand. The meaning is the same.

[80]M lacks the end of this line through the middle of B, a case of haplography.

units.} Come and learn [M. R.H. 4:9: *If] one sounded the first Tekiah-blast [of the set of three] and then sustained the second blast for twice as long, he [still] has credit only for one.* {That is, he cannot count the sustained blast half for the first set and half for a later set.}

[B] Why [does he get credit for only one]?

[C] [Rather] you should [deem the blast to] be divided into two parts [so as to allow credit for two separate blasts]!

[D] [This cannot be done, since] we do not divide a single blast. {The implication is that what unit **VIII**.A-B describes comparably should not be permitted. Since a blast is indivisible, in order to fulfill one's obligation to hear the shofar, he must hear the entire blast.}

[X.A] Come and learn [a refutation of Rabbah's notion, unit **VII**, that one who hears only half of the blast has fulfilled his obligation. M. R.H. 3:7 states]: *He who sounds the shofar into a cistern, cellar, or large jar—*

[B] *if he heard the sound of the shofar, he has fulfilled his obligation.*

[C] *But if he heard the sound of the echo, he has not fulfilled his obligation.*

[D] But why?

[E] [Contrary to C, and in accordance with the perspective of Rabbah, unit **VII**], let him [be deemed] to have fulfilled his obligation [by having heard] the beginning of the blast, before it became mixed up with the sound [of the echo]! {This would be in line with Rabbah's explicit statement at unit **VII**.A. There he states that one who hears part of the blast while in the cistern and, having stepped out, hears the rest of the blast on the edge of the cistern has fulfilled his obligation.}

[F] {We now find that Rabbah in fact agrees with M. R.H. 3:7's rule, cited at C. The circumstance at unit **VII**, where Rabbah deems the individual to have fulfilled his obligation, is not comparable to the circumstance in which M. R.H. 3:7 holds that the person has not fulfilled his obligation.} When Rabbah spoke [at unit **VII**.A, he referred to a case] in which [the person standing in the cistern] himself blew [the shofar] while he stepped [out of the cistern]. {In this situation, it is clear that the person heard the entire blast and has fulfilled his obligation. This is different from the circumstance described at M. R.H. 3:7, cited above a C, where the person does not hear the entire blast. Despite his view at unit **VII**, and contrary to A's claim, Rabbah agrees with M. R.H. 3:7's rule. That rule in no way conflicts with Rabbah's perspective.}

[G] {F's interpretation of Rabbah's position is rejected as rendering Rabbah's statement obvious. Since, in the case described at F, the person blowing the shofar certainly hears the entire blast, the fact that, while blowing, he steps out of a cistern seems irrelevant.} If this [is what Rabbah means], what does he mean to say [that is not anyway obvious]?

[H] [Had we not heard Rabbah's statement] what might you have thought?

[I] At times [the person in the situation described at F] sticks his head [out of the cistern] while the shofar [he is blowing] still is in the cistern, and as a result the sound [of the shofar] becomes mixed up [with the sound of the echo, so that even the person playing the shofar cannot distinguish between the two].

[J] Therefore we are informed [by Rabbah, unit **VII**.A, that even in this situation, the person has fulfilled his obligation to hear the shofar].

[**XI**.A] Said Rab Judah, "One may not sound a shofar from [an animal used as] a burnt-offering, but if he sounded [such a shofar], he has fulfilled [his obligation].

[B] "One may not sound a shofar from [an animal used as] a peace-offering, and if he sounded [such a shofar], he has not fulfilled [his religious obligation]."

[C] What is the reason [for the distinction]?

[D] A burnt-offering [A] is subject to the laws regarding trespass [that is, the use of a holy thing for a secular purpose].

[E] [Therefore] once one committed an act of trespass with it, it has entered the status of that which is unconsecrated [such as to comprise a valid shofar].

[F] Peace-offerings [B] are not subject to the laws regarding trespass.

[G] [Therefore] they are saddled with the prohibition [that applies to them as consecrated things], and [even if used for a secular purpose] they do not enter the status of that which is unconsecrated.[81]

[H] Rava objected to this [claim, A, that, if used, a shofar from a burnt-offering is valid]: "At[82] what point has he committed an act of trespass?

[I] "Once he [already] has blown [the shofar].

[J] "[Therefore] when he blew, he blew that which was forbidden [and, contrary to A, cannot be deemed to have fulfilled his obligation]!"

[K] Rather, said Rava, "The rule is the same in both cases: [Whether he used a shofar from a burnt-offering, A, or peace-offerings, B], he has not fulfilled [his obligation]."

[L] [Later Rava][83] reconsidered and said, "The rule is the same in both cases: [Whether he used a shofar from a burnt-offering, A, or peace-offerings, B], he *has* fulfilled [his obligation]."

---

[81] In P the final clause here is bracketed. These words are lacking in M and other sources.

[82] M introduces the quotation: In the final analysis....

[83] The name "Rava" appears explicitly in M.

[M]   [He took this position because[84] religious] obligations are not for purposes of enjoyment. {Since blowing the shofar entails no personal enjoyment or material benefit, using a shofar from a consecrated animal does not comprise trespass. Contrary to A-B, the use of such a shofar is permitted in the first place.}

[XII.A] Said Rab Judah,[85] "With a shofar from [an animal used for] idolatry one should not blow, but if he blew [such a shofar], he has fulfilled [his obligation].

[B]   "With a shofar from [an animal from] a dedicated city [Dt. 13:12-17], one should not blow, and if he blew [such a shofar], he has not fulfilled [his obligation]."

[C]   What is the reason [for the distinction]?

[D]   [In the case of] a dedicated city, [all of] its measures have been crushed [that is, no horn of appropriate size for a shofar remains]. {Dt. 13:12-17 requires the destruction of everything in a city the inhabitants of which have engaged in idolatry.}

[XIII.A] Said Rava, "[As for] one who vows not to benefit [literally: derive enjoyment] from his neighbor—[that neighbor in all events] is permitted to sound the required Tekiah[86] for him. {As we know from unit XI.M, hearing the shofar is not deemed to entail personal benefit.}

[B]   "[Comparably] one who vows not to benefit from a [particular] shofar is permitted to sound the required Tekiah on it."

---

[84]M introduces this line by asking: What is the reason?

[85]In place of "Judah," M has: Rava.

[86]In place of "Tekiah," M has the word: shofar.

[C] And [along the same lines] said Rava, "[As for] one who vows not to benefit from his neighbor—[that neighbor[87] in all events] may sprinkle on him the water of the sin-offering [derived from the red heifer, which purifies from corpse uncleanness].

[D] "[This applies] in the rainy season, but not in the sunny-season." {The ritual act of sprinkling the water so as to cleanse the person of corpse uncleanness is deemed not to involve physical benefit and so, despite the vow, is permitted. But in the summer, as a secondary result of the ritual act, the person who is sprinkled enjoys the cooling affect of the waters. For this reason, at that time, a person from whom he has vowed not to benefit may not sprinkle him.}

[E] {The following case is parallel to C-D.} A person who vows not to benefit from a [particular] spring may [anyway] dunk in it for purposes of an obligatory immersion [that is, using the spring as a ritual bath, a *mikveh*].

[F] [This applies] in the rainy season but not in the sunny-season [when the bather will enjoy the cool water].

[XIV.A] They sent to the father of Samuel [saying: If on Passover] they compelled [a person] to eat unleavened bread, [by doing so] he fulfilled [his obligation to eat unleavened bread]. {This is the case even though he did not intend to fulfill the religious obligation.}

[B] Who compelled him?

[C] Might I say [it was] a demon?

[D] Now, [that would be unacceptable, since, to the contrary], thus it is taught on Tannaitic authority [T. Ter. 1:3: **If one is] at times lucid and at times crazy—whenever he is lucid, lo, he is equivalent to a person of sound senses in every respect; when he is crazy, lo, he is**

---

[87]M has "neighbor" explicitly.

BAVLI ROSH HASHANAH CHAPTER THREE [28b] 353

deemed crazy in every respect. {In the case at A, if the person believes a demon forced him to eat unleavened bread, he is deemed crazy and therefore not subject to the fulfillment of religious obligations anyway. A thus cannot refer to a case such as is proposed by C.}

[E] Said Rab Ashi, "[It refers to a case] in which the Persians compelled him."[88]

[F] Said Rava, "This [rule at A, explained by E, which states that an act not intended to fulfill a religious obligation still is efficacious] suggests: One who blows [a shofar simply] to produce music [in all events] fulfills his obligation."

[G] This is obvious, [since the cases at A+E and F] are [exactly] the same!

[H] {G is shown to be incorrect.} [Had Rava not explicitly stated the rule at F] what might you have said?

[I] There [in the situation described at A], the merciful [simply] said, "Eat unleavened bread," and [in fact] the individual ate [unleavened bread]. {Even though he was compelled, he carried out the requirement and therefore has fulfilled his obligation.}

[J] [28b] But here [regarding the hearing of the shofar, at Lev. 23:24], "a memorial proclaimed with blast of trumpets" is written.

[K] Now, this one[89] [referred to by Rava, F] is [simply] fooling around [and so does not fulfill the biblical requirement of producing "a memorial"].

[L] Therefore we are informed [by Rava, F, that, even so, he has fulfilled his obligation].

---

[88]M records Rava as saying: No! [This rule is] necessary, for instance in a case in which the Persians compelled him.

[89]M lacks the biblical citation at J through this point.

[XV.A] {The implication of Rava's view is drawn out and evaluated.} [Based upon the preceding] can I say that Rava reasons [that] the [performance of religious] obligations does not require intention.

[B] [There is] an objection[90] [to A's perspective, that religious obligations do not require intention, based upon M. Ber. 2:1: *If] one was reading [the verses of the Shema] in the Torah and the time for the recitation [of the Shema] arrived:*

[C] *if he directed his heart, he fulfilled his obligation [to recite].*

[D] *But if not, he has not fulfill his obligation.*

[E] {On the surface, the Mishnaic passage, B-D, seems to state explicitly that, to fulfill a religious duty, one must "direct his heart," that is, formulate the intention to carry out that obligation. The following rejects this interpretation, suggesting instead that M. Ber. 2:1 does not provide evidence against A's claim that intention is not required.} What [does D mean? Does it] not [mean]: "If he did [not] direct his heart [towards the fulfillment of the obligation, then, he has not fulfilled that obligation]"?

[F] No, [rather, the deficiency is that he did not direct his heart] to read [the passage]! {In this reading, M. Ber. 2:1 says nothing about a requirement of intention towards the fulfillment of a religious obligation. At B, the person has not fulfilled his obligation because he paid no attention to the reading itself. If he had paid attention to the reading, the fact that he had no consciousness of performing a religious obligation would have been irrelevant. He in all events would have been deemed to have fulfilled the obligation to read the Shema.}

[G] {For the reason given at G-H, F's reading of M. Ber. 2:1 seems unacceptable.} [Can it in fact be as F claims that, "The

---

[90]M and other manuscripts have: Abayye objected. The name is lacking from all printed editions except Cracow.

BAVLI ROSH HASHANAH CHAPTER THREE [28b] 355

deficiency is that he did not direct his heart] to read [the passage]"!?

[H] [How can this be since, in the case described at A] he was [in fact] in the middle of reading [the required passage]? {Since the individual was in fact reading, it seems unreasonable to claim that because he was not paying attention to reading, he has not fulfilled his obligation to recite the Shema.}

[I] {The Talmud explains why the individual's failure to turn his attention to reading is in fact the concern here.} [At[91] issue here is a case] in which he is reading [a Torah scroll] so as to correct [it]. {Such an individual does not pay attention to the act of reading but, rather, to the checking of the scroll for errors. In this case H's consideration is a concern. The individual has not fulfilled the obligation to read the Shema because of his failure to direct his attention to the act of reading. His lack of intention towards fulfilling the religious obligation is irrelevant. A's contention stands. The rule of M. Ber. 2:1 does not prove that, contrary to A, the fulfillment of religious obligations requires intention.}

[XVI.A] {M. R.H. 3:7D-H provides a second challenge to unit XV.A, which states that the performance of religious obligations does not require intention.} Come and learn [a second challenge to unit XV.A. M. R.H. 3:7 states]: *He who was going along behind a synagogue, or whose house was near a synagogue, and who heard the sound of the shofar or the sound of [the reading of] the Scroll [of Esther]—*

[B] *if he directed his heart, he has fulfilled his obligation.*

[C] *But if not, he has not fulfilled his obligation.*

[D] {On the surface, the Mishnaic passage, B-C, seems explicit that, to fulfill a religious duty, one must "direct his heart," that is, formulate the intention to perform that obligation. The

---

[91]M and other manuscripts introduce this line: Perhaps.

following rejects this interpretation.} What [does C mean? Does it] not [mean]: "If he did [not] direct his heart [towards the fulfillment of the obligation, then, he has not] fulfilled that obligation"?

[E]⁹² No, [rather, the deficiency is that he did not direct his heart] to hear [the blast]! {In this reading, M. R.H. 3:7 says nothing about a requirement of intention in the fulfillment of a religious obligation. At C, the person has not fulfilled his obligation because he paid no attention to hearing the blast. If he had paid attention to hearing, the fact that he had no consciousness of performing a religious obligation would have been irrelevant. He in all events would have been deemed to have fulfilled the obligation to hear the shofar.}

[F] {For the reason given in the following, E's reading of M. R.H. 3:7 seems unacceptable.} [Is it reasonable to claim that, "The deficiency is that he did not direct his heart] to hear [the shofar]"!?

[G] [How can this be the issue since, in the case described at A] he did [in fact] hear [the shofar]? {The fact of the case is that the individual heard the shofar. It therefore seems unreasonable to declare that, since he was not paying attention to hearing, he has not fulfilled his obligation.}

[H] {The Talmud explains why the individual's failure to turn his attention to hearing is in fact the concern here.} [The failure to direct one's attention to hearing is an issue here since otherwise] he might think [that he simply is hearing] a donkey [braying and not a shofar at all]. {Since the individual described at M. R.H. 3:7 might not even realize that he is hearing a shofar, he has not fulfilled his obligation. But if he

---

⁹²At E-G, M and other manuscript sources read: Is it not so that, if he directed his heart to hear [the shofar], he would [in fact] hear it? L lacks the word "if," so that its reading is the same as that of P, except that it explicitly has the words found in brackets at E.

did direct his attention to the hearing, he would be deemed to have fulfilled that obligation. This would be the case despite his lack of intention towards fulfilling a religious obligation. Unit **XV**.A's contention stands. The rule of M. R.H. 3:7 does not prove that the fulfillment of religious obligations requires intention.}

[**XVII**.A] There is [another] objection [to unit **XV**.A, which holds that the performance of religious obligations does not require intention. A Tannaitic source states: If] the one who hears [the blast] directed [his heart], but the one who sounds [the blast] did not direct [his heart];

[B] [or if] the one who sounds [the blast directed his heart], but the one who hears [the blast] did not direct [his heart]—

[C] he did not fulfill his obligation [to hear the shofar].

[D] [This is the case] until the point at which [both] the one who hears and the one who sounds [the blast] direct [their hearts].

[E] Granted, [B-C's rule, which states, "If] the one who sounds [the blast] directed [his heart], but the one who hears [the blast] did not direct [his heart, he has not fulfilled his obligation," makes sense].

[F] [This is as **XVI**.H already has explained, that the hearer] might think[93] [that he simply is hearing] a donkey [braying and not a shofar at all].

[G] But [the case at A+C, which states, "If] the one who hears [the blast] directed [his heart], but the one who sounds [the blast] did not direct [his heart, he did not fulfill his obligation]"—how can this occur?

[H] Is it not [an instance in which the individual] blows [the shofar simply] to produce music [see above, unit **XIV**.F, 28a]? {In this case, the person has directed his attention towards playing but not towards fulfillment of the religious

---

[93]M lacks: might think.

obligation of hearing the shofar. Since, as we see at B-C, under this circumstance he has not fulfilled that religious obligation, this rule appears to challenge the contention of unit XV.A. The fulfillment of religious obligations does require intention.}

[I] {H's interpretation of B-C is rejected.} Perhaps [B refers to a case in which he simply] made a barking sound. {To accomplish this, the individual did not even focus his intention upon playing the shofar. For this reason he does not fulfill the religious obligation. Again, the fact that he did not formulate the intention to fulfill that obligation is irrelevant.}

[XVIII.A] {This challenge to the proposition that religious obligations do not require intention, unit XV.A, argues that if intention is not required to fulfill religious obligations, it also should not be a requisite in cases in which people are deemed to transgress religious precepts.} Abayye said to him [that is, to Rava, the authority behind unit XV.A], "Based upon this [notion, that the performance of religious obligations does not require intention], one who [inadvertently] sleeps in a booth [constructed for the festival of Tabernacles] on the eighth night [when doing so is not required] should be flogged." {Rashi: The individual transgressed the prohibition against extending biblical commandments. Abayye argues that, in Rava's theory that intention does not matter, this individual is culpable even though he did not intentionally extend the Bible's rule.}

[B] {Rava rejects Abayye's conclusion that the individual described at A. is culpable for transgressing the prohibition against extending commandments. But, since Rava's response focuses upon the nature of what this particular person did, not upon the larger question of whether or not violating religious precepts requires intention, the issue introduced by Abayye remains unresolved.} [Rava] said to him,[94] "[The circumstance you describe is different and not subject to the prohibition against extending commandments], since I say [that, as for religious] obligations—one does not transgress them except during their own period [of applicability]." {Once Tabernacles is over, a person under no circumstance can be deemed culpable for extending the holiday. A person is culpable for transgressing this prohibition only by adding to what is required while it is required, for instance (Rashi) by placing five fringes on a prayer shawl instead of the required four.}

[C] Objected Rab Shaman b. Abba[95] [to Rava, B, "The following legal source invalidates your claim that the prohibition against extending a religious obligation applies only during the period of that obligation]:

[D] "From what [verse in Scripture do we know] that a priest who mounts the stage [from which the priestly benediction is recited][96] should not say, 'Since the Torah has given me the right to bless [the people of] Israel, I shall add a blessing of my own, for instance, [citing Dt. 1:11]: "May the Lord, the God of your fathers, make you [a thousand times as many as you are, and bless you, as he has promised you!]"'?

---

[94]M lacks: said to him. In place of the rest of this line, it has: The circumstance for [extending] commandments is different, since one does not transgress them except during their own period [of applicability]. The variant perhaps resulted from the scribe's reading the phrase "since I," found in P and other sources, as "different," which is spelled the same way.

[95]M and other manuscripts read: Shimi bar Ashi. Since Shaman b. Abba was a student of Yohanan and active in the Land of Israel, he should not appear in debate with Rava. Rabbinovicz accordingly rejects the reading of the printed editions as a printer's corruption of the abbreviation of Shimi bar Ashi's name.

[96]M adds: and who completes all of his benedictions, how do we know he.... In the following, M lacks the word, "Torah," reading instead: Since I was given....

[E] "[We know this is impermissible, since] Scripture states [Dt. 4:2]: 'You shall not add to the word [that I command you].'[97]

[F] {Shaman b. Abba continues by explaining explicitly why the rule at D-E disproves Rava's claim at B.} "Now, here, since he [already] has blessed them [that is, the people, with the words of the priestly benediction], the time [of the obligation to bless the people] has passed!

[G] "But [anyway] it is taught on Tannaitic authority that [by adding his own blessing at this point] he transgresses!" {This suggests that Rava's claim, B, is unacceptable. Abayye, A, is correct.}

[H] {Shaman b. Abba's case is shown not to prove the point on which he concludes.} Here [in the case described at D-E] with what [circumstances] are we dealing?

[I] [It is a case] in which [the priest] did not conclude [the priestly benediction prior to adding his own prayer]. {The fact that his addition is prohibited does not disprove Rava's claim, B. Since he had not completed the required liturgy, the additional prayer was recited while he still was obligated to bless the people.}

[J] {I seems unacceptable.} But thus it is [explicitly] taught on Tannaitic authority: [If] he completed [his required benediction, he still may not add a blessing of his own].

[K] [I's consideration still applies, since the Tannaitic source at J indicates only that] he had finished [only] one [of the three] benedictions!

[L] {I+K is challenged.} But thus it is [explicitly] taught on Tannaitic authority:[98] [If] he completed all his [required] benedictions, [he still may not add a blessing of his own].

---

[97]M has the bracketed conclusion of the verse explicitly.

[98]M places the formula indicating the Tannaitic statement after the citation.

[M] {We find a final reason that D-E does not disprove Rava's claim, B.} This [case of a priest who recites the priestly benediction] is distinctive [and not subject to evaluation under the regular rule].

[N] Since, if he [later] chances upon another community, he goes and blesses [them as well], the entire day is treated as the time [for the performance of this religious obligation]. {The general principle stands: one transgresses the prohibition against extending a commandment only if one does so during the period of that obligation's applicability. In the case of the priestly benediction, the entire day is treated as its period of applicability.}

[XIX.A] {The argument of the preceding unit continues on a new basis.} On what grounds do you say this [that is, that one transgresses the prohibition against extending a commandment only while it still is in affect]?

[B] For we have taught on Tannaitic authority [M. Zeb. 8:10: *Blood of a sacrifice] that is to be tossed in a single act of tossing that was mixed up with [blood] that is to be tossed in a single act of tossing—let them be tossed in a single act of tossing.*

[C] *[Blood] that is to be tossed in four acts of tossing [that was mixed up] with [blood] that is to be tossed in four acts of tossing—let them be tossed in four acts of tossing.*

[D] *[Blood] that is to be tossed in four acts of tossing [that was mixed up] with [blood] that is to be tossed in one act of tossing—*

[E] *R. Eliezer says, "Let them be tossed in four acts of tossing."*

[F] *R. Joshua says, "Let them be tossed in a single act of tossing."*

[G] *Said to him R. Eliezer, "But, lo, [in your approach] he transgresses the rule against diminishing [that which God requires; Dt. 4:2]."*

[H] *Said to him R. Joshua, "But, lo, [in your approach] he transgresses the rule against adding [to that which God requires; Dt. 4:2]."*

[I] *Said to him R. Eliezer, "The prohibition against adding applies only [if the additional act is performed] with the same object [through which the obligation already was completed]."* {Eliezer's ruling that the blood be tossed four times does not comprise a prohibited extension of the number of times the blood meant to be tossed once actually is tossed. This is because each amount of blood, once tossed, is not itself tossed again. Each quantity of blood taken from the basin is tossed only once.}

[J] *Said to him R. Joshua, "The prohibition against diminishing applies only [if that which was meant to be done is withheld] from the same object."* {Since, once thrown, the same blood in all events could not be tossed again, the priest has not transgressed the prohibition against diminishing. This is the case even though the blood of that particular sacrifice, which was meant to be thrown four times, winds up being thrown only once.}

[K] *And further did R. Joshua say, "If [as I require] you did not toss [the blood four times, then, even if, as you say], you [thereby] transgress the prohibition against diminishing, [at least] you did not do [any prohibited] deed with your own hand.*

[L] *"But if [as you require] you tossed [the blood four times, then, as I have explained], you transgressed the prohibition against adding, and you [also] did the [forbidden] deed with your own hand [by tossing four times blood meant to be tossed once]."*

[M] {We now examine the implication of the cited passage for the question of whether or not the prohibition against extending applies after the time within which an obligation applies has passed.} Now, here, as soon as he tossed [the blood once]

[N] for the firstling, the time period within which he was subject to the obligation [to toss the blood] had passed.

[N] Yet [even so] it is taught on Tannaitic authority that, [in Joshua's view, an individual who continues to toss such blood] has transgressed the prohibition against adding [to required actions]! {Joshua appears to reject the principle first articulated at unit **XVIII**.B, that the prohibition against extending pertains only during an obligation's period of applicability.}

[O] {O suggests that, in the case of the tossing of the blood of a firstling, an as yet unidentified consideration applies. Joshua indeed holds that the prohibition against extending pertains only during an obligation's period of applicability.} Is not [the reason that Joshua deems this individual culpable] that we say that, since, if [the priest] chances upon another firstling, he goes and [upon its being sacrificed] tosses its [blood as well], the entire day is treated as the time [for the performance of this religious obligation]!? {Joshua concurs with the principle phrased by Rava, unit **XVIII**.B. One transgresses a commandment only by extending it while it still is in affect. The commandment to toss the firstling's blood is treated as though it pertained all day, even after some blood from a particular firstling already has been tossed.}

[P] {O's explanation of Joshua's view is rejected.}[99] Perhaps R. Joshua [in fact] reasons [that, as for religious] obligations—one does transgress them even outside of their period [of applicability]!

[Q] Thus we can state [as at O, to show that P is incorrect and that Joshua indeed holds that one transgresses a commandment only by extending it while it still is in affect].

---

[99]In the printed the edition, the phrase "From whence do we know this" occurs here in brackets.

[R] {O's explanation of Joshua's position again is challenged. If Joshua at M. Zeb. 8:10 intends what O states, why did Shaman bar Abba not adduce that case in his challenge to Rava, recorded in unit **XVIII**.D-G?} [If matters are as O claims, then, as for] Rab Shaman bar Abba,[100] for what reason did he ignore [the more authoritative Mishnaic passage, M. Zeb. 8:10] and object [to Rava's principle, unit **XVIII**.B] on the basis of a [non-Mishnaic] Tannaitic statement, [which he cites at unit **XVIII**.G]?

[S] [If Joshua's position at M. Zeb. 8:10 means what O claims, Shaman] should have objected [to Rava's view] on the basis of this Mishnaic passage!

[T] [As for] the Mishnaic passage—what is the reason [Shaman] did not [use it as the foundation for his] objection [to Rava's view]?

[U] {This was because M. Zeb. 8:10 is subject to a special consideration, such that it does not in fact challenge Rava's perspective.} [M. Zeb. 8:10 was not an appropriate basis for the objection], since, if [the priest] chances upon another firstling, he goes and [upon its being sacrificed] tosses its [blood as well], the entire day is treated as the time [for the performance of this religious obligation].

[V] [For the reason given here, U's explanation seems unacceptable. The same consideration applies in the case of the Tannaitic rule that Shaman did cite.} Also [n the case of] the Tannaitic statement [cited at unit **XVIII**.G], if he [later] chances upon another community, he goes and blesses them [as well]; therefore the entire day is treated as the time [for the performance of this religious obligation]. {Since there seems to be no difference between the cases cited at unit **XVIII**.G and M. Zeb. 8:10, the reason for Shaman's use of the non-Mishnaic Tannaitic statement remains open.}

---

[100]See note 95.

BAVLI ROSH HASHANAH CHAPTER THREE [28b] 365

[W] Now, [how does] Rab Shaman bar Abba [respond so as to explain his use of the Tannaitic rule instead of M. Zeb. 8:10]?

[X] There [at M. Zeb. 8:10] there is no possibility of [the priest's] not tossing [the blood of a firstling that later is sacrificed]. {In this case, Shaman concurs that the reasoning given at O applies. The entire day is deemed the period of the tossing of the blood, so that whenever a priest tosses more times than are required, he has transgressed the prohibition against adding. This case cannot serve to disprove Rava's view, unit **XVIII**.B, that the prohibition against adding applies only during an obligation's period of applicability.}

[Y] [By contrast] here [in the case of the priestly benediction, unit **XVIII**.G], if [a priest who, having blessed one group later chances upon a different group]—if he wishes, he blesses them [as well]; if he wishes, he does not bless [them]. {For this reason, in the case of the priestly benediction, Shaman rejects the contention, unit **XVIII**.N, that the entire day is deemed the obligation's period of applicability. His challenge to Rava, unit **XVIII**.B, therefore stands. In the case of the priestly benediction, the prohibition against adding applies even after the period of the obligation's applicability. This is contrary to the principle Rava articulates, that this prohibition applies only so long as the religious obligation itself pertains.}

[**XX**.A] Rava said, "The fulfillment [of a religious obligation] does not require intention.

[B] "Transgression [of the prohibition against adding] does require intention."

[C] But [contrary to B, in the case of] the sprinkling of the blood [of a firstling]—according to R. Joshua, [M. Zeb. 8:10, by sprinkling the blood of a firstling four times instead of once], he transgresses [the prohibition against adding] and [for this to be deemed a transgression] does not require intention. {See unit **XIX**.F+H. By sprinkling four times, the priest here certainly does not intend to transgress the prohibition against adding. Even so, Joshua deems him culpable for that prohibited act.}

[D] [Responding to C's challenge and revising his original statement], rather, said Rava, "The fulfillment [of a religious obligation] does not require intention.

[E] "Transgression [of the prohibition against adding to a religious obligation] during its period of applicability [also] does not require intention.

[F] "[But transgression of the prohibition against adding to a religious obligation] outside of its period of applicability does require intention."[101]

[XXI.A] Said R. Zera to his servant, [29a] "Focus your intention [upon fulfilling the religious obligation] and [then] blow the shofar for me [to hear]."

[B] [Based on this] I can say he reasoned [that] the one who sounds [the blast] must have the intention [to fulfill the obligation].

[C] They objected [on the basis of M. R.H. 3:7: *If] he was going along behind a synagogue, or [if] his house was near a synagogue, and he heard the sound of the shofar or the sound of [the reading of] the Scroll [of Esther]—*

[D] *if he directed his heart, he has fulfilled his obligation.*

[E] *But if not, he has not fulfilled his obligation.*

[F] {On the surface, the Mishnaic passage, C-E, seems explicit that the performance of the religious obligation does not require that the one sounding the shofar formulate the intention to fulfill that obligation; the one hearing it, rather, must do so.} And [even] if [as at D, the one who hears the shofar] does [in fact need to] direct his heart, what [does this teach us]?

---

[101]In M, E and F are reversed.

[G] [So far as the passage before us is concerned, this one, who hears the shofar, has fulfilled his obligation even though] the other one [who is blowing the shofar] has not himself formulated intention [to fulfill the commandment]! {It seems clear that, contrary to A-B, the one who sounds the shofar need not formulate the intention to fulfill his religious obligation.}

[H] {F-G's interpretation of M. R.H. 3:7's case is rejected.} Here [in the Mishnah] we deal with a [professional] representative of the community, who [always] intends [to fulfill religious obligations] on behalf of all [of the community]. {A-B's phrasing of matters stands.}

[XXII.A] Come and learn [from the following Tannaitic statement: If] the one who hears [the blast] directed [his heart], but the one who sounds [the blast] did not direct [his heart];

[B] [or if] the one who sounds [the blast] directed [his heart], but the one who hears [the blast] did not direct [his heart]—

[C] he did not fulfill his obligation [to hear the shofar].

[D] [This is the case] until the point at which [both] the one who hears and the one who sounds [the blast] direct [their heart].

[E] That which is taught on Tannaitic authority draws an analogy between[102] the one who sounds [the blast] and the one who hears [the blast]—

[F] Just as the one who hears [the blast] hears [it only] to [fulfill] his own [religious obligation], so [if] the one who sounds [the blast] sounds [it] only for himself [without formulating the intention for his blast to fulfill the obligation of others], it is

---

[102] Literally: the one who sounds [the blast] is similar to the one who hears [it]. M reverses the terms "sounds" and "hears."

	taught on Tannaitic authority [A+C] that he does not fulfill [those others people's religious obligation].[103]
[G]	There is [a dispute] among Tannaitic authorities [regarding this matter].
[H]	For [in contrast to F] it is taught on Tannaitic authority: The one who hears [the blast] hears [it only] to [fulfill] his own [religious obligation], but the one who sounds [the blast] does so according to his own practice [and need not formulate the intention to fulfill the obligation on behalf of others].
[I]	Said R. Yose, "For what case is this [rule at H] stated?
[J]	"For the case of an agent of the community. {As a matter of practice, the agent intends to fulfill religious obligations on behalf of others. Whether or not he is conscious of formulating the intention to do this, his actions are efficacious on behalf of others.}
[K]	"But [in the case of] an [ordinary] individual, he did not fulfill his obligation [to hear the shofar] unless [both] the one who hears and the one who sounds [the blast] direct [their heart]."

3:8

[A]	*"Now it happened that when Moses held up his hand, Israel prevailed, [and when he let his hand fall, Amalek prevailed;" Ex. 17:11].*
[B]	*Now do Moses' hands make war or break it off?*
[C]	{They do not.} *Rather, [the point of the verse is] to say this to you:*[104]

---

[103]M, Rashi, and other sources read: he has fulfilled [their obligation]. It is unclear whether the point in this reading is that the one who blows the shofar must formulate the intention to allow others to fulfill the obligation to hear the shofar, or whether it is sufficient simply to formulate the intention to fulfill his own obligation. The marginal gloss in P of Bezalel Ronsburg argues that the latter is the case, so that F serves to challenge Zera's approach, A.

[104]M and some manuscripts of the Mishnah lack this line.

[D] *So long as the Israelites would set their eyes upward and submit[105] their hearts to their Father in heaven, they would grow stronger. And if not, they fell.*

[E] *Similarly, you may say [the following, citing Num. 21:8]:[106] "Make yourself a fiery serpent and set it on a standard, and it shall come to pass that every one who is bitten, when he sees it, shall live."*

[F] *Now does that serpent [on the standard] kill or give life?*

[G] *{It does not.} Rather: So long as the Israelites would set their eyes upward and submit to their Father in heaven, they would be healed. And if not, they decayed [from the bites].*

[H] *[The shofar blasts of] a deaf-mute, idiot, and minor do not fulfill the obligation of the community.*

[I] *This is the governing principle: Whoever is not obligated to carry out a particular deed cannot effect the obligation of the community either.*

M. R.H. 3:8A-G apparently intends to illustrate the principle of M. R.H. 3:7, concerning the centrality of intention.[107] The point at M. R.H. 3:8H-I, which is the focus of the Talmudic materials that follow, is separate. Only an individual who is himself obligated to carry out a certain deed may act on behalf of some other person as well (see M. Ter. 1:1-2).

Unit **I** introduces a passage from the Tosefta that supplements M. R.H. 3:8H-I, listing people who are obligated to hear the shofar and detailing categories of individuals who may not carry out religious obligations on behalf of others. The conclusion of unit **I** begins to explain this Toseftan material, indicating why it was necessary to indicate explicitly that priests are obligated to hear the

---

[105]Here and at H, M and some manuscripts of the Mishnah read: direct.

[106]M has the beginning of the verse, "The Lord said to Moses," but lacks the conclusion of the verse, following the word "serpent."

[107]So Albeck, p. 320.

shofar. Unit **II** continues the explanation of the passage, questioning the rule for one who is half slave and half freeman. Phrasing the issue of the preceding in general terms, units **III-V** describe various circumstances in which one may or may not repeat a religious act so as to fulfill the obligation on behalf of others.

[I.A] Our rabbis have taught on Tannaitic authority [T. R.H. 2:5]: **All are obligated regarding sounding the shofar: priests, Levites, Israelites, converts, freed slaves, [disqualified priests, *netins*,[108] *mamzers*],[109] one of uncertain sex, hermaphrodites,** and one who is half slave and half free.

[B] **One of uncertain sex does not [perform a religious act so as to] exempt [from that act] either one of his own kind or one who is not of his own kind.**

[C] **A hermaphrodite may [perform a religious act so as to] exempt [from that act] one who is of his own kind but not one who is not of his own kind.**

[D] **One who is half slave and half free does not [perform a religious act so as to] exempt [from that act] either one of his own kind or one who is not of his own kind.**

[E] A master said, "[T. R.H. 2:5 states]: **All are obligated regarding sounding the shofar: priests, Levites, Israelites.**

[F] "This is obvious [and goes without saying]!

[G] "[For], if these[110] [three categories of people] are not obligated, who is?"

---

[108]Reference is to the descendants of the Gibeonites, deemed dedicated to the Temple and excluded from marriage into the Israelite community. See Josh. 9.

[109]The offspring of a union forbidden by Scripture.

[110]M adds: priests, Levites, and Israelites.

[H]   {The list's inclusion of priests is explained.} [As for] priests—they needed [to be explicitly mentioned].

[I]   You might have thought, since it is written [Num. 29:1: "On the first day of the seventh month you shall have a holy convocation; you shall do no laborious work]. It is a day for you to sound the blast [of the shofar]"—

[J]   [this means] one who has only one day that is a day of blowing is obligated [regarding the sounding of the shofar].

[K]   But [as for] these priests, since they have [occasion] for blowing the shofar all through the year,

[L]   as it is written [Num. 10:10]: "You shall blow the trumpets[111] over your burnt offerings [and over the sacrifices of your peace offerings],"

[M]   you might have said, they should not be obligated [regarding the sounding of the shofar on New Year].

[N]   Therefore we are informed [by T. R.H. 2:5, cited at A, that even priests are so obligated].

[O]   {I-N is challenged, based on a question of the pertinence of Num. 10:10 to a discussion of the obligation to sound the shofar.} Are [the requirements indicated by Num. 29:1 and Num. 10:10] analogous?

[P]   There [at Num. 10:10 we speak of] trumpets; but here [at Num. 29:1 we speak of] the shofar! {One should not imagine that the priest's obligation indicated by Num. 10:10 has an impact upon his being subject to the requirement indicated at Num. 29:1. The question raised at F-G regarding priests stands.}

[Q]   {A second explanation for the inclusion of priests is given.} Rather, [as for] priests—they needed [to be mentioned explicitly for the following reason]:

[R]   [Had they not been mentioned] you might have thought, since we have taught on Tannaitic authority [M. R.H. 3:5]: *The*

---

[111]M lacks the remainder of the verse.

[proclamation of the] year of Jubilee is equivalent to the New Year in regard to the sounding of the shofar and to the blessings—

[S] [therefore] one who is subject to the obligations of the year of Jubilee also is subject to the obligations of the New Year.

[T] But these priests, since they are not subject to the obligations of the year of Jubilee—

[U] as we have taught on Tannaitic authority [M. Ar. 9:8]: *Priests and Levites sell at any time and redeem at any time* [without regard for the Jubilee's restrictions listed at M. Ar. 9:1, M. Ar. 9:5, and M. Ar. 9:7]—

[V] I might have said [that to] the obligations of the New Year, they should not be obligated.

[W] Therefore we are informed[112] [by T. R.H 2:5, that they are obligated].

[II.A] [T. R.H. 2:5:] **One who is half slave and half free does not [perform a religious act so as to] exempt [from that act] either one of his own kind or one who is not of his own kind.**

[B] Said Rab Huna, "But he may [perform a religious act so as to] exempt himself."

[C] Said Rab Nahman to Rab Huna, "What is distinctive about the case of others, such that [he may] not [perform a religious act so as to exempt them]?

[D] "For [his] enslaved side cannot act [on behalf of others'] freed side."

[E] [Huna responds, rejecting this explanation: "If matters are as D claims, then], regarding himself as well, his enslaved side cannot act [on behalf of] his own freed side."

---

[112]M and other manuscripts add: they are exempt from the release of property and the release of debts. But to the freeing of slaves, they are however obligated.

[F] {Nahman responds by agreeing to E's premise and stating that the law in fact is as E states.} Rather, said Rab Nahman, "[Indeed] he may not even [perform a religious act so as to] exempt himself [from that obligation]."

[G] That which is taught on Tannaitic authority makes the same point: One who is half slave and half free may not [perform a religious act so as to] exempt himself [from that obligation].

[III.A] Ahabah the son of R. Zera taught on Tannaitic authority: "[As for] all blessings[113]—even though one [already has recited them, so as to have] fulfilled [his own obligation], he [still] may [recite them again, so as to] exempt [others from the obligation].

[B] "[This applies] except for the blessings over bread and wine, in the case of which, if he has not [yet] fulfilled [his obligation], he may fulfill the obligation [on behalf of others], but if he [already] fulfilled [his own obligation], he may not fulfill the obligation [on behalf of others]."

[C] Asked Rava, [29b] "[As for] the blessing over bread [said] upon [eating] unleavened bread and the blessing over wine [said] on [the occasion of] the sanctification [of the Sabbath]—what is the law [whether or not these blessings may be recited by one who already has fulfilled his own obligation in order to fulfill the obligation on behalf of others]?

[D] "Since [the occasions on which these blessings are said] are obligatory, [do we hold that, in contrast to the case described at B] he may fulfill the obligation [on behalf of others]?

[E] "Or, perhaps, [we hold that] the blessing is not obligatory,[114] [and that, as at B, one who already fulfilled his own obligation may not fulfill the obligation on behalf of others]?"

---

[113] M reads: commandments.

[114] In place of the preceding clause, M reads: there is no difference.

[F]   Come and learn [an answer to Rava's question]: For Rab Ashi said, "When we were in the house of Rab Pappi,[115] he would say the sanctification on our behalf.

[G]   "And [later] when the laborers came from the field, he would say the sanctification [again], on their behalf." {In contrast to what is described at B, in the case of the sanctification or other obligatory blessings, even though one already fulfilled his own obligation, he still may fulfill the obligation on behalf of others.}

[IV.A] {The Talmud develops the general theme of the preceding.} Our rabbis have taught on Tannaitic authority: A person should not break bread [and say the blessing] for visitors unless he is going to eat with them.

[B]   But he may break bread [and say the blessing] for his children and the members of his household [even if he is not going to eat with them],

[C]   in order to teach them about [the performance of religious] obligations.

[V.A] And regarding the [recitation of the] Hallel and [the reading of] the Scroll [of Esther]—even though he [already has performed these duties and] fulfilled [his religious] obligation, he may [perform the duty again so as to] fulfill the obligation [on behalf of others].

---

[115]M reads: Pappa.

CHAPTER FOUR

ROSH HASHANAH CHAPTER FOUR

4:1

[A] [**29b**] *[As for] the festival day of the New Year which coincided with the Sabbath—*

[B] *in the Temple they would sound the shofar.*

[C] *But not in the provinces.*

[D] *When the Temple was destroyed, Rabban Yohanan b. Zakkai ordained that they should sound the shofar in every locale in which there was a court.*

[E] *Said R. Eleazar,[1] "Rabban Yohanan b. Zakkai ordained only for the case of Yavneh alone."*

[F] *They said to him, "All the same are Yavneh and every locale in which there is a court."*

4:2

[A] *And in this regard also was Jerusalem ahead of Yavneh:*

[B] *in every town that is within sight and sound [of Jerusalem], and nearby, and [the residents of which are] able to come up [to Jerusalem], they sound the shofar.*

[C] *But as to Yavneh, they sound the shofar only in the court alone.*

The Talmud begins by establishing the source of the rule implicit at M. R.H. 4:1-2, that the shofar normally is not sounded on the Sabbath at all. An initial attempt to derive this rule from Scripture is challenged, leading to the determination that this restriction, as well as those precluding the performance on the Sabbath of certain other rituals that had been carried out in the Temple, derives from the rabbis themselves. Unit **II** explains how Yohanan b. Zakkai, M. R.H. 4:1D, prevailed against authorities who, after the destruction of the

---

[1] So all manuscripts and early printings of B. and M. P reads: Eliezer

Temple, desired to prohibit entirely the sounding of the shofar on the Sabbath. Unit **III** argues that the authorities behind M. R.H. 4:1F disagree both with the view of Eleazar, M. R.H. 4:1E, and with that of Yohanan b. Zakkai, M. 4:1D, which, in the Mishnah's phrasing of matters, they claim only to explain. Unit **IV** continues the interpretation of M. R.H. 4:1F, explaining the rule that the shofar may be sounded on the Sabbath only in a locale "in which there is a court."

Units **V-VIII** take up M. R.H. 4:2. Alongside materials directly pertinent to understanding this Mishnaic passage occurs a long discussion, at unit **VI**, of the nature and extent of the obligation to sound the shofar. The Talmud asks who must do so and indicates when are they obligated to do so. Alongside its line-by-line exegesis of M. R.H. 4:1-2, the Talmud thus also addresses the broader legal concerns left open by the Mishnah's authorities.

[I.A] What is the source [in Scripture] of this rule [M. R.H. 4:1A+C, that the shofar is not sounded on the Sabbath]?

[B] Said R. Levi bar Lahma said R. Hama bar Hanina, "One verse [Lev. 23:24] says: '[In the seventh month, on the first day of the month, you shall observe] a day of solemn rest, a memorial of the blast [of trumpets].'

[C] "And a different verse says [Num. 29:1: 'On the first day of the seventh month you shall have a holy convocation; you shall do no laborious work]. It is a day for you to blow [the trumpets].' {Lev. 23:24, cited at B, states that New Year is a "memorial" of the blast of the shofar, suggesting that, on that day, the shofar is not actually sounded. Num. 29:1, by contrast, seems clear that, on New Year, the shofar actually is sounded.}

[D] "There is no contradiction [between the two verses]:[2]

---

[2]M lacks this line.

[E]   "Here [at Lev. 23:24 we speak] of [an occasion on which] the festival day coincides with the Sabbath. {In this case, New Year marks a memorial of the blast of the shofar. But on that day the shofar is not actually sounded.}

[F]   "Here [at Num. 29:1, by contrast, we speak] of [an occasion on which] the festival day is a [regular] week day." {In this instance, the shofar is sounded on New Year.}

[G]   {D-F's solution to A's problem seems unacceptable.} Said Rava,[3] "If [the law precluding the sounding of the shofar on Sabbath derives] from Scripture, how is it that, in the sanctuary, they sound the shofar [even on the Sabbath, M. R.H. 4:1B]?

[H]   "And furthermore, is [sounding the shofar[4] a kind of] work that requires a verse of Scripture to be excluded [from the general prohibition against working on the Sabbath]?!

[I]   "For it is taught on Tannaitic authority in the house of Samuel: [When Num. 29:1 states: 'On the first day of the seventh month you shall have a holy convocation]. You shall do no laborious work. [It is a day for you to blow the trumpets]'—this excludes [from the prohibition against labor] the sounding of the shofar and the removal of bread [from an oven], which are skills and not labor." {Rava's point is that, contrary to B-F's explanation, there are conclusive arguments proving that the shofar *may* be sounded when New Year coincides with the Sabbath. 1) A prohibition against doing so cannot derive from Scripture since, while such a prohibition would apply in the Temple as well as in the provinces, we know that, in the Temple, the shofar was sounded on the Sabbath (M. R.H. 4:1B). 2) Num. 29:1 explicitly excludes the sounding of the shofar from the category of labors prohibited on the Sabbath.

---

[3] M lacks the attribution.

[4] So M and, it appears, Rashi. P adds: not.

In light of Rava's rejection of the argument at B-F, a different explanation for M. R.H. 4:1A-C's rule is required.}

[J] Rather [to explain M. R.H. 4:1A-C] said Rava, "According to Scripture [sounding the shofar when New Year coincides with the Sabbath] is certainly permitted.

[K] "But it is the rabbis who enacted a prohibition against this,

[L] "as is [explained] by Rabbah, for said Rabbah, 'All are obligated to sound the shofar, but not all are skilled in the sounding of the shofar.

[M][5] "'[The rabbis enacted] a prohibition [against sounding the shofar on the Sabbath] lest [someone who is not an expert] take [a shofar] in his hand and go to an expert to learn and [in doing so wind up] carrying it four cubits in public domain [in violation of the Sabbath law].' {The reason for this prohibition would not pertain within the Temple. As M. R.H. 4:1A-C states, when New Year coincides with the Sabbath, the shofar was sounded within the Temple, but not in other areas.}

[N] "And this same reasoning applies to the lulab [used on Tabernacles] and to the Scroll [of Esther]." {These items comparably were used inside, but not outside of the Temple on the Sabbath.}

[II.A] *When the Temple was destroyed, Rabban Yohanan b. Zakkai ordained [that they should sound the shofar in every locale in which there was a court;* M. R.H. 4:1D].

[B] Our rabbis have taught on Tannaitic authority: Once, New Year coincided with the Sabbath, and [the people of] all the

---

[5]M adds: Why did they say that one may not sound [the shofar]? Other manuscripts add: What is the reason?

	cities⁶ came together [in Yavneh, to hear a representative of the court sound the shofar, as described at M. R.H. 4:1D].
[C]	Said Rabban Yohanan b. Zakkai to the sons of Beterah,⁷ "Let us sound [the shofar]!"
[D]	They said to him, "Let us discuss [the issue, to determine whether the prohibition against sounding the shofar on the Sabbath should extend even to cities in which there is a court]."
[E]	[Yohanan] said to them, "Let us sound [the shofar first] and discuss afterwards!"
[F]	After they had sounded [the shofar] they said to him, "[Now] let us discuss [the matter]!"
[G]	[Yohanan] said to them, "The horn already has been heard in Yavneh, and, after the fact, one does not reconsider."

[III.A] *Said R. Eleazar, "Rabban Yohanan b. Zakkai ordained only for the case of Yavneh alone."*⁸ *They said to him, "All the same are Yavneh and every locale in which there is a court"* [M. R.H. 4:1E-F].

[B] [The authorities introduced by the statement] *"They said to him"* hold the same [view] as the first cited Tannaitic authority [Yohanan b. Zakkai, M. R.H. 4:1D, who says that wherever there is a court, the shofar is sounded on the Sabbath].

[C] {B is rejected.} They disagree concerning [the sounding of the shofar where there is] a temporary court. {Yohanan b. Zakkai, M. R.H. 4:1D, permits the sounding of the shofar wherever there is a court, even a temporary one. The

---

⁶M lacks: the cities. Other manuscripts and early printings, except Cracow, lack the entire clause: and all [the people of] the cities came together. Those words appear to have entered the Talmud from the text of Rashi.

⁷See B. Pes. 66a and B. B.M. 85a. Reference is to a family of community leaders and legal authorities.

⁸M lacks the remainder of this line.

anonymous authority at M. R.H. 4:1F permits the sounding of the shofar on the Sabbath only where there is a permanent court, such as in Yavneh.}

[IV.A] *They said to him, "All the same are Yavneh and every locale in which there is a court"* [M. R.H. 4:1F].

[B] Said R. Huna [**30a**], "Now, [the point of M. R.H. 4:1F is that the shofar is sounded on the Sabbath only] with a court."

[C] What [is the meaning of] "with a court"?

[D] [It means it must be sounded] in the presence of the court,

[E] which excludes [any sounding of the shofar on the Sabbath] that is not in the presence of a court.[9]

[V.A] Objected Rava[10] [to the statement at M. R.H. 4:2A-C]: *And in this regard also was Jerusalem ahead of Yavneh: [in every town that is within sight and sound (of Jerusalem), and nearby so that (the residents are) able to come up to Jerusalem, they sound the shofar. But as to Yavneh, they sound the shofar only in the court alone].*

[B] "What [is the significance of the words]: *And in this regard also*?

[C] "Shall I say [the text means exactly] what it says [without the need to interpolate any additional considerations]?

[D] "[If that is the case] it should [lack the word *also* and] say simply: *[In] this [regard was Jerusalem ahead of Yavneh]*.

[E] "Rather [if you argue that the point is that Jerusalem *also* is ahead] in that in Jerusalem individuals may sound [the shofar on the Sabbath] whereas in Yavneh, individuals may not sound [it]—

---

[9]In place of "in the presence of a court," M reads: at a time the court is in session.

[10]An apparent error, M reads: Rabbah

[F] "[Is it in fact the case that] in Yavneh, individuals may not sound [the shofar on the Sabbath]?[11]

[G] "But,[12] [indicating the contrary], when Rab Isaac bar Joseph came [to Babylonia from the land of Israel] he said, 'When at Yavneh [on a New Year that coincided with the Sabbath] the representative of the community concluded his sounding [of the shofar], one could not hear his own voice because of the noise of the sounding [of shofars] by individuals.'" {In this regard, Yavneh and Jerusalem are comparable. We still need to account for the word "also" at M. R.H. 4:2A.}

[H] [Rava continues], "Rather [the additional difference must be that] in Jerusalem they sound [the shofar on the Sabbath] both when the court was in session and when the court was not in session, while in Yavneh: while the court was in session, indeed [they sounded the shofar], but while the court was not in session, [they did] not [sound it]!"

[I] {While based on H, the issue in the following is separate.} [Is H's point that, in Yavneh], when the court is in session, they sound [the shofar] even out of the presence of the court? {This would contradict the statement of Huna, unit **IV**, that the shofar may be sounded on the Sabbath only in the actual presence of the court.}

[J] No! [Additionally indicating the superiority of Jerusalem, it means] that in Jerusalem, they sound [the shofar on the Sabbath] both in the presence of and not in the presence of the court,

[K] while in Yavneh, in the presence of the court, indeed [they sound it]; outside of the presence of the court [they do] not [sound it].[13]

---

[11] All manuscripts lack this line.

[12] M begins with a question: Is this so? See the preceding note.

[13] M presents a slightly different wording of H-K. The meaning is the same.

[VI.A] There are those who, on Tannaitic authority, relate[14] this [statement] of Rab Huna [unit IV.B, that the shofar is sounded on the Sabbath only in the presence of a court] to that which is written[15] [Lev. 25:9]: "On the Day of Atonement you shall make proclamation with the shofar throughout all your land."

[B] [This] teaches that each and every individual is obligated to sound [the shofar]. {On the following, see unit IV.}

[C] Said Rab Huna, "Now, [the shofar is sounded on the Sabbath only] with a court."

[D] What [is the meaning of] "with a court"?

[E] [It means it must be sounded] when the court is in session,

[F] which excludes [any sounding of the shofar on the Sabbath] when the court is not in session.[16]

[G] Objected Rava, "The sounding [of the shofar] on New Year and the Jubilee supersedes the Sabbath in the provinces [for] a man and his household."

[H] What [is the meaning of] "a man and his household"?

[I] Shall I say [it means] "a man and his wife"?

[J] [This is unacceptable, since] is a woman obligated [to the sounding of the shofar]?

[K] For this is a positive commandment the time [for the fulfillment] of which is fixed.

[L] And women are exempt from all positive commandments the time [for the fulfillment] of which is fixed.

[M] Rather [must it] not [mean] "a man in his household"?

[N] Now, [contrary to Huna's claim, C+D-F, this would imply that the obligation applies] even during a time at which the court is not in session.

---

[14] Literally: teach.

[15] All manuscripts lack: that which is written.

[16] This line is added in the margin of M.

[O]　No! In all instances it applies [only] at a time when the court is in session.

[P]　{Sheshet responds to O's claim that the obligation to sound the shofar on the Sabbath applies for both the Jubilee and New Year only when the court is in session.} Objected Rab Sheshet, "[M. R.H. 3:5A states]: *The [proclamation of the] year of Jubilee is equivalent to the New Year in regard to the sounding [of the shofar] and to the blessings—*

[Q]　"except that [in announcing] the Jubilee [on the Sabbath], they sound [the shofar] before a court that sanctified the month and a court that did not sanctify the month, and each and every individual is obligated to sound [the shofar].

[R]　"But for the New Year [that coincided with the Sabbath], they did not sound [the shofar] except before a court that sanctified the month, and each and every individual was not obligated to sound [the shofar]."

[S]　What [is the meaning of], "each and every individual was not obligated to sound [the shofar]"?

[T]　Shall I say that, on the Jubilee [that coincides with the Sabbath] individuals sound [the shofar], whereas on New Year [that coincides with the Sabbath] individuals do not sound [the shofar]?

[U]　But [indicating the contrary] when Rab Isaac bar Joseph came [to Babylonia from the land of Israel] he said, "When at Yavneh [on a New Year that coincided with the Sabbath] the representative of the community concluded his sounding [of the shofar], one could not hear his own voice because of the noise of the sounding [of shofars] by individuals."[17]

---

[17]M adds: Shall I [therefore] say that each and every individual is obligated to sound [the shofar]? This appears to be a marginal gloss that was copied into the body of the text (Rabbinovicz).

[V]   {S's statement does not mean what T claims.} Rather, [does it] not[18] [mean: In announcing] the Jubilee, they sound [the shofar on the Sabbath] both when the court is in session and when the court is not in session,

[W] while in [the case of] New Year, when the court is in session, indeed [they sound the shofar]; when the court is not in session, no [they do not sound the shofar]?

[X] {The way in which Sheshet's statement contradicts Huna's view, as expressed at O, is made explicit.} It is taught here [at V] that in fact, on the Jubilee, whether or not it is at the time the court is in session, [they sound the shofar]. {This contradicts O, which states that only when the court is in session may the shofar be sounded on the Sabbath.}

[Y] {X's reading of the preceding is rejected.} No. In all events [the shofar may be sounded] only when the court is in session.

[Z] And here is what [Sheshet's opinion at P-R] means: On the Jubilee, [if it is the Sabbath], at a time at which the court is in session, they sound [the shofar] both within and outside of the presence of the court.

[AA] [By contrast] on a New Year [that coincides with the Sabbath], they sound [the shofar only] while the court is in session and in the presence of the court.[19]

[BB] It also has been stated on Amoraic authority: Said Rab Hiyya bar Gamda, said R. Yose b. Saul, said Rabbi [Judah the Patriarch], "They do not sound [the shofar] except during the time when the court sits in session."

[VII.A] {We turn to a secondary issue regarding the sounding of the shofar on the Sabbath in the presence of a court.} Inquired R. Zera, "[If the members of the court] had gotten ready to rise,

---

[18]M lacks this word, probably with no difference in meaning.

[19]All manuscripts and, it seems, Rashi lack Z-AA.

but had not yet risen, what is the rule [whether or not the shofar may be sounded]?

[B] "[If] we require the court to be sitting in session, since here [that condition] is fulfilled [the shofar may still be sounded].

[C] "Or perhaps we require it to be the time that the court is in session, [which condition here] is not fulfilled [insofar as the court's members are ready to leave]." {If this is the case, the shofar may not any longer be sounded.}

[D][20] [The question] stands!

[VIII.A] *And in this regard also was Jerusalem ahead of Yavneh: [In every town that is within sight and sound of Jerusalem, and nearby and the residents of which are able to come up to Jerusalem, they sound the shofar; M. R.H. 4:2A].*

[B] [The reference to] *sight* excludes [from sounding the shofar on the Sabbath] one located in a valley.

[C] [The reference to] *sound* excludes one located on the top of a mountain.

[D] [The reference to being] *nearby* excludes one who dwells beyond the Sabbath limit [that is, 2,000 cubits from the wall of Jerusalem].

[E] [The reference to] *being able to come* [to Jerusalem] excludes one separated from it [that is, the city] by a river.

4:3

[A] *In olden times*[21] *the lulab was taken up in the Temple for seven [days] and, in the provinces, for one day.*

[B] *When the Temple was destroyed, Rabban Yohanan b. Zakkai made the rule that in the provinces the lulab should be taken up for seven [days, as a] memorial to the Temple;*

---

[20]M adds: What [is the decision]?

[21]Literally: At first.

[C] *and that the day [on which the omer] is waved [that is, the sixteenth of Nisan] should be wholly prohibited [in regard to the eating of new produce; M. Suk. 3:12].*

The Talmud focuses upon Yohanan b. Zakkai's two ordinances, which, in the aftermath of the destruction of the Temple, altered previously standard practice. Unit **I** proves from Scripture that changing the law "as a memorial to the Temple" (M. R.H. 4:3B) is appropriate. Units **II-III** provide distinct interpretations of M. R.H. 4:3C. Unit **II** suggests a practical explanation for Yohanan's edict. Prohibiting consumption of new grain on the sixteenth of Nisan was necessary to assure that, when the Temple is rebuilt, people do not unknowingly err and eat this produce before the *omer* is waved. Unit **III**, by contrast, suggests that in this rule Yohanan b. Zakkai simply makes explicit a scriptural prohibition. This being the case, the rule appears not to respond to the particular needs of the people in the period following the destruction of the Temple at all.

[I.A] Now, from what [verse in Scripture] do we [know that we should] create a memorial to the Temple?

[B][22] For Scripture says [Jer. 30:17]: "For I shall restore health to you, and your wounds I shall heal, says the Lord, because they have called you an outcast: 'It is Zion, [about whom] no one cares!'"

[C] [This suggests] the principle that [Zion] should be cared about.

[II.A] *And that the day [the sixteenth of Nisan on which the omer] is waved should be wholly prohibited [in regard to the eating of new produce;* M. R.H. 4:3C].

[B] What is the reason [for this]?

---

[22]All manuscripts and Cracow introduce the following with an attribution: Said R. Yohanan.

[C] The Temple may soon be rebuilt, and [the people] will say, "Last year did we not eat [the new grain on the sixteenth of Nisan] beginning with day break? Now too let us eat [it immediately after day break on the sixteenth]."

[D] And [they will suggest this, since] they will not realize that, last year, [when, in the absence of the Temple],[23] there was no [waving of the] *omer*, day break [on the sixteenth indeed] rendered [the new grain] permitted [for consumption].

[E] But now [that the Temple is rebuilt, such] that there is [a waving of the *omer*, the waving of the] *omer* [is needed to] render [the new grain] permitted [for consumption]. {This is based upon Lev. 23:14: "And you shall eat neither bread nor grain parched or fresh until this same day, until you have brought the offering of your God." In order to assure that, in the event of the Temple's being rebuilt, people do not make a wrong assumption regarding when new grain may be consumed, Yohanan b. Zakkai, M. R.H. 4:3, ordained that the new grain may not be eaten at all on the sixteenth of Nisan.}

[F] {B-E's explanation of Yohanan's action is challenged. In order to prevent people from eating new grain before it is permitted to do so, one should not need to prohibit its consumption on the whole of the sixteenth of Nisan.} [In the preceding interpretation] when [is it assumed] that [the Temple] will be rebuilt?

[G] If I say it is rebuilt [that is, completed] on the sixteenth [itself], lo, [despite the Temple's being rebuilt], day break [on the sixteenth still] renders [the new grain] permitted [for consumption]. {At day break, the Temple had not yet been completed and waving of the *omer* could not take place. Day break renders the new grain permitted just as in the previous

---

[23] In M, the beginning of the line is garbled.

388 BAVLI ROSH HASHANAH CHAPTER FOUR [30a]

year, before the Temple was rebuilt. In this circumstance, Yohanan's ordinance is needless.}

[H] Rather [even if I say] that it is rebuilt [that is, completed] on the fifteenth [so that the waving of the *omer* can take place on the sixteenth, even then] it is permitted [to eat the new grain] from midday [on the sixteenth, by which time it is assumed that the *omer* has been waved in the Temple].

[I] [We know that, while the Temple stood, the new grain was eaten beginning at midday on the sixteenth] for thus we have taught on Tannaitic authority[24] [M. Men. 10:5: *After the omer was offered, new produce was permitted forthwith. And for] people who are distant [from Jerusalem and do not know exactly when the omer was waved] it is permitted from midday and thereafter...because the court did not put off [fulfillment of the requirement that the omer be waved]*. {Since in all events, people are permitted to eat the new grain after midday on the sixteenth, it appears to have been needless for Yohanan b. Zakkai to have prohibited the eating of new grain on the whole of that day. The potential circumstance that necessitated his prohibition is identified in the following.}

[J] No, [contrary to what G-I argues, Yohanan's ordinance] was necessary.

[K] [It precludes people from acting incorrectly in a case] in which [the Temple] is rebuilt on the fifteenth[25] close to sunset.

[L] Comparably [it is needed to prevent incorrect practice in a case] in which [the Temple] is rebuilt at night [prior to the morning of the sixteenth]. {In the cases described at K and L, the Temple will be completed by the morning of the sixteenth, so that the *omer* must be waved. But its late completion will

---

[24]In place of "we have taught on Tannaitic authority," all manuscripts, Cracow, Rashi, and Ramban read: A master said.

[25]All manuscripts and Cracow lack: on the fifteenth. The phrase appears to have entered the Talmud from the text of Rashi.

delay the actual waving until late on the sixteenth. To prevent people who live a distance from the Temple from developing a practice that potentially would lead them to eat new grain prior to this late waving of the *omer*, Yohanan ordained that in no circumstance may it be eaten on the day of the sixteenth.}

[III.A] {Nahman bar Isaac presents a different explanation of Yohanan b. Zakkai's ordinance.} Said Rab Nahman bar Isaac, "[At M. R.H. 4:3C] Rabban Yohanan b. Zakkai [30b] followed the legal perspective [later expressed] by R. Judah.

[B] "For [Judah] said,[26] '[Lev. 23:14 states: "And you shall eat neither bread nor grain parched or fresh] until this same day"—[this means that one may not eat it] until [the end of] the substance of that day.'

[C] "And [Judah] reasoned [on the grounds that Lev. 23:14 uses the word] 'until'—and [he held that the term] 'until' encompasses [the period to which it refers, such that 'until this same day' in all circumstances means 'until the end of this day']."

[D] {A-C is challenged.} But does [Judah in fact] concur with it [that is, with Yohanan b. Zakkai's rule regarding when new grain may be consumed on the sixteenth of Nisan]?

[E] For, indeed, [Judah] disagrees concerning this,

[F] as we have taught on Tannaitic authority [M. Men. 10:5]: *After the Temple was destroyed, Rabban Yohanan b. Zakkai ordained that the day of waving [of the omer] should be wholly prohibited [in respect to new produce].*

[G] *Said R. Judah, "And is it not so that it is prohibited by the Torah,[27] as it is written [Lev. 23:14], 'Until this same day'?"*

---

[26]M and other sources add: This day itself is forbidden by the Torah, as it is written.

[27]M lacks the end of this line.

[H] {The Talmud explains that regarding actual practice, Judah did not disagree with Yohanan b. Zakkai.} There, R. Judah erred.

[I] This one [that is, Judah] thought that Rabban Yohanan b. Zakkai declared [consumption of new grain on the sixteenth of Nisan prior to sunset] to be [forbidden only as] a rabbinic ordinance. {Judah disagreed with this, as indicated at G, holding that the rule derives from Scripture.}

[J] But this [claim, that Yohanan intended only a rabbinic ordinance] is not correct.

[K] [Yohanan b. Zakkai][28] phrased it as a [prohibition] based on Scripture!

[L] {K seems unacceptable.} But [suggesting the contrary, in the Mishnah] it is taught on Tannaitic authority [that Yohanan] "ordained" [the prohibition against eating new grain on the sixteenth]. {The term "ordained" generally indicates a rabbinic rule.}

[M] {L's misunderstanding is corrected.} [In this case] what [is the meaning of] "ordained"?

[N] He interpreted [Scripture] and [on that basis] ordained [an appropriate rule, which was in the status of a scriptural injunction].

4:4a

[A] *In olden times[29] they would receive testimony about the new moon all day long.*

[B] *One time the witnesses came late, and the Levites [consequently] were mixed up as to [what] psalm [they should sing].*

[C] *They made the rule that they should receive testimony [about the new moon] only up to the afternoon offering.*

---

[28] All manuscripts have the bracketed name explicitly.

[29] Literally: At first.

BAVLI ROSH HASHANAH CHAPTER FOUR [30b]   391

[D]   *And if witnesses came after the afternoon offering, they would treat that day as holy and the next day as holy [too].*

[E]   *When the Temple was destroyed, Rabban Yohanan b. Zakkai made the rule that they should [once more] receive testimony about the new moon all day long.*

Unit I asks of the nature of the "mix up" referred to at M. R.H. 4:4B. With this issue out of the way, the Gemara turns to only loosely related questions. Developing unit I's reference to the psalm for Thursday, unit II discusses which psalm is recited on each day of the week and indicates why. Units III-V develop this theme, detailing the psalms recited at the times of the Sabbath sacrifices.

Unit VI has no apparent thematic association with the prior materials or with M. R.H. 4:4. It argues that the divine presence left the soon to be destroyed Temple in ten stages and suggests that, in ten corresponding stages, the Sanhedrin was removed from Jerusalem into a place of exile.

[I.A] In what way were the Levites mixed up as to [what] psalm [they should sing, M. R.H. 4:4B]?

[B]   Here [in Babylonia] they interpreted it [to mean] that they did not recited any psalm at all.

[C]   R. Zera [by contrast] said that [the mix up was in the fact that] they recited the psalm [appropriate] for a weekday in conjunction with the afternoon tamid-offering. {The error was that, since it turned out to be a festival, they should have song the festival psalm.}

[D]   [To prove his point] R. Zera said to Ahabah his son,[30] "Go, teach [the Babylonians][31] on Tannaitic authority: They ordained that [the court] should not accept testimony[32]

---

[30]M introduces this line: Is this really so? But thus said R. Zera....

[31]M reads: them.

[32]All manuscripts read: witnesses.

regarding the appearance of the new moon unless there was enough time left in the day to [allow the necessary] sacrifice of tamid-offerings, additional-offerings, and their drink-offerings[33] and to recite the [correct] psalm without confusion."[34]

[E] "If you say, 'Granted, [the problem was that they] said the weekday psalm [when the festival psalm was required]'—it would [certainly] be a case of confusion, [represented in the fact that the Levites did the wrong thing].

[F] "But, if you say, '[Not knowing what was required] they said no psalm at all'—in what regard is there confusion?" {Zera argues that the Levites' choosing to say no psalm at all is a logical response to their not knowing whether a weekday or festival psalm is required. This should not be termed "confusion" at all.}

[G] {Zera's approach is deemed unacceptable.} [Contrary to Zera's claim, F] if they said no [psalm] at all—you have no greater case of confusion[35] than that!

[H] Objected Rab Aha bar[36] Huna [to G's view that doing nothing can be termed "confusion"]: "The tamid-offering for the morning of New Year was offered in the usual manner.

[I] "For the additional offering, what [psalm] does one recite?

[J] "[Ps. 81, which begins]: 'Sing aloud to God our strength. Shout for joy to the God of Jacob!'

---

[33] A scribal error, M lacks: and their drink offerings.

[34] A scribal error, M lacks: without confusion.

[35] As Simon correctly points out, p. 144, notes 6 and 7, at issue here is the meaning of the Hebrew term *šbwš*, translated as "confusion." Zera takes it to refer to a reversal of what should be done for some other action. The anonymous authorities, represented here at G, by contrast, take the term simply to mean "error." Not reciting any psalm is certainly an error. At issue is whether or not it also suggests "confusion."

[36] M adds the honorific: Rab.

[K]	"For the afternoon offering, what [psalm] does one recite?
[L]	"[Ps. 29, which, in vs. 8, states]: 'The voice of the Lord shakes the wilderness, [the Lord shakes the wilderness of Kadesh].'[37]
[M]	"Now, on an occasion on which New Year[38] falls on Thursday, for which the morning psalm is [Ps. 81, beginning], 'Sing aloud to God our strength,'[39] one would not say [that psalm]—'Sing aloud [to God our strength]'—in the morning,
[N]	"since [later in the day, at the time of the additional offering, I-J] he repeats this passage.
[O]	"Rather [on a Thursday morning that is New Year], what [psalm] does one recite?
[P]	"[The passage beginning with Ps. 81:6]: 'I relieved your shoulder of the burden. [Your hands were freed from the basket].'
[Q]	"But if [the day were being treated as a regular weekday and] witnesses [testifying to the appearance of the new moon] came after the morning tamid-offering [such that, as the daily psalm was about to be recited, it was not yet known whether or not the day would wind up being treated as New Year], one [still] recites [Ps. 81, beginning] 'Sing aloud....'[40]
[R]	"[This psalm is used] even though [should it turn out to be New Year, then, for the additional offering] he repeats the passage, [as I-J indicates].
[S]	{Based on the facts cited at I-R, Aha bar Huna now appears to prove the point he stated at H, that doing nothing at all cannot

---

[37]M has the bracketed conclusion of the verse explicitly.

[38]M lacks: New Year

[39]M concludes this line slightly differently from P: they would not say [that psalm] at all.

[40]M has the continuation of the verse.

be called "confusion." But the point of the proof as well as of the retort, at U, is unclear.} "If you say [that], granted, wherever there is a doubt, we recite the psalm for a regular weekday, it is for this reason that [the law at Q-R] says that [in a case in which it is not clear whether or not the day will wind up being New Year] one says it and then [when it in fact turns out to be New Year] repeats it.

[T] "But, if you say that [in a case of uncertainty] one does not recite anything, what [at Q-R is the meaning of the notion that] one recites it and then repeats it?"

[U] [31a] The situation there [at Q-R] is different, since it is the psalm of the day, [which is recited regardless of the doubt]. {But, in other cases of doubt, no psalm would be recited at all, as B originally argued.}

[II.A] It is taught on Tannaitic authority [see M. Tam. 7:4]: R. Judah says in the name of R. Aqiba:

[B] "On the first day what would they recite?[41] [Ps. 24, which begins]: 'The earth is the Lord's and the fullness thereof, [the world and they who live therein.'[42] This psalm was used] because [on Sunday, God] took possession and gave possession and was ruler over his world [without the heavenly hosts, who were created on the second day].

[C] "On the second [day] what would they recite? [Ps. 48, beginning]: 'Great is the Lord and highly to be praised [in the city of our God, even upon his holy hill.' This psalm was used] because [on Monday, God] divided that which he created [into the upper and lower worlds] and[43] was sovereign over them.

---

[41] Throughout the following, in place of "what did they recite?" M reads: what does one recite?

[42] M has the bracketed conclusion of the verse explicitly.

[43] M ends the line: and went up and dwelled on the heights.

[D] "On the third [day] they would recite [Ps. 82, which begins]: 'God stands in the congregation of God, [he is a judge among the gods.' This psalm was used] because [on Tuesday, God] revealed the dry land in his wisdom and prepared the earth for his congregation.[44]

[E] "On the fourth [day] they would recite [Ps. 94, which begins]: 'Lord God to whom vengeance belongs, [you God to whom vengeance belongs, show yourself.'[45] This psalm was used] because [on Wednesday, God] created the sun and moon and was destined to exact punishment from those who serve them.

[F] "On the fifth [day] they would recite [Ps. 81, which begins], 'Sing aloud to God our strength, [make a joyful noise to the God of Jacob.' This psalm was used] because [on Thursday, God] created birds and fish, which bring glory to his name.

[G] "On the sixth [day] they would recite [Ps. 93, which begins], 'The Lord reigns; he is robed in majesty.' [This psalm was used] because [on Friday, God] finished his work and ruled over [all he created].

[H] "On the seventh [day] they would recite [Ps. 92, which begins], 'A psalm, a song for the Sabbath day'—[a psalm] for the day[46] that is wholly Sabbath rest [for eternity]."

[I] {Nehemiah rejects H's explanation of the use of Ps. 92 on the Sabbath.} Said R. Nehemiah, "What was sages'[47] understanding [that led them] to distinguish between these passages? {Why do they say that the first passages refer to

---

[44]In place of "for his congregation," M reads: for the world. This appears to be a scribal error, since the same reading as is found in the printed edition and other sources appears below at line M (Rabbinovicz).

[45]M has the bracketed conclusion of the verse explicitly.

[46]In place of "for the day," M reads: for the future time.

[47]M, Rashi, and others read: R. Aqiba's.

God's acts in the past, at the time of creation, while the passage for the Sabbath, they say, refers to the future?}

[J] "Rather [the passages should be explained as follows]:

[K] "On the first [day Ps. 24 was used] because [on Sunday, God] took possession and gave possession and was ruler over his world [without the heavenly hosts, who were created on the second day].

[L] "On the second [day Ps. 48 was used] because [on Monday, God] divided that which he created [into the upper and lower worlds] and was sovereign over them.[48]

[M] "On the third [day Ps. 82 was used] because [on Tuesday, God] revealed the dry land in his wisdom and prepared the earth for his congregation.

[N] "On the fourth [day Ps. 94 was used] because [on Wednesday, God] created the sun and moon and was destined to exact punishment from those who serve them.

[O] "On the fifth [day Ps. 81 was used] because [on Thursday, God] created birds and fish, which bring glory to his name.

[P] "On the sixth [day Ps. 93 was used] because [on Friday, God] finished his work and ruled over all [he created].

[Q] "On the seventh [day Ps. 92 was used] because [on the Sabbath, God] rested."

[R] {The dispute between Nehemiah, I-Q, and the sages who transmitted A-H is evaluated.} Now, they disagree[49] concerning that which Rab Kattina [said].

[S] For said Rab Kattina, "[For] six thousand years the world will exist, and [for] one [thousand years] it will be desolate, as it says [Is. 2:11: 'The haughty looks of man shall be brought low, and the pride of men shall be humbled]. And the Lord alone will be exalted in that day.'

---

[48] See note 43.

[49] M phrases this as a question: Concerning what do they disagree?

[T] Said Abayye, "[For] two [thousand] it will be desolate, as it says [Hos. 6:2]: 'After two days he will revive us; [on the third day he will raise us up, that we may live before him].'" {Rashi: Nehemiah, I+Q, agrees with Abayye, understanding his position to mean that a single day cannot represent an eternal Sabbath. Nehemiah rejects H's interpretation, which depends upon Kattina's understanding of matters.}

[III.A] At the Sabbath additional sacrifice, what would they say?

[B] Said Rab Hanan[50] bar Rava said Rab, "[They recited parts of Dt. 32, represented by the mnemonic] 'The splendor, [God], is yours.'" {The Hebrew expression "*hzyw lk*" is comprised of the first letters of Dt. 32:1, 7, 13, 19, 27, and 36,[51] indicating the divisions of the passage as it was used in the Temple.}

[C] And said Rab Hanan bar Rava said Rab,[52] "Just as [Dt. 32] is broken up here, so they divide it [into portions for reading] in the synagogue."

[IV.A] At the afternoon sacrifice on the Sabbath, what would they say?[53]

[B] Said R. Yohanan, "[They recited Ex. 15:1-10, which begins]: 'Then [Moses[54] and the people of Israel] sang [this song to the Lord;' followed by the rest of the Song of the Sea, Ex. 15:11-19, which begins]: 'Who is like you, [Lord, among the

---

[50]So L and other sources, as below at C. P reads: Anan. Here and at C, M reads: Nahman.

[51]M here explicitly lists the first words of these verses. The printer has inset this same material into the body of the text in P, noting that it is found in manuscripts and the text of Rashi.

[52]M reads: Rava.

[53]M has the question in the passive: what was said?

[54]M has this word explicitly.

gods?[55] Who is like you, majestic in holiness, terrible in glorious deeds, doing wonders?; followed by the Song at the Well, Num. 21:17ff., which begins]: 'Then Israel sang [this song: "Spring up, O well!"]'"

[V.A] {The preceding units' description of the psalms recited on the Sabbath is evaluated.} They asked them, "[Regarding] these [passages referred to at units **III-IV**], are they all recited on every Sabbath or, perhaps, on each Sabbath they recite only one [passage]?

[B] Come and learn:

[C] Since it is taught on Tannaitic authority: Said R. Yose,[56] "By the time that the first [passages, referred to at unit **III**, which lists six parts] have been recited[57] once, the second [passages, referred to in unit **IV**, which lists three readings] have been repeated twice—

[D] learn from this that on each Sabbath they recite only one [passage at the time of each sacrifice].

[E] [So you must] learn from this![58]

[VI.A] Said Rab Judah bar Idi said R. Yohanan, "The divine presence [Shechina] made ten journeys [in leaving Israel prior to the destruction of the first Temple]. {Simon, p. 147: "The Divine Presence left Israel by ten stages."}

[B] "[This we know from] Scripture.

[C] "And corresponding to these [stages], the Sanhedrin was exiled [successively to ten places of banishment].

[D] "[This we know from] tradition."

---

[55]M has "among the gods" explicitly.

[56]M reads: R. Judah says.

[57]All manuscripts and Rashi read: repeated.

[58]M and other sources lack this line.

[E] {A-B and C-D now are elaborated.} The divine presence made ten journeys [in leaving Israel prior to the destruction of the first Temple. This we know from] Scripture:

[F] [It went] (1) from the ark-cover to the cherub; [delete:[59] and from (one) cherub to the (other) cherub;] (2) and from the cherub to the threshold [of the Holy-of-Holies]; (3) and from the threshold to the [Temple-]court; (4) and from the court to the altar; (5) and from the altar to the [Temple-]roof; (6) and from the roof to the wall; (7) and from the wall to the city; (8) and from the city to the mountain; (9) and from the mountain to the wilderness; (10) and from the wilderness it ascended and dwelled in its place [in heaven]—

[G][60] as it is said [Hos. 5:15]: "I will return[61] again to my place, [until they acknowledge their guilt and seek my face]."

[H] {The Talmud now locates the source in Scripture for F(1).} From the ark-cover to the cherub; [delete:[62] and from (one) cherub to the (other) cherub;] (2) and from the cherub to the threshold [of the Holy-of-Holies]—

[I] as it is written [Ex. 25:22, proving that the original location of the divine presence was above the ark-cover]: "There I will meet with you, and from above the ark-cover, [from between the two cherubim that are upon the ark of the testimony], I will speak with you."

---

[59]So M, the parallel in Abot deR. Nathan, and numerous commentators, in order to yield the required ten items in the list.

[60]M and other sources lack this line, which in all events repeats below, AA.

[61]The root of the word "return"—ŠWB—plays on the root of the word "dwelled"—YŠB— in the preceding line.

[62]See note 59. M lacks the entire remainder of this line, placing the words "from the cherub to the threshold" before K.

[J] And [showing that, later, the divine presence had moved to the cherub] it is written [2 Sam. 22:11]: "He rode on a cherub and flew."[63]

[K] And [proving that the divine presence then moved to the threshold] it is written [Ezek. 9:3]: "Now the glory of the God of Israel had gone up from the cherubim on which it rested to the threshold of the house."

[L] (3) And from the threshold to the [Temple-]court—

[M] as it is written [Ezek. 10:4]: "And the house was filled with the cloud, and the court was full of the brightness of the glory of the Lord."

[N] (4) And from the court to the altar—

[O] as it is written [Amos 9:1]: "I saw the Lord standing beside the altar."

[P] (5) And from the altar to the [Temple-]roof—

[Q] as it is written [Prov. 21:9]: "It is better to live in a corner of the roof [than in a house shared with a contentious woman]."[64]

[R] (6) And from the roof to the wall—

[S] as it is written [Amos 7:7: "He showed me]: now, the Lord was standing beside a wall built with a plumb line."

[T] (7) And from the wall to the city—

[U] as it is written [Micah 6:9]: "The voice of the Lord cries to the city."

[V] (8) And from the city to the mountain—

[W] as it is written [Ezek. 11:23]: "And the glory of the Lord went up from the midst of the city and stood upon the mountain which is on the east side of the city."[65]

[X] (9) And from the mountain to the wilderness—

---

[63]Simon follows Rashi in deleting this line.

[64]M has the bracketed conclusion of the verse explicitly.

[65]M and other sources lack: on the east side of the city.

[Y]	as it is written [Prov. 21:19]: "It is better to live in a land of wilderness [than with a contentious and troublesome woman]."
[Z]	(10) And from the wilderness it ascended and dwelled in its place [in heaven]—
[AA]	as it is written [Hos. 5:15]: 'I will return again to my place, [until they acknowledge their guilt and seek my face].'[66]
[BB]	{BB-DD develops AA. Then the Talmud turns to elaborate C-D.} Said R. Yohanan, "For sixth months, the divine presence waited in the wilderness for [the people of] Israel, hoping lest they might repent.
[CC]	"When they did not repent, it said, 'May their souls expire.'[67]
[DD]	"[We know this] as it says [Job 11:20]: 'But the eyes of the wicked will fail, all means of escape will elude them, and their [only] hope will be for their souls to expire.'"
[EE]	{We turn to an analysis of C-D:} "And corresponding to these [stages through which the divine presence left Israel], the Sanhedrin was exiled [successively to ten places of banishment; this we know] from tradition."[68]
[FF]	[The Sanhedrin was banished] (1) from the Chamber of Hewn Stone [in the inner court of the Temple] to the market;[69] and (2) from the market into Jerusalem [proper], and (3) from Jerusalem to Yavneh, [31b] and (4) from Yavneh to Usha, and (5) from Usha [back] to Yavneh, and (6) from Yavneh [back] to Usha,[70] (7) and from Usha to Shefar'am, and (8)

---

[66]M has the bracketed conclusion of the verse explicitly.

[67]So Simon, p. 149, reading this in light of the proof text that follows. Literally: may they languish.

[68]M lacks: from tradition.

[69]So Jastrow, p. 482, s.v., *ḥnwt*. Simon, p. 149, takes it as a place name, Hanuth, referring to a location on the Temple mount.

[70]M lacks items 5 and 6, presumably the result of haplography.

	from Shefar'am to Beth[71] Shearim, and (9) from Beth Shearim to Sepphoris, and (10) from Sepphoris to Tiberias.
[GG]	And Tiberias is the lowest of them all [at the Sea of Galilee, symbolic of the complete abasement of the Sanhedrin's authority].
[HH]	[We know of the lowered physical location and reduced status of the Sanhedrin] as it is said [Is. 29:4]: "And deep from the earth you shall speak."
[II]	[Proposing a different description of the banishment of the Sanhedrin] R. Eleazar says, "There were [only] six [places of] banishment,
[JJ]	"as it says [Is. 26:5]: 'For (1) he has brought low the inhabitants of the height, the lofty city.[72] (2) He lays it low, (3) lays it low (4) to the ground, (5) he casts it (6) to the dust.'"
[KK]	Said R. Yohanan,[73] "And from there they are destined to be redeemed,
[LL]	"as it says [Is. 52:2]: 'Shake yourself from the dust; arise!'"[74]

4:4b

[F]	*Said R. Joshua b. Qorha, "This rule too did Rabban Yohanan b. Zakkai make:*
[G]	*"Even if the head of the court is located somewhere else, the witnesses should come only to the location of the council [to give testimony, and not to the location of the head of the court]."*

---

[71] In error, here and at item 9, M lacks this word.

[72] M lacks this first item.

[73] M lacks the attribution.

[74] M has the following word of the verse: Jerusalem.

Unit I indicates that M. R.H. 4:4G's rule applies only to witnesses who wish to give testimony regarding the new moon. Other individuals who have business before the court are obligated to go wherever the head of the court happens to be. Unit II speaks generally about ordinances enacted by Yohanan b. Zakkai. While eight such ordinances are agreed to derive from Yohanan, Amoraic authorities dispute regarding which of two additional ordinances Yohanan in fact enacted.

[I.A] [As for] a certain woman who was summoned to appear in court[75] before Amemar in Nehardea—

[B] [before she appeared] Amemar went to Mahoza, but she did not follow him [and, hence, failed to appear].

[C] He[76] [therefore] wrote out a warrant[77] against her.

[D] [Arguing that this was not an appropriate response] said Rab Ashi to Amemar, "But [to the contrary] have we not taught on Tannaitic authority [M. R.H. 4:4G]: *Even if the head of the court is located somewhere else,*[78] *the witnesses should come only to the location of the council [to give testimony, and not to the location of the head of the court]?*"

[E] [Claiming that M. R.H. 4:4G's rule does not apply in the case described at A-C, Amemar] said to him, "This rule [cited at D] applies [only] in the case of [a witness who comes to give] testimony regarding the [new][79] moon,

---

[75] M lacks: in court.

[76] M has: Amemar.

[77] Jastrow, p. 1253, s.v. *ptyhh*; reference is to a preliminary legal decision demanding either a court appearance or adherence to a court's decision.

[78] M and other manuscript sources lack the beginning of the citation of the Mishnah.

[79] M has the bracketed word explicitly.

[F] "for if this [other procedure were followed, that the witness should go to wherever the head of the court might be], it would wind up creating a problem in the future. {Witnesses might decide not to go to the trouble of traveling to wherever the head of the court happens to be and, as a result, the court would not obtain information regarding the appearance of the new moon. Therefore Yohanan b. Zakkai ruled that witnesses always should go to the usual location of the court.}

[G] "But here [in the case described at A-C, a different rule applies, insofar as, citing Prov. 22:7], 'The borrower is the slave of the lender.'" {To obtain testimony regarding the appearance of the new moon, the court depends upon witnesses. Their convenience must be taken into account, as F argues. But in other matters, people are dependent upon or subject to the will of the court. In these other matter, as at A-C, people must do whatever is convenient to the court. This means traveling to wherever the head of the court happens to be.}

[II.A] Our rabbis have taught on Tannaitic authority: Priests are not permitted to go up to the priests' platform [in the Temple, from which they recite the priestly benediction] in their sandals.

[B] And this is one of nine ordinances that Rabban Yohanan b. Zakkai enacted: six [found] in this chapter [of M. R.H.],[80]

[C] one in a preceding chapter,[81]

[D] and the other,[82] as it is taught on Tannaitic authority: A proselyte who converts [to Judaism] at the present time [that is, after the destruction of the Temple] must set aside a quarter

---

[80] These rules are at (1) M. R.H. 4:1D, (2) M. R.H. 4:3B, (3) M. R.H. 4:3C, (4) M. R.H. 4:4E, (5) M. R.H. 4:4G, and (6) in this unit, at A.

[81] At B. R.H. 1:4 III.C-D, 21b.

[82] M adds: what is his [view]?

	[sheqel][83] for his nest [of pigeons, required as a sacrifice, should the Temple be rebuilt].
[E]	Said R. Simeon b. Eleazar, "Rabban Yohanan [b. Zakkai][84] already has taken a vote and annulled this [rule], since [it creates] a stumbling block [insofar as the money set aside for the offering might accidentally be put to a secular purpose]."
[F]	And the [identification of the] other, [ninth, ordinance] is subject to dispute by Rab Pappa and Rab Nahman bar Isaac.[85]
[G]	Rab Pappa said, "[Reference is to an ordinance Yohanan enacted concerning the fruit of] a vineyard in its fourth year of growth [see Lev. 19:23-25]."
[H]	Rab Nahman bar Isaac said, "[Reference is to an ordinance Yohanan enacted concerning] the crimson thread [literally, 'tongue']."
[I]	Rab Pappa said, "[Reference is to an ordinance Yohanan enacted concerning the fruit of] a vineyard in its fourth year of growth."
[J]	[This is] as it is taught on Tannaitic authority [M. M.S. 5:2:[86] *Produce of] a vineyard in its fourth year [of growth, which must be brought to Jerusalem and consumed there] was brought physically to Jerusalem [if it was grown] within one day's [journey of the city] in any direction.* {If the produce was grown further from the city, it would be sold, and the money received would be taken to the holy city and used there to purchase food, eaten in place of the original fourth year produce.}

---

[83] So Rashi; cf., Tosafot.

[84] M and the parallel at B. Ker. 9a have the bracketed patronymic explicitly.

[85] In place of this line, M reads simply: And the other [enactment]—what is it?

[86] So P and the parallel at B. Bes. 1:1 **XVII.D**, 5a. The marginal note in P suggests reading: For we have taught on Tannaitic authority. That is the usual introduction to a citation of the Mishnah.

[K] *And what is*[87] *the extent [of a day's journey from Jerusalem]?*

[L] *Elat*[88] *to the south, Aqrabah to the north,*[89] *Lud to the west, and the Jordan [River] to the east.*[90]

[M] Now, said Ulla, and some say it was Rabbah bar Ulla,[91] said R. Yohanan, "What is the reason [that sages ordained that, within these boundaries, the fruit itself should be brought instead of being redeemed]?

[N] "It was so that the markets of Jerusalem could be decorated with produce." {The rule of J-L thus was tied to the joy involved in visiting the holy city and gladdening all of its inhabitants.}

[O] And it is [further] taught on Tannaitic authority: R. Eliezer had a vineyard in its fourth year of growth to the east of Lud, next to Kefar Tabi [and thus within the area demarcated as a day's journey to Jerusalem].

[P] And [to avoid needing himself to carry the produce to Jerusalem] R. Eliezer[92] sought to declare [the grapes] ownerless, for the benefit of the poor, [who thus could themselves take the fruit to Jerusalem and eat it there].

---

[87]So sources for the Mishnah. Here and in B. Bes., P reads: And this is. There is no difference in meaning. The variant is caused by the shifting of only one letter.

[88]The name occurs in two different spellings. M and MSS. of the Mishnah have *'ylt*. V and P have *'lt*. Jastrow, p. 50, holds that the name should be *Ayyelet*. On the location of this site, see Haas, p. 215, n. 9.

[89]So sources for the Mishnah and as required by the actual location of the sites. MSS. and editions of the Talmud switch the words north and south. The correct reading is indicated by a marginal note in P. Aqrabah is 30 miles southwest of Damascus.

[90]So P and as required by the actual location of the sites. M, Venice, and Silia reverse the words "east" and "west."

[91]M, other manuscripts, and the parallel at B. Bes. 5a read: Rabbah bar bar Hana.

[92]M and the parallel at B. Bes. 5a lack the name, implying the word: he

[Q] His students said to him, "Rabbi,[93] your colleagues already have voted on this matter and rescinded [the previous prohibition against redeeming fourth year produce within a day's journey of Jerusalem]." {Rashi: After the destruction of the city, there was no concern for decorating the markets with produce. Thus Eliezer did not need to give the produce away. He could sell it and take the proceeds to Jerusalem to purchase produce to be eaten there.}

[R] Who are referred to as "your colleagues"?

[S] Rabban Yohanan b. Zakkai.

[T] {The second proposal concerning Yohanan's ninth ordinance follows.} Rab Nahman bar Isaac said, "[Reference is to an ordinance Yohanan enacted concerning] the crimson thread [literally, 'tongue']."

[U] {U-BB describes the ordinance Nahman bar Isaac credits to Yohanan b. Zakkai.} For it is taught on Tannaitic authority: In olden times, [on the Day of Atonement, after the high priest performed his special worship], they would tie a crimson thread to the outside of the door of the [Temple] entranceway.

[V] [If] it turned white, [the people] would rejoice;

[W] [if] it did not turn white, [the people] would be grieved.

[X] They ordained that they should tie it to the inside of the door of the [Temple] entranceway,

[Y] but still [the people] would peek and see [it].

[Z] [If] it turned white, [the people] would rejoice;

[AA] [if] it did not turn white, [the people] would be grieved.

[BB] They ordained that they should tie half of it to the rock and half of it between the horns of the goat sent [to the wilderness].

[CC] {The reasons for Pappa and Nahman bar Isaac's disagreement now are given.} [As for] Rab Nahman bar Isaac—why does he not agree with Rab Pappa [above at R-S, that Yohanan b.

---

[93]M lacks the honorific.

Zakkai stands behind the decree that fourth year produce may be redeemed even if it grew within a day's journey of Jerusalem]?

[DD] [Nahman bar Isaac] can say to you: "If you imagine [that it was] Rabban Yohanan b. Zakkai [who reversed the rule concerning fourth year produce, this does not make sense, since] was he the colleague of R. Eliezer [as Q-S suggests]?

[EE] "[No!] He was his teacher." {Since Yohanan b. Zakkai was not Eliezer's colleague, but, rather, his teacher, Q cannot refer to him.}

[FF] But the other [that is, Pappa, will respond to this argument by stating]: "Since they were [Eliezer's own] students [who reminded Eliezer that the law had been changed]—it is not polite to say to one's teacher,[94] 'Your teacher [did such and so].'" {Rather, out of respect, Eliezer's students referred to Yohanan b. Zakkai as Eliezer's colleague. Nahman bar Isaac's argument at DD-EE therefore is inconclusive.}

[GG] [Now, as for] Rab Pappa—why does he not agree with Rab Nahman bar Isaac [above at U-BB, that Yohanan b. Zakkai stands behind the decree concerning the crimson thread]?

[HH] [Rab Pappa] can say to you, "If you imagine [that it was] Rabban Yohanan b. Zakkai [who enacted the decree concerning the crimson thread, this would be impossible, since],[95] during Rabban Yohanan b. Zakkai's day, was there [still] a crimson thread [that turned white]?[96]

[II] "[Indicating that there was not] thus it is taught on Tannaitic authority: Rabban Yohanan b. Zakkai's lived one hundred and

---

[94]M lacks: to one's teacher.

[95]M has the preceding in a shorter form: If you imagine that there was [still] a crimson thread in the time of Yohanan b. Zakkai....

[96]The bracketed words "that turned white" apparently were found explicitly in Rashi's text of the Talmud.

	twenty years. For forty years he engaged in business, for forty years he studied, and for forty years he taught.
[JJ]	"And it is [additionally] taught on Tannaitic authority: For forty years prior to the destruction of the Temple, the crimson thread did not turn white but, rather, remained red.
[KK]	"And we have taught on Tannaitic authority [M. R.H. 4:1D]: *After the destruction of the Temple, Rabban Yohanan b. Zakkai made the rule.....*" {M. R.H. 4:1D suggests that all of Yohanan b. Zakkai's ordinances were ordained after the destruction of the Temple, during the forty year period in which he "taught," II. Yet, as JJ indicates, by that time, the crimson thread already had ceased changing color. Therefore, contrary to Nahman b. Isaac, U-BB, Yohanan b. Zakkai cannot stand behind ordinances necessitated by the people's response to the changing color of the crimson thread.}
[LL]	But the other [that is, Nahman b. Isaac, will respond to this argument by stating]: "During those forty years that [Yohanan b. Zakkai] studied [while the Temple still stood], he was a disciple who sat before his teacher.
[MM]	"And he would make a statement [regarding the law] and it would appear reasonable, [**32a**] and his teacher[97] would institute [this practice] in his [Yohanan's] name." {In Nahman b. Isaac's view, contrary to KK, the rules at U-BB were enacted by Yohanan b. Zakkai while the Temple stood, during the period in which he was still a student.}

4:5

[A] *The order of the blessings [of the New Year additional service*[98] *is as follows]:*

---

[97]M and Rashi lack: his teacher.

[98]That is, Musaf, recited on Sabbaths and holidays in recognition of the additional sacrifice offered in the Temple on these days. The central component of the Musaf service is the Amidah ("standing prayer;" "eighteen benedictions") which occurs in

[B] "One says the Patriarchs,[99] Powers,[100] the Sanctification of the Name,[101] and includes the Sovereignty-verses[102] with them but does not sound [the shofar];

[C] "[then] the Sanctification of the Day,[103] and one [now] sounds [the shofar], the Remembrance-verses,[104] and one sounds [the shofar], the Shofar-verses,[105] and one sounds [the shofar];

[D] "then one says the blessing of the sacrificial service,[106] the thanksgiving,[107] and the priestly blessing"[108]—the words of R. Yohanan b. Nuri.

---

all worship services. While its initial and concluding benedictions are always the same, the middle benedictions change to reflect the theme of the particular day.

[99] Always the first benediction of the Amidah, recalling God's protection of the patriarchs.

[100] The second benediction, which speaks of God's power to resurrect the dead.

[101] The third benediction, in which the congregation declares God's holiness.

[102] Ten verses from Scripture that refer to God's sovereignty. The first three verses are taken from the Pentateuch and are followed by three from the Prophets, three from the Writings, and a final verse from the Pentateuch.

[103] Referring to God's sanctifying of the people of Israel and the Day of Remembrance, that is, New Year.

[104] Ten verses from Scripture that refer to God's being mindful of the people of Israel. As with the Sovereignty verses, the first three Remembrance verses are taken from the Pentateuch and are followed by three from the Prophets, three from the Writings, and a final verse from the Pentateuch.

[105] Ten verses that mention occasions on which the shofar was, or will be, sounded. The verses are taken from Scripture following the format already described.

[106] This refers to God's eventual restoring of the sacrificial cult.

[107] This notes that God is deserving of prayer and thanksgiving.

[108] The three-part blessing found at Num. 6:24-26, which comprises the second to last benediction of each Amidah.

[E] *Said to him R. Aqiba,*[109] *"If he does not sound [the shofar] in connection with the Sovereignty-verses, why does he make mention [of them at all]?*

[F] *"Rather, one says the Patriarchs, the Powers, the Sanctification of the Name, and includes the Sovereignty-verses with the Sanctification of the Day,*[110] *and then sounds [the shofar];*

[G] *"the Remembrance-verses and sounds [the shofar]; the Shofar-verses and sounds [the shofar],*

[H] *"then the blessing of the sacrificial service, the thanksgiving, and the priestly blessing."*

We again begin with exegetical materials, concerned, in this instance, with the meaning of Aqiba's statement at M. R.H. 4:5E (unit I). The remainder of the Talmudic discussion of this Mishnaic passage refers broadly to the themes raised here. Unit II identifies the passages in Scripture that instruct about the recitation of the benedictions of the Amidah and the Sovereignty, Remembrance, and Shofar-verses. Citing material from the Tosefta, unit III discusses in terms distinct from the Mishnah the proper placement of the sanctification of the day. Units IV-V again cite Toseftan materials, here describing how Tannaitic masters followed either the view of R. Yohanan b. Nuri, M. R.H. 4:5A-D, or Aqiba, M. R.H. 4:5E-H.

[I.A] {Aqiba's challenge to Yohanan b. Nuri, M. R.H. 4:5B vs. M. R.H. 4:5E-H, is explained.} [M. R.H. 4:5E states]: *Said to him R. Aqiba, "If he does not sound [the shofar] in connection with the Sovereignty-verses, why does he make mention [of them at all]?"*

---

[109] At D-E, M reverses the authorities' names.

[110] In error, M reads "Name" instead of "Day."

[B] [Aqiba's challenge to Yohanan b. Nuri], *"Why does he make mention [of them at all]?,"* [appears unconvincing, since the answer to this question is obvious]:

[C] [One mentions the Sovereignty-verses because God], the merciful, said that they must be recited! {God's command applies without regard to whether or not the shofar is sounded in conjunction with these verses.}

[D] {In order to clarify Aqiba's challenge to Yohanan b. Nuri, Aqiba's question is interpreted differently.} Rather, [Aqiba's challenge to Yohanan b. Nuri is as follows]: "Why are there[111] ten [verses]?

[E] "[If matters are as you—Yohanan b. Nuri—propose, people instead] should recite [only] nine [Sovereignty-verses, three each from the Pentateuch, Prophets, and Writings],

[F] "since if [as you say, the Sovereignty-verses] differ [from the Remembrance-verses and Shofar-verses in that they are not accompanied by the sounding of the shofar], then they should also be different [in regards to the number of verses that are said]." {Aqiba states that since the Sovereignty-verses contain the same number of citations as the Remembrance and Shofar-verses, they should also be the same in that they too are accompanied by the sounding of the shofar. This is contrary to what Yohanan b. Nuri proposes.}

[II.A] Our rabbis have taught on Tannaitic authority: From what [verse in Scripture do we know] that we are to recite [the first benediction of the Amidah, which refers to God's protection of] the Patriarchs?

[B] For it says [Ps. 29:1]: "Ascribe to the Lord, mighty ones [lit.: sons of gods]...." {The term "mighty ones" is understood to refer to the patriarchs, so that the verse as a whole is read to mean: Recall the patriarchs in the presence of God.}

---

[111]In place of "are there," M reads: does he recite.

[C] And from what [verse in Scripture do we know] that we are to recite [the second benediction of the Amidah, which refers to God's] Powers [in resurrecting the dead]?

[D] For it says [Ps. 29:1]: "Ascribe to the Lord glory and strength."

[E] And from what [verse in Scripture do we know] that we are to recite Sanctifications [that is, the third benediction of the Amidah]?

[F] For it says [Ps. 29:2]: "Ascribe to the Lord the glory of his name, bow down to the Lord in holy array."

[G][112] And from what [verse in Scripture do we know] that [in the New Year additional service] we are to recite the Sovereignty, Remembrance, and Shofar-verses?

[H] [T. R.H. 2:10:] R. Eliezer says,[113] "As it is written[114] [Lev. 23:24: 'In the seventh month, on the first day of the month, you shall observe] a day of solemn rest, a memorial proclaimed with blast of trumpets, a holy convocation.'

[I] "'A day of solemn rest'—this refers to [recitation of] the sanctification of the day.[115]

[J] "'A memorial'—this refers to [recitation of] the Remembrance-verses.

[K] "'Proclaimed with blast of trumpets'—this refers to [recitation of] the Shofar-verses.

[L] "'A holy convocation'—[this means that] you must sanctify it by [abstaining from] doing work."

---

[112] The text of M here is garbled.

[113] T. reads: R. Judah says R. Eliezer says.

[114] T. and M lack this clause. At the conclusion of the cited verse, M also lacks: a holy convocation.

[115] This line is added in the margin of M.

[M] Said to him R. Aqiba, "Why do we not say [contrary to I+L]: 'A day of solemn rest'—[this refers to] cessation of work?

[N] "[This interpretation makes sense] since with this [characteristic] Scripture commenced [its description of New Year, and abstaining from work is a primary element of observance of New Year (Rashi)].

[O] "Thus [contrary to the interpretation given at I-L, here is how Lev. 23:24 should be read]:

[P] "'A day of solemn rest'—sanctify [New Year by abstaining from] doing work.

[Q] "'A memorial'—this refers to [recitation of] the Remembrance-verses.

[R] "'Proclaimed with blast of trumpets'—this refers to [recitation of] the Shofar-verses.

[S] "'A holy convocation'—this refers to the sanctification of the day."

[T] {We turn to the source of the Sovereignty-verses, so far ignored.} And from what [verse in Scripture do we know] that [in the New Year additional service] we are to recite the Sovereignty-verses?

[U] It is taught on Tannaitic authority: Rabbi [Judah the Patriarch] says, "[Lev. 23:22 concludes], 'I am the Lord your God,'[116] [which is followed by the statement at Lev. 23:24], 'In the seventh month....'

[V] "This [juxtaposition of the concept of God's rule and the commandment to observe New Year indicates that, on New Year, the people must recite] the Sovereignty-verses."

[W] R. Yose bar Judah says, "This [interpretation] is unnecessary.

---

[116]In M, a complete citation of Lev. 23:22 ("You shall leave them for the poor and for the stranger: I am the Lord your God") has been crossed out.

[X] "Lo, [Scripture] says [explicitly, Num. 10:10: 'On the day of your gladness and at your appointed feasts...you shall blow the trumpet...] they shall serve you for remembrance before your God: [I am the Lord your God].'

[Y] "Now [having referred to a remembrance before God] Scripture did not need to [conclude the verse by adding the] state[ment], 'I am the Lord your God.' {That concept is implicit in the requirement that people "remember."}

[Z] "Why, then, does Scripture add, 'I am the Lord your God'?

[AA] This creates a general rule regarding all circumstances under which Remembrance-verses are recited, [that] Sovereignty-verses should be recited with them."

[III.A] Now, where [in the worship service] does one say the sanctification of the day?

[B] It is taught on Tannaitic authority [T. R.H. 2:11]: **Rabbi says,** "One says it with the Sovereignty-verses.

[C] **"Just as we find that in every circumstance [that is, on other festivals] it is the fourth [benediction of the Amidah], so here it is the fourth [benediction, which, on New Year, is where the Sovereignty-verses are recited as well; see M. R.H. 4:5F]."**

[D] [Disagreeing] Rabban Simeon b. Gamaliel[117] says, "With the Remembrance-verses one says it."

[E] "Just as we find in every circumstance [that is, on other festivals, when the Amidah in the additional service has seven benedictions] it is the middle [benediction], so here [on New Year, when the Amidah in the additional service has nine benedictions] it is the middle [benediction]." {Hence, while on other festivals the sanctification of the day is fourth, on New Year, it is fifth.}

---

[117]At T. R.H. 2:11 Simeon b. Gamaliel makes the same point in different words entirely.

[IV.A] [T. R.H. 2:11:] **Now, when the court sanctified the[118] year in Usha, R. Yohanan b. Beroqah went down [before the ark]** in the presence of Rabban Simeon b. Gamaliel[119] **and acted in accordance with [the view of] R. Yohanan b. Nuri**[120] [M. R.H. 4:5A-D]. {He recited the Sovereignty-verses with the third benediction and did not sound the shofar after them.}

[B] **Said to him Rabban Simeon [b. Gamaliel],**[121] **"That was not the custom that we followed in Yavneh."**

[C] **On the second day [of the festival] R. Hanina, son of R. Yose the Galilean, went down [before the ark] and acted in accordance with [the view of] R. Aqiba**[122] [M. R.H. 4:5E-H]. {He recited the Sovereignty-verses along with the sanctification of the day and sounded the shofar with them.}

[D] **Said Rabban Simeon b. Gamaliel, "That was the custom that we followed in Yavneh."**

[E] This suggests that Rabban Simeon b. Gamaliel concurred with R. Aqiba.[123]

[F] But [this seems impossible], for R. Aqiba said that the Sovereignty-verses were to be recited along with the sanctification of the day [M. R.H. 4:5F],

[G] and Rabban Simeon b. Gamaliel says that the sanctification of the day was to be recited along with Remembrance-verses [see above, unit **III.D**].

---

[118]All manuscripts add: New.

[119]The preceding clause is lacking in T.

[120]M reads: Aqiba. See above, note 109.

[121]So T. and M.

[122]M reads: Yohanan b. Nuri. See above, note 109.

[123]Here and at F, M reads: Yohanan. See the preceding note.

[H] [Explaining] said R. Zera, "This is to say that [in the view of Simeon b. Gamaliel] they sound [the shofar] for the Sovereignty-verses." {In this he agrees with Aqiba, M. R.H. 4:5F. Regarding the placement of the Sovereignty-verses, he does not agree.}

[V.A] {The Tannaitic statement at unit IV.C is cited and then explained.} **On the second [day of the festival] R. Hanina [son of R. Yose the Galilean] went down [before the ark and acted in accordance with the view of R. Aqiba].**

[B] What [is the meaning of] "second"?

[C] Shall I say[124] [it means] "the second [day] of the festival,"

[D] which would suggest that Elul had been intercalated [so that the thirtieth was treated as New Year out of doubt, but the new month was not actually sanctified until the following day]?

[E] But [this cannot be] for thus said R. Hanina bar Kahana: "Since the days of Ezra, we have not found [a case in which the month of Elul] has been intercalated."

[F] {A different explanation is required.} Said R. Hisda, "What [is the meaning of] '**second**'?

[G] "[It means] the second [occurrence of the same] holiday, in the following year."

4:6a

[A] *They do not say fewer than ten Sovereignty-verses, ten Remembrance-verses, ten Shofar-verses.*

[B] *R. Yohanan b. Nuri says, "If one has said three of each, he has fulfilled his obligation."*

---

[124] In place of A-B through this point in C, M reads simply: What [is the meaning of], "On the second [day of the festival R. Hanina son of R. Yose the Galilean] went down?" This appears to be the result of a scribal error (Rabbinovicz).

Unit **I** gives two different explanations for why ten of each kind of verse is required, M. R.H. 4:6A. Unit **II** explains an ambiguity in Yohanan b. Nuri's statement, M. R.H. 4:6B. Yohanan b. Nuri requires a total of three of each kind of verse, Sovereignty, Remembrance, and Shofar. He does not require that, for each of these categories of verses, the individual choose three examples from the Torah, Writings, and Prophets, yielding a total of nine verses in each category.

[I.A] These ten Sovereignty-verses [required by M. R.H. 4:6A]—to what do they correspond?

[B] Said R. Levi,[125] "[They] correspond to the ten praises that David stated in the book of Psalms."

[C] [This seems unacceptable, since, in the Psalms] there are many praises [of God, not just ten]!

[D] [Levi means that the Sovereignty-verses correspond specifically to] those [praises] among which are written [the statement, Ps. 150:3]: "Praise him with the sound of the shofar." {The meaning of this retort is not clear, since Ps. 150 lists more than ten ways in which people are to praise God.}

[E] [Offering a different explanation] Rab Joseph said, "[They] correspond to the ten commandments, which were spoken to Moses at Sinai [and which were introduced by the sounding of the shofar]."

[F] R. Yohanan said, "[They] correspond to the ten statements through which the world was created."

[G] {F seems unacceptable, since the creation account consists of only nine statements by God.} Which are these?!

[H] [The phrase] "And [God] said" occurs [only] nine [times] in the story [that describes what occurred] "in the beginning"!

---

[125]So the parallel at B. Meg. 21b. P here lacks: Levi.

[I] [Responding to H, Yohanan can argue that the words with which the creation account begins, that is], "In the beginning [God created the heaven and the earth]," also refer to a statement [of God].

[J] [We know that the heaven and earth were created through a statement of God], since it is written [Ps. 33:6]: "By the word of the Lord the heavens were made."

[II.A] [M. R.H. 4:6B:] *R. Yohanan b. Nuri says, "If one has said three of each, he has fulfilled his obligation."*

[B] The question was posed: What is the meaning [of Yohanan b. Nuri's statement]?

[C] [Does Yohanan b. Nuri mean that, to fulfill the obligation of each category of verses, one need only recite] three [verses] from the Pentateuch, three from the Prophets, and three from the Writings, which equals a total of nine [verses], such that the difference between them [that is, between the views of Yohanan b. Nuri and the anonymous view at M. R.H. 4:6A, which requires ten of each type of verse] is [only] one verse?

[D] Or perhaps [Yohanan b. Nuri means that, to fulfill the obligation for each category of verses, one need only recite] one [verse] from the Pentateuch, one from the Prophets, and one from the Writings, which equals a total of three [verses], such that the difference between them [that is, between the views of Yohanan b. Nuri and the anonymous view at M. R.H. 4:6A] is greater, [specifically, seven verses]?

[E] Come and learn [which interpretation is correct]:

[F] For it is taught on Tannaitic authority [see T. R.H. 2:12]: *They do not say fewer than ten Sovereignty-verses, ten Remembrance-verses, ten Shofar-verses.*

[G] **But if one said seven of each [kind of verse], he has fulfilled his obligation,**

[H] corresponding to the seven heavens.

[I] R. Yohanan b. Nuri says, "One who [wishes to say] fewer [verses], should not say fewer than seven. *But if he has said three of each, he has fulfilled his obligation,*

[J] "corresponding to the Torah, Prophets, and Writings,

[K] "or, others say, corresponding to the [three classes of Jews]: priests, Levites, and Israelites." {This appears to support D's interpretation of Yohanan b. Nuri's statement.}

[L] Said Rab Huna said Samuel, "The decided law follows [the view of] R. Yohanan b. Nuri."

4:6b

[C] *They do not make mention of verses of Remembrance, Sovereignty, or Shofar that speak of punishment.*

[D] *One begins with [verses deriving from] the Pentateuch and completes the matter with [verses deriving from] the Prophets.*

[E] *R. Yose says, "If one completed [the matter] with [verses deriving from] the Pentateuch, he has fulfilled his obligation."*

The Talmud refers in turn to the distinct issues introduced at M. R.H. 4:6C and M. R.H. 4:6D-E. Unit **I** exemplifies the sorts of verses, referring to punishment, excluded from use by M. R.H. 4:6C. Unit **II** develops this theme, indicating that verses that refer to the punishment of idolaters may be used and giving examples of such verses. Units **III-IV** offer cognate rules. Verses concerning the remembrance of a single individual may not be used in the Remembrance-verses, unit **III**. The question of whether verses that refer to visitations of God are in the category of Remembrance-verses is disputed, unit **IV**.

Units **V-VI** complete the discussion of M. R.H. 4:6C, illustrating how particular verses fulfill the obligation to recite Sovereignty, Remembrance, and Shofar-verses. Unit **V** presents a number of passages that contain more than one reference to God's sovereignty. Yose and Judah disagree concerning how one counts these multiple references. These authorities comparably disagree, unit **VI**, concerning the appropriate use of verses that fulfill the obligation of more than one category, for instance, referring both to remembrance and the sounding of the shofar.

The long discussion at unit **VII** interprets the view of Yose, M. R.H. 6:4E, that one fulfills the obligation to recite Sovereignty, Remembrance, and Shofar-verses by concluding with a verse taken from the Pentateuch. An initial discussion of what Yose means introduces the secondary question of whether or not the Pentateuch contains four Sovereignty-verses, needed if one is to cite an initial three and then, after reciting verses from the prophets and writings, conclude with another one. Yose holds that sufficient verses can be found; Judah disagrees.

[I.A] [32b] [What does M. R.H. 4:6C meant by] Sovereignty-verses [that speak of punishment]?

[B] [Verses] such as [Ezek. 20:33]: "As I live, says the Lord God, surely with a mighty hand and an outstretched arm and with wrath poured out, I shall be king over you."

[C] And even though [indicating that this verse does not describe a totally pessimistic future] Rab Nahman said, "Let the holy one, blessed be he, be as angry as all this with us, just that he should [eventually] redeem us"—

[D] [despite this fact], since [the verse] was said in anger, it is not recited at the beginning of the year.

[E] [What does M. R.H. 4:6C mean by] Remembrance-verses [that speak of punishment]?

[F] [Verses] such as [Ps. 78:39]: "And he remembered that they are but flesh [a wind that passes and comes not again]."

[G] [What does M. R.H. 4:6C mean by] Shofar-verses [that speak of punishment]?

[H] [Verses] such as [Hos. 5:8, which refers to the use of the shofar to sound an alarm when God acts as Israel's enemy]: "Blow the horn in Gibeah."

[II.A] {The Talmud develops the theme of the preceding.} But if one wished to recite Sovereignty, Remembrance, or Shofar-verses that speak of the punishment of idolaters, one may recite [them].

[B] [What is meant by] Sovereignty-verses [that speak of punishment of idolaters]?

[C] [Verses] such as [Ps. 99:1]: "The Lord reigns, let the nations tremble."

[D] And [verses] such as [Ps. 10:16]: "The Lord is king for ever and ever. The nations shall perish from his land."

[E] [What is meant by] Remembrance-verses [that speak of punishment of idolaters]?

[F] [Verses] such as [Ps. 137:7]: "Remember, Lord, against the Edomites."

[G] [What is meant by] Shofar-verses [that speak of punishment of idolaters]?

[H] [Verses] such as [Zech. 9:14]: "The Lord God will sound the shofar and march forth in the whirlwinds of the south."

[I] And [following that] it is written [Zech. 9:15]: "The Lord of hosts will protect them [that is, the Israelites, in battle against the nations]."

[III.A] They do not recite [a verse that concerns] the remembrance of an individual, even if it is favorable,

[B] for instance [Ps. 106:4]: "Remember me, Lord, when you show favor to your people,"

[C] or, for instance, [Neh. 5:19]: "Remember for good, my God, [all that I have done for this people]."

[IV.A] [T. R.H. 2:13: "**Verses referring to**] **visitations are equivalent to [verses that refer to] remembrance,**

[B] "**for instance [Gen. 21:1]: 'The Lord visited Sarah [as he had said, and the Lord did to Sarah as he had promised];'**

[C] "and such as [Ex. 3:16]: 'I have surely visited you'"—the words of R. Yose.

[D] [Disagreeing] R. Judah says, "[Verses referring to visitations] are not equivalent to [verses that refer to] remembrance."

[E] {Yose's inclusion of Gen. 21:1, cited at B, as a Remembrance-verse is challenged.} Now, [even in the view] of R. Yose, [who holds] that [verses referring to] visitations are equivalent to [verses that refer to] remembrance, [Gen. 21:1, which states] "The Lord visited Sarah," [should not be included among Remembrance-verses, since] it [refers to] the visitation of an individual. {Use of that verse would contradict the rule at unit III.A, which prohibits the use of verses that concern the remembrance of an individual.}

[F] {The Talmud argues that unit III.A's rule does not apply in this case.} Since [as a result of this visitation] a multitude [of people] issued from her, it is equivalent to [the visitation of] a multitude [of people and hence, in Yose's view, may be recited as a Remembrance-verse].

[V.A] {Ps. 24:7-10 is analyzed to determine the number of references it contains that may be used as Sovereignty-verses. Cf., T. R.H. 2:13.} [Ps. 24:7-10 reads:] "Lift up your heads, O gates, and rise up, O ancient doors, that the king of glory may come in. Who is the king of glory? The Lord, strong and mighty, the Lord, mighty in battle! Lift up your heads, O gates, and be lifted up, O ancient doors, that the king of glory may come in! Who is this king of glory? The Lord of hosts, he is the king of glory. Selah."

[B] "The first [segment of the passage contains] two [references to God's sovereignty, indicated by the words 'king of glory'],

[C] "[and] the second [segment contains] three [such references]"—the words of R. Yose.

[D] [Leaving out of the count the question "Who is the king of glory?" (Rashi)] R. Judah says, "The first [segment of the passage contains] one [reference to God's sovereignty],

[E] "[and] the second [segment contains] two [references]."

[F] {A similar dispute follows.} [Ps. 47:6-7 reads:] "Sing praises to God, sing praises! Sing praises to our king, sing praises! For God is the king of all the earth."

[G] "Two [references to God's sovereignty occur here]"—the words of R. Yose. {Yose includes in his count the words "our king" and the words "king of all the earth."}

[H] [Disagreeing] R. Judah says, "[There is only] one [such reference]." {Rashi: Judah excludes the words "our king," which refer to God's rule over Israel but not over the entire world.}

[I] [Unlike their disputes at A-E and F-H, Judah and Yose] concur in [their readings of Ps. 47:8, which states], "God reigns over the nations, God sits on his holy throne," that this [contains only] one [reference to God's sovereignty]. {Rashi: Neither Judah nor Yose holds that the phrase "God sits on his holy throne" refers to God's sovereignty.}

[VI.A] [T. R.H. 2:13: **A verse referring to] remembrance that contains [an allusion to] the sounding of the shofar—**

[B] **such as [Lev. 23:24: "In the seventh month, on the first day of the month, you shall observe] a day of solemn rest, a memorial proclaimed with blast of trumpets, a holy convocation"—**

[C] **"One recites it [either] among the Remembrance-verses or among the Shofar-verses"—the words of R. Yose.**

[D] **R. Judah says, "One recites it only among the Remembrance-verses."**

[E] **[A verse referring to] sovereignty that contains [an allusion to] the sounding of the shofar—**

[F] **such as** [Num. 23:21, "The Lord their God is with him, and the shout [lit.: blast, the word normally used to indicate the sounding of the shofar] of a king is among them"—[126]

[G] **"One recites it either with the Sovereignty-verses or with the Shofar-verses"**—the words of R. Yose.

[H] **R. Judah says, "One recites it only among the Sovereignty-verses."**

[I] **[A verse referring to] the sound of the shofar that contains no reference to anything else**—[127]

[J] **such as [Num. 29:1]: "You shall have a day for you to sound the shofar"**—

[K] **"One recites it with the Shofar-verses"—the words of R. Yose.**

[L] **R. Judah says, "One does not recite it at all."**

[VII.A] [M. R.H. 4:6D-E:] *One begins with verses deriving from the Pentateuch and completes the matter with verses deriving from prophetic writings.*

[B] *R. Yose says, "If one completed the matter with verses deriving from the Pentateuch, he has fulfilled his obligation."*

[C] [Yose says specifically], "*If one completed [the matter with verses deriving from the Pentateuch, he has fulfilled his obligation].*"

[D] [This means that] *post facto*, indeed [he has fulfilled his obligation]; but *de jure*, [he may] not [do this].

[E] But [suggesting that Yose holds a view contrary to D] thus we have taught on Tannaitic authority: R. Yose says, "One who completes [the matter] with [verses deriving from] the Pentateuch—lo, this is praiseworthy."

---

[126]T. R.H. 2:13 uses as an example Ps. 98:6: "With trumpet and the sound of the horn make a joyful noise before the king, the Lord."

[127]T. reads: A verse referring to the sound of the shofar without an accompanying reference to remembrance.

[F] [Based on this Tannaitic tradition] I must say [that, contrary to D, Yose's view is that] one *may* complete [the verses with a citation of the Torah]!

[G] But, [indicating the contrary, at M. R.H. 4:6E, Yose explicitly states], "If *one completed [the matter with verses deriving from the Pentateuch, he has fulfilled his obligation]*."

[H] [This means that] *post facto*, indeed [he has fulfilled his obligation]; but *de jure*, [he may] not [do this].

[I] [To resolve the contradiction] this is how [the dispute at M. R.H. 4:6D-E] should be stated:

[J] One begins with [passages from] the Pentateuch and concludes with [passages from] the prophets.

[K] R. Yose says, "He [should] conclude with [passages from] the Pentateuch, but if he concludes with [passages from] the prophets, he has fulfilled [his obligation]."

[L] A Tannaitic statement makes the same point: Said R. Eleazar b. R. Yose, "The men of old would conclude it with [passages from] the Pentateuch."

[M] Granted, [this proposal, that one should conclude with verses from the Pentateuch, makes sense for the case of] the Remembrance and Shofar-verses, [since the Pentateuch] contains many [appropriate references].

[N] But [in the case of] the Sovereignty-verses [this seems impossible, since] there are only three [appropriate verses in the Pentateuch]!

[O] [The verses are: Num. 23:21], "The Lord his God is with him, and the shout of a king is among them;" [Dt. 33:5], "Thus he became king in Jeshurun;" [and Ex. 15:18], "The Lord will reign for ever and ever."

[P] Now, we require ten [verses in all] and [if verses from the Pentateuch are to complete the selections, such that we would need at least four Pentateuchal verses], there are not sufficient [verses to fulfill this purpose]!

[Q] [Suggesting that, contrary to N-P, in Yose's view there are other passages in the Pentateuch that can be used as

Sovereignty-verses] said R. Huna, "Come and learn[128] [T. R.H. 2:13]: 'Here O Israel, the Lord our God, the Lord is one' [Dt. 6:4]—

[R] "'[This is] a Sovereignty verse'—the words of R. Yose.
[S] "R. Judah says, 'It is not a Sovereignty verse.'
[T] "'Know therefore this day and lay it to your heart that the Lord is God [in the heaven above and on the earth beneath]: there is no other' [Dt. 4:39][129]—
[U] "'[This is] a Sovereignty verse'—the words of R. Yose.
[V] "R. Judah says, 'It is not a Sovereignty verse.'
[W] "'To you it was shown, that you might know that the Lord is God, there is no other besides him' [Dt. 4:35]—
[X] "'[This is] a Sovereignty verse'—the words of R. Yose.
[Y] "R. Judah says, 'It is not a Sovereignty verse.'"

4:7

[A] *He who goes before the ark on the festival day of the New Year—*
[B] *the second [who leads the additional prayer orders the] sounding of the shofar.*
[C] *And at a time of saying the Hallel, the first one [who says the morning service] proclaims the Hallel psalms.*

Unit I explains why the sounding of the shofar, unlike the recitation of the Hallel, occurs late in the worship service. Unit II explains why, as M. R.H. 4:7 implies, the Hallel is not recited on New Year and the Day of Atonement.

---

[128]Rosh reads: It is taught on Tannaitic authority.

[129]In T., this verse follows the citation of Dt. 6:4, given here at N. The point is the same.

[I.A] What is the reason that *the second [who leads the additional prayer orders the] sounding of the shofar* [M. R.H. 4:7B]? {Why is the shofar not sounded during the earlier service?}

[B] This is based upon [Prov. 14:28]: "In a multitude of people is the glory of a king." {The shofar is sounded in the later service, when more people are present. The understanding here is that most people do not come to the synagogue early for the beginning of the worship.}

[C] {B is challenged.} If this were the case, then Hallel also would be said by the second [reader, during the additional service],

[D] on the basis of [Prov. 14:28]: "In a multitude of people is the glory of a king."

[E] Rather, what is special[130] about the Hallel that it is [recited] by the first [reader, during the earlier service]?

[F] This is based upon [the precept that] those who are zealous come early to perform religious obligations.

[G] {F is challenged.} [If this were the case, then] the shofar also would be sounded [early in the worship, at the order of] the first [reader],

[H] on the basis of [the precept that] those who are zealous come early to perform religious obligations.

[I] {The parallel units at A-D and E-H have failed to explain why the shofar is sounded late in the service. Yohanan now answers that question.} Said R. Yohanan, "[The rule that the shofar is sounded by the second reader] was decreed at a time when the [gentile] government had enacted a restrictive ordinance [outlawing the sounding of the shofar]." {The Talmud proposes that 1) violation of this ordinance would be less likely to be noticed if the shofar were sounded later in the service, and 2) even after the ordinance was rescinded, the practice of sounding the shofar late continued.}

---

[130]The Aramaic phrase is the same as that translated "What is the reason" at A.

[II.A] Insofar as [M. R.H. 4:7C] states, *"And at a time of saying the Hallel,"* we can deduce that on New Year there is no [recitation of the] Hallel. {Otherwise, the clause would read: *And when they say the Hallel*, referring to New Year day, as in the previous lines.}

[B] What is the reason [that Hallel is not recited on New Year day]?

[C] Said R. Abbahu, "The ministering angles said in the presence of the holy one, blessed be he, "Master of the universe! Why do [the people of] Israel not recite songs of praise before you on New Year and on the Day of Atonement?"

[D] He said to them, "Is it logical that the king should sit on the throne of judgment, with the books of the living and books of the dead open before him, and have [the people of] Israel recite songs of praise?!"

4:8

[A] *[On account of making provision for] the shofar to be used at the New Year:*

[B] *(1) they do not cross the [Sabbath] boundary;*

[C] *(2) and they do not dig up debris [that has fallen on it];*

[D] *(3) they do not climb a tree [to get it];*

[E] *(4) and they do not ride on a beast;*

[F] *(5) and they do not swim in the water;*

[G] *(6) and they do not cut it either with a tool that is forbidden on account of the rules of Sabbath rest or with a tool that is [explicitly forbidden] by a negative commandment of the Torah.*

[H] *But if one wanted to put water or wine in it, he may do so.*

[I] *They do not keep children from sounding the shofar.*

[J] *But they practice with them until they learn [how to do it].*

[K] *And one who is practicing has not [thereby] fulfilled his obligation [to sound the shofar].*

[L] *And the one who hears [the shofar] sounded by the person who is practicing [also] has not fulfilled his obligation.*

Unit **I** explains M. R.H. 4:8B-G. The prohibition against working on New Year is on a stronger footing than the requirement that one sound the shofar and so takes precedence. Units **II-IV** explain specific items listed in the Mishnah, including the reason that one is permitted to place water or wine (the Talmud adds: but not urine) in a shofar, M. R.H. 4:8H.

Unit **V** turns to the implications of M. R.H. 4:8I, detailing the rule for a woman, which the Mishnah itself does not consider. Units **VI-VIII** consider the fulfilling of the commandment to hear the shofar in cases in which the individual who is sounding the shofar either intends only to practice or is playing only for himself, without a concern for fulfilling other people's obligation. These discussions propose that, to fulfill the religious obligation, an individual who sounds the shofar must formulate the intention to satisfy his own as well as other listeners' obligations to hear the blast.

[I.A]   What is the reason [that the actions listed at M. R.H. 4:8B-G are forbidden]?

[B]   [The reason is that the obligation to sound] the shofar [derives only from] a positive commandment. {Reference is to Num. 29:1: "It shall be a day of sounding of the horn to you."}

[C]   But [the rules that apply to] the festival day [derive from both] positive and negative commandments. {The positive precept is at Lev. 23:24: "In the seventh month...you shall observe a day of solemn rest." The negative commandment appears at Lev. 23:25: "You shall do no laborious work."}

[D]   And [the obligation to fulfill] a positive commandment does not [empower the individual to] set aside both a negative and a positive commandment.

[II.A]   *[On account of making provision for the shofar to be used at the New Year...] they do not climb a tree [to get it]; and they do not ride on a beast* [M. R.H. 4:8:D-E].

[B]   Insofar as [in precluding bringing the shofar from beyond the Sabbath limit or removing it from debris, M. R.H. 4:8B-C] you have said that [to make provision for its use] rabbinic ordinances [may] not [be violated],

[C] need [the violation of] Pentateuchal ordinances [such as climbing or riding] be mentioned [at all]? {These proscriptions should be obvious and go without saying.}

[D] "This [breaking of rabbinic ordinances, such as are listed at M. R.H. 4:8B-C, is forbidden] and, needless to say, this [violation of Pentateuchal ordinances, such as are listed at M. R.H. 4:8D-E, is forbidden] as well" is [the point of] what is taught in the Mishnah.

[III.A] [33a] *And they do not cut it either with a tool that is forbidden on account of the rules of Sabbath rest or with a tool that is [explicitly forbidden] by a negative commandment of the Torah* [M. R.H. 4:8G].

[B] *"[With] a tool that is forbidden on account of the rules of Sabbath rest"*—

[C] [This refers to use of]¹³¹ a sickle. {Jastrow, p. 728: "an implement combining knife and saw." Since such a tool would not normally be used on a shofar, its use on the festival—"Sabbath"—is not technically forbidden under the category of "work." Such use is prohibited only because of the rabbinical extension of the prohibition against work to include any action that is not in keeping with a broad notion of holiday "rest."}

[D] *"[With a tool] that is [explicitly forbidden] by a negative commandment of the Torah"* [M. R.H. 4:8G]—

[E] [This refers to use of] a knife. {A knife regularly is used on a shofar, so that its use on the festival is precluded under the biblical prohibition against work.}

---

¹³¹M reads: such as. In the following a number of words have dropped out of M through haplography.

[F] {The Talmud questions why the Mishnah needed explicitly to list both of the prohibitions cited here at A.} Insofar as you have said [use of a tool on a shofar is forbidden] if it violates the rules of the Sabbath rest, do we need [also] to note that [use of a tool is forbidden if it violates] a negative commandment of the Torah? {This should be obvious. If the rules regarding Sabbath rest apply, certainly the Pentateuchal rules prohibiting work apply.}

[G] "This [breaking of the rabbinical ordinance regarding Sabbath rest is forbidden] and, needless to say, this [violation of the Pentateuchal prohibition against work is forbidden] as well" is [the point of] what is taught in the Mishnah.

[IV.A] *But if one wanted to put water or wine in it, he may do so* [M. R.H. 4:8H].

[B] Water or wine [one may] indeed [use],

[C] [but] urine [he may] not [use].

[D] This Tannaitic teaching [at B-C derives from] whom?

[E] It is Abba Saul,

[F] for it is taught on Tannaitic authority: Abba Saul says, "Water or wine are permitted, in order to clean it,

[G] "[but] urine is forbidden, because of the honor [due the shofar]."

[V.A] *They do not keep children from sounding the shofar* [M. R.H. 4:8I].

[B] This implies that they do prevent women.

[C] But [indicating the contrary] has it not been taught on Tannaitic authority: They do not keep women or children from sounding the shofar on a festival?[132]

[D] Said Abayye, "There is no contradiction.

---

[132]M and all manuscripts lack: on a festival.

[E] "One [view represents the opinion of] R. Judah; the other [follows] R. Yose and R. Simeon."

[F] For it is taught on Tannaitic authority: [Lev. 1:2 introduces the regulations regarding sacrifices by stating], "Speak to the sons[133] of Israel...."

[G] "[This means that male] 'sons of Israel' may lay hands [on a sacrifice], but [female] 'daughters of Israel' may not lay on hands"—the words of R. Judah.

[H] R. Yose and R. Simeon say, "Women lay on hands [not as an obligation but] as an optional act." {Yose and Simeon would hold, comparably, that women may sound the shofar.}

[VI.A] *But they practice with them until they learn [how to do it; M. R.H. 4:8J].*

[B] Said R. Eleazar, "[This applies] even on the Sabbath."

[C] A Tannaitic statement makes the same point [T. R.H. 2:16]: *They practice with them until they learn even on the Sabbath,*

[D] and *they do not keep*[134] **children from sounding the shofar** [even] **on the Sabbath** [M. R.H. 4:8I],

[E] **and it goes without saying on a festival day [that is not a Sabbath].**

[F] This [Tannaitic statement] contradicts itself!

[G] [First, at C] you said: *"They practice with them until they learn*[135] *even on the Sabbath."*

[H] This implies that, *de jure*, we tell them, "[Go ahead], blow!"

[I] But then it is taught on Tannaitic authority [at D]: *"They do not keep [children from sounding the shofar* **even on the Sabbath**]."

---

[133]"*Bny*," a masculine word, usually rendered "people."

[134]M adds: women or.

[135]M lacks the end of D through this point, the result of haplography.

[J] [This implies that, if they start to sound the shofar on their own] one does not prevent them [from doing so], but, *de jure*, we do not tell them, "[Go ahead], blow!"

[K] There is no contradiction.

[L] One [rule] [**33b**] applies in the case of a minor who has reached the age at which he is taught [the proper performance of religious obligations].

[M] [But] the other [rule] applies in the case of a minor who has not reached the age at which he is taught [the proper performance of religious obligations]. {The question of which rule applies to which child is disputed by Rashi and Tosafot. Rashi says that one may help the older child to learn. Unlike in the case of the younger child, this is permitted as an important aspect of his religious education. Tosafot reject this view, holding that the older child should not be encouraged to violate a rabbinical prohibition. This consideration is of less weight in the case of the younger child, who will not be subject to the commandments for some time.}

[VII.A] *And one who is practicing has not [thereby] fulfilled his obligation [to sound the shofar;* M. R.H. 4:8K].[136]

[B] This implies that one who sounds [the shofar] to produce proper notes [lit.: a song] does fulfill his obligation.[137] {The individual's intention to produce the correct sound is sufficient. He need not formulate the intention to fulfill his religious obligation.}

[C] Should I say that this supports [the view of] Rava?

---

[136]Rashi's text apparently had here the added words: "It is one who is practicing who has not fulfilled his obligation." The meaning is the same.

[137]M and other manuscripts read this as a question and answer: [As for] one who sounds [the shofar] to produce proper notes—what [is the rule]? He does fulfill his obligation!

[D]   For said Rava, "One who sounds [the shofar] to produce proper notes fulfills his obligation."

[E]   Perhaps [this authority]¹³⁸ deems sounding [the shofar] to produce proper notes also to be in the category of practicing. {This statement appears to challenge B's assumption, that A's authority would deem one who intends to make proper notes as fulfilling his obligation regarding the sounding of the shofar. Contrary to B, the Mishnaic authority may in fact deem making proper notes to be the same as practicing and, absent of intention to fulfill the religious obligation, to be of no legal weight. E does not however appear to respond to C-D.}

[VIII.A] {B proposes that, since M. R.H. 4:8L, cited here, does not specifically refer to one who sounds the shofar for himself, the rule for that person must be different from the rule for one who is practicing, the category of people the Mishnah specifically mentions. E rejects this approach. It argues that even though one who sounds the shofar for himself is not explicitly mentioned at M. R.H. 4:8L, such a person may be included in the same category.} *And the one who hears [the shofar sounded] by the person who is practicing [also] has not fulfilled his obligation* [M. R.H. 4:8L].

[B]   But [as for] one who hears [the shofar being sounded] by one who sounds it [only] to [fulfill] his own [obligation], what [is the rule? Is it that the listener has in this way] fulfilled his obligation? {This appears to be the case.}

[C]   [If he has fulfilled his obligation], you can say this refutes [the view] of R. Zera.

[D]   For said R. Zera to his attendant, "Formulate [the required] intention [to fulfill the obligation on my behalf] and sound the

---

¹³⁸M and other manuscripts explicitly state: Perhaps this Tannaitic authority also....

shofar for me!" {Contrary to the implication of M. R.H. 4:8L, expressed at B, Zera clearly holds that, for the act to be efficacious, one who sounds the shofar must explicitly formulate the intention to act on behalf of other people who hear him.}

[E] {B's inference is rejected.[139] Contrary to B, the authority of M. R.H. 4:8L may not purposely have failed to refer to an individual who sounds the shofar only for himself.} [Rather than purposely omitting reference to an individual who sounds the shofar only for himself], perhaps since the initial Tannaitic statement [at M. R.H. 4:8K refers to] "practice"[140] the final Tannaitic statement [at M. R.H. 4:8L] also [uses the term] "practice" [even though that term does not encompass all of the cases to which its rule applies]. {Contrary to B, the rule in fact was meant to include one who intends to sound the shofar only for himself.}

4:9

[A] *The order of sounding the shofar is [to sound] three sets of three each.*[141] {A set is sounded with each of the three special sections of the Musaf worship: the Sovereignty, Remembrance, and Shofar-verses.}

[B] *The length of the sustained blast is [equal to] three quavering blasts.*

[C] *The length of the quavering blast is [equal to] three alarm blasts.*

---

[139]M states this explicitly, adding: No! I shall in all events state that he has not fulfilled his obligation

[140]M concludes this line slightly differently from P: the Tannaitic authority [at M. R.H. 4:8L] also [referred to] "one who hears [the shofar sounded] by the person who is practicing." The meaning is the same.

[141]M lacks the repetition of the word for "three," rendered here as "each."

BAVLI ROSH HASHANAH CHAPTER FOUR [33b] 437

[D] *[If] one sounded the first sustained blast and then sounded the second [sustained blast] for twice as long, he has credit only for one [set].* {The lengthened blast does not count as the beginning of the next set.}

[E] *He who said the blessings [of the Musaf worship] and afterward was assigned a shofar should sound a sustained blast, a quavering blast, and a sustained blast, three times, [once each for the Sovereignty, Remembrance, and Shofar-verses].*

[F] *Just as the congregation's agent is liable [to recite the daily prayers], so each individual is liable.*

[G] *Rabban Gamaliel*[142] *says, "The agent of the community carries out the obligation on behalf of the community [and therefore individuals do not have to recite the prayers themselves."*

Units **I-IV** begin with general definitions 1) of the shofar-blasts referred to at M. R.H. 4:9B-D and 2) of the source in Scripture of the notion that these sounds are produced with a ram's horn and always are introduced with a sustained blast. Units **V-IX** summarize and then reevaluate these initial materials, covering in many regards the same exegetical interests found in the initial Talmudic units.

Units **X-XI** introduce secondary problems regarding the sounding of the shofar. How do we account for an uncertainty regarding the correct sequence of sounds, unit **X**? Can people fulfill their obligation by hearing the shofar's blasts over a long period of time or, conversely, by hearing shofars sounded by nine people all at the same time, unit **XI**? Units **XII-XIII** provide the general principle governing these cases: on New Year and the Day of Atonement, all prayers and sounding of the shofar must take place at the proper time, in the correct order, and without omissions. The same strict rule does not apply on other ritual occasions.

---

[142]M reads: Rabban Simeon b. Gamaliel.

438   BAVLI ROSH HASHANAH CHAPTER FOUR [33b]

Units **XIV-XVIII** turn to M. R.H. 4:9F-G, the recitation of required prayers or the sounding of the shofar by one person on behalf of a different individual. Of concern is whether or not a designated agent in fact can carry out these responsibilities on behalf of other members of the community, especially those who are able to carry out the obligation themselves. All agree that the shofar may be sounded by a designated agent, unit **XIV**. The dispute regarding the rule for the liturgy, M. R.H. 4:9F-G, by contrast, engenders extended discussion, units **XV-XVIII**. Gamaliel's position, that the agent of the congregation carries out the obligation on behalf of the congregation, is accepted as authoritative for New Year and the Day of Atonement, since the complexity of the liturgy for these holidays makes it extremely difficult for most people correctly to fulfill the obligation themselves. Units **XIX-XX** discuss secondary issues related to this conclusion. Before reciting unfamiliar prayers, people should go over the material to prepare themselves, unit **XIX**. Only people who cannot recite prayers themselves are exempted by the recitation of the agent of the community, unit **XX**. People who can themselves go to the synagogue and pray must do so.

[I.A] {M. R.H. 4:9B states: *The length of the sustained blast is [equal to] three quavering blasts.*} But [indicating the contrary] thus it has been taught on Tannaitic authority: The length of the sustained blast is [equal to] the quavering blast.

[B]   [To resolve the contradiction] said Abayye, "Our Tannaitic authority [at M. R.H. 4:9B] counted all of the sustained blasts and all of the quavering blasts. {His point is that the length of a single sustained blast is the same as the length of each of the three quavering blasts heard in a complete cycle of three sets.}

[C]   "The other Tannaitic authority [cited here at A] counted one set and no more." {His point is the same as that made by M. R.H. 4:9B: the sustained blast heard in each set is the same length as the quavering blast heard in each set.}

[II.A] *The length of the quavering blast is [equal to] three alarm blasts* [M. R.H. 4:9C].

[B] But [indicating the contrary] thus it is taught on Tannaitic authority: The length of a quavering blast is [equal to] three fragmented blasts. {Fragmented blasts are slightly longer than alarm blasts.}

[C] Said Abayye, "Concerning this there certainly is a dispute.

[D] "For it is written [Num. 29:1: 'On the first day of the seventh month you shall have a holy convocation....] It is a day for you [to sound] quavering blasts.'[143]

[E] "Now, we translate [this into Aramaic as], 'It is a day for you [to sound] *yebaba* [that is, alarm, blasts].'

[F] {The disagreement cited at A vs. B results from a dispute over the character of a *yebaba* blast.} "Now, it is written regarding the mother of Sisera [Judges 5:28]: 'Out of the window the mother of Sisera[144] looked forth and *tybb*.'[145] {At issue is the meaning of the final word, which derives from the same root as *yebaba*.}

[G] "One authority [B] reasoned [it means that she] made a long sigh. {Thus he holds that the quavering blast is the length of three fragmented blasts, which are slightly longer than three alarm blasts.}

[H] "But [the other] authority [A] reasoned [it means that she] made a piercing lamentation [comparable to the shorter alarm blasts]."

[III.A] Our rabbis have taught on Tannaitic authority: From what [verse in Scripture do we know that the trumpet sounds on New Year must be made with] a shofar?

---

[143]The verse normally is rendered: It is a day for you to blow the trumpets.

[144]M lacks: the mother of Sisera.

[145]RSV: peered.

[B] Scripture says [Lev. 25:9, referring to the announcement of the Jubilee Year]: "Then you shall make proclamation with the blast of the shofar [on the tenth day of the seventh month]."[146]

[C] [Based on Lev. 25:9] I know the rule only for the Jubilee Year.

[D] Regarding New Year—how [do I know that a shofar is used]?

[E] [In the cited verse] Scripture adds,[147] "of the seventh month," even though [there is here] no [need for] Scripture to add, "of the seventh month." {Indication of the month is unnecessary since, immediately afterwards, the verse continues, "on the Day of Atonement."}

[F] So why does Scripture add, "of the seventh month"?

[G] To [instruct] that all of the blasts [required] in the seventh month should be alike, [sounded on a shofar].

[IV.A] And from what [verse in Scripture do we know that the trumpet sounds on New Year all] are preceded by a plain blast?

[B] Scripture says [Lev. 25:9, referring to the announcement of the Jubilee Year]: "Then you shall make proclamation with the blast (*teru'ah*) of the shofar." {The word *teru'ah* refers to the quavering blast. The word shofar is understood to refer to an additional sound, a plain blast.}

[C] From what [verse in Scripture do we know that the trumpet sounds on New Year all] are followed by a plain blast?

[D] Scripture says [Lev. 25:9, in the second half of the verse]: "You shall send abroad the shofar." {Here, since the word shofar occurs for the second time, it is understood to refer to a concluding blast.}

---

[146]M explicitly has part of the bracketed conclusion of the verse.

[147]Lit.: says.

[E] But [based on Lev. 25:9] I know the rule only for the Jubilee Year.

[F] Regarding New Year—how [do I know that a shofar is used]?

[G] [In the cited verse] Scripture adds, "of the seventh month," [34a] even though [there is here] no [need for] Scripture to add, "of the seventh month." {Indication of the month is unnecessary since, immediately afterwards, the verse continues, "on the Day of Atonement."}

[H] So why does Scripture add, "of the seventh month"?

[I] To [instruct] that all of the blasts [required] in the seventh month should be alike, [sounded on a shofar].

[V.A] And from what [verse in Scripture do we know that there must be] *three sets of three [blasts] each* [M. R.H. 4:9A]?

[B] {We know this since Scripture three times refers to the use of the shofar.} Scripture says [in reference to the Jubilee year, Lev. 25:9]: "Then you shall make proclamation with the blast of the shofar;" [in reference to New Year, Lev. 23:24]: "...a day of solemn rest, a memorial proclaimed with the blast of trumpets;" [and, again in reference to New Year, Num. 29:1]: "It is a day for you to blow the trumpet."

[C] And from what [verse do we know that one can] apply that which is stated in conjunction with this [event, the Jubilee] to this [other event, New Year] and *vice versa*[148] [so as to ascertain that, on each occasion, there must be three sets of blasts]?

[D] Scripture says [regarding New Year] "seventh [month," Lev. 23:24, and, regarding the Jubilee, it also says], "seventh [month," Lev. 25:9], so as to create an analogy based on verbal congruities.[149]

---

[148]M lacks: and *vice versa.*

[149]*Gezerah shavah.*

[E] {E-H appears to summarizes the conclusions of units **I-V**.} How, then, [is the shofar sounded]?

[F] Three [sets of blasts], which equal [a total of] nine [blasts].

[G] The length of the sustained blast is [equal to] the quavering blast [see above, unit **I**.A].

[H] The length of a quavering blast is [equal to] three fragmented blasts [see above, unit **II**.B].

[**VI**.A] {The Talmud explores a contradiction internal to the preceding units.} Lo, the Tannaitic authority [whose view is understood to be represented in the preceding units] first made his point through a correspondence between two biblical verses[150] [units **III-IV**],

[B] but now [at unit **V**] he makes his point through an analogy based on verbal congruities.

[C] This is his point:[151] If there were no possible analogy based on verbal congruities, I could teach [the same point] by using the correspondence between two biblical verses.

[D] [But] now, since there is an analogy based on verbal congruities, the [argument based on the] correspondence between two biblical verses is not needed.

[**VII**.A] {A different biblical foundation is given for the rule that the sequence of sounding the shofar always begins with a plain blast, unit **IV**.} Now this [following] Tannaitic authority derives this [rule] through an analogy based on verbal congruities involving the [use of the shofar in the] wilderness [to sound a military alarm]:

[B] For it is taught on Tannaitic authority:[152] [Num. 10:5 states], "And you shall sound [*TQ'*] a blast [*TR'*].

---

[150]*Heqesh.*

[151]M lacks the remainder of this line.

[152]In place of "For it is taught on Tannaitic authority," M reads: As it is written.

[C] [This signifies] a sustained blast [TQ'] by itself and a quavering blast [TR'] by itself.

[D] Should you say [this refers to] a sustained blast by itself and a quavering blast by itself?

[E] Or does it [rather] refer to a sustained blast and a quavering blast [sounded] as one?

[F] Insofar as [elsewhere] it says [Num. 10:7], "But when the assembly is to be gathered together, you shall blow [a sustained blast, TQ'], but you shall not sound a quavering blast[153] [TR']," thus you must say [that, at Num. 10:5, reference is to] a sustained blast by itself and a quavering blast by itself.

[G] And from what [verse in Scripture do we know that] a plain blast precedes it?

[H] Scripture states [Num. 10:5], "And you shall sound [TQ'] a blast [TR']."

[I] And from what [verse in Scripture do we know that] a plain blast follows it?

[J] Scripture states [Num. 10:6], "A blast you shall blow."

[K] R. Ishmael the son of R. Yohanan b. Beroqah says, "This [exposition] is not necessary!

[L] "Lo, it says [Num. 10:6], 'And when you blow a blast the second time....'

[M] "Now Scripture does not [need to] state [the words] 'a second time.' {Since an initial sounding of the shofar has just been mentioned, reference obviously is to a second blast.}

[N] "Therefore, why does Scripture say, 'a second time'?

[O] "This creates a general rule,[154] that each time a quavering blast is mentioned, a second sustained blast will accompany it."

---

[153] RSV: You shall not sound an alarm.

[154] Lit.: father.

[P] [So far] I know only the rule for [the use of the shofar to assemble the people] in the wilderness.

[Q] For New Year, what [is the foundation of the rule]?

[R] Scripture uses [the term] "blast" [in connection with the wilderness and] "blast" [in connection with New Year], to create an analogy based on verbal congruities.[155] {Since the word "blast" is used in both contexts, the same rules apply to each.}

[VIII.A] Now, three quavering blasts are mentioned in connection with the New Year—[Lev. 23:24]: "...a day of solemn rest, a memorial proclaimed with the blast of trumpets;" [Num. 29:1]: "It is a day for you to blow the trumpet;" [and Num. 25:9, referring to the announcement of the Jubilee Year]: "Then you shall make proclamation with the blast of the shofar [on the tenth day of the seventh month]."[156]

[B] And two sustained blasts accompany each quavering blast.

[C] We wind up learning [that] three quavering blasts and six sustained blasts were prescribed for the New Year.

[D] Two of them [derive] from the [written] Torah and one [derives] from the words of scribes.

[E] [This is as follows: The blasts referred to at Lev. 23:24, which reads], "...a day of solemn rest, a memorial proclaimed with the blast of trumpets," [and Num. 25:9, which reads], "Then you shall make proclamation with the blast of the shofar [on the tenth day of the seventh month," derive] from the [written] Torah.[157]

---

[155] Connecting this unit to the one that follows, M and other sources add: Here it says "quavering blast" and below it says "quavering blast." Just as here [there is] a sustained [blast] before and after it, so below [there is] a sustained [blast] before and after it. How does this work? Three quavering blasts....

[156] M reverses the order of the citations of Num. 29:1 and Num. 25:9.

[157] M reverses the order of the two biblical citations in this line.

[F]   [Num. 29:1, which reads], "It is a day for you to blow the trumpet," is included to teach its own lesson. {This verse allows the analogy between the rules for sounding the shofar on the New Year and those that apply to the announcement of the Jubilee year. Lev. 23:24 and Num. 25:9 in conjunction with Num. 29:1 thus represent the Biblical foundation for two blasts of the shofar on the New Year. The third blast must be based on a scribal ordinance.}

[G]   [Disagreeing with D] R. Samuel bar Nahmani said R. Jonathan[158] [said], "One [of them derives] from the [written] Torah and two [derive] from the words of scribes.

[H]   "[Num. 25:9], "Then you shall make proclamation with the blast of the shofar [on the tenth day of the seventh month," signifies one sounding of the shofar that derives] from the [written] Torah.

[I]   "[Lev. 23:24], '...a day of solemn rest, a memorial proclaimed with the blast of trumpets,' and [Num. 29:1], 'It is a day for you to blow the trumpet,' [each] is included to teach its own lesson."

[J]   What is the meaning of, "[each] is included to teach its own lesson"? {What lesson other than that explained at F is taught by Num. 29:1, such that the verse does not represent a Scriptural foundation for sounding the shofar on New Year.}

[K]   It is needed [to prove that the shofar is sounded] during the *day* and not at night.

[L]   But [as for] the other [Tannaitic authority, at D-F, as regards the rule that the shofar is sounded] during the *day* and not at night—from where [does he derive it]?

[M]   He derives it from [Lev. 25:9, the second half of which reads], "On the Day of Atonement [you shall make

---

[158]M and other sources lack: R. Jonathan.

proclamation with the trumpet...]."¹⁵⁹ {The use of the word "day" here shows that the shofar is sounded by day and not at night.}

[N] If he derives this from [Lev. 25:9's citing of the words], "On the Day of Atonement [you shall make proclamation with the trumpet...]," he should also learn from this [couplet of texts cited at I that there is] a plain blast [sounded] before and after [the other shofar sounds]! {See above, unit **IV**.A-D, which derives this point from Lev. 25:9.}

[O] [Lev. 25:9, the two halves of which read], "Then you shall make proclamation [with the blast of the trumpets].... You shall make proclamation [with the blast of the trumpets]" does not have this meaning for him.

[P] Rather, how does he interpret these [clauses]?¹⁶⁰

[Q] [He explains the words], "Then you shall make proclamation [with the blast of the trumpet]" in the same way as Rab Mattenah,

[R] for said Rab Mattenah, "[The words] 'Then you shall make proclamation' [mean that this should be done] in the usual manner of a proclamation. {Rashi: Mattenah derives from this verse the rule that the shofar may not be sounded while being held upside down.}

[S] "[And the phrase], 'You shall make proclamation,' which the Merciful One stated, [suggests that the shofar] should be taken by hand."

[T] But [as for] the other [authority, how does he respond to this]?

[U] [He holds that the point made] by Rab Mattenah [can be derived] from [the fact that the text uses] the word, "You shall

---

¹⁵⁹M explicitly has the bracketed conclusion of the verse.

¹⁶⁰All manuscripts and the Venice and Silia printings lack this line.

[V]	make proclamation." {This term indicates that the shofar must be used in the usual manner.}
	But [contrary to Mattenah] you cannot argue that [this means that the shofar must be taken] by hand!
[W]	[Rather] you must learn [the meaning of the operative language at Lev. 25:9], "make proclamation," from the use of the same term by Moses.
[X]	It is written here, "And you shall make proclamation with the blast of the trumpets;"
[Y]	and it is written there [Ex. 36:6], "So Moses gave command, and a sound[161] was proclaimed throughout the camp."
[Z]	[We deduce from this that] just as later on [the use of the word "proclaimed" means that there was] a sound, so here [in the context of the use of the shofar on New Year] there [must be] a sound.
[IX.A]	{We take up a point internal to the previous unit.} But according to that Tannaitic authority who derived [the rule for sounding the blast] from [the blast commanded in] the wilderness, [we might object that, if this analogy were appropriate then], just as there [the blast is to be made with] trumpets, so here [in the case of New Year it should be made with] trumpets!
[B]	Scripture states [Ps. 81:3]: "Blow the shofar at the new moon, at the full moon [Heb. root: *KSH*], on our feast day."
[C]	Which is the festival on which the moon is hidden [Heb. root: *KSH*]?
[D]	We must say it is New Year, [which falls on the new moon, unlike other festivals, which come in the middle of the month].
[E]	And the Merciful One [thus explicitly] stated that a shofar [is to be sounded on it].

---

[161]Literally: voice.

[X.A] R. Abbahu ordained in Caesaria [that there would be] a sustained blast, three fragmented blasts, a quavering blast, [and] a [final] sustained blast.

[B] Why do this? {At issue is why Abbahu required both the fragmented and quavering blasts.}

[C] If [what is needed is] a wailing [sound], let him make a sustained blast, a quavering blast [which is known as a wailing sound, above, unit **II**], and a [final] sustained blast;

[D] and if [what is needed is] a groaning [sound], let him make a sustained blast, three fragmented blasts, and a [final] sustained blast!

[E] [Abbahu required both sounds since] he was unsure if [the required sound] was a groaning [sound] or a wailing [sound].

[F] Objected Rab Avirah[162] to this [approach taken by Abbahu]: "But perhaps [in fact what is required is] a wailing [sound], and [in Abbahu's approach] the three[163] fragmented blasts separate the [required] quavering blast from the [closing] sustained blast[164] [so as to render the sequence of sounding the shofar entirely invalid]."

[G] {This objection is not probative.} [We assume] that [after following Abbahu's procedure], he goes back and makes a sustained blast, quavering blast, and [final] sustained blast.

[H] [Taking an approach similar to that of F] objected Rabina to this [procedure required by Abbahu]: "But perhaps [in fact what is required is] a groaning [sound], and [in Abbahu's method] the quavering blast separates the [required] fragmented blasts from the [closing] sustained blast [so as to render the sequence of sounding the shofar entirely invalid]."

---

[162] At F+H, M and other sources reverse the names—Avirah and Ravina—and the types of sounds—wailing and groaning.

[163] M and other sources, including Rashi, lack this word.

[164] M and most exegetical sources reverse the terms "quavering blast" and "sustained blast."

BAVLI ROSH HASHANAH CHAPTER FOUR [34a]   449

[I]   {This objection too is not probative.} [We assume] that [after following Abbahu's procedure], he goes back and makes a sustained blast, fragmented blasts,[165] and [final] sustained blast.

[J]   [In light of G and H we ask]: but what [then is the point of] that which R. Abbahu ordained [requiring a sequence of four blasts]?

[K]   [This seems unnecessary since] if [what is required is] a groaning [sound], he already has made it [as at I], and if [what is required is] a wailing [sound], he [also] already has made it [as at G]. {If the shofar in all events is to be sounded in two different sequences of three kinds of blasts, once with a quavering blast in the middle and once with fragmented blasts in the middle, why should the sequence of four blasts, referred to at A, be used at all?}

[L]   [Abbahu requires the sequence referred to at A] because he was unsure whether [perhaps] a groaning [sound] and [then] a wailing [sound is needed].

[M]   If this [in fact] were [Abbahu's] reason, then [he would] also [require] the opposite—a sustained blast, a quavering blast, three fragmented blasts, and a [final] sustained blast—lest [what is required] is a wailing [sound] followed by a groaning [sound]. {Since Abbahu does not require this, his reason presumably is not as is given at L.}

[N]   {Abbahu would have good reason to require the blasts to be sounded in only one order. M thus is rejected.} Generally, when a man has a pain, first he groans, then he wails. {Abbahu requires the shofar to be sounded in this same order, a groaning sound followed by a wailing sound, as at A. Contrary to M, he has no reason to require the reverse order.}

---

[165]M and other sources read: three fragmented blasts.

[XI.A] *[If] one sounded the first sustained blast and then sounded the second sustained blast for twice as long, [he has credit only for one set; M. R.H. 4:9D].*

[B] Said R. Yohanan, "[If] one heard [**34b**] nine sustained blasts at nine [different] hours of the day, he has fulfilled his obligation [to hear the sounding of the shofar]."

[C] A Tannaitic statement makes the same point: [If] one heard nine sustained blasts at nine [different] hours of the day, he has fulfilled his obligation [to hear the sounding of the shofar].

[D] [But if he heard nine blasts made][166] by nine [different] people at the same time, he has not fulfilled his obligation.

[E] [If] he heard a sustained blast [sounded] by this one, and a quavering blast [sounded] by this [other] person,[167] he has fulfilled his obligation.

[F] And [this is the case] even [if he hears the sounds] at intervals, and even [if the intervals extend] over the entire day.[168]

[G] But did R. Yohanan really say this [A]?

[H] But [on the contrary] thus said R. Yohanan in the name of R. Simeon b. Yehozadeq, "In the [reading of the] Hallel-psalms and the scroll[169] [of Esther, on Purim], if one paused long enough to have finished the entire [reading], he must go back to the beginning." {This contradicts the rule Yohanan proposes for the shofar, A.}

[I] There is no contradiction [between Yohanan's opinions].

---

[166]M has the bracketed words explicitly.

[167]In place of the end of this line, M, other manuscripts, and many exegetical sources read: and this one after the other he heard nine sustained blasts from nine [different] people one after the other....

[168]Reading this line as the end of the sentence begun at E, M and other sources add: he has fulfilled his obligation.

[169]M reverses the terms "scroll" and "Hallel-psalms."

[J]   Here [at A, Yohanan was stating] his own [opinion], while here [at H, he was stating] his teacher's [view].

[K]   But does his [own perspective in fact] not [contradict that which is reported in his name at A]?

[L]   For [suggesting that Yohanan does hold a contradictory view] R. Abbahu [once][170] took up [his cloak] and followed after R. Yohanan and was reciting the Shema. When he came upon some dirty alleys, he [ceased[171] the recitation and] remained silent. After he passed [the alleys] he said to him [that is, to Yohanan], "What is the rule [regarding whether or not it is permitted] to finish [the recitation]?"

[M]   [Yohanan] said to him, "If you paused long enough to have finished the entire [recitation, you] must go back to the beginning!"

[N]   {Again Yohanan is shown not to have contradicted himself.} This is what he meant to say to him: "As for me, I do not hold this view [that you may not continue].

[O]   "[But] as for you, who does hold [the view expressed by Simeon b. Yehozadeq, H], if you paused long enough to have finished the entire [recitation, you] must go back to the beginning!"

[XII.A]   Our rabbis have taught on Tannaitic authority: [On most occasions, the omission of some] blasts [of the shofar] does not impair [the validity of other] blasts, and [the omission of some] blessings does not impair [the validity of other] blessings.[172]

---

[170]In error, M adds: said.

[171]M and other manuscripts have this word explicitly but lack the remainder of the sentence.

[172]M lacks this line.

[B]   [But] the [omission of some] blasts or blessings on New Year and the Day of Atonement does impair[173] [the validity of other blasts and blessings]. {On these days, to be valid, everything must be done in order, with no omissions.}

[C]   What is the reason?

[D]   {On the following, see above, B. R.H. 1:2 **VI**.G-J, 16a. It is not clear how Rabbah's statement here responds to the question posed at A-C+D.} Said Rabbah,[174] "Said the holy one, blessed be he,[175] 'Say before me on New Year[176] [the Scriptural passages concerning] sovereignty, remembrance, and [the sounding of] the shofar:

[E]   "'Sovereignty—so that you will proclaim me king over you.

[F]   "'Remembrance—so that memory of you may rise favorably[177] before me.

[G]   "'And through what [will that memory be made to rise]? Through the shofar.'"

[XIII.A] *He who said the blessings [of the Musaf worship] and afterward was assigned a shofar should sound a sustained note, a quavering note, and a sustained note, [three times, once each for the Sovereignty, Remembrance, and Shofar-verses; M. R.H. 4:9E].*

[B]   The reason [for the rule in this case] is that he did not have a shofar at the beginning [of the Musaf worship].[178]

---

[173]All manuscripts and Rif add: one another.

[174]Manuscripts, Rif, Rosh, and Ritba read: Rava.

[175]Manuscripts, Rif, Ritba, and Rosh add: to [the people of] Israel.

[176]M lacks: on New Year.

[177]M and other sources lack this word.

[178]M and other sources make the same point through a different wording: The reason [for the rule in this case] is that he recited the blessings and [only] afterwards a shofar was assigned to him.

[C]   [This implies that] if he had a shofar at the beginning [of the Musaf worship], if he is to hear those [required blasts], during the course of the blessings he must hear them, [and not at the end, after the blessings all have been recited].

[D]   {D supports C.} Rab Pappa bar Samuel arose to pray.[179] He said to his attendant, "When I give you a sign [that I have completed a blessing that is to be followed by the sounding of the shofar], sound [the shofar] on my behalf."

[E]   [E suggests that, while Pappa bar Samuel had the general rule correct, it did not apply to him as an individual.} Said to him Rava, "They stated [this rule, that the shofar is sounded during the course of the blessings] only for the case of a congregation."

[F]   A Tannaitic statement makes the same point: When one hears them [that is, the required blasts], he must hear them in order and during the course of the blessings.

[G]   In what circumstance does this apply?

[H]   In the case of a congregation.

[I]   But if [he is] not [praying] within a congregation, he must hear them in order but need not [hear them] during the course of the blessings.[180]

[XIV.A] And [as for] an individual who has not sounded [the shofar]—his fellow may sound it on his behalf.

[B]   But [as for] an individual who has not recited the blessings—his fellow may not recite the blessings on his behalf.

[C]   The greater commandment concerns the sounds of the shofar than concerns the recitation of the blessings.

[D]   How [does this work in a concrete case]?

---

[179]M and other sources read: When Rab Pappa would pray alone....

[180]In error (Rabbinovicz), M reads: But if [he is praying] alone, when he hears them, [if] he hears them out of order and not in the course of the blessings, he has fulfilled his obligation.

[E] [If there are] two villages, in one of which they are sounding [the shofar] and in the other of which they are reciting the blessings, [people] should go to the place in which they are sounding [the shofar], but [people] should not go to the place in which they are reciting the blessings.

[F] This is obvious [and goes without saying, since]

[G] this [obligation to sound the shofar] derives from Scripture, [while] this [obligation to recite the blessings] derives from the rabbis.

[H] No! [Contrary to F-G] one needs [explicitly to phrase the rule at C-E in order to indicate that one must go to the place in which the shofar is being sounded] even though it is certain [that if he went to the town in which the blessings were being said, he would be able to recite those blessings, which requires nothing more than locating nine other individuals], while this [chance for him actually to hear the shofar] is uncertain, [since he might arrive after it already has been sounded].

[XV.A] *Just as the congregation's agent is liable [to recite the daily prayers], so each individual is liable* [M. R.H. 4:9F]. {The passage continues at M. R.H. 4:9G: *Rabban Gamaliel says, "The agent of the community carries out the obligation on behalf of the community [and therefore individuals do not have to recite the prayers themselves]."*}

[B] It is taught on Tannaitic authority: They said to Rabban Gamaliel,[181] "In your view, why does the public need to pray [the Amidah prior to the community's designated agent's recitation of the required prayers]?" {Based on Gamaliel's argument at M. R.H. 4:9G, that the community's agent carries out the community's obligation, individuals should not say anything themselves.}

---

[181] In place of "to Rabban Gamaliel," M reads simply: to him.

[C]   He said to them, "It is [to give] the agent of the community [time] to get himself ready for prayer."

[D]   Said to them [that is, to the authorities behind M. R.H. 4:9F] Rabban Gamaliel,[182] "In your view, why does the agent of the community need to go down before the ark[183] [that holds the Torah scroll]?" {If each person is individually responsible for the prayers, then the agent of the community need not take a position of prominence over the congregation as a whole.}

[E]   They said to him, "It is so that he can fulfill the obligation of anyone who is not familiar [with the prayers]."

[F]   [Gamaliel] said to them, "Just as he fulfills the obligation [of prayer] for anyone who is not familiar [with the prayers], so he fulfills the obligation for one who is familiar ."

[XVI.A] {Discussion of M. R.H. 4:9F-G continues.} Said Rabbah bar bar Hannah said R. Yohanan, "Sages [who stand behind M. R.H. 4:9F] concede to Rabban Gamaliel,[184] [so that the dispute is resolved in favor of Gamaliel]."

[B]   But Rab said, "This [issue] remains under dispute."[185]

---

[182]In error, M reads: Rabban Simeon b. Gamaliel.

[183]M and other manuscripts lack: before the ark.

[184]In error, M reads: Rabban Simeon b. Gamaliel. See above, note 182.

[185]The body of the text of M lacks this line, rightly according to Rabbinovicz (who is followed by Simon). It is added in M's margin.

[C] R.[186] Hiyya son of Rabbah bar Nahmani heard. He went and recited[187] what he heard[188] in the presence of Rab Dimi bar Hinena.[189]

[D] [Dimi] said to him, "Thus said Rab, 'This [issue] remains under dispute.'"

[E] [Hiyya] said to him,[190] "Rabbah bar bar Hannah also said this, that when R. Yohanan made this statement [attributed to him at A, that the dispute was resolved in favor of Gamaliel], Resh Laqish disagreed with him and said [to the contrary], 'This [issue] remains under dispute.'"

[XVII.A] {A problem internal to the preceding unit is analyzed.} Now, did R. Yohanan [really] say this [that the dispute was resolved in favor of Gamaliel] at all?

[B] But [indicating the contrary] thus said R. Hannah[191] of Sepphoris, "Said R. Yohanan,[192] 'The decided law follows [the view of] Rabban Gamaliel.'"

[C] [Insofar as Yohanan deemed it necessary to indicate] the decided law, this indicates that there is [in fact] a dispute! {Had sages conceded to Gamaliel, there would no longer be a

---

[186]M, Rashi (manuscript), and all early printings except Cracow lack the honorific.

[187]Literally: said.

[188]In place of "He went and recited what he heard," M reads simply: and he recited it....

[189]In error, M reads: Hanina.

[190]M lacks this attribution, reading the following as the continuation of the statement of Dimi, D.

[191]M and other sources read: Rab Huna.

[192]Through haplography, M lacks the following through the repetition of the attribution to Yohanan below at G.

	dispute, and Yohanan would not need to indicate which view is authoritative.}
[D]	[**35a**] When R. Abba returned from the sea, he explained it: "Sages concede to Gamaliel in the case of the blessings of the New Year and the Day of Atonement.
[E]	"And 'The decided law [follows the view of Gamaliel]'—from which one may logically deduce that there was a dispute—in the case of the blessings of all [the rest] of the year." {In Abba's understanding, both statements attributed to Yohanan are accurate. They refer to different prayers.}
[F]	Is this correct?
[G]	But [suggesting the contrary] thus said R. Hannah of Sepphoris, "Said R. Yohanan, 'The decided law follows [the view of] Rabban Gamaliel for the case of the blessings of New Year and the Day of Atonement.'" {In light of this statement, the distinction Abba draws at D-E is incorrect. Sages continued to disagree with Gamaliel on all matters.}
[H]	Rather [to resolve the contradiction between Yohanan's two statements] said Rab Nahman bar Isaac, "Who [does Yohanan hold] conceded [to Rabban Gamaliel]?
[I]	"[It was] R. Meir.
[J]	"But [Yohanan still finds it necessary to say], 'The decided law [follows Gamaliel],' from which one may logically deduce that the rabbis [that is, sages, continue to] disagree." {Hence Yohanan's two statements are not contradictory: one sage conceded; the others did not.}
[K]	{Proof of H-I's claim, that Meir and sages are in disagreement, follows.} For it is taught on Tannaitic authority: "[In the case of][193] the blessings of New Year and the Day of Atonement, the agent of the congregation carries out the obligation on behalf of the congregation"—the words of R. Meir.

---

[193] A scribal error, M adds: shofar blasts and.

[L] *But sages say, "Just as the congregation's agent is liable [to recite the prayers], so each individual is liable"* [M. R.H. 4:9F].

[XVIII.A] {We turn to a problem internal to the preceding unit.} Why are these [prayers, of New Year and the Day of Atonement, subject to a][194] different [rule]?

[B] I might say it is because they contain numerous verses of Scripture.

[C] But [to the contrary] thus said Rab Hananel said Rab, "Once [in the holiday prayers] one has recited [the words], 'In your Torah it is written...', he need not [recite any more Scriptural verses]." {Reference is to the passage in the Additional Service that introduces a recitation of the Bible's description of the sacrifices offered on the particular festival day. If individuals were not required to recite these verses, then, contrary to B, the fact that the prayers for New Year and Day of Atonement contain many citations of Scripture is irrelevant.}

[D] Rather, [the reason is simply] that [on these days] the blessings are lengthy.[195]

[E] The text [cited at C says]:

[F] Said Rab Hananel said Rab, "Once [in the holiday prayers] one has recited [the words], 'In your Torah it is written...', he need not [recite any more Scriptural verses]."

[G] It was presumed that this statement [applies] to an individual; but, as for the congregation [as a whole], no. {Rab's statement, F, was interpreted to mean that while individuals may abbreviate their silent prayer, in the public repetition, the entire biblical passage must be recited.}

---

[194]M has the bracketed interpolation explicitly.

[195]See Jastrow, p. 35, s.v., 'wš: "the benedictions are numerous and lengthy." Apparently in error, M reads: the [citations of] Scripture are lengthy.

[H] [Indicating that this is not the case] it is said on Amoraic authority: Said R. Joshua b. Levi, "The same rule applies to an individual and to the congregation. Once one has recited [the words], 'In your Torah it is written...', he need not [recite any more Scriptural verses]."[196]

[XIX.A] Said R. Eleazar, "A person always should [first] put his prayer in order[197] and then pray."

[B] Said R. Abba,[198] "The statement of R. Eleazar makes sense in respect to the blessings of New Year, the Day of Atonement, and the periodical [prayers[199] for festivals].

[C] "But for the rest of the year, no!"[200] {The individual need not engage in special preparation for every-day prayer. Such preparation is required only in the case of special liturgies that are infrequently used.}

[D] Is this so?

[E] For, [to the contrary], Rab Judah [always] would put his prayer in order and [then] pray!

[F] [The case of] Rab Judah is different.

[G] Since he would pray only every thirty days, [his prayers] were similar to periodical prayers.

[XX.A] Said Rab Aha bar Avirah,[201] "Said R. Simeon the Pious, '[On the basis of the recitation of the liturgy by the agent of

---

[196]M has the bracketed words explicitly.

[197]Simon, p. 173: "prepare himself for prayer."

[198]For "R. Abba," M and others read: Rava.

[199]So Jastrow, p. 1239, s.v., *prk*, followed by Simon, p. 174.

[200]M reads: But on the other days of the year, he need not.

[201]In place of the name "Avirah," M reads: Abba.

the community] Rabban Gamaliel[202] would deem even the people in the fields exempt [from prayer].

[B] "'And, it goes without saying, [this applies to] those located here [in the town].'"

[C] [Rejecting B]: To the contrary, these [people in the fields] are prevented [by their work from coming to the synagogue and therefore receive a special dispensation, so as to be deemed to have fulfilled their obligation].

[D] [But][203] these [people in the town] are not prevented [from coming to the synagogue]. {If they choose not to come, the recitation of the community's agent does not fulfill their obligation to pray.}

[E] This [D] is as Abba, son of Rab Benjamin bar Hiyya,[204] taught on Tannaitic authority: "[In the synagogue] the people [who stand] behind the priests are not covered by the [priestly] blessing." {No one in the synagogue needs to stand behind the priests rather than in front of them. Those who choose not to move in front of the priests therefore are not covered by their blessing, just as those who could come to the synagogue but do not are not exempted by the recitation of the community's agent.}

[F] {In light of C-E, the practice attributed to Gamaliel at B appears incorrect. A corrected version of A-B is provided.} Rather when Rabin came [to Babylonia from the land of Israel] he said [in the name of] R. Jacob bar Idi,[205] "Said R. Simeon the Pious,[206] '[On the basis of the recitation of the

---

[202]M reads: Simeon b. Gamaliel.

[203]M has this word explicitly.

[204]M reads: Minyamin bar Hama. In the parallel at B. Sot. 38b, the name appears as: Minyamin bar Hiyya.

[205]M lacks: [in the name of] R. Jacob bar Idi.

[206]Apparently in error, M lacks: the Pious.

liturgy by the agent of the community] Rabban Gamaliel[207] deemed only the people in the fields exempt [from prayer].' {Contrary to the report at B, he did not include the people in the town.}

[G] "What is the reason?

[H] "It is[208] because [the people in the fields] are prevented by their work[209] [from coming to the synagogue].

[I] "[But people] in the town are not [prevented from coming to the synagogue]."

---

[207] M reads: Simeon b. Gamaliel.

[208] M lacks all of G and H through this point, reading the following as a continuation of G. There is no difference in meaning.

[209] M lacks: by their work.

INDEX TO BIBLICAL AND TALMUDIC REFERENCES

Bible

Amos
7:7, 400
9:1, 400

2 Chronicles
3:2, 74, 76

Daniel
5:23, 83
11:16, 172
12:2, 208

Deuteronomy
1:3, 70-71, 75
1:4, 71, 72, 75
1:11, 359
4:2, 360-362
4:7, 226
4:35, 427
4:39, 427
5:12, 332
6:4, 427
10:17, 221, 222
11:12, 118, 131, 143, 203, 219
12:2, 133
12:5-6, 87, 101, 110
13:12-17, 351
14:22, 128
14:23, 98
14:29, 166
16:1, 113, 114, 115, 263, 272
16:7, 90
16:13, 172, 178
16:13-15, 87, 88

16:16, 86, 87, 88, 89, 90, 91, 92
17:9, 311
18:9, 304
19:15, 269
23:21, 85, 94-101, 110, 112
23:23, 100, 101, 103
26:12, 164, 165
31:2, 154
31:10, 167
32:1, 397
32:7, 397
32:13, 397
32:19, 397
32:27, 397
32:36, 397
33:5, 426
33:17, 320
34:10, 22, 268, 269

Ecclesiastes
2:14, 182
7:10, 311
12:10, 268, 269

Esther
2:16, 115
3:7, 115, 116
7:10, 162
8:9, 115

Exodus
3:16, 423
6:6, 158, 159
12, 322
12:1-2, 270, 271, 318

12:2, 118, 133, 144, 254, 255
12:2-6, 113
12:18, 259
12:42, 159
15:1-10, 397
15:11-19, 398
15:18, 426
17:11, 368
19:1, 73, 76
20:4, 301, 302
20:8, 332
20:23, 299-302
23:16, 168, 169, 172
23:26, 155
24:9, 305, 309
25:22, 399
32:32, 207
34:6, 21, 216, 217
34:6-7, 217
34:10, 217
34:21, 137
36:6, 447
40:17, 73, 75

Ezekiel
1:10, 300
9:3, 400
11:23, 400
20:33, 421
24:1-2, 233
33:21, 234

Ezra
6:4, 82
6:9, 80
6:10, 81
6:15, 79

7:8, 79
7:21-22, 84

Genesis
1:11, 150, 151
1:12, 151
2:4, 152
2:6, 151
7:11, 160, 161
8:1, 162
8:13, 148, 149
12:1, 205
12:1-2, 205
12:2, 205
16:15, 204
17:15, 204
17:16, 205
18:14, 155
21:1, 157, 158, 423
21:17, 203
23:2, 204
30:22, 157
33:19, 320, 325
50:5, 326

Haggai
1:15, 78, 79
2:1, 78, 79

Hosea
2:6, 288
5:8, 422
5:15, 399, 401
6:2, 397

Isaiah
2:11, 396
5:2, 290
6:10, 218
14:23, 328
26:5, 402

27:13, 159
29:4, 402
33:21, 285
41:19, 284, 286
52:2, 402
55:6, 226
60:17, 287
64:10, 286
66:24, 210

Jeremiah
2:22, 224, 226
4:14, 224
30:17, 386
40:1, 290
41:1-2, 233
52:5-7, 232

Job
7:17-18, 197, 199
11:20, 401
25:2, 292
37:24, 213
38:36, 326

Joel
3:21, 287

Jonah
3:10, 205

Joshua
4:19, 170
5:11, 170
6:5, 320, 325
15:7, 279

Judges
5:28, 439

1 Kings
6:1, 69, 75, 153, 154
6:36, 82
7:12, 82
8:2, 152-154
8:13, 210
8:59, 132, 199, 200
8:66, 90
11:26, 210

2 Kings
4:22-23, 205

Lamentations
3:9, 288
4:19, 263

Leviticus
1:2, 433
1:3, 99, 101, 102
7:16, 94
7:18, 99, 100
11:8, 206
15, 169
16:4, 321
16:12, 322
16:23, 321
19:23, 61, 143
19:23-25, 405
19:24, 143, 144
19:24-25, 145
21:1, 206
22:27, 106
22:31, 309
23:2, 296, 297, 309
23:4, 14, 266, 274, 296, 305, 309
23:10, 170
23:14, 123, 387, 389

INDEX TO BIBLICAL AND TALMUDIC REFERENCES 465

23:15, 91
23:16, 91, 92
23:17, 123
23:22, 414
23:23-25, 1, 2
23:24, 7, 157, 202, 353, 376, 377, 413, 414, 424, 430, 441, 442, 444, 445
23:25, 430
23:26-28, 2
23:32, 137-139, 258
23:36, 89
23:39, 114
23:44, 296
25:4, 133
25:4-5, 137
25:9, 15, 134, 142, 382, 440-442
25:10, 17, 134, 135, 139, 140-143, 297
25:11, 135, 136
25:21, 173
25:22, 173
25:30, 108
27:32, 61

Malachi
3:8, 327
4:3, 209

Micah
6:2, 152, 153
6:9, 400
7:18, 214, 215
7:19, 214

Nehemiah
1:1, 76, 77

1:1-3, 77
1:15-2:1, 79
2:1, 76, 77
2:1-6, 78
2:6, 83
5:19, 422

Numbers
6:24-26, 410
6:26, 221, 222
10:2, 335
10:5, 443
10:6, 443
10:10, 371, 415
10:11, 73, 75
11:19-20, 91
18:26, 165, 166
20:29, 72
21:1, 71, 72, 75
21:17, 398
23:21, 425, 426
24:21, 152
25:9, 342, 444-447
28:11, 91
28:14, 118
29:1, 7, 371, 376-378, 425, 430, 439, 444-446
29:1-6, 1
29:39, 88
33:38, 69-71, 75
35:24-25, 319

Proverbs
4:8, 328
10:2, 204
14:28, 14, 428
21:9, 400
21:19, 401
22:27, 100, 404

Psalms
8:5, 268
8:14, 13
10:16, 422
12:6, 14, 268
16:1, 209
24, 394, 386
24:7-10, 24, 423
29:1, 412, 413
29:2, 413
29:8, 393
33:6, 419
33:14-15, 228
33:15, 194
45:9, 83
47:6-7, 424
47:8, 424
48, 394, 396
48:2, 326
49:14, 210
55:22, 328
62:12, 216
65:13, 13, 127, 128, 151
69:28, 207
69:31, 321
78:39, 421
81, 393, 396
81:3, 131, 159, 202, 448
81:3-4, 276
81:3-5, 158
81:4, 131, 132, 276, 316, 317
81:5, 276
81:6, 158, 393
82, 395, 396
89:36-37, 307
92, 395, 396
93, 395, 396

94, 395, 396
98:6, 337, 425
99:1, 422
99:6, 310
104:19, 306
106:4, 422
107:6, 204
107:23-31, 220
116:1, 212
116:6, 212
137:7, 422
145:17, 216
150:3, 418

1 Samuel
1:19, 157
1:20, 156
1:21, 157
2:6, 209
2:10, 210
2:21, 158
2:33, 226
3:14, 225
12:6, 310
12:11, 310
25:5-8, 227
25:38, 227

2 Samuel
5:21, 281
22:11, 400

Song of Songs
2:8, 153

Zechariah
1:7, 115
7:1, 115
8:19, 232, 233, 235, 238

9:14, 422
13:9, 208, 211, 212

Mishnah

Baba Mesia
8:6, 121

Bekhorot
9:5, 121

Berakhot
2:1, 354

Bikkurim
2:6, 181, 183, 185

Eduyyot
7:6, 105
7:7, 117

Hagigah
1:6, 90

Maaser Sheni
5:2, 405

Maaserot
1:3, 14, 167
1:5, 164

Megillah
1:6, 104
2:2, 327

Menahot
10:5, 388, 389

Pesahim
9:6, 93

Qinnim
1:1, 104

Rosh Hashanah
1:1, 3, 9, 12, 13, 15, 19, 20, 24, 25, 33-35, 61, 63-65, 69, 84, 85, 116, 117, 120-125, 127, 129, 130, 131, 133, 134, 143, 144, 162, 163, 166, 180, 181, 185, 186
1:1-2, 6
1:2, 2, 3, 26, 36, 194-198, 200, 227
1:3, 4, 12, 18, 25, 37, 228, 229, 244-246, 264, 265
1:4, 4, 14, 15, 25, 38, 248, 249, 264-266
1:5, 4, 14, 38, 267, 268
1:6, 4, 15, 38, 267-269
1:7, 4, 12, 14, 10, 38, 270-272
1:8, 4, 10, 39, 273
1:9, 4, 39, 273, 274
2:1, 4, 10, 22, 39, 275-279
2:2, 4, 14, 15, 39, 280
2:3, 4, 22, 40, 280, 284

INDEX TO BIBLICAL AND TALMUDIC REFERENCES 467

2:4, 4, 10, 40, 280, 281, 287, 288
2:5, 5, 15, 41, 289, 290, 283
2:6, 5, 10, 41, 290-292
2:7, 5, 10, 14, 18, 41, 42, 295-298, 305
2:8, 5, 10, 42, 298, 299, 302, 304, 306
2:9, 5, 15, 43, 304, 306, 308, 309, 311
3:1, 5, 10-11, 25, 43, 44, 297, 313-319
3:2, 5, 11, 14, 15, 44, 320, 323-325
3:3, 5, 11, 15, 25, 45, 328-335
3:3-5, 14, 336, 340
3:4, 5, 45, 329, 335
3:5, 5, 46, 329, 330, 337, 338, 372, 383
3:6, 5, 17, 46, 338, 339, 341, 342, 343
3:7, 5, 11, 46, 47, 333, 339, 345, 346, 348, 349, 355, 356, 366, 369
3:8, 5, 47, 368, 369
4:1, 6, 12, 16, 48, 375-380, 404, 409
4:1-2, 375, 380, 381
4:1-4, 7
4:2, 6, 11, 48, 375, 376, 380, 385
4:3, 6, 14, 49, 385, 386, 389, 404
4:4, 6, 24, 49, 390, 391, 402-404
4:5, 6, 11, 50, 51, 409, 411, 415-417
4:6, 6, 11, 16, 25, 51, 52, 417-421, 425, 426
4:7, 6, 11, 14, 52, 427-429
4:8, 6, 12, 24, 25, 52, 53, 429-436
4:9, 6, 12, 15, 16, 25, 53-55, 332, 333, 347, 437-439, 441, 450, 453, 455, 456, 458

Sanhedrin
4:1, 316, 318

Shebiit
1:4, 136, 137
2:6, 145
2:7, 174
2:9, 179
5:1, 192
9:1, 327
10:5, 15, 65, 129

Sukkah
3:12, 386

Taanit
4:6, 231

Tamid
7:4, 394

Terumot
1:1-2, 369
1:5, 175

Zebahim
8:10, 361, 364, 365

Tosefta

Avodah Zarah
5:2, 303

Arakhin
1:9, 16
1:11, 110
3:17, 12, 86, 92-95, 111
3:18, 86, 107, 108

Eduyyot
2:3, 182

Megillah
3:20, 334

Rosh Hashanah
1:1, 16, 67-69
1:2, 16, 85, 122
1:7, 162, 166
1:8, 15, 144
1:9, 14, 16, 164, 185, 186
1:10, 16, 166
1:12, 201
1:13, 197

1:14, 245
1:15, 16, 279
1:16, 277
1:17, 281, 293, 294
1:18, 309
2:4, 15, 17, 329, 331, 340, 341, 342, 344
2:5, 17, 370-372
2:10, 413
2:11, 11, 415, 416
2:12, 16, 419
2:13, 17, 422, 424, 425, 427
2:16, 25, 433

Sanhedrin
2:7, 25, 116
3:6, 98
13:3, 208

Shebiit
2:3, 144
2:5, 175
4:21, 190

Sotah
6:6, 232
6:10, 232

Sukkah
3:18, 201

Taanit
2:5, 235, 236

Terumot
1:3, 352

Babylonian Talmud

Avodah Zarah
43a-b, 299
43b, 300, 302, 303

Baba Batra
80b, 284, 285

Baba Mesia
60b, 336
85a, 379
87a, 156
109b, 336

Baba Qamma
84a, 336
93a, 204

Berakhot
43b, 154

Besah
5a, 405, 406
16a, 131, 132, 158

Erubin
7a, 182, 183
45a, 289

Hagigah
17a, 89, 90, 92

Hullin
139a, 104

Keritot
9a, 405

Ketuvot
112a, 172

Moed Qatan
24b, 89

Megillah
21a, 334
21b, 418
29b, 118

Menahot
66a, 92
79b, 96
103b, 169

Nedarim
38a, 268
49a, 200

Pesahim
66a, 379
97b, 93

Rosh Hashanah
2a, 61, 66
2b, 66, 145
3a, 71
3b, 70, 71, 75
4a, 80
4b, 86
5a, 90
5b, 93
6a, 99
6b, 106, 256
7a, 112
7b, 119
8a, 125, 158, 162, 180, 186, 263, 337
8b, 124, 131, 200
9a, 136
9b, 139

Index to Biblical and Talmudic References

10a, 145
10b, 131, 147, 337
11a, 150
11b, 158
12a, 160
12b, 164
13a, 168
13b, 173
14a, 176
14b, 180, 186
15a, 185
15b, 190
16a, 194, 224, 452
16b, 202
17a, 208
17b, 215
18a, 222
18b, 230
19a, 238
19b, 242
20a, 248
20b, 256
21a, 260
21b, 264, 404
22a, 269

22b, 275
23a, 282
23b, 287
24a, 135, 292
24b, 299
25a, 304
25b, 310, 313
26a, 319
26b, 326
27a, 331, 347
27b, 339
28a, 346, 357
28b, 353
29a, 366
29b, 373, 375
30a, 380
30b, 389
31a, 394
31b, 401
32a, 409
32b, 421
33a, 431
33b, 434
34a, 441

34b, 450
35a, 457

Shabbat
13b, 234
135b, 112

Sukkah
12a, 172
37a, 284

Taanit
25b, 284

Yoma
65b, 118

Zebahim
29a, 98

Jerusalem Talmud

Rosh Hashanah
3:8, 203

GENERAL INDEX

Abayye: announcement of new moon, 265; definition of shofar, 323-324; delayed payment of obligation, 112; God's judgment, 225; intention to fulfill commandments, 358-359; interpretation of Hos. 6:2, 397; new year for tithes, 175; power of repentance, 218; prohibition against images, 299-301; rule for festivals, 259; rule for Sabbatical year, 187-188; sanctification of new moon, 297-298; Scroll of Fasting, 236; sounding of shofar, 439-440; witnesses to the new moon, 290, 295

Abba: agent of the congregation, 457; intercalation of calendar, 257; New Year liturgy, 458-459; rule for Sabbatical year, 192-193

Abba bar Benjamin bar Hiyya: agent of the congregation, 460

Abba Saul: preparation of shofar, 432

Abbahu: function of shofar, 202; meaning of *alil*, 268; meaning of Num. 20:29, 72; new year for kings, 79; new year for tithes, 179; rule for Hallel, 429; sounding of shofar, 448-451

Abin: God's judging of the world, 204, 207

Abtolemos: citron in Sabbatical year, 190

Adar: intercalation of, 116, 247-251

Aha bar Avirah: agent of the congregation, 460

Aha bar Hanina: God's judging of the world, 215; intercalation of Elul, 251-252

Aha bar Huna: psalms for Temple-offerings, 392-394, 397; Scroll of Fasting, 237-238

Aha bar Jacob: delayed payment of obligation, 112; new year for months, 115

Ahabah: fulfilling a commandment on behalf of another, 373; witnesses to the new moon, 391-392

Aibo bar Nagri: two day festival in the diaspora, 261

Amemar: rule for court appearances, 403-404

Ami: intercalation of calendar, 255

Amida: order of benedictions, 409-411; sources in Scripture, 412-413

Aqiba: definition of fast days, 232-234; definitions of words, 325; new year for tithes, 178-179; new year for trees, 180-184; order of blessings on New Year, 411-412, 416; power of repentance, 222-223; psalms recited in the Temple, 394-395; reason for *omer*, 201; rule for Sabbatical year, 137; rule for testimony, 319; rule for Yom Kippur, 139; sanctification of the new moon, 304-306, 308-309; Scriptural sources of Amida, 414; witnesses to the new moon, 267, 269

Artaxerxes: 76-77

Ashi: commandment fulfilled on behalf of another, 374; commandment fulfilled under compulsion, 353; intercalation of calendar, 258; meaning of *qaba'an*, 326-327; new year for months, 115; rule for court appearances, 403-404; Scroll of Fasting, 240-241; witnesses to the new moon, 277

Assi: new year for produce, 167-168

Avirah: sounding of shofar, 448-449

Beterah, sons of: sounding of shofar, 379

Bonds: antedated and postdated, 129

Burnt-offering: delayed payment of, 86, 95, 99, 101-102; designation of birds as, 104; shofar from, 349; substitute for, 95, 97

Charity: delayed payment of, 101, 104-105

Commandments: fulfillment on behalf of another, 369-374; negative, 100-101, 107; positive, 100-101, 105; prohibition against extending, 361-366; requirement of intention, 353-368

Creation: dating of, 131, 149-151; nature of, 152

Cyrus: character of, 80-84; other names for, 80; reign of, 79

Day of Atonement: determination of correct day, 260-261; God's judgment at, 196-198; liturgy for, 459; period of self-affliction, 137-138; use of shofar on, 330, 331

Dimi: intercalation of calendar, 256; kinds of cedar, 284

Dimi bar Hinena: agent of the congregation, 456

Dosa b. Harkinas: sanctification of the new moon, 309; witnesses to new moon, 304-305

Eleazar: definition of bullock, 146; nature of God's judging of world, 216; new year for tithing Cattle, 61, 63, 122, 127-129; New Year liturgy, 458-459; power of repentance, 224; sounding of shofar, 375, 379, 433

Eleazar (Amora): delayed payment of obligation, 100; new year for kings, 74; new year for trees, 180; rule for sacrifice omitted on Pentecost, 89

Eleazar b. R. Yose: rule for Shofar, Sovereignty, and Remembrance-verses, 426

Eleazar b. Sadoq: sanctification of the new moon, 295, 297-298

Eli, House of: early death, 225-226

Eliezer: blood of sacrifices, 361-362; chronology of Israelite history, 150-154, 159-160; God's judgment, 214; nature and cause of Flood, 160-161; new year for trees, 146-147, 181, 184; Sanhedrin's route into exile, 402; Scriptural sources of Amida , 413; Scroll of Fasting, 235-236; vineyard in its fourth year, 406-407; world created in Tishre, 131, 337-338

Eliezer b. Jacob: delaying payment of obligation, 86-89

Eliezer b. Simeon: delaying payment of obligation, 88
Elul: intercalation of, 244-245, 251-253, 417
Ena: New Year liturgy, 337

Fast days: use of shofar on, 329, 335
Festivals: need for purification on, 206; new year for, 34, 61, 63, 84, 116, 118, 121-122, 125; two days in the diaspora, 260-262
Firstlings: payment of, 86, 95, 98, 108, 112
Flood: astrological cause of, 160; date of, 162
Forgotten sheaves: payment of, 86-87, 95
Freewill offering: delayed offering of, 94, 101, 103-104

Gamaliel: agent of the congregation, 437-438, 455-456, 460-461; new year for trees, 181, 183-185; power of repentance, 221-222; prohibition against images, 302-303; sanctification of the new moon, 308, 311-312; witnesses to new moon, 269, 289, 298, 304-306
Gleanings: payment of, 86, 95
God: attributes of, 215-217
Guilt-offerings: payment of, 86, 95, 101

Halafta: use of shofar, 336
Hallel: rule for recitation, 427-429
Hama bar Hanina: sounding shofar on Sabbath, 376-377
Hamnuna: rule for Sabbatical year, 188-190

Hanan bar Rava: psalms for Temple offerings, 397; witnesses to new moon, 271-272
Hananel: New Year liturgy, 458-459
Hanania b. Teradion: use of shofar, 336
Hanina: new year for tithes, 172-173; new year for trees, 183; order of blessings on New Year, 416, 417; Scroll of Fasting, 234-236
Hanina bar Kahana: intercalation of Elul, 417
Hanna bar Biznah: nature of fast days, 230-231
Hannah: God's visitation of, 150, 156-157
Hannah of Sepphoris: agent of the congregation, 457
Heave-offering of the Sheqel: new year for, 34, 113, 116, 118, 120
Hillel, House of: nature of God's judgment, 209, 211-213; new year for trees, 61, 64, 180-183
Hinena bar Kahana: intercalation of Elul, 244
Hisda: definition of shofar, 321; definition of wrongdoers, 213; God's judgment, 199-200; missed Passover offering, 93; nature of Flood, 161-162; new year for festivals, 85; new year for kings, 65, 76, 130; new year for months, 114; order of blessings on New Year, 417
Hiyya: delayed payment of obligation, 111; rule for thank-offering, 96; sanctification of the new moon, 307
Hiyya bar Abba: produce forbidden as *orlah*, 145; rules for Jubilee,

142; two day festival in the diaspora, 261
Hiyya bar Gamda: sanctification of the new moon, 296
Hiyya bar Rab: rule for Yom Kippur, 139
Hiyya bar Rabbah bar Nahmani: agent of the congregation, 456
House: new year for renting, 113, 121
Huna: nature of God's judgment, 216; rule for witnesses to new moon, 271-272; sounding of shofar, 345-346, 372, 380, 382
Huna bar Abin: intercalation of year, 263
Huna, son of Idi: prohibition against images, 300
Huna, son of Joshua: recovery from illness, 214-215

Ilpa: God's judgment, 216-217
Images: prohibition against, 299-304
Isaac: character of Cyrus, 80, 82; God's judgment, 203-205; honor due teacher, 205-206; purification for festival, 206; reason for shofar, 202-203
Isaac bar Abin: nature of God's judgment, 210
Isaac bar Joseph: sounding of shofar, 381, 383
Isaac bar Nahmani: new year for tithes, 176-177
Isaac (Patriarch): dating birth of, 155-156
Ishmael: rule for Sabbatical year, 137
Ishmael b. Yohanan b. Beroqa: new year for Jubilee, 124, 134-135; sounding of shofar, 443

Ishmael, House of: God's judging of the world, 198
Israelite nation: dating redemption of, 150, 159; dating release from bondage of, 150, 158-159

Jacob bar Idi: agent of the congregation, 461
Jeremiah: new year for produce, 169
Jonah: delaying payment of obligation, 88
Jonathan: sounding of shofar, 445
Jonathan b. Joseph: new year for tithing, 173
Joseph: character of Cyrus, 82; identification of Mishnaic authority, 122; meaning of term Exile, 287; new year of kings, 78; prayers for the sick, 200; Scroll of Fasting, 236
Joseph (Patriarch): dating release from prison, 150, 158
Joshua: blood of sacrifices, 361-365; cause of Flood, 160-161; chronology of Israelite history, 150-154, 159-160; intercalation of year, 117; rule for peace-offerings, 105; sanctification of the new moon, 308-309, 311-312; Scroll of Fasting, 235-236; witnesses to new moon, 304-405
Joshua b. Levi: calendar for tithing, 164-165, 172; intercalation of Adar, 247; intercalation of calendar, 255; nature of creation, 152; New Year liturgy, 458-459; Scroll of Fasting, 235
Joshua b. Qorha: witnesses to new moon, 402

Josiah: heave-offering of the sheqel, 118

Jubilee: dismissal of slaves in, 140-142; nature of, 139-141; new year for, 34-35, 61, 64, 122, 124, 134-136; outside the land of Israel, 143; release of fields on, 141-142; use of shofar on, 140-142, 329, 372, 382-384

Judah: God's judging of world, 197-198; meaning of word *deror*, 142; new year for trees, 147; psalms recited in the Temple, 394-395; rule for Jubilee, 142; rule for *omer*, 201, 389-390; rule for Remembrance-verses, 423, 425; rule for Sovereignty-verses, 424-425, 427

Judah: rule for tithing, 166; sounding of shofar, 433; use of shofar, 329, 330-331

Judah (Amora): blessing for trees in bloom, 154; communal sacrifices, 119; God's judgment, 228; kinds of cedar, 284; power of repentance, 227; preparation for prayer, 459-460; prohibition against images, 302; sanctification of the new moon, 297; sounding of Shofar, 349-351

Judah b. Shammua: fights government's decree, 241-243

Judah bar Idi: Shechina's departure from Israel, 398-401

Judah the Patriarch: definitions of words, 325, 327-328; delayed payment of obligation, 108-109; intercalation of calendar, 245-246, 248, 255; order of blessings on New Year, 415; rules for new years, 122; sanctification of the new moon, 296, 307; Scriptural sources of Amida, 414

Judgment: dating of, 34, 131; nature of, 2-3, 30-32, 132, 207-228

Kahana: announcing the new moon, 278; intercalation of Adar, 250-251; names of Cyrus, 80; new year for months, 115; payment of obligations, 107; Scroll of Fasting, 235; source of first *omer*, 170-171

Kattina: interpretation of Is. 2:11, 396-397

King: judgment of, 132-133; new year for, 33-34, 61, 63, 65-81, 116, 118, 122, 129-130

Kruspedai: God's books of judgment, 207

Leap Year: new year for, 34, 113, 116, 118, 120

Levi: meaning of *qaba'an*, 326-327; prohibition against images, 303; two day festival in the diaspora, 260-261; use of shofar, 330-331; witnesses to new moon, 270-271

Levi bar Lahma: sounding shofar on the Sabbath, 376-377

Lulab: use of, 6, 49, 385

Mattenah: repair of shofar, 342; sounding of shofar, 446-447

Meir: agent of the congregation, 457-458; definitions of calf, bullock, 146; delaying payment of obligation, 86-89, 97, 110-111; God's judging of world, 197; new year for tithe of cattle, 121, 127; new year for trees, 145-149; power of repentance, 223; Scroll of Fasting, 243

Months: intercalation of, 313, 316; new year for, 63, 113-116, 118, 120; sanctification of, 91

Nahman: dating of final judgment, 131; intercalation of calendar, 248-250, 258-259, 263; new year for trees, 147-148, 187; power of repentance, 227; sounding of shofar, 372-373; two day festival in the diaspora, 262

Nahman bar Hisda: intercalation of Adar, 247-248

Nahman bar Isaac: agent of the congregation, 457; determination of new year days, 123; flares to announce new moon, 288; intercalation of year, 117; nature of God's judgment, 207-208, 228; rule for crimson thread, 405, 407-409; rule for *omer*, 389

Nathan: God's judging of the world, 197, 199; repair of shofar, 343

Nehemiah: new year for trees, 191-192; psalms recited in the Temple, 395-396

Nehorai: witnesses to new moon, 277

New Moon: flares to announce, 4, 39-40, 280-285, 287-288; messengers sent forth on, 4, 37, 228-232, 244-251, 261-262, 264-265; proclamation of, 1, 41-43, 295-298, 313-315; witnesses to, 4-5, 38-39, 41, 44, 49, 264-267, 269, 270-274, 275-280, 289-295, 298, 304, 306, 313-315, 317-319, 390-391

New Year: God's judging of world at, 2-3, 194, 197; liturgy for, 6, 50-52, 337, 409-413, 415, 458-459; use of shofar on, 328, 330-332, 335, 372, 427-428; which falls on the Sabbath, 375, 378-381

Omer: after the destruction of the Temple, 386-390; new year for, 123; reason for, 201

Oshaia: new year for trees, 180; sacrifice omitted on Pentecost, 89

Pappa: counting of years from Exodus, 70; determination of new year days, 123-124; nature of fast days, 231; new year for kings, 130; new year for years, 129; power of repentance, 218; reign of Artaxerxes, 77-78; repair of shofar, 342; responds to Huna's illness, 214-215; sanctification of the new moon, 296; vineyard in its fourth year, 405-409; witnesses to new moon, 276

Pappa bar Samuel: sounding of shofar, 335, 453

Pappias: intercalation of year, 117; sacrifice of peace-offerings, 105-106

Passover: God's judging of world at, 32, 194-197; making up missed offering, 92

Patriarchs: dating birth, death of, 150, 152-154

Peace-offering: rule for substitute, 95, 97, 101; shofar from, 350; payment of, 86, 95

Pentecost: dating of, 92, 109-110; God's judging of world at, 32, 194, 197; making up missed offering, 91

Polemo: sanctification of new moon, 297

Rab: agent of the congregation, 455-456; collecting coral, 285; definition of wrongdoers, 213; intercalation of Elul, 244; Moses' greatness, 268; New Year liturgy, 458-459; power of repentance, 227; prohibition against images, 303; psalms for Temple-offerings, 397; Scroll of Fasting, 234-236, 239

Rab, House of: kinds of cedar, 284

Rabbah: new year for tithes, 174-175; rule for Sabbatical year, 187-190; sounding of Shofar, 346-349, 378; Sovereignty, Remembrance, and shofar-verses, 452-453

Rabbah bar Abbuha: new year for trees, 147-148; power of repentance, 227

Rabbah bar bar Hannah: agent of the congregation, 456; definitions of words, 328; God's judging of the world, 228

Rabbah bar Huna: kinds of cedar, 284; new year for trees, 184-186

Rabbah bar Lema: character of Cyrus, 84

Rabbah bar Samuel: counting days of month, 91; intercalation of calendar, 254-255

Rabbah bar Ulla: vineyard in its fourth year, 406

Rabin: agent of the congregation, 460

Rabina: new year for kings, 74; new year for months, 115; new year for trees, 184; rule for sounding shofar, 449

Rachel: God's visitation of, 150, 156-157

Rava: counting days to Pentecost, 92; determination of new year days, 122; fulfilling commandment on behalf of another, 373-374; God's judging of the world, 198, 211-214, 225; intention to fulfill commandments, 358-361; intercalation of calendar, 254, 263; meaning of *qaba'an*, 326-327; new year for tithing cattle, 128; new year for trees, 146, 187; payment of obligations, 97, 104, 105, 107; prohibition against extending commandments, 358-360, 363-365; significance of vow, 351-352; sounding of shofar, 336, 350, 353, 378, 380-382, 435, 453; two day festival in the diaspora, 262

Remembrance-verses: number of, 417, 419-420; reason for, 202, 453; rule for reciting, 52-53, 420-424; sounding shofar during, 50, 437, 453

Repentance: power of, 36, 218-221, 223-227

Resh Laqish: agent of the congregation, 456; nature of God's judgment, 227-228; rule for festivals, 259; rule for Sabbatical year, 191-193

Retribution: 62

Sabbatical year: consumption of produce in, 173-174; new year for, 34, 61, 64, 122, 133-134; produce subject to, 188-190

Sacrifices: rule for communal, 119-120

Samuel: commandment fulfilled under compulsion, 352; intercalation of calendar, 256-257; Moses' greatness, 268-269; nature of God's judging of the world, 228; new year for tithes, 176-177; prohibition against images, 303; sanctification of the new moon, 297

Samuel bar Imi: nature of God's judgment, 225

Samuel bar Inia: nature of God's judging of world, 226-227

Samuel bar Isaac: New Year liturgy, 337-338

Samuel bar Nahmani: sounding of shofar, 445

Sanctified time: extension into secular time, 135-139

Sanhedrin: route into exile, 401-402

Sarah: God's visitation of, 150, 156-157

Satan: confused by shofar, 203

Scroll of Fasting: 229, 234-244

Second Tithe: payment of, 98

Shaman b. Abba: intention to fulfill commandments, 359-360, 364-365

Shammai, House of: nature of God's judgment, 208-209; new year for trees, 61, 64, 180-183

Shechina: departure from Israel, 398-401

Shemayah: dating of Pentecost, 109-110

Shemini Azeret: as independent festival, 89-90

Sheshet: missed Passover offering, 93; rule for thank-offering, 96; sounding of Shofar, 383

Shisha: determination of new year days 125; New Year liturgy, 338

Shizpar: witnesses to new moon, 269

Shofar: definition of, 5, 45, 319-324, 328-329, 344; repair of, 5, 44, 46, 338-344; sounding of, 1, 6, 202-203, 329-337, 339, 345-353, 367, 370-371, 427-455; sounding on Sabbath, 6, 48, 375-384

Shofar-verses: number of, 417, 419-420; reason for, 202, 453; rule for reciting, 50-51, 420, 421-422, 424; sounding shofar during, 50, 437, 453

Simeon: delaying payment of vow, 85, 86-89; new year for festivals, 122; new year for tithing cattle, 61, 63, 122, 127-129; new year for trees, 147-149; sounding of shofar, 433; witnesses to new moon, 270, 271

Simeon b. Eleazar: flares to announce new moon, 287; new year for trees, 185; rule for proselyte, 405

Simeon b. Gamaliel: definition of shofar, 344; intercalation of calendar, 246-247; order of blessings on New Year, 415, 416

Simeon b. Judah: rule for Sabbatical year, 188-189

Simeon b. Laqish: definitions of words, 325; meaning of Num. 20:29, 72

Simeon b. Yehozadeq: sounding of shofar, 452

Simeon b. Yohai: definition of fast days, 232-244; rule for Sabbatical year, 188-189

Simeon Shezuri: new year for tithes, 176-177

Simeon the Pious: agent of the congregation, 460-461; nature of fast days, 230-231

Sin-offering: delayed payment of, 86, 95, 99, 101; rule for substitute, 95

Sovereignty-verses: number of, 417-420; reason for, 201, 452; rule for reciting, 51-52, 420-424; sounding shofar during, 50, 437, 453

Tabernacles: God's judging of the world at, 32, 194, 197

Teacher: honor due, 205-206

Testimony: rules for, 313-319

Thank-offering: rule for substitute, 95-96

Tithe of cattle: new year for, 34, 61, 63, 121-122, 127-129; payment of, 86

Tithes: designation in third year, 165-166; new year for, 162, 176-178; payment of, 108, 164; point of liability to, 167

Torah-study: power of, 225-226, 286

Tovi bar Mattenah: Scroll of Fasting, 241

Trees: new year for, 34, 61, 64, 122, 143-148, 180-186, 191

Ulla: announcing new moon, 278; intercalation of Elul, 251-252; vineyard in its fourth year, 406

Uqba: intercalation of Adar, 248-249

Valuations: payment of, 86, 94

Vegetables: new year for, 35, 61, 64, 143, 162-172

Vows: delayed payment of, 30, 31, 34, 62, 65, 85-113, 125; new year for, 162, 166-167

Woman: delayed payment of obligation, 111-112; period of purification, 146-147

World: God's judging of, 2-3, 31, 194-228

Yannai: new year for trees, 186; produce forbidden as *orlah*, 145

Year: intercalation of, 116-17; new year for, 61, 63, 122, 129

Yohanan: agent of the congregation, 456-457; citron in Sabbatical year, 191; delayed payment of obligation, 100; flares to announce new moon, 288; God showed Moses the order of prayers, 217; God's books of judgment, 207; idol-worshippers have no atonement, 286; intercalation of calendar, 255; nature of God's judgment, 228; new year for kings, 69, 74; new year for produce, 167-168; new year for tithe of cattle, 127; new year for trees, 186; power of repentance, 218-220; produce forbidden as *orlah*, 145; psalms appropriate to Temple offerings, 397-398; repair of shofar, 343; restoration of Jerusalem, 286; rule for festivals, 258-259; rule for Jubilee, 142; rule for Sabbatical year, 192-193; Sanhedrin's route into exile, 402; Scroll of Fasting, 235; sounding of shofar, 428-429, 450-452; two day festival in diaspora, 261-262; value of Torah-study, 286; witnesses to new moon, 292, 306

Yohanan b. Beroqah: order of blessings on New Year, 416

Yohanan b. Nuri: number of Shofar, Sovereignty, and Remembrance-verses, 417, 419-420; order of blessings on New Year, 410, 412; Sovereignty-verses, 419; witnesses to new moon, 304

Yohanan b. Zakkai: power of Torah-study, 225-226; priests' appearance on platform, 404; rule for crimson thread, 405, 407-408; rule for lulab, 385; rule for *omer*, 386-390; rule for proselyte, 404-405; sounding of shofar, 375, 378-380; vineyard in its fourth year, 405-409; witnesses to new moon, 266, 391

Yom Kippur: see Day of Atonement

Yose: citron in Sabbatical year, 190; definition of shofar, 319-321, 323-324; God's judging of the world, 197, 199-200; nature of Jubilee, 140; new year for trees, 147; rule for Jubilee, 142; rule for Shofar, Sovereignty, and Remembrance-verses, 420, 422-427; sounding of shofar, 368, 433; witnesses to new moon, 270-271

Yose b. Kiper: ripening of harvest, 175

Yose b. Saul: sanctification of the new moon, 296

Yose bar Hanina: God's judging of the world, 214

Yose bar Judah: new year for trees, 181, 183; prohibition against images, 299; Scriptural sources of Amida, 414-415

Yose the Galilean: new year for produce, 167-168; new year for tithes, 178-179; order of blessings on New Year, 416, 417

Yose the Priest: power of repentance, 221-222; rule for Sabbatical year, 192

Zebid: sacrifice of peace-offerings, 106

Zera: delayed payment of obligation, 110, 111; flares to announce new moon, 282; intention to fulfill commandment, 366; intercalation of calendar, 257, 259; new year for produce, 168-169; new year for tithes, 173, 176; new year for years, 130; order of blessings on New Year, 417; sounding of shofar, 384-385, 436; witnesses to the new moon, 391-392

Brown Judaic Studies

140001	*Approaches to Ancient Judaism I*	William S. Green
140002	*The Traditions of Eleazar Ben Azariah*	Tzvee Zahavy
140003	*Persons and Institutions in Early Rabbinic Judaism*	William S. Green
140004	*Claude Goldsmid Montefiore on the Ancient Rabbis*	Joshua B. Stein
140005	*The Ecumenical Perspective and the Modernization of Jewish Religion*	S. Daniel Breslauer
140006	*The Sabbath-Law of Rabbi Meir*	Robert Goldenberg
140007	*Rabbi Tarfon*	Joel Gereboff
140008	*Rabban Gamaliel II*	Shamai Kanter
140009	*Approaches to Ancient Judaism II*	William S. Green
140010	*Method and Meaning in Ancient Judaism I*	Jacob Neusner
140011	*Approaches to Ancient Judaism III*	William S. Green
140012	*Turning Point: Zionism and Reform Judaism*	Howard R. Greenstein
140013	*Buber on God and the Perfect Man*	Pamela Vermes
140014	*Scholastic Rabbinism*	Anthony J. Saldarini
140015	*Method and Meaning in Ancient Judaism II*	Jacob Neusner
140016	*Method and Meaning in Ancient Judaism III*	Jacob Neusner
140017	*Post Mishnaic Judaism in Transition*	Baruch M. Bokser
140018	*A History of the Mishnaic Law of Agriculture: Tractate Maaser Sheni*	Peter J. Haas
140019	*Mishnah's Theology of Tithing*	Martin S. Jaffee
140020	*The Priestly Gift in Mishnah: A Study of Tractate Terumot*	Alan. J. Peck
140021	*History of Judaism: The Next Ten Years*	Baruch M. Bokser
140022	*Ancient Synagogues*	Joseph Gutmann
140023	*Warrant for Genocide*	Norman Cohn
140024	*The Creation of the World According to Gersonides*	Jacob J. Staub
140025	*Two Treatises of Philo of Alexandria: A Commentary on* De Gigantibus *and* Quod Deus Sit Immutabilis	Winston/Dillon
140026	*A History of the Mishnaic Law of Agriculture: Kilayim*	Irving Mandelbaum
140027	*Approaches to Ancient Judaism IV*	William S. Green
140028	*Judaism in the American Humanities I*	Jacob Neusner
140029	*Handbook of Synagogue Architecture*	Marilyn Chiat
140030	*The Book of Mirrors*	Daniel C. Matt
140031	*Ideas in Fiction: The Works of Hayim Hazaz*	Warren Bargad
140032	*Approaches to Ancient Judaism V*	William S. Green
140033	*Sectarian Law in the Dead Sea Scrolls: Courts, Testimony and the Penal Code*	Lawrence H. Schiffman
140034	*A History of the United Jewish Appeal: 1939-1982*	Marc L. Raphael
140035	*The Academic Study of Judaism*	Jacob Neusner
140036	*Woman Leaders in the Ancient Synagogue*	Bernadette Brooten
140037	*Formative Judaism I: Religious, Historical, and Literary Studies*	Jacob Neusner
140038	*Ben Sira's View of Women: A Literary Analysis*	Warren C. Trenchard
140039	*Barukh Kurzweil and Modern Hebrew Literature*	James S. Diamond
140040	*Israeli Childhood Stories of the Sixties: Yizhar, Aloni, Shahar, Kahana-Carmon*	Gideon Telpaz
140041	*Formative Judaism II: Religious, Historical, and Literary Studies*	Jacob Neusner
140042	*Judaism in the American Humanities II: Jewish Learning and the New Humanities*	Jacob Neusner

140043	*Support for the Poor in the Mishnaic Law of Agriculture: Tractate Peah*	Roger Brooks
140044	*The Sanctity of the Seventh Year: A Study of Mishnah Tractate Shebiit*	Louis E. Newman
140045	*Character and Context: Studies in the Fiction of Abramovitsh, Brenner, and Agnon*	Jeffrey Fleck
140046	*Formative Judaism III: Religious, Historical, and Literary Studies*	Jacob Neusner
140047	*Pharaoh's Counsellors: Job, Jethro, and Balaam in Rabbinic and Patristic Tradition*	Judith Baskin
140048	*The Scrolls and Christian Origins: Studies in the Jewish Background of the New Testament*	Matthew Black
140049	*Approaches to Modern Judaism I*	Marc Lee Raphael
140050	*Mysterious Encounters at Mamre and Jabbok*	William T. Miller
140051	*The Mishnah Before 70*	Jacob Neusner
140052	*Sparda by the Bitter Sea: Imperial Interaction in Western Anatolia*	Jack Martin Balcer
140053	*Hermann Cohen: The Challenge of a Religion of Reason*	William Kluback
140054	*Approaches to Judaism in Medieval Times I*	David R. Blumenthal
140055	*In the Margins of the Yerushalmi: Glosses on the English Translation*	Jacob Neusner
140056	*Approaches to Modern Judaism II*	Marc Lee Raphael
140057	*Approaches to Judaism in Medieval Times II*	David R. Blumenthal
140058	*Midrash as Literature: The Primacy of Documentary Discourse*	Jacob Neusner
140059	*The Commerce of the Sacred: Mediation of the Divine Among Jews in the Graeco-Roman Diaspora*	Jack N. Lightstone
140060	*Major Trends in Formative Judaism I: Society and Symbol in Political Crisis*	Jacob Neusner
140061	*Major Trends in Formative Judaism II: Texts, Contents, and Contexts*	Jacob Neusner
140062	*A History of the Jews in Babylonia I: The Parthian Period*	Jacob Neusner
140063	*The Talmud of Babylonia: An American Translation XXXII: Tractate Arakhin*	Jacob Neusner
140064	*Ancient Judaism: Debates and Disputes*	Jacob Neusner
140065	*Prayers Alleged to Be Jewish: An Examination of the Constitutiones Apostolorum*	David Fiensy
140066	*The Legal Methodology of Hai Gaon*	Tsvi Groner
140067	*From Mishnah to Scripture: The Problem of the Unattributed Saying*	Jacob Neusner
140068	*Halakhah in a Theological Dimension*	David Novak
140069	*From Philo to Origen: Middle Platonism in Transition*	Robert M. Berchman
140070	*In Search of Talmudic Biography: The Problem of the Attributed Saying*	Jacob Neusner
140071	*The Death of the Old and the Birth of the New: The Framework of the Book of Numbers and the Pentateuch*	Dennis T. Olson
140072	*The Talmud of Babylonia: An American Translation XVII: Tractate Sotah*	Jacob Neusner
140073	*Understanding Seeking Faith: Essays on the Case of Judaism II: Literature, Religion and the Social Study of Judiasm*	Jacob Neusner
140074	*The Talmud of Babylonia: An American Translation VI: Tractate Sukkah*	Jacob Neusner
140075	*Fear Not Warrior: A Study of 'al tira' Pericopes in the Hebrew Scriptures*	Edgar W. Conrad

140076	Formative Judaism IV: Religious, Historical, and Literary Studies	Jacob Neusner
140077	Biblical Patterns in Modern Literature	Hirsch/Aschkenasy
140078	The Talmud of Babylonia: An American Translation I: Tractate Berakhot	Jacob Neusner
140079	Mishnah's Division of Agriculture: A History and Theology of Seder Zeraim	Alan J. Avery-Peck
140080	From Tradition to Imitation: The Plan and Program of Pesiqta Rabbati and Pesiqta deRab Kahana	Jacob Neusner
140081	The Talmud of Babylonia: An American Translation XXIII.A: Tractate Sanhedrin, Chapters 1-3	Jacob Neusner
140082	Jewish Presence in T. S. Eliot and Franz Kafka	Melvin Wilk
140083	School, Court, Public Administration: Judaism and its Institutions in Talmudic Babylonia	Jacob Neusner
140084	The Talmud of Babylonia: An American Translation XXIII.B: Tractate Sanhedrin, Chapters 4-8	Jacob Neusner
140085	The Bavli and Its Sources: The Question of Tradition in the Case of Tractate Sukkah	Jacob Neusner
140086	From Description to Conviction: Essays on the History and Theology of Judaism	Jacob Neusner
140087	The Talmud of Babylonia: An American Translation XXIII.C: Tractate Sanhedrin, Chapters 9-11	Jacob Neusner
140088	Mishnaic Law of Blessings and Prayers: Tractate Berakhot	Tzvee Zahavy
140089	The Peripatetic Saying: The Problem of the Thrice-Told Tale in Talmudic Literature	Jacob Neusner
140090	The Talmud of Babylonia: An American Translation XXVI: Tractate Horayot	Martin S. Jaffee
140091	Formative Judaism V: Religious, Historical, and Literary Studies	Jacob Neusner
140092	Essays on Biblical Method and Translation	Edward Greenstein
140093	The Integrity of Leviticus Rabbah	Jacob Neusner
140094	Behind the Essenes: History and Ideology of the Dead Sea Scrolls	Philip R. Davies
140095	Approaches to Judaism in Medieval Times III	David R. Blumenthal
140096	The Memorized Torah: The Mnemonic System of the Mishnah	Jacob Neusner
140097	Knowledge and Illumination	Hossein Ziai
140098	Sifre to Deuteronomy: An Analytical Translation I: Pisqaot 1-143. Debarim, Waethanan, Eqeb	Jacob Neusner
140099	Major Trends in Formative Judaism III: The Three Stages in the Formation of Judaism	Jacob Neusner
140101	Sifre to Deuteronomy: An Analytical Translation II: Pisqaot 144-357. Shofetim, Ki Tese, Ki Tabo, Nesabim, Ha'azinu, Zot Habberakhah	Jacob Neusner
140102	Sifra: The Rabbinic Commentary on Leviticus	Neusner/Brooks
140103	The Human Will in Judaism	Howard Eilberg-Schwartz
140104	Genesis Rabbah I: Genesis 1:1 to 8:14	Jacob Neusner
140105	Genesis Rabbah II: Genesis 8:15 to 28:9	Jacob Neusner
140106	Genesis Rabbah III: Genesis 28:10 to 50:26	Jacob Neusner
140107	First Principles of Systemic Analysis	Jacob Neusner
140108	Genesis and Judaism	Jacob Neusner
140109	The Talmud of Babylonia: An American Translation XXXV: Tractates Meilah and Tamid	Peter J. Haas
140110	Studies in Islamic and Judaic Traditions I	Brinner/Ricks

140111	*Comparative Midrash: The Plan and Program of Genesis Rabbah and Leviticus Rabbah*	Jacob Neusner
140112	*The Tosefta: Its Structure and its Sources*	Jacob Neusner
140113	*Reading and Believing*	Jacob Neusner
140114	*The Fathers According to Rabbi Nathan*	Jacob Neusner
140115	*Etymology in Early Jewish Interpretation: The Hebrew Names in Philo*	Lester L. Grabbe
140116	*Understanding Seeking Faith: Essays on the Case of Judaism I: Debates on Method, Reports of Results*	Jacob Neusner
140117	*The Talmud of Babylonia: An American Translation VII: Tractate Besah*	Alan J. Avery-Peck
140118	*Sifre to Numbers: An American Translation and Explanation I: Sifre to Numbers 1-58*	Jacob Neusner
140119	*Sifre to Numbers: An American Translation and Explanation II: Sifre to Numbers 59-115*	Jacob Neusner
140120	*Cohen and Troeltsch: Ethical Monotheistic Religion and Theory of Culture*	Wendell S. Dietrich
140121	*Goodenough on the History of Religion and on Judaism*	Neusner/Frerichs
140122	*Pesiqta deRab Kahana I: Pisqaot 1-14*	Jacob Neusner
140123	*Pesiqta deRab Kahana II: Pisqaot 15-28 and Introduction to Pesiqta deRab Kahana*	Jacob Neusner
140124	*Sifre to Deuteronomy: Introduction*	Jacob Neusner
140126	*A Conceptual Commentary on Midrash Leviticus Rabbah: Value Concepts in Jewish Thought*	Max Kadushin
140127	*The Other Judaisms of Late Antiquity*	Alan F. Segal
140128	*Josephus as a Historical Source in Patristic Literature through Eusebius*	Michael Hardwick
140129	*Judaism: The Evidence of the Mishnah*	Jacob Neusner
140131	*Philo, John and Paul: New Perspectives on Judaism and Early Christianity*	Peder Borgen
140132	*Babylonian Witchcraft Literature*	Tzvi Abusch
140133	*The Making of the Mind of Judaism: The Formative Age*	Jacob Neusner
140135	*Why No Gospels in Talmudic Judaism?*	Jacob Neusner
140136	*Torah: From Scroll to Symbol Part III: Doctrine*	Jacob Neusner
140137	*The Systemic Analysis of Judaism*	Jacob Neusner
140138	*Sifra: An Analytical Translation I*	Jacob Neusner
140139	*Sifra: An Analytical Translation II*	Jacob Neusner
140140	*Sifra: An Analytical Translation III*	Jacob Neusner
140141	*Midrash in Context: Exegesis in Formative Judaism*	Jacob Neusner
140142	*Sifra: An Analytical Translation IV*	Jacob Neusner
140143	*Oxen, Women or Citizens? Slaves in the System of Mishnah*	Paul V. Flesher
140144	*The Book of the Pomegranate*	Elliot R. Wolfson
140145	*Wrong Ways and Right Ways in the Study of Formative Judaism*	Jacob Neusner
140146	*Sifra in Perspective: The Documentary Comparison of the Midrashim of Ancient Judaism*	Jacob Neusner
140147	*Uniting the Dual Torah: Sifra and the Problem of the Mishnah*	Jacob Neusner
140148	*Mekhilta According to Rabbi Ishmael: An Analytical Translation I*	Jacob Neusner
140149	*The Doctrine of the Divine Name: An Introduction to Classical Kabbalistic Theology*	Stephen G. Wald
140150	*Water into Wine and the Beheading of John the Baptist*	Roger Aus
140151	*The Formation of the Jewish Intellect*	Jacob Neusner
140152	*Mekhilta According to Rabbi Ishmael: An Introduction to Judaism's First Scriptural Encyclopaedia*	Jacob Neusner

140153	Understanding Seeking Faith: Essays on the Case of Judaism III: Society, History, and Political and Philosophical Uses of Judaism	Jacob Neusner
140154	Mekhilta According to Rabbi Ishmael: An Analytical Translation II	Jacob Neusner
140155	Goyim: Gentiles and Israelites in Mishnah-Tosefta	Gary P. Porton
140156	A Religion of Pots and Pans?	Jacob Neusner
140157	Claude Montefiore and Christianity	Maurice Gerald Bowler
140158	The Philosophical Mishnah III: The Tractates' Agenda: From Nazir to Zebahim	Jacob Neusner
140159	From Ancient Israel to Modern Judaism I: Intellect in Quest of Understanding	Neusner/Frerichs/Sarna
140160	The Social Study of Judaism I	Jacob Neusner
140161	Philo's Jewish Identity	Alan Mendelson
140162	The Social Study of Judaism II	Jacob Neusner
140163	The Philosophical Mishnah I: The Initial Probe	Jacob Neusner
140164	The Philosophical Mishnah II: The Tractates' Agenda: From Abodah Zarah Through Moed Qatan	Jacob Neusner
140166	Women's Earliest Records	Barbara S. Lesko
140167	The Legacy of Hermann Cohen	William Kluback
140168	Method and Meaning in Ancient Judaism	Jacob Neusner
140169	The Role of the Messenger and Message in the Ancient Near East	John T. Greene
140171	Abraham Heschel's Idea of Revelation	Lawerence Perlman
140172	The Philosophical Mishnah IV: The Repertoire	Jacob Neusner
140173	From Ancient Israel to Modern Judaism II: Intellect in Quest of Understanding	Neusner/Frerichs/Sarna
140174	From Ancient Israel to Modern Judaism III: Intellect in Quest of Understanding	Neusner/Frerichs/Sarna
140175	From Ancient Israel to Modern Judaism IV: Intellect in Quest of Understanding	Neusner/Frerichs/Sarna
140176	Translating the Classics of Judaism: In Theory and In Practice	Jacob Neusner
140177	Profiles of a Rabbi: Synoptic Opportunities in Reading About Jesus	Bruce Chilton
140178	Studies in Islamic and Judaic Traditions II	Brinner/Ricks
140179	Medium and Message in Judaism: First Series	Jacob Neusner
140180	Making the Classics of Judaism: The Three Stages of Literary Formation	Jacob Neusner
140181	The Law of Jealousy: Anthropology of Sotah	Adriana Destro
140182	Esther Rabbah I: An Analytical Translation	Jacob Neusner
140183	Ruth Rabbah: An Analytical Translation	Jacob Neusner
140184	Formative Judaism: Religious, Historical and Literary Studies	Jacob Neusner
140185	The Studia Philonica Annual 1989	David T. Runia
140186	The Setting of the Sermon on the Mount	W.D. Davies
140187	The Midrash Compilations of the Sixth and Seventh Centuries I	Jacob Neusner
140188	The Midrash Compilations of the Sixth and Seventh Centuries II	Jacob Neusner
140189	The Midrash Compilations of the Sixth and Seventh Centuries III	Jacob Neusner
140190	The Midrash Compilations of the Sixth and Seventh Centuries IV	Jacob Neusner
140191	The Religious World of Contemporary Judaism: Observations and Convictions	Jacob Neusner
140192	Approaches to Ancient Judaism VI	Neusner/Frerichs
140193	Lamentations Rabbah: An Analytical Translation	Jacob Neusner
140194	Early Christian Texts on Jews and Judaism	Robert S. MacLennan
140196	Torah and the Chronicler's History Work	Judson R. Shaver

140197	Song of Songs Rabbah: An Analytical Translation I	Jacob Neusner
140198	Song of Songs Rabbah: An Analytical Translation II	Jacob Neusner
140199	From Literature to Theology in Formative Judaism	Jacob Neusner
140202	Maimonides on Perfection	Menachem Kellner
140203	The Martyr's Conviction	Eugene Weiner/Anita Weiner
140204	Judaism, Christianity, and Zoroastrianism in Talmudic Babylonia	Jacob Neusner
140205	Tzedakah: Can Jewish Philanthropy Buy Jewish Survival?	Jacob Neusner
140206	New Perspectives on Ancient Judaism I	Neusner/Borgen/Frerichs/Horsley
140207	Scriptures of the Oral Torah	Jacob Neusner
140208	Christian Faith and the Bible of Judaism	Jacob Neusner
140209	Philo's Perception of Women	Dorothy Sly
140210	Case Citation in the Babylonian Talmud: The Evidence Tractate Neziqin	Eliezer Segal
140211	The Biblical Herem: A Window on Israel's Religious Experience	Philip D. Stern
140212	Goodenough on the Beginnings of Christianity	A.T. Kraabel
140213	The Talmud of Babylonia: An American Translation XXI.A: Tractate Bava Mesia Chapters 1-2	Jacob Neusner
140214	The Talmud of Babylonia: An American Translation XXI.B: Tractate Bava Mesia Chapters 3-4	Jacob Neusner
140215	The Talmud of Babylonia: An American Translation XXI.C: Tractate Bava Mesia Chapters 5-6	Jacob Neusner
140216	The Talmud of Babylonia: An American Translation XXI.D: Tractate Bava Mesia Chapters 7-10	Jacob Neusner
140217	Semites, Iranians, Greeks and Romans: Studies in their Interactions	Jonathan A. Goldstein
140218	The Talmud of Babylonia: An American Translation XXXIII: Temurah	Jacob Neusner
140219	The Talmud of Babylonia: An American Translation XXXI.A: Tractate Bekhorot Chapters 1-4	Jacob Neusner
140220	The Talmud of Babylonia: An American Translation XXXI.B: Tractate Bekhorot Chapters 5-9	Jacob Neusner
140221	The Talmud of Babylonia: An American Translation XXXVI.A: Tractate Niddah Chapters 1-3	Jacob Neusner
140222	The Talmud of Babylonia: An American Translation XXXVI.B: Tractate Niddah Chapters 4-10	Jacob Neusner
140223	The Talmud of Babylonia: An American Translation XXXIV: Tractate Keritot	Jacob Neusner
140224	Paul, the Temple, and the Presence of God	David A. Renwick
140225	The Book of the People	William W. Hallo
140226	The Studia Philonica Annual 1990	David Runia
140227	The Talmud of Babylonia: An American Translation XXV.A: Tractate Abodah Zarah Chapters 1-2	Jacob Neusner
140228	The Talmud of Babylonia: An American Translation XXV.B: Tractate Abodah Zarah Chapters 3-5	Jacob Neusner
140230	The Studia Philonica Annual 1991	David Runia
140231	The Talmud of Babylonia: An American Translation XXVIII.A: Tractate Zebahim Chapters 1-3	Jacob Neusner
140232	Both Literal and Allegorical: Studies in Philo of Alexandria's Questions and Answers on Genesis and Exodus	David M. Hay
140233	The Talmud of Babylonia: An American Translation XXVIII.B: Tractate Zebahim Chapters 4-8	Jacob Neusner

140234	The Talmud of Babylonia: An American Translation XXVIII.C: Tractate Zebahim Chapters 9-14	Jacob Neusner
140235	The Talmud of Babylonia: An American Translation XXIX.A: Tractate Menahot Chapters 1-3	Jacob Neusner
140236	The Talmud of Babylonia: An American Translation XXIX.B: Tractate Menahot Chapters 4-7	Jacob Neusner
140237	The Talmud of Babylonia: An American Translation XXIX.C: Tractate Menahot Chapters 8-13	Jacob Neusner
140238	The Talmud of Babylonia: An American Translation XXIX: Tractate Makkot	Jacob Neusner
140239	The Talmud of Babylonia: An American Translation XXII.A: Tractate Baba Batra Chapters 1 and 2	Jacob Neusner
140240	The Talmud of Babylonia: An American Translation XXII.B: Tractate Baba Batra Chapter 3	Jacob Neusner
140241	The Talmud of Babylonia: An American Translation XXII.C: Tractate Baba Batra Chapters 4-6	Jacob Neusner
140242	The Talmud of Babylonia: An American Translation XXVII.A: Tractate Shebuot Chapters 1-3	Jacob Neusner
140243	The Talmud of Babylonia: An American Translation XXVII.B: Tractate Shebuot Chapters 4-8	Jacob Neusner
140244	Balaam and His Interpreters: A Hermeneutical History of the Balaam Traditions	John T. Greene
140245	Courageous Universality: The Work of Schmuel Hugo Bergman	William Kluback
140246	The Mechanics of Change: Essays in the Social History of German Jewry	Steven M. Lowenstein
140247	The Talmud of Babylonia: An American Translation XX.A: Tractate Baba Qamma Chapters 1-3	Jacob Neusner
140248	The Talmud of Babylonia: An American Translation XX.B: Tractate Baba Qamma Chapters 4-7	Jacob Neusner
140249	The Talmud of Babylonia: An American Translation XX.C: Tractate Baba Qamma Chapters 8-10	Jacob Neusner
140250	The Talmud of Babylonia: An American Translation XIII.A: Tractate Yebamot Chapters 1-3	Jacob Neusner
140251	The Talmud of Babylonia: An American Translation XIII.B: Tractate Yebamot Chapters 4-6	Jacob Neusner
140252	The Talmud of Babylonia: An American Translation XI: Tractate Moed Qatan	Jacob Neusner
140253	The Talmud of Babylonia: An American Translation XXX.A: Tractate Hullin Chapters 1 and 2	Tzvee Zahavy
140254	The Talmud of Babylonia: An American Translation XXX.B: Tractate Hullin Chapters 3-6	Tzvee Zahavy
140255	The Talmud of Babylonia: An American Translation XXX.C: Tractate Hullin Chapters 7-12	Tzvee Zahavy
140256	The Talmud of Babylonia: An American Translation XIII.C: Tractate Yebamot Chapters 7-9	Jacob Neusner
140257	The Talmud of Babylonia: An American Translation XIV.A: Tractate Ketubot Chapters 1-3	Jacob Neusner
140258	The Talmud of Babylonia: An American Translation XIV.B: Tractate Ketubot Chapters 4-7	Jacob Neusner
140259	Jewish Thought Adrift: Max Wiener (1882-1950)	Robert S. Schine
140260	The Talmud of Babylonia: An American Translation XIV.C: Tractate Ketubot Chapters 8-13	Jacob Neusner

140261	The Talmud of Babylonia: An American Translation XIII.D: Tractate Yebamot Chapters 10-16	Jacob Neusner
140262	The Talmud of Babylonia: An American Translation XV. A: Tractate Nedarim Chapters 1-4	Jacob Neusner
140263	The Talmud of Babylonia: An American Translation XV.B: Tractate Nedarim Chapters 5-11	Jacob Neusner
140264	Studia Philonica Annual 1992	David T. Runia
140265	The Talmud of Babylonia: An American Translation XVIII.A: Tractate Gittin Chapters 1-3	Jacob Neusner
140266	The Talmud of Babylonia: An American Translation XVIII.B: Tractate Gittin Chapters 4 and 5	Jacob Neusner
140267	The Talmud of Babylonia: An American Translation XIX.A: Tractate Qiddushin Chapter 1	Jacob Neusner
140268	The Talmud of Babylonia: An American Translation XIX.B: Tractate Qiddushin Chapters 2-4	Jacob Neusner
140269	The Talmud of Babylonia: An American Translation XVIII.C: Tractate Gittin Chapters 6-9	Jacob Neusner
140270	The Talmud of Babylonia: An American Translation II.A: Tractate Shabbat Chapters 1 and 2	Jacob Neusner
140271	The Theology of Nahmanides Systematically Presented	David Novak
140272	The Talmud of Babylonia: An American Translation II.B: Tractate Shabbat Chapters 3-6	Jacob Neusner
140273	The Talmud of Babylonia: An American Translation II.C: Tractate Shabbat Chapters 7-10	Jacob Neusner
140274	The Talmud of Babylonia: An American Translation II.D: Tractate Shabbat Chapters 11-17	Jacob Neusner
140275	The Talmud of Babylonia: An American Translation II.E: Tractate Shabbat Chapters 18-24	Jacob Neusner
140276	The Talmud of Babylonia: An American Translation III.A: Tractate Erubin Chapters 1 and 2	Jacob Neusner
140277	The Talmud of Babylonia: An American Translation III.B: Tractate Erubin Chapters 3 and 4	Jacob Neusner
140278	The Talmud of Babylonia: An American Translation III.C: Tractate Erubin Chapters 5 and 6	Jacob Neusner
140279	The Talmud of Babylonia: An American Translation III.D: Tractate Erubin Chapters 7-10	Jacob Neusner
140280	The Talmud of Babylonia: An American Translation XII: Tractate Hagigah	Jacob Neusner
140281	The Talmud of Babylonia: An American Translation IV.A: Tractate Pesahim Chapter I	Jacob Neusner
140282	The Talmud of Babylonia: An American Translation IV.B: Tractate Pesahim Chapters 2 and 3	Jacob Neusner
140283	The Talmud of Babylonia: An American Translation IV.C: Tractate Pesahim Chapters 4-6	Jacob Neusner
140284	The Talmud of Babylonia: An American Translation IV.D: Tractate Pesahim Chapters 7 and 8	Jacob Neusner
140285	The Talmud of Babylonia: An American Translation IV.E: Tractate Pesahim Chapters 9 and 10	Jacob Neusner
140286	From Christianity to Gnosis and From Gnosis to Christianity	Jean Magne
140287	Studia Philonica Annual 1993	David T. Runia
140288	Diasporas in Antiquity	Shaye J. D. Cohen, Ernest S. Frerichs
140289	The Jewish Family in Antiquity	Shaye J. D. Cohen
140290	The Place of Judaism in Philo's Thought	Ellen Birnbaum

140291	*The Babylonian Esther Midrash, Vol. 1*	Eliezer Segal
140292	*The Babylonian Esther Midrash, Vol. 2*	Eliezer Segal
140293	*The Babylonian Esther Midrash, Vol. 3*	Eliezer Segal
140294	*The Talmud of Babylonia: An American Translation V. A: Tractate Yoma Chapters 1 and 2*	Jacob Neusner
140295	*The Talmud of Babylonia: An American Translation V. B: Tractate Yoma Chapters 3-5*	Jacob Neusner
140296	*The Talmud of Babylonia: An American Translation V. C: Tractate Yoma Chapters 6-8*	Jacob Neusner
140297	*The Talmud of Babylonia: An American Translation XXII.D: Tractate Baba Batra Chapters Seven and Eight*	Jacob Neusner
140298	*The Talmud of Babylonia: An American Translation XXII.E: Tractate Baba Batra Chapters Nine and Ten*	Jacob Neusner
140299	*The Studia Philonica Annual, 1994*	David T. Runia
140300	*Sages, Stories, Authors, and Editors in Rabbinic Judaism*	Richard Kalmin
140301	*From Balaam to Jonah: Anti-prophetic Satire in the Hebrew Bible*	David Marcus
140302	*The History of Sukkot in the Second Temple and Rabbinic Periods*	Jeffrey L. Rubenstein
140303	*Tasting the Dish: Rabbinic Rhetorics of Sexuality*	Michael L. Satlow
140304	*The School of Moses: Studies in Philo and Hellenistic Religion*	John Peter Kenney
140305	*The Studia Philonica Annual, 1995*	David T. Runia
140306	*The Talmud of Babylonia, An American Translation IX, Tractate Rosh Hashanah*	Alan J. Avery-Peck

Brown Studies on Jews and Their Societies

145001	*American Jewish Fertility*	Calvin Goldscheider
145002	*The Impact of Religious Schooling: The Effects of Jewish Education Upon Religious Involvement*	Harold S. Himmelfarb
145003	*The American Jewish Community*	Calvin Goldscheider
145004	*The Naturalized Jews of the Grand Duchy of Posen in 1834 and 1835*	Edward David Luft
145005	*Suburban Communities: The Jewishness of American Reform Jews*	Gerald L. Showstack
145007	*Ethnic Survival in America*	David Schoem
145008	*American Jews in the 21st Century: A Leadership Challenge*	Earl Raab

Brown Studies in Religion

147001	*Religious Writings and Religious Systems I*	Jacob Neusner, et al
147002	*Religious Writings and Religious Systems II*	Jacob Neusner, et al
147003	*Religion and the Social Sciences*	Robert Segal

BM
499.5
.E4
1984
39452s
v.9